Tupolev Tu-134

The USSR's Short-Range Jet Airliner

Dmitriy Komissarov

An imprint of
Ian Allan Publishing

Tupolev Tu-134:
The USSR's Short-Range Jet Airliner
© 2004 Dmitriy Komissarov
ISBN 1 85780 159 8

Published by Midland Publishing
4 Watling Drive, Hinckley, LE10 3EY, England
Tel: 01455 254 490   Fax: 01455 254 495
E-mail: midlandbooks@compuserve.com

Midland Publishing and Aerofax are imprints of
Ian Allan Publishing Ltd

Worldwide distribution (except North America):
Midland Counties Publications
4 Watling Drive, Hinckley, LE10 3EY, England
Telephone: 01455 254 450   Fax: 01455 233 737
E-mail: midlandbooks@compuserve.com
www.midlandcountiessuperstore.com

North American trade distribution:
Specialty Press Publishers & Wholesalers Inc.
39966 Grand Avenue, North Branch, MN 55056
Tel: 651 277 1400   Fax: 651 277 1203
Toll free telephone: 800 895 4585
www.specialtypress.com

Design concept and layout
© 2004 Midland Publishing and
Stephen Thompson Associates

Printed in England by
Ian Allan Printing Ltd
Riverdene Business Park, Molesey Road,
Hersham, Surrey, KT12 4RG

Contents

Title page: **Russia State Transport Co Tu-134AK
RA-65921 on short finals to runway 24 at
Moscow-Vnukovo on 20th May 2000.** Author

Below: **The Russian Air Force's quasi-civil VIP
transports are beginning to shed their pseudo-
Aeroflot looks. Tu-134AK RA-65685 (seen here
parked at Domna AB near Chita on 9th
September 2003) wears an absolutely non-
standard colour scheme. Contrary to some
reports, this aircraft was never converted into a
Tu-134 Balkany ABCP.** Vyacheslav Martyniuk

Foreword

The Tu-134, which has given sterling service for 35 years now, surely deserves a separate monograph. This workhorse of the airways has played a major role in Soviet/Russian civil aviation (and continues to do so); it was the first jet type operated by the flag carriers of several nations affiliated with the Soviet Union, taking the civil aviation of these countries to new levels of comfort and efficiency. If one includes the nations that appeared after the break-up of the Soviet Union, the Tu-134 has seen service in 42 countries of Europe, South-East Asia, the Middle East, Africa and South America. Apart from scheduled and charter passenger flights, its multifarious activities include VIP transportation, support of Air Force, Army and Navy headquarters, military pilot and navigator training, astronaut training, agricultural and geophysical research, and miscellaneous test and development work. What's more, the last chapter in the history of this aircraft is not yet written.

It took seven years to conceive and write this book, and there are two reasons why it was written in the first place. Firstly, I have a soft spot for this aircraft. The Tu-134 is a damn beautiful aeroplane! Besides, this was the aircraft in which yours truly made his first air trip as a kid back in 1975. That was an unforgettable experience (no reference to Aeroflot's service standards!).

The second reason is a feeling of injustice. Even a brief look at the bookstalls creates the impression that Russian aviation writers and aviation enthusiasts are absolutely military-minded! Combat aircraft are always the rage, while airliners and transports tend to get neglected; only recently has the situation begun to improve. True, militaria sells better – partly because military aircraft were a closely guarded secret until the early 1990s and very little information was available to John Q Public (the 'forbidden fruit' syndrome); yours truly still remembers Soviet-era aviation magazines with crudely retouched photos and captions like 'Jet fighter'. Still, it's a shame that Soviet/Russian civil aircraft remain largely unsung, though many of them deserve attention no less than many a fighter does. And civil aviation enthusiasts are not so few, after all.

For various reasons the book was completed years later than originally intended. Still, this enforced delay has made it possible to eliminate some errors and make the book as detailed and up-to-date as possible. I hope you will not be disappointed.

Acknowledgements

The author wishes to thank all those who assisted and contributed (in whatever degree) to the making of this book:

Yevgeniy R Polzovskiy, Maximilian B Saukke and the late Leonid L Selyakov at the Tupolev Design Bureau who supplied a lot of information on the type's development history; Aleksandr V Androsov, Aleksandr I Kirpichenko, Aleksandr V Lebedev, Stanislav I Looschchik, Viktor A Mashkin, Nikolai V Nalobin, Ivan D Nosych, Mikhail I Pronyakin, Aleksey V Romanov, Andrey D Sizykh and Boris N Terekhov (Vnukovo Airport Aviation Security), as well as Aleksandr P Boonaryov, Vladislav N Korzh, Aleksandr V Zaïtsev and Aleksandr I Zhoochkov (East Line Aviation Security) who gave ramp access at Moscow-Vnukovo and Moscow-Domodedovo, allowing valuable photos to be taken; Lydia N Anghelova, Ivan G Faleyev, Rudolf A Teymurazov and Natal'ya I Titova (CIS Interstate Aviation Committee) for providing access to the official records of civil Tu-134s which allowed a lot of production data (notably manufacture dates), operational details and accident reports to be included; Aleksandr A Katyukha, Vladimir F Oostinovich, Anatoliy V Panfilenko, Sergey Yu Panov, Vladimir I Seleznyov and Vladimir I Shevko who gave an insight of Tu-134 operations in the Russian Air Force; Vladislav A Golubenko, Nikolai N Ionkin, Yuriy Kirsanov, Yuriy A Kotel'nikov and Viktor G Kravchenko who did the often risky job of spotting when the author was otherwise engaged, supplying photos and hot information on aircraft movements; Aleksandr I Balashov and Vladimir A Toorchak (Menatep Bank); Pavel V Novikov, Sergey S Tsvetkov and Vasiliy V Zolotov (Mir Aviatsii); Pavel S Minyutko and Taïsia Soormenkova (Kvand Aircraft Interiors); Pyotr B Batooyev, Valeriy A Belov, Vladimir F Filippov, Sergey L Ghafner (Aeroflot Plus), Aleksey V Ivanov, Ernest V Katayev (Aviatsiya magazine), Dmitriy Ye Kolesnik, Sergey D Komissarov, Viktor P Kulikov, Vyacheslav Martynyuk, Dmitriy A Petrochenko, Ghennadiy F Petrov, the late Anatoliy F Tischchenko, Il'dar A Valeyev (Kazan' Aircraft Production Association), Aleksey B Vool'fov (Domodedovo Airlines), Nikolai V Yakubovich, Aleksey M Yankitov (Nizhegorodskiye Airlines), Sergey S Yeriomin (Komiinteravia), Peter Davison (London Science Museum), Nigel Eastaway (Russian Aviation Research Trust), Ryszard Jaxa-Małachowski, Thomas Müller, Bob Ogden and Helmut F Walther who also provided assorted data and/or photos without which the book would have been so much the poorer; Andrey A Yurgenson who completed the line drawings used in this book; Russell Strong at Midland Publishing; and Dmitriy S Makovenko who printed many of the photos used in this book with excellent quality.

Special thanks go to my friend and colleague Yefim I Gordon and Mikhail M Kvashnin who provided valuable assistance with getting the photos scanned and sorted, as well as supplying some of his own, and to Vladimir G Rigmant (Tupolev Design Bureau) who provided some rare original photos and data.

Special thanks also go to the editorial team of the Soviet Transports reference book (Peter Hillman, Stuart Jessup, Guus Ottenhof and Tony Morris) who have painstakingly collected data on Tu-134 operations worldwide. Not only did they kindly give permission to use this information but they also supplied monthly updates to Scramble magazine, which has been vital in making the book as up-to-date as possible.

Dmitriy Komissarov
Moscow, December 2003

Russian Language and Transliteration

The Russian language is phonetic – pronounced as written, or 'as seen'. Translating into English gives rise to many problems and the vast majority of these arise because English is not a straightforward language, with many pitfalls of pronunciation!

Accordingly, Russian words must be translated through into a phonetic form of English and this can lead to different ways of helping the reader pronounce what he sees. Every effort has been made to standardise this, but inevitably variations will occur. While reading from source to source this might seem confusing and/or inaccurate but it is the name as pronounced that is the constancy, not the spelling of that pronunciation!

The 20th letter of the Russian (Cyrillic) alphabet looks very much like a 'Y' but is pronounced as a 'U' as in the word 'rule'.

Another example is the train of thought that Russian words ending in 'y' are perhaps better spelt out as 'yi' to underline the pronunciation, but it is felt that most Western speakers would have problems getting their tongues around this!

This is a good example of the sort of problem that some Western sources have suffered from in the past (and occasionally even today) when they make the mental leap about what they see approximating to an English letter.

Chapter One

Mistaken Identity

Every aircraft has its *raison d'être*. To clarify the circumstances which led to the development of the Tu-134 we will have to travel back in time for half a century – all the way back to the beginning of the jet age in civil aviation. On 27th July 1949 the prototype of the world's first jet airliner to enter service, the 44-seat de Havilland DH.106 Comet 1 (G-ALVG) performed its maiden flight; after a lengthy test period the British Overseas Airways Corporation (BOAC) commenced scheduled services with the type on 2nd May 1952.

The DH.106 was one of the first passenger aircraft to feature a pressurised cabin; however, the operating conditions of such aircraft – specifically, the effect of the pressure differential on the fuselage structure and the resulting fatigue stresses – had not yet been studied. Hence the Comet 1 had a traditional safe-life fuselage design and thin fuselage skins were used to save weight. On 10th January 1954 one of BOAC's Comets, G-ALYP, disintegrated in mid-air over the Mediterranean. The cause was traced to fatigue failure; a crack originating at the flightdeck escape hatch had spread with overwhelming speed, the fuselage splitting open like a pea pod.

Hardly had the 'tin kickers' found the cause of the crash when another Comet 1, G-ALYY, was lost for the same reason on 8th April 1954. In consequence, production of the Comet 1 was stopped and all surviving examples broken up. The American Boeing and Douglas companies were quick to learn from de Havilland's mistake: the Boeing 707 and the DC-8 which entered flight test on 20th December 1957 and 30th May 1958 respectively both featured a fail-safe fuselage design precluding such catastrophic failures. (True, the much-improved DH.106 Comet 4 was brought out in October 1958, followed in January 1959 by the Comet 4B, but too late – the USA had become king of the hill on the world airliner market and the new Comet found few customers.)

Meanwhile, in the Soviet Union the advent of the Comet 1 immediately created the need to match the progress of the British by developing an indigenous jet airliner. This politically important task was entrusted to the nation's leading designer of commercial aircraft – the design bureau led by Andrey Nikolayevich Tupolev (OKB-156).[1] The first Soviet commercial jet was designated Tu-104 (NATO reporting name *Camel*). Thus was born a tradition – all subsequent Tupolev airliners were designated in the 1x4 (and later the 2x4 and 3x4) series, the Soviet answer to Boeing's 7x7 system.

To save time A N Tupolev opted for maximum structural and systems commonality with the Tu-16 medium bomber ('aircraft 88'; NATO codename *Badger*) – in effect, the fuselage was the only all-new component. Predictably, this approach led to an over-strengthened and overweight airframe, but this was not the only drawback. As was the case with the Tu-16 (and the Comet), the engines were buried in the wing roots, which led to high cabin noise levels.

Registered CCCP-Л5400 (ie, SSSR-L5400 in Cyrillic characters),[2] the Tu-104 prototype took to the air on 17th June 1955. Just over a year later, on 15th September 1956, the jet age really began for Aeroflot, the sole Soviet airline, when the Tu-104 performed the first revenue service from Moscow to Irkutsk via Omsk. The type soon replaced the ponderous piston-engined Lisunov Li-2P *Cab*, Il'yushin IL-12 *Coach* and IL-14 *Crate* on Aeroflot's long-haul routes, cutting travel times dramatically. For instance, the Li-2P took 28 hours to fly from Leningrad to Yuzhno-Sakhalinsk, with nine stops en route. The Tu-104 covered the distance in eight and a half hours, making two refuelling stops. For many years the Tu-104 was touted by the Soviet press as 'the world's first jet airliner'; no mention was made of the Comet – obviously it was acceptable to bend the facts a little for propaganda purposes.

Inspired by the success of the Tu-104 on transcontinental and international routes, Aeroflot was now eager to introduce jet hardware on other services, too. The airline issued a request for proposals concerning a short-to-medium haul twinjet airliner – and, not unexpectedly, a Tupolev product was selected. Although a 'clean sheet of paper' design, in general arrangement the new aircraft – designated Tu-124 (NATO codename *Cookpot*) – was a scaled-down Tu-104, utilising low-mounted wings, conventional swept tail surfaces and engines buried in the wing roots. Originally it was designed to seat 44 in all-economy configuration as this was then considered to be the optimum seating capacity for such an aircraft. The OKB-19 aero engine design bureau led by Pavel Aleksandrovich Solov'yov and located in the city of Perm' (now the Aviadvigatel' Production Association) developed the D-20P turbofan[3] with a take-off rating of 5,400kgp (11,904 lbst) for the Tu-124. This was the first-ever commercial turbofan engine, making the Tu-124 the world's first turbofan-powered airliner.

Academician Andrey Nikolayevich Tupolev, head of OKB-156, in his study in the late 1960s. His jacket is adorned by two Gold Star Orders that went with his two Hero of Socialist Labour titles.
Tupolev JSC

The Tu-124 short-haul airliner was the starting point. How many differences can you count? This particular aircraft, CCCP-45025, is now on display at the Russian Air Force Museum in Monino. Sergey Komissarov

The other starting point – the Aérospatiale SE210 Caravelle that prompted development of the Tu-134. B-1856 (c/n 170) is a Caravelle III, exactly like the one in which Nikita S Khrushchov flew in 1960. Sergey and Dmitriy Komissarov archive

The first prototype Tu-124 (CCCP-45000) made its maiden flight on 30th March 1960; production began in the same year at the Khar'kov aircraft factory No 135 named after the Lenin Young Communist League (KhAZ – *Khar'kovskiy aviatsionnyy zavod*) in the Ukraine.[4] After a 30-month test and evaluation programme the type joined the Aeroflot inventory, making the first scheduled flight on the Moscow-Tallinn route on 2nd October 1962. The 44-seat capacity soon proved insufficient, which led to the development of the 56-seat Tu-124V with a take-off weight increased from 34.5 tons (76,058 lb) to 38 tons (83,774 lb). Other versions included the 36-seat Tu-124K-36 VIP aircraft and the more luxurious 22-seat Tu-124K2-22, two navigator trainers for the Soviet Air Force – the Tu-124Sh-1 for strategic bomber crews and the Tu-124Sh-2 for tactical bomber crews and so on.

Meanwhile, France lost no time either. SNCASE (Société Nationale de Constructions Aériennes Sud-Est which later became part of Aérospatiale) brought out the SE210 Caravelle twinjet short-haul airliner. It was an unconventional design by the day's standards, featuring a cruciform tail unit and having the engines mounted on the aft fuselage sides on short horizontal pylons – a pioneering feature which was to become quite popular in the years to come.

Unlike the Comet and the Tu-104, the Caravelle underwent a long gestation period: the prototype (F-WHHH) took off on 27th May 1955, almost a month before the Tu-104, but revenue services did not begin until 12th May 1959. Yet the French engineers consciously chose a 'slowly but surely' approach in order to eliminate as many bugs as possible, not wishing a repetition of the British scenario with the explosive Comet.

What's the Caravelle got to do with this, you may ask? Well, in January 1960 the Soviet leader Nikita Sergeyevich Khruschchov paid an official visit to France where, among other things, he was given a demonstration flight in a Caravelle III. Khruschchov liked the airliner; he was especially impressed by the low noise and vibration levels in the cabin as compared to the Tu-104V which took him to France and back. To be perfectly honest, however, the comparison is not entirely objective because the Tu-104 was powered by much bigger engines; the Caravelle III's Rolls-Royce Avon RA.527s developed 5,300kgp (11,680 lbst) each whereas the Tu-104's Mikulin AM-3s were rated at 9,500kgp (20,940 lbst).

On returning to Moscow Khruschchov had a meeting with General Designer[5] Tupolev, asking him to start work on an aircraft similar to the Caravelle. Considering that such instructions came from the head of state, the design process was initiated at once. The bureaucratic machine was rather slower: on 1st August 1960 the Soviet Council of Ministers issued directive No 846-341 tasking the Tupolev OKB with creating a short-haul jet airliner *à la* Caravelle. According to this document the new aircraft was to have a top speed of 1,000km/h (621mph) and a cruising speed of 800-900km/h (497-559mph) at 10,000-12,000m (32,810-39,370ft). The required range at cruising speed with 30-minute fuel reserves was defined as 1,500km (930 miles) and the take-off/landing run as 800m (2,625ft). The aircraft was to have a payload of 5 tons (11,020 lb) and accommodate a maximum of 40 passengers plus three or four crewmembers. No mention was made of operating economics (this aspect was generally of secondary importance under the Soviet planned economy system).

The preliminary design (PD) section of OKB-156 chose the same basic approach as with the Tu-104 – the new airliner was to be derived from an existing design; this saved time and offered the advantage of lower production costs thanks to structural commonality. The as-yet unflown Tu-124 was chosen as the starting point, since its seating capacity was very similar to the government's demands. Hence the

'Soviet Caravelle' was provisionally designated Tu-124A.

The fuselage was borrowed from the basic Tu-124 almost unchanged; hence the Tu-124A retained the extensively glazed navigator's station in the extreme nose and the chin-mounted ROZ-1 Lotsiya (Navigational directions) weather/navigation radar[6] (NATO codename *Toad Stool*) in a small teardrop radome. (This 'bomber nose' was typical of nearly all Soviet passenger and transport aircraft designed in the late 1950s and early 1960s – the Antonov An-8 *Camp*, An-10 Ookraïna (the Ukraine/*Cat*), An-12 *Cub*, An-22 Antey (Antheus/*Cock*), Tupolev Tu-104, Tu-107, Tu-110 *Cooker*, Tu-114 Rossiya (Russia/*Cleat*), Tu-116 and Tu-124. In the case of the Tupolev aircraft this was indeed bomber heritage, since the Tu-104/-107/-110 and the Tu-114/-116 were derivatives of the Tu-16 and the Tu-95 *Bear-A* respectively.) A curious side effect of this arrangement was that the captain and the first officer each had his own pair of throttles.

The fuselage diameter was 2.9m (9ft 6⅛in), which meant the seating could be four-abreast only; by comparison, the Tu-104 had a fuselage diameter of 3.5m (11ft 5¾in), which allowed six-abreast seating. Speaking of which, the choice of the Tu-124's fuselage diameter was not a matter of chance. In terms of overall dimensions the *Cookpot* was an 80% scale copy of the *Camel*; multiplying the latter's fuselage diameter by 0.8 gives you 2.8m (9ft 2¼in).

An artist's impression of the Tu-124A (Tu-134) from the advanced development project documents. Tupolev JSC

This preliminary three-view of the Tu-134 from the advanced development project documents shows well the characteristic Tupolev wing design with the rearward-projecting main gear fairings. Tupolev JSC

The wings were outwardly similar to those of the basic Tu-124. The main landing gear units retracted into elongated fairings extending beyond the wing trailing edge (these fairings introduced on the Tu-16 became a trademark feature of Tupolev aircraft designed in the 1950s and 1960s). The trailing edge had a pronounced kink, running at right angles to the fuselage inboard of the landing gear fairings; the leading edge also featured a slight kink. Two boundary layer fences were installed on each wing's upper surface to limit spanwise flow, delaying tip stall and improving aileron efficiency; this feature was also typical of many Tupolev aircraft.

The same general arrangement was shared by Western airliners in the same class as the Tu-124A which appeared about the same time – the BAC One-Eleven, Douglas DC-9 and Fokker F.28 Fellowship. Generally the low-wing, T-tail, rear-engine layout was popular in the 1960s, finding use on the three-engined Yakovlev Yak-40 *Codling*, Tu-154 *Careless*, de Havilland DH.121 Trident and Boeing 727, as well as the four-engined Il'yushin IL-62 *Classic* and Vickers VC-10.

The chosen layout offered a number of advantages. Removing the engines from the wings allowed relative flap area and wing efficiency to be increased. The aft fuselage and tail unit were less affected by vibration and tailplane buffet (caused by jet efflux), a phenomenon which could cause fatigue problems. Likewise, the high-set stabilisers were less affected by wing upwash, which improved longitudinal stability in cruise flight. In addition, this improved engine operating conditions thanks to the short inlet ducts, reduced foreign object damage (FOD) risk and facilitated engine maintenance and change. Passenger comfort was greatly enhanced by the low noise and vibration. Finally, there was no danger of fragments entering the cabin in the event of an uncontained engine failure.

Yet the rear-engine, T-tail arrangement had some serious shortcomings, too. The wings were positioned further aft as compared to the normal layout, increasing fuselage area ahead of the centre of gravity (CG); this meant vertical tail area had to be increased to ensure adequate directional stability, with an attendant increase in structural weight. The fuselage and fin had to be reinforced, increasing empty weight and reducing the payload. CG travel was increased, and the high position of the thrust line produced a pitch-down force that increased rotation speed on take-off and elevator control forces.

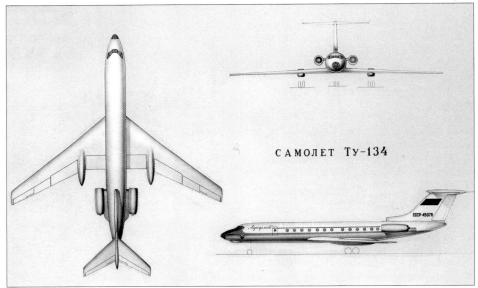

С А М О Л Е Т Ту-134

Earlier, however, three Soviet aircraft factories (though not the one building the Tu-124) had built the Tu-4 *Bull* heavy bomber – a copy of the Boeing B-29 Stratofortress whose fuselage diameter was 2.9m, and this was selected for the Tu-124 for the sake of simplifying production. (Thus the Tu-124 and Tu-124A can be considered *very* distant relatives of Boeing!)

In many other respects, however, the Tu-124A differed markedly from the 'pure' Tu-124. The engines were housed in nacelles attached to the aft fuselage sides by short pylons, as was the case with the Caravelle. True, this was not the first Tupolev jet with aft-mounted engines; in 1957 the OKB had brought out the 'aircraft 105' supersonic bomber which, after a deal of redesigning, became the '105A', entering production and service as the Tu-22 *Blinder*. However, the Tu-22 had the engines mounted directly on top of the aft fuselage, flanking the fin root.

The new engine location dictated the need for a T-tail, with the stabilisers mounted atop the fin; the Caravelle-style cruciform arrangement was rejected because the sound waves

impinging on the relatively low-set stabilisers could cause fatigue problems. The vertical tail now had a much wider chord and a prominent bullet fairing at the fin/tailplane junction; vertical tail area was nearly doubled as compared to the Tu-124, being 21.25m² (228.49ft²) versus 12.0m² (129.0ft²). The rudder was enlarged accordingly and, for the first time in Tupolev OKB practice, provided with a hydraulic actuator. Conversely, horizontal tail area was reduced over the Tu-124, as it was believed that the engine nacelles and their pylons would contribute a stabilising influence. (Later events, however, showed this was a bad decision, but more about this later.)

Thanks to the new layout the Tu-124A had aerodynamically 'clean' wings unencumbered by the engines. As with previous Tupolev swept-wing jets (both civil and military), wing sweep at quarter-chord was 35°. However, the aspect ratio was increased as compared to the Tu-124 by increasing the wing span from 25.55m (83ft 10in) to 29.01m (95ft 2¼in); wing area increased accordingly from 115.0m² (1,236.56ft²) to 125.5m² (1,349.46ft²).

A highly dangerous (and as yet unknown) deep stall problem was inherent in the T-tail layout. Besides, maintenance of the tail unit became complicated, a tall work platform being required to reach the horizontal tail.

The aerodynamically 'clean' wings made it possible to delete the steps in the middle of the cabin characteristic of the basic Tu-124. These steps, which were due to the wing centre section spars passing over the engines, had been a major source of annoyance for passengers who kept tripping over them; the smooth cabin floor of the Tu-124A eliminated this problem. However, for better integration between wings and cabin floor the designers lopped off the top of the wing airfoil inboard of the landing gear fairings, creating a flat upper surface. This feature simplified production but created unnecessary vortices, increasing drag.

By trying to ensure maximum commonality with the basic Tu-124 in order to simplify production and cut costs (a point pressed by the OKB's chief technologist S A Vigdorchik) the OKB did itself a disservice. Attempts to incorporate wing camber while retaining the Tu-124's wing torsion box resulted in a unique S-shaped airfoil: the leading edge was curved downwards while the trailing edge portion was bent upwards. This unique solution approved by TsAGI (*Tsentrahl'nyy aero- i ghidrodinameecheskiy instituut* – the Central Aerodynamics & Hydrodynamics Institute named after Nikolay Yegorovich Zhukovskiy) proved to be a double-edged weapon. The leading-edge curvature delayed the onset of stall at high angles of attack, improving the lift/drag ratio at low speed; on the other hand, the upward-bent trailing edge created a strong negative pressure in cruise flight at speeds around Mach 0.7, considerably increasing drag. Moreover, wind tunnel tests showed the need to increase the angle between the engine pylons and the fuselage waterline. However, instead of tilting the pylons bodily the engineers chose to simply twist the leading edges upwards; this minimised the changes to the pylon/rear fuselage structure but again increased drag and fuel consumption.

True enough, operating economics were not an issue of particular importance in the USSR with its state-controlled economy. The air enterprises constituting Aeroflot got all the fuel they wanted; all they had to do was make sure the annual and five-year plan targets were met. In the long run, however, the aerodynamic imperfections of the Tu-134 caused by this 'quick fix' approach resulted in a colossal waste of fuel and money. The excess fuel consumption amounted to 300kg/hr (660 lb/hr); with a 30,000-hour designated service life a single Tu-134 would guzzle an extra 9,000 tons (19,840 lb) of fuel. Considering that Aeroflot's Tu-134 fleet was roughly 400 units, the aggregate figure is 3.6 million tons (7,936,507,940 lb). In Soviet times a ton of jet fuel cost 68 roubles; thus the total excess costs for the fleet (if all aircraft were to be operated until time-expired) would be a whopping 244.8 million roubles! In comparison, reworking the manufacturing drawings and tooling would have cost 20,000 roubles at the most.

Like its progenitor, the Tu-124A featured a large ventral speedbrake under the wing centre section; this was deployed together with the flaps to increase the glideslope angle. Unlike the Tu-124, however, the speedbrake was of almost square shape rather than elongated and convex, not concave (because it was no longer wrapped around the engine nacelles flanking the fuselage).

As already noted, the landing gear design was typical of Tupolev aircraft of the 1950s and 1960s; the main units retracted aft, the bogies rotating through 180° to lie inverted in streamlined fairings. Yet again, unlike the predecessors, the new airliner featured semi-levered suspension; the main gear oleos were inclined when extended and a prominent telescopic retraction strut was attached to the front of the oleo. This allowed the main gear bogies to move aft by virtue of oleo compression in the

The rear-engine, T-tail layout selected for the Tu-134 was popular in the 1960s. One example is the BAC One-Eleven; this is a Romanian-built Rombac 111-561RC of TAROM Romanian Airlines (YR-BRC, c/n 403) pictured at Copenhagen-Kastrup in August 1998. Author

One more Tu-134 look-alike designed in the same period is the Douglas DC-9, illustrated by Finnair DC-9-51 OH-LYP (c/n 47969, f/n 808) taking off from runway 22R at Copenhagen-Kastrup in July 1998. Author

Yet another contemporary look-alike, the Fokker F.28 Fellowship, illustrated here by Air Botnia Fellowship Mk 4000 SE-DGO (c/n 11190). Author's collection

The Tu-124A designation was short-lived; Tupolev soon decided that the changes were serious enough to warrant a new designation. Pursuant to an order dated 20th February 1963 the aircraft was renamed Tu-134,[7] which puzzled Western aviation experts mightily. Interestingly, the new designation leaked to the West surprisingly quickly; in March 1963 *Flying Review International* wrote that *'the Tu-124A, a derivative of the current Tu-124 (Cookpot) with twin aft-mounted turbofan engines, has been abandoned in favour of the larger Tu-134 which reportedly features three turbofans arranged in a similar fashion to the engines of the Hawker Siddeley Trident'*. This misunderstanding was cleared the following month, however, and the Tu-134 received a separate NATO reporting name, *Crusty* (C for commercial).

Assembly of the first prototype began in the spring of 1963 at the OKB's experimental plant, MMZ No 156 'Opyt' (MMZ = *Moskovskiy mashinostroitel'nyy zavod* – Moscow Machinery Plant; the name translates as either 'experiment' or 'experience'). The aircraft was registered CCCP-45075 and bore the construction number 00-00, that is, batch zero, aircraft zero (hence the first prototype was known in-house as *noolyovka* – 'Aircraft Zilch').

Curiously, the registration reflected the aircraft's original designation (apparently it was allocated before the Tu-124A was renamed Tu-134). Under the five-digit registration system in use since 1958 the first two digits are usually a type designator introduced for flight safety reasons (this allows air traffic control officers to identify the aircraft type by its registration and thus avoid placing excessive demands on the crew).[8] Since the 45xxx registration block was allocated to Tu-124s, it is logical that the Tu-124A should be registered in this block. Yet when a new registration block (65xxx) was issued go with the new Tu-134 designation, the prototype was never reregistered – possibly because nobody wanted to mess around with additional paperwork.

Usually Soviet/Russian design bureaux build prototypes and static test airframes themselves and then pass the drawings and tooling to aircraft factories for production, sending a team of experts to solve problems coming up during the learning curve. However, since the Tu-124 and Tu-134 had a lot in common, a different *modus operandi* was chosen. Stock Tu-124 subassemblies were converted and delivered by rail and road from the Khar'kov aircraft factory and other plants to MMZ No 156 for assembly. Thus both factories – or neither factory – can claim to be the manufacturer of

event of hard braking or jolts, providing a very smooth touchdown and a smoother ride on the ground – which was just as well, considering the less-than-perfect condition of the runways and taxiways at many Soviet airports.

A brake parachute was housed in the tailcone to shorten the landing run on wet or icy runways or in an emergency. The parachute was a leftover from the basic Tu-124 which had inherited this feature from the Tu-104; it was nearly eight years yet before thrust reversers would appear on Soviet jets.

The powerplant comprised two Solov'yov D-20P-125 turbofans; this was a version of the D-20P uprated to 5,800kgp (12,790 lbst) and with a specific fuel consumption (SFC) reduced from 0.89kg/kgp·hr to 0.815kg/kgp·hr. (It may be said at this stage that three standard Tu-124s were fitted with the new D-20P-125 engines in late 1962 and early 1963. Designated Tu-124B, this version performed well but did not enter production, becoming a stepping stone towards the more advanced Tu-124A.)

The preliminary specifications issued by Aeroflot in September 1960 called for a seating capacity of 46 or 58 (in all-tourist and all-economy configuration respectively) and a flight crew of four – two pilots, a flight engineer and a navigator. The speed, range and field performance figures stated in the aforementioned CofM directive of 1st August 1960 were confirmed; the service ceiling was specified as 10,000-12,000m (32,810-39,370ft), the dry weight as 22.6 tons (49,820 lb), the empty operating weight as 23.1 tons (50,925 lb) and the payload as five to six tons (11,025-13,230 lb).

An advanced development project (ADP) meeting these specifications was completed on schedule by 1st April 1961 (some April Fool's Day joke, indeed). However, small airliners have a habit of growing before they get off the drawing board, and the Tu-124A was a case in point. After reviewing the project Aeroflot changed its requirements, issuing new specs between 7th and 13th October 1961. Now the aircraft was to have the same 1,500-km (930-mile) range with a 7-ton (15,430-lb) maximum payload or a 3,000-km (1,860-mile) maximum range with a 4-ton (8,820-lb) payload and 30-minute fuel reserves, a 900-m (2,950-ft) take-off/landing run and a seating capacity of 65-70. It was back to the drawing board for Tupolev; the work of defining and refining the project continued well into 1962.

Initially Dmitriy Sergeyevich Markov was the Tu-124A's chief project engineer. But then the Tupolev OKB embarked on numerous military programmes and many engineers, including Markov, were reassigned to bombers. Overall responsibility for the airliner passed to Leonid Leonidovich Selyakov who joined Tupolev in December 1962 after working with the rival OKB-23 led by Vladimir Mikhaïlovich Myasishchev, and he remained project chief until he passed away in October 2002. Tupolev's long-time aide Aleksandr Aleksandrovich Arkhangel'skiy, Leonid L'vovich Kerber, Sergey Mikhaïlovich Yeger, Aleksandr Sergeyevich Shengardt (he became Tu-134 project chief after Selyakov's death), Kurt Vladimirovich Minckner, M G Pinegin, M D Lebedev and Boris F Petrov were also on the Tu-124A team.

The flightdeck of Tu-134 CCCP-45075, showing clearly the passage into the glazed navigator's station and the eyebrow windows inherited from the Tu-124. The large round 'box' on the captain's control wheel is associated with test equipment. Tupolev JSC

The cabin of the first prototype following refurbishment to representative airline configuration – a typical 1960s interior with patterned wall upholstery. The curtains at the rear close the passage to the toilets. Tupolev JSC

CCCP-45075, which is why the factory number is not stated in the c/n. The fuselage was lengthened by 660mm (2ft 2in); the original intention was to stretch it by 2m (6ft 6¾in).

There were 12 cabin windows of 40cm (15¾in) diameter to port (an entry door incorporating a window+3 windows+4+4) and 11 to starboard (3+4+4) but as yet no overwing emergency exits; the latter was Tu-124 heritage. A square-shaped baggage loading door opening inwards and up was located on the starboard side aft of the flightdeck, with two smaller windows of 30cm (11¾in) diameter above it to admit some daylight into the galley and forward baggage compartment. There were four windows high on the rear fuselage sides next to the engines; these were for the toilets and the rear baggage compartment. A ram air intake for the air conditioning system heat exchanger protruded at the junction of the fin and the fin fillet. The fairing at the fin/tailplane junction had a rounded front end and a pointed rear end; a wire aerial for an HF radio ran from the fin top to the centre fuselage.

The prototype was 33.84m (111ft 0in) long and 9.017m (29ft 7in) high, with a wing span of 29.01m (95ft 2in); the landing gear track was 9.45m (31ft 0in) and the wheelbase 13.4m (43ft 11½in). The OEW was 24.25 tons (53,460 lb) and the fuel capacity 14,400 litres (3,168 Imp gals) or 11.5 tons (25,350 lb). The cabin could accommodate 52-56 passengers and the flight crew consisted of four or five persons. ICAO Cat I blind landing capability was provided (decision altitude 60m/200ft, horizontal visibility 800m/2,600ft), which facilitated night and poor-weather operations considerably.

The longer fuselage, 'clean' wings and T-tail made the Tu-134 rather more elegant and aesthetically pleasing than the tubby Tu-124 which seemed to be weighed down by the engines installed in the wing roots. 'Aircraft Zilch' was painted white with a dark blue cheatline underlined in blue, a dark blue fin/tailplane fairing, natural metal undersurfaces, black Aeroflot titles in italics and the customary round 'Tu' badge aft of the navigator's glazing. Black phototheodolite calibration markings were carried on the fin and forward fuselage.

Chapter Two

Pains of Birth

Before tests could begin CCCP-45075 had to be delivered to the Flight Research Institute named after Mikhail Mikhaïlovich Gromov (LII – *Lyotno-issledovatel'skiy institoot*) in the town of Zhukovskiy south of Moscow where OKB-156 had its flight test facility. Sergey Vladimirovich Il'yushin's OKB-240 was better off than most others: it was (and still is) located at the Central Airfield named after Mikhail Vasil'yevich Frunze (better known as Moscow-Khodynka) with its 1,700-m (5,577-ft) runway. Hence most Il'yushin prototypes were flown from there straight to Zhukovskiy, as were production IL-18 *Coot* airliners built by MMZ No 30 'Znamya truda' (Banner of Labour, pronounced *znahmya troodah*)[1] located right across the field. The Tupolev OKB, however, did not enjoy this proximity, having its premises at Radio Street which is a long way off. There was no choice but to disassemble the aircraft and take it to LII by road. Besides, making a flight from downtown was a risk the OKB could do without, especially since the Nuclear Physics Research Institute with its reactors was directly in the flight path.

After reassembly the aircraft underwent systems checks and taxiing tests. Finally, on 29th July 1963 the Tu-134 successfully performed its maiden flight, captained by Distinguished Test Pilot[2] Aleksandr Danilovich Kalina, Hero of the Soviet Union – the man who had taken the Tu-124 into the air three years earlier. The crew also included Distinguished Test Pilot Ye A Goryunov, Boris F Petrov and test engineer Vyacheslav Aleksandrovich Revyakin.

The crew was pleased with the aircraft's handling, reporting that the Tu-134 was stable and easy to fly. Newspaper reporters waxed lyrical about the new airliner: the first news items about the Tu-134 (which, incidentally, did not appear until September 1964!) were full of clichés like 'silver arrow', 'conquering the skies with ease' and so on. This was the usual style of Soviet newspapers when extolling the achievements of the socialist economy.

Distinguished Test Pilot Nikolay Nikolayevich Kharitonov acted as co-pilot in subsequent test flights. The aircraft had a 38-ton (83,770-lb) take-off weight, a 33.5-ton (73,850-lb) landing weight and a cruising speed of 800km/h (497mph/432kts). Range was 2,000km (1,240 miles) with a 1,500-kg/3,306-lb payload (16 passengers) or 1,500km (930 miles) with a 2,000-kg/4,410-lb payload (20 passengers); the take-off run was 950m (3,120ft) and the landing run 700m (2,300ft).

Like most aircraft, the Tu-134 had its share of bugs; for instance, excessive aileron compensation was discovered, necessitating a redesign. The flap drive failed on several occasions, causing asymmetrical deployment and forcing a flapless landing. Flights with wool tufts glued to the wings to visualise the airflow showed that the flaps were inefficient (that is, 'leaky'); the flaps had to be modified by reducing the cutouts for the flap tracks (these were not replicated on the wind tunnel models). Nevertheless, the wide slots along the aileron leading edges (8-12mm; $^5/_{16}$ to $^{15}/_{32}$ in) were still there; on Western airliners in the same class the ailerons were sealed to cut drag.

Contrary to reports perpetuated by Western authors, the first prototype did *not* crash on 22nd October 1963 (on the same day as the BAC 111 prototype). Instead, it flew without mishap, completing manufacturer's flight tests on 6th November 1964 and logging 274 hours in 225 flights, whereupon it was transferred to Aeroflot for evaluation. Later it was used by OKB-156 for various development work. After retirement by mid-1968 Tu-134 CCCP-45075 was put on display at the VDNKh fairground (*Vystavka dostizheniy narodnovo khoziaystva* – National Economy Achievements Exhibition) in Moscow, succeeding Tu-124V CCCP-45052 which had been there since at least 1965. The Tu-134 graced the fairground's central plaza together with a pre-production Yakovlev Yak-40 *Codling* feederliner (CCCP-19661) until 1977 when they gave way to Tu-154 CCCP-85005 and Yak-42 CCCP-42304 which are still there. After that CCCP-45075 became a 'gate guard' at an aircraft engineers' school on the eastern outskirts of Moscow (9 Napol'nyy Proyezd, a couple of bus stops from Novogireyevo subway station). Regrettably the aircraft is now in a rather sorry state, weather and local vandals having taken their toll. Incidentally, the man behind the opening of the school and the transfer of the aircraft thereto was Aleksey Andreyevich Tupolev, the General Designer's son and successor.

However, all this happened much later. Meanwhile the Khar'kov aircraft factory completed the second prototype, known as *dooblyor* (lit. 'understudy'; the Soviet term for second prototypes used until the late 1960s) in mid-1964. This aircraft again wore a Tu-124-type registration, CCCP-45076 (c/n 4350001).[3]

An air-to-air study of the first prototype cruising above the clouds. Note the photo calibration markings on the fin and forward fuselage.
Tupolev JSC

The *dooblyor* differed considerably from the first prototype, featuring a further 0.5-m (1ft 7in) fuselage stretch at fuselage frame 37 increasing overall length to 34.3m (112ft 6⅜in), the wheelbase to 13.9m (45ft 7¼in) and the seating capacity to 64. Other external differences included 14 cabin windows to port (door+7+6) and 13 to starboard (2 small windows+7+6) – but still no emergency exits. The outer boundary layer fences were moved slightly outward in line with the inboard ends of the ailerons. The rear ends of the engine nacelles were recontoured, the heat exchanger air intake was cut down flush with the fin leading edge, and the HF wire aerial now ran all the way to the flightdeck. The rear doors of the nosewheel well now closed when the gear was down.

Other changes were not so obvious. The outer wings incorporated additional integral tanks increasing the fuel capacity to 13.0 tons (28,660 lb) or 16,300 litres (3,586 Imp gals). Empty weight increased to 24.9 tons (54,894 lb).

The colour scheme was different, too, featuring a bright blue cheatline below the windows with a blue 'lightning bolt' underneath and a red pinstripe above the windows, a white fin top fairing, smaller Aeroflot titles, a restyled Soviet flag and 'inverted-T' calibration markings.

CCCP-45076 took to the air on 9th September 1964[9] and the manufacturer's flight tests of the *dooblyor* officially lasted from 20th February to 7th April 1965. At this stage the rear end of the fin/tailplane fairing was fattened considerably to improve aerodynamics; this feature was retained on production aircraft. The second prototype had an MTOW of 42 tons (92,592 lb) and a maximum landing weight of 35 tons (77,160 lb); cruising speed was 850-880km/h (528-546mph; 459-475kts) and top speed 920km/h (571mph; 497kts). With 64 passengers and a fuel load of seven or ten tons (15,432 or 22,045 lb) the Tu-134 could travel 1,300 or 2,200km (807 or 1,366 miles) respectively; maximum range was recorded as 3,000km (1,863 miles).

The required runway length in max range configuration was 1,800m (5,900ft) and the landing roll was 800-1,000m (2,625-3,280ft). It was envisaged that the aircraft would be used on regional routes between airports with short runways and even operate from unpaved runways, the position of the engines relative to the wings and main gear bogies preventing FOD.

The manufacturer's flight tests of CCCP-45076 involved only 36 flights totalling 60 hours. On 11th December 1964 the State Commission which was to clear the Tu-134 for production and service had its first session; the second, decisive session followed on 7th March 1965 and Stage 1 of the flight test programme was declared successfully completed. The Commission ruled that the aircraft presented no problems for average-skilled pilots but demanded that special high-alpha (angle of attack) tests be held and that vibrations arising when the flaps were deployed be eliminated.

TU-134 CONSTRUCTION NUMBERS

Three systems were used, and the first one was straightforward. For instance, Tu-134 CCCP-65640 manufactured on 6th April 1970 is c/n 0350919 – that is, year of manufacture 1970,[4] Khar'kov aircraft factory No 135 (the first digit is omitted for security reasons to confuse would-be spies), Batch 9, 19th aircraft in the batch. This system remained in use until late April 1974; the last civil example to use it was Tu-134A LZ-TUR (c/n 4352308).

In mid-April 1974 the factory switched to what yours truly calls the 'damn fool system' devised in 1973 (certainly by the KGB to make life harder for spies!) and used by most Soviet aircraft factories. For instance, Tu-134A-1 OK-IFN manufactured on 28th February 1978 is c/n 8360282. The first digit again denotes the year of manufacture; the second is always a 3 and may be an in-house product code (*izdeliye* 3).[5] The remaining five digits do not signify *anything at all*; the idea is to confuse would-be spies so that the c/n would not reveal how many aircraft have been built. The first two digits of these 'famous last five', as they are often called, change independently from the final three. Only the 'famous last five' are usually quoted in paperwork. In these cases the missing two digits at the front will be given in parentheses – for example, Tu-134A CCCP-65840, c/n (43)18118; the '4' means 1974 in this case.

Additionally, Tu-134s with c/ns under System 2 have four-digit fuselage numbers (f/ns); security is all very well but the manufacturer has to keep track of production, after all. Typically of Soviet aircraft, the f/n is not just a sequential line number (as in the case of Boeing and Douglas aircraft) but consists of a batch number and the number of the aircraft in the batch. The aforementioned Tu-134A-1 OK-IFN is f/n 4409; thus it would have been c/n 8354409 if the 'rational' System 1 had continued in use.

As regards civil versions, Batch 0 had six aircraft (that is, not counting the two static airframes which had no c/ns for some reason); batches 1 through 7 consisted of five aircraft, Batch 8 had ten and Batch 9 had 28. This is because all remaining 'short' Tu-134s were crammed into Batch 9, since production of the stretched Tu-134A was planned to start from Batch 10. This and subsequent batches consisted of ten aircraft, except Batch 63 (the final one for civil aircraft) which comprised no fewer that 75 aircraft – again because production of the Tu-134UBL military

trainer was to begin with Batch 64. Different civil versions were often mixed within a single batch.

The Tu-134Sh military navigator trainer originally used System 1 but had a separate c/n sequence with batch numbers starting from 00 all over again (which caused much confusion in the West). The last known example is an aircraft with the tactical code '87 Blue'[6] (c/n 3350403). Late-production aircraft have eight-digit c/ns which are a cross-breed between systems 1 and 2 (and hence have fuselage numbers as well). For instance, Tu-134Sh-1 '84 Red' manufactured on 17th September 1976 is c/n 63550720; the first digit denotes the year of manufacture, the next two refer to factory No 135 and the rest are the 'famous last five'; the f/n is unknown.[7] Normally there were five aircraft to a batch, except batches 0 and 18 (the last one), both of which had only two aircraft, and Batch 2, which comprised eight aircraft.

The Tu-134UBL military pilot trainer used System 2 but, unlike civil versions, the 'famous last five' invariably commenced with 64; for example, an example coded '15 Red' which was built in 1982 is c/n (23)64270. Some sources claim that batches 64 through 71 were reserved for this version, with ten aircraft to a batch.

The c/n is found at the top of a small metal plate riveted to the forward bulkhead of the nosewheel well; the last four digits under System 1, the 'famous last five' under System 2 or the complete c/n under System 3 are embossed there. The c/n is *extremely* hard to read, as the nose gear oleo hinders access to the plate (ideally, you have to stand on the nosewheel) and the digits are really tiny. Aircraft featuring the standard glazed nose have an identical plate in the flightdeck (on the left side of the passage leading to the navigator's station). The Tu-134Sh went one better than the others. Virtually all civil-registered aircraft carry the registration on a plate or sticker in the cockpit/flightdeck as a reminder to facilitate working with air traffic control; the Tu-134 has two such plates affixed to the captain's and first officer's instrument panel shrouds. Well, on the Tu-134Sh these plates carry the last four digits of the c/n under System 1 or the complete c/n under System 3 instead of a registration! Conversely, the f/n is usually found only in the aircraft's record card or other papers, but Soviet/CIS Air Force examples often have it – or the last five of the c/n – marked on air intake covers, wheel chocks etc to prevent them from being stolen.[8] A production list is provided in Appendix 1.)

Above: **The first prototype at Sochi-Adler in 1967 during service tests.** Tupolev JSC

Left: **Still in pristine condition, the first prototype is seen here on display in VDNKh's Central plaza in August 1968.** Sergey Komissarov

Below left: **CCCP-45075 in its latter days as a gate guard at technical school No 164 in Moscow. The students are examining one of the aircraft's D-20P-125 turbofans removed for use as a teaching aid.** ITAR-TASS

Below right: **CCCP-45076, the second prototype, joined the flight test programme on 9th September 1964. It is seen here in its original colour scheme. Note the slightly different window arrangement and the revised ACS air intake.** Tupolev JSC

The second prototype at Moscow-Sheremet'yevo in the early spring of 1965 with modified engine nacelles. *Sergey Komissarov*

A rare photo of both prototypes in formation flight, showing the different colour schemes. *Tupolev JSC*

Occasionally both prototypes could be seen together at Moscow-Sheremet'yevo. *Sergey Komissarov*

On 4th May it was decided to unveil the Tu-134 at the 25th Paris Air Show. After a full month's preparations involving removal of the test equipment, installation of passenger seats and cabin trim, and repainting CCCP-45076 made the type's international debut at Le Bourget. Immediately after the show the aircraft visited Warsaw, Berlin and Prague on a sales trip.

Tests revealed that the Tu-134 was underpowered. On 10th February 1965 the Solov'yov OKB started work on the uprated D-20P-125 Srs 5, and soon after Le Bourget it was decided to launch production of the airliner with these engines. But then OKB-19 dropped the idea, proposing a more radical redesign – the D-30 turbofan rated at 6,800kgp (14,990 lbst), with a design life of 7,500 hours and a time between overhauls (TBO) of 2,500 hours. A 72-seat version of Tu-134 with a 44-ton (97,000-lb) TOW powered by D-30s was quickly developed; the project was approved by Yevgeniy F Loginov, Chairman of the Civil Air Fleet Main Directorate (GU GVF – **Glahv**noye oopra**vlen**iye Grazh**dahn**skovo vozdoosh**novo flot**a), on 17th July 1965 and by Minister of Aircraft Industry Pyotr V Dement'yev four days later. The engine entered full-scale development in September.

Meanwhile, the manufacturer's flight tests were terminated in order to speed up service entry. On 18th July 1965 CCCP-45076 was loaned to the Soviet Air Force State Research Institute named after Valeriy Pavlovich Chkalov (GK NII VVS – Gosoo**dar**stvennyy krasnozna**myon**nyy na**ooch**no-is**sled**ovatel'skiy inst**itoot** voye**nno**-vozd**oosh**nykh seel) at Chkalovskaya airbase about 30km (18.5 miles) east of Moscow.[10] All new airliners were tested by this institution to evaluate possible military uses. On 14th January 1966 disaster struck: the *dooblyor* crashed near Moscow with an Air Force pilot at the controls, killing all four crewmen and four test engineers.

The OKB claims that grave pilot error was the cause; contrary to all flight manuals and common sense the captain, S V Yevseyev, gave full 25° rudder deflection at never-exceed speed (Mach 0.86). This was possible because, unlike the manual elevators and ailerons, the rudder had a hydraulic actuator – for the first time on a Soviet airliner. A curious quirk of the Tu-134 was that the aircraft displayed reverse roll reaction to rudder inputs at speeds above Mach 0.84 (that is, it rolled right instead of left when left rudder was applied). As a result, CCCP-45076 side-slipped, entering a dive from which

the pilots could not recover in time due to insufficient elevator area. By sheer bad luck, Yevgeniy Vasil'yevich Gloobokov, the Tupolev OKB's engineer in charge of the tests, was late for the flight on that day; had he been aboard, he would surely have prevented the fatal error.

The crash led the OKB to introduce an artificial-feel unit limiting rudder deflection in cruise mode to 5° into the rudder control circuit and impose a Mach 0.82 operational speed limit. Also, tests at GK NII VVS were terminated for the time being. By Government decision all further testing of new civil aircraft was transferred to the Civil Air Fleet Research Institute (NII GVF – Na**ooch**no-is**sled**ovatel'skiy inst**itoot** Grazh**dahn**skovo vozd**oosh**novo **flot**a) at Moscow-Sheremet'yevo, now called the State Civil Aviation Research Institute (GosNII GA – Gosoo**dar**stvennyy na**ooch**no-is**sled**ovatel'skiy inst**itoot** grazh**dahn**skoy avi**ahts**ii).

Meanwhile the Khar'kov aircraft factory completed a static test airframe and a fatigue test airframe in the spring of 1965. On 14th August 1965 the first pre-production Tu-134 (CCCP-65600, c/n 5350002) made its first flight from the factory's Sokol'nikovo airfield. This and the second pre-production aircraft (CCCP-65601, c/n 5350003) were still powered by D-20P-125s (but later re-engined with D-30s); the nacelle shape was identical to the first prototype's – apparently the changes made on the second prototype gave unsatisfactory results. The fin/tailplane fairing also had the original shape at first.

Sporting its definitive colour scheme, CCCP-45076 comes in to land at Paris-Le Bourget in June 1965 to make its international debut. A very similar livery was originally worn by production examples. *Flug Revue*

The inevitable crunch as the Tu-134 static test airframe undergoes destructive testing at TsAGI. The airframe already incorporates one overwing emergency exit on each side but still features a protruding air conditioning system air intake on the fin leading edge. Tupolev JSC

Seen here in 1965 during service tests with the original D-20P-125 engines and small horizontal tail, CCCP-65600, the first pre-production Tu-134, shares the ramp at Moscow's Vnukovo-2 VIP terminal with a Tu-124K, an Il'yushin IL-18 and a Mil' Mi-4S (CCCP-36338).
Novosti Press Agency

Tu-134 CCCP-65600 introduced overwing emergency exits measuring 0.586 x 0.6m (23 x 23⅝in, that is, Type IV in current ICAO classification), although the first production aircraft had only two of these. Thus the window placement was as follows: door+5+exit+1+6 to port and 2 small windows+5+exit+1+6 to starboard.

The first aircraft to have D-30 engines from the start and the envisaged 44-ton TOW was the third pre-production example, CCCP-65602 (c/n 6350004), which took off on 21st July 1966. The new turbofan had entered production in 1965 at the aero-engine factory No 19 named after Yakov Mikhaïlovich Sverdlov in Perm'.[11]

As already mentioned, the T-tail, rear-engine layout was not yet fully studied at the time (the Caravelle with its cruciform tail offered no analogy). Soon, the deep stall phenomenon (the blanketing of the horizontal tail by the engine nacelles at high alpha which reduces elevator efficiency) came to light. On 22nd October 1963, four months after the Tu-134's maiden flight, the BAC One-Eleven 200AB prototype (G-ASHG) crashed near Chicklade, Wiltshire, during low-speed trials, killing the crew. The aircraft had entered a deep stall and there was insufficient elevator authority to recover from it.

Designers all over the world learn from the mistakes of their colleagues. The solution was to increase the horizontal tail span and hence the portion of the elevators which would not be blanketed by the nacelles during a stall. The Douglas Company urgently increased the horizontal tail area of the as-yet unflown DC-9 by 30%. So did the Tupolev OKB; at Leonid L Selyakov's insistence a new horizontal tail of by 30% greater area and a span increased from 9.2m (30ft 2¼in) to 11.8m (38ft 8½in). After tests in the TsAGI wind tunnel the new structure was manufactured in Khar'kov and installed on CCCP-65602 which first flew in this guise on 25th October 1966.

CCCP-65600 was also retrofitted with the larger horizontal tail. In July 1966 the aircraft was further modified at the OKB's flight test facility in Zhukovskiy for high-alpha, stall and spin tests (these became a mandatory part of the test programme after several Tu-104s stalled and crashed at low speed). The tailcone was replaced by a long thick fairing with external stiffening ribs which housed a large anti-spin parachute canister with a downward-hinging hemispherical cover; electric cables ran along the port side of the fuselage and fairing to the parachute release mechanism. The forward baggage door was modified to serve as an escape hatch for bailing out, should spin recovery become impossible.

The trials proceeded from October 1966 to February 1967, involving flights with various flap settings; the engines ran steadily all the time, indicating that their position with respect to the wings had been well chosen (they did not ingest turbulent air at high angles of attack). Aleksandr D Kalina was project test pilot, with N N Kharitonov and Distinguished Test Pilot

The second pre-production Tu-134, CCCP-65601, as originally flown. Note the square-shaped baggage hatch and the high position of the galley windows above it. Boris Vdovenko

An air-to-air of CCCP-65600, showing the short nacelles of the D-20P-125 engines and original short-span horizontal tail. Sergey and Dmitriy Komissarov archive

In 1966 CCCP-65600 was refitted with D-30 engines and increased-span stabilisers and modified for low-speed/high-alpha handling tests. This picture taken at the Minsk overhaul plant shows the large spin recovery parachute container and the new engines.
Yefim Gordon archive

The forward fuselage of CCCP-65600 with a cine camera fairing aft of the nosewheel well. Note the small size of the entry door.
Yefim Gordon archive

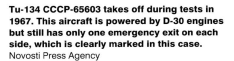

Tu-134 CCCP-65603 takes off during tests in 1967. This aircraft is powered by D-30 engines but still has only one emergency exit on each side, which is clearly marked in this case.
Novosti Press Agency

P A Malinin acting as co-pilots. As a result, the new horizontal tail became standard.

About the same time a cine camera in a teardrop fairing was installed on the lower fuselage of CCCP-65600 just aft of the nose gear to check the operation of the shimmy damper. To prevent reflections which might dazzle the camera the nose gear doors and the forward half of the fairing were painted matt black.

An extra cabin window on each side was introduced from the first production aircraft (CCCP-65604 No 1, c/n 6350101) onwards (that is, door+6+exit+1+6 to port and 2 small windows+6+exit+1+6 to starboard), followed by a second pair of emergency exits from CCCP-65607 No 1 (c/n 6350104)[12] onwards; all four exits were identical (Type IV). The windows were now located thus: door+6+exit+1+exit+5 to port and one small window+6+exit+1+exit+5 to starboard. Now the exterior of the initial production version was defined at last. The Mikoyan/Gurevich MiG-23 *Flogger* tactical fighter had a version known among pilots as ***dvahdsat' tretiy 'bez bookvy'*** – 'MiG-23 with no [suffix] letter', or *sans suffixe*;[13] by analogy the original version of the Tu-134 will hereinafter be called Tu-134 *sans suffixe*.

The colour scheme of the first nine Khar'kov-built aircraft was almost identical to the first prototype's, save that the fin fillet and leading edge were painted blue and the Aeroflot winged logo was carried on the engine nacelles instead of the fuselage. Starting with the sixth production aircraft (CCCP-65609 No 1, c/n 6350201), the

The first two production Tu-134s *sans suffixe*, CCCP-65604 No 1 and CCCP-65605 No 1, parked at Moscow-Vnukovo in 1968 with Tu-124s and an IL-18 visible beyond. Note the extra window ahead of the wing introduced in Batch 1, the original shape of the fin top fairing and the 'cut here in emergency' markings.
Novosti Press Agency

colours changed *again*; the bright blue cheatline had a dark blue pinstripe below and a red one above, the fin was all-white (the fin top fairing was still blue), the Aeroflot logo was moved back to the fuselage and replaced by blue stripes on the nacelles. This livery became standard for Aeroflot's Tu-134s *sans suffixe*.

A limited certification programme held by the Ministry of Aircraft Industry (MAP – *Ministerstvo aviatseeonnoy promyshlennosti*) began on 24th March 1967 and was completed in July. V D Popov was project test pilot; the leading engineers involved were A Daniliuk, I S Maiboroda, A Teterikov and Rudolf A Teymurazov. CCCP-65601 was used for wet-runway tests, the last pre-production aircraft (CCCP-65603, c/n 6350005) for avionics electromagnetic compatibility tests and CCCP-65607 No 1 (c/n 6350104) for ICAO Cat I automatic landing tests. The latter aircraft was written off in an accident on 17th July 1972 but this was not associated with the autoland system (see Appendix 2).

The wing flaps continued to cause trouble at this stage. On one occasion the port inboard flap of CCCP-65613 No 1 failed to retract during a test flight at GosNII GA and the aircraft rolled sharply to starboard. Cancelling flap retraction, V D Popov managed with difficulty to make a circuit of the airport and land, and the damaged flap broke away after touchdown! Consequently changes were made to the flight manual, limiting speed dependent on the flap setting.

Ten early-production Tu-134s were then transferred for evaluation to Aeroflot's Vnukovo United Air Detachment (UAD) of the Moscow Territorial Civil Aviation Directorate (CAD) – traditionally the first to receive the latest types. Between 1st April and 7th August 1967 they logged 2,600 hours on mail and cargo flights between Moscow and the southern regions. The crews made good use of this assignment,

bathing in the Black Sea and buying fresh fruit at the southern bazaars. A conversion training course for flight and ground crews was set up at Moscow-Vnukovo.

(Note: Aeroflot's organisation closely resembled an air arm's order of battle – unsurprisingly, considering that the Soviet civil air fleet constituted an immediately available military reserve (and considering the militarisation of the Soviet economy at large). There was a number of Civil Aviation Directorates (UGA – *Oopravleniye grazhdahnskoy aviahtsii*), several of which were in the Russian Federation and one in each of the other Soviet republics. These were broadly equivalent to the air forces of the USAF or the air armies of the Soviet Air Force. Each CAD consisted of several United Air Detachments (OAO – *obyedinyonnyy aviaotryad*) based in major cities; these were equivalent to an air group (USAF) or an air division (SovAF). Each UAD had several Flights (LO – *lyotnyy otryad*) similar to an air wing (USAF) or an air regiment (SovAF). Finally, a Flight comprised up to four, or maybe more, squadrons (yes, squadrons – *aviaeskadril'ya*!); not infrequently different squadrons of the same Flight operated different aircraft types.)

Aeroflot pilots involved in the tests included Boris Pavlovich Boogayev who went on to become Minister of Civil Aviation (he held office in 1980-87). This is how he described the Tu-134: *'During my flying career I had a chance to fly many of our aircraft types. I will not dwell on all the Tu-134's qualities; suffice it to say the new aircraft is very easy to fly. I believe it can be quickly and accurately put on the right course from any attitude (sic). The Tu-134 will require minimum airfields (sic; this probably means 'minimum ground support facilities' – Auth.) The aircraft has a very smooth ride when taxying. It should be put into service as soon as possible.'* From then on it was green light for the new Tupolev airliner.

Chapter Three

Version Variety

The Tu-134 turned out to be a truly versatile aircraft, spawning numerous versions, which no doubt partly accounts for its long career.

Tu-134 Short/Medium-haul Airliner

The basic Tu-134 was progressively improved as test results and operational experience were accumulated. Starting with Batch 2 (that is, CCCP-65609 No 1) the forward baggage door measuring 1.1 x 0.9m (43¼ x 35½in) gave way to a 1.25 x 0.75m (49¼ x 29½in) forward-sliding rectangular service door incorporating a 30-cm window, and the second small window in the galley was reinstated; these windows were now placed slightly lower. From CCCP-65612 No 1 (c/n 7350205) onwards the SPM-1 rotating anti-collision beacons were replaced with more effective SMI-2KM strobe lights.

From CCCP-65618 No 1 (c/n 7350301) onwards the oval port side entry door was enlarged to 1.61 x 0.7m (63⅜ x 27½in) to increase headroom. Previously it had been identical to that of the Tu-124, measuring 1.3 x 0.7m (51⅛ x 27½in), and you really had to mind your head when boarding and deplaning; this was a liability during emergency evacuation

when a crowd could build up at the door. (Even so, the doorway still is a bit low...)

Sixty-eight Tu-134s *sans suffixe*, including the two prototypes, were built in passenger configuration. The final aircraft in Batch 9, including CCCP-65639 (c/n 9350917), had a *Mikron* (Micron) HF radio replacing the old 1RSB-70 radio. Outwardly it could be identified by a forward-pointing probe aerial at the top of the fin (dubbed *klyoov*, 'beak') replacing the earlier wire aerial. Earlier examples were retrofitted during overhauls.

Tu-134 with Groza-M134 Radar

A late-production Tu-134 *sans suffixe* ordered by the Yugoslav charter carrier Aviogenex (YU-AHS, c/n 0350921) was custom-built with a Groza-M134 weather radar – the latest version of the Groza (Thunderstorm, pronounced *grozah*) developed for the Antonov An-24 *Coke* twin-turboprop airliner.[1]

The need for such a modification was long overdue. Firstly, a weather radar should 'look straight ahead'; however, the chin-mounted ROZ-1 scanned the forward lower quadrant and was of little use as a weather radar. Sec-

ondly, in the West it was considered uneconomical to have a navigator on an aircraft in this class, and Western short-haul airliners were flown by crews of three or even two.

The Tupolev OKB was *very* reluctant to eliminate the navigator's station and install a weather radar instead, refusing a demand from the Polish airline LOT on the grounds that it was too complicated and inadvisable. However, after taking delivery of two standard 'glass-nosed' Tu-134s *sans suffixe* Aviogenex became adamant: get rid of the navigator and fit the Groza radar, period. Trying to brush off the pesky customer, the OKB and MAP pretended they had never heard of this radar. The Yugoslavs, however, would not be put off *and produced an advertising brochure from an industrial fair in Ljubljana where the Groza had been displayed!* Finding themselves in an embarrassing situation, the OKB and MAP had no choice but to meet the demands; thus the third and final Tu-134 *sans suffixe* for Aviogenex was manufactured on 24th April 1970 as a 'radar-nosed' aircraft.

The radar set was housed in a pressurised equipment bay replacing the navigator's station, with a forward-opening ventral access door where the chin radome used to be. A forward pressure bulkhead mounting the radar scanner and a pointed radome supplanted the nose glazing. This increased the overall length from 34.95m (114ft 8in) to 35.17m (115ft 4⅝in) because the radome could not be kept within the dimensions of the navigator's station glazing due to the need to avoid internal reflections impairing the radar's performance. If you look closely, you will see the radome is not blended completely into the nose contour – there is a slight 'waist' at the joint line.

The crew was reduced to three, the navigator's duties being performed by the first officer; to this end the radar display was built into a panel between the pilots' seats where the

Tu-134 CCCP-65610 No 1 taxies in at Moscow-Shermet'yevo, still wearing the Le Bourget exhibit code 232. Note the revised cheatline and the white fin leading edge; this was the standard livery of Aeroflot's Tu-134s *sans suffixe* until 1973. Boris Vdovenko

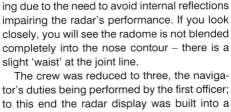

YU-AHS, the only Tu-134 *sans suffixe* to feature the Groza-M134 radar in place of a glazed navigator's station, at Belgrade International airport. The lack of thrust reversers and 14 cabin windows to starboard typical of the short version are plainly visible. Aviaexport

CCCP-65626, the second prototype Tu-134A, on the factory apron in Khar'kov displaying the new colour scheme developed for Aeroflot's Tu-134As. The colouring of the engine nacelles was to change yet. ITAR-TASS

entrance to the navigator's station used to be. YU-AHS remained a one-off and was returned to the USSR in 1971 as CCCP-65963 when the airline traded in its Tu-134s for stretched Tu-134As. However, it paved the way for a similarly equipped version of the latter (see below).

Tu-134K VIP Aircraft

Chronologically the first derivative was a VIP version of the Tu-134 *sans suffixe* brought out in 1967. By analogy with its precursors – the 36-seat Tu-124K-36 and the 22-seat Tu-124K2-22 – the aircraft was designated Tu-134K, the K standing for *komfort* – (enhanced) comfort.

Two interior layouts existed. The 29-seat version for Aeroflot's 235th Independent Air Detachment (*otdel'nyy aviaotryad*) – the Soviet federal government flight – had two cabins for the VIPs (referred to as the *main passengers*), seating five and four respectively, and a 20-seat rear cabin for the escorting staff. The 37-seat version supplied to all other customers had 13 seats for the VIPs and 24 seats for the retinue. The galley was enlarged at the expense of baggage space; there was a wardrobe and an extra toilet for the VIPs ahead of the forward cabin. The wing centre section housed two auxiliary bag tanks holding 750 litres (165 Imp gals) each, bringing the total fuel amount to 17,800 litres (3,916 Imp gals) or 14.2 tons (31,305 lb).

12 Tu-134Ks were built in 1967-70. The first four (CCCP-65618 No 1 and CCCP-65614 No 1 through -65616 No 1, c/ns 7350301 through 7350304) were delivered to the 235th IAD at Moscow-Vnukovo; in 1969 they were retrofitted with special secure HF communications equipment. CCCP-65616 was later transferred to the Soviet Air Force as '77 Blue'. One Tu-134K serialled '050 Red' (the first to have this serial) was operated by the Bulgarian Air Force, four aircraft (DM-SCE through -SCG and '177 Black')

by the East German Air Force, two more (HA-LBG and -LBH) by the Hungarian government flight and the final one (YI-AED) by the Iraqi government. All of them were ultimately converted to regular passenger aircraft.

Tu-134A Short/Medium-haul Airliner

Building on operational experience with the Tu-134 *sans suffixe*, in 1968 the Tupolev OKB started work on an improved version designated Tu-134A. The objective was to increase the payload to 8.2 tons (18,080 lb) and the seating capacity to 76; the aircraft was to have a 1,700-km (1,055-mile) range, a cruising speed of 800-900km/h (497-559mph) and operate from runways 2,200-2,400m (7,200-7,880ft) long. The maximum take-off and landing weights were 47 and 43 tons (103,615 and 94,800 lb) respectively.

Foreign customers insistently demanded that the baggage hold volume be increased to 16-17m³ (565-600ft³); the 13m³ (459ft³) of the Tu-134 *sans suffixe* were clearly inadequate. Therefore the fuselage was stretched by inserting a 2.1-m (6ft 10⅝in) plug at the manufacturing break at frame 15. This mostly affected the forward baggage hold which was enlarged from 4.5 to 6m³ (from 159 to 212ft³); only a single row of seats was added, increasing capacity from 64-72 to 68-76.

The cabin windows were now located thus: entry door+7+exit+1+exit+5 to port and service door+1+7+exit+1+exit+5 to starboard. Also, the centre pair of cockpit eyebrow windows (a leftover from the Tu-124) was deleted because a new overhead circuit breaker panel was installed there.

Of course, the landing gear wheelbase also grew, reaching 16.03m (52ft 7⅛in). To provide an adequate turning radius a new shimmy damper/nosewheel steering mechanism was developed, increasing the nosewheel steering angle from ±35° to ±55°.

The Tu-134A was powered by new D-30-II (D-30 Srs II) engines featuring cascade-type thrust reversers to shorten the landing run (an absolute necessity, regarding the higher landing weight) and the anachronistic brake para-

chute was finally deleted. For one thing, a brake parachute produces a sharp jolt when it opens, with a planeload of angry passengers as a result. For another, the 'chute has to be released at the end of the landing run and picked up by a ground crew, which airport authorities abroad would not appreciate. The thrust reversers increased nacelle length by 0.76m (2ft 6in). As noted earlier, each pilot had his own set of throttles; however, on the Tu-134A only the captain's throttles featured reverse thrust control levers.

Unlike the original D-30, which was started electrically, the D-30-II had a low-pressure air starter. Hence a compact TA-8 auxiliary power unit (TA = *toorboagregaht* – lit. 'turbo unit') was installed in the former brake 'chute bay for self-contained engine starting and power supply. It breathed via two upward-opening intakes at the base of the rudder or, when these were closed in flight, via a ventral intake grille. The APU was specially developed by the Stoopino Machinery Design Bureau (SKBM – *Stoopinskoye konstrooktorskoye byuro mashinostroyeniya*), alias KB-120,[2] located near Moscow. The new powerplant was tested on a modified Tu-134 *sans suffixe*, CCCP-65601 (see below).

An added bonus was the possibility to air-condition the cabin on the ground; on the Tu-134 *sans suffixe* the air conditioning system worked only when the engines were running or a ground AC was hooked up. One of the strengths of the TA-8 is its relatively quiet operation, though the upturned nozzle clearly helps. Of course, you have to speak louder when the APU is running but at least you don't have to plug the ears.

Interestingly, OKB engineers had proposed fitting an APU from the start but Andrey N Tupolev axed the idea, believing the APU would be too heavy. However, when ground tests of 'Aircraft Zilch' began it transpired that the single DC battery fitted initially could not crank up the engines at all! A second battery was added and then a third; still, engine starting problems at below-zero temperatures persisted. Tupolev was always reluctant to admit his mistakes, and when he learned the whole

story he gave his design staff a dressing-down, as recounted by Leonid L Kerber in *Tupolev – the Man and the Aircraft*:

'How much do your three bloody batteries weigh?'
'The batteries themselves weigh 360kg [790 lb], and with the wiring and relays it adds up to at least 500kg [1,100 lb]!' (In comparison, the TA-8 APU minus GS-12TO generator weighs 165kg/360 lb – *Author*)
'Then why the hell didn't you insist on installing an auxiliary turbine?'
*'Now hold it! We **did** insist!'*
*'But you didn't ram it home, and now I'm the one to blame, of course. That's the way it always works: there's lots of you people involved but I'm the only one who gets the blame. You **should** have convinced me, and I mean it! Now we've got a whole can of worms!'*

Other changes included an improved fuel system which increased the engines' acceleration rate, an SEUZ-1 flap synchroniser preventing asymmetric deployment in the event of flap drive failure, and a duplex cabin pressure control system. The Mikron HF radio with its characteristic 'beak' at the top of the fin became a standard fit on the Tu-134A. The flight crew was reduced from five to four by eliminating the radio operator (the pilots were now responsible for communications).

Not all of the proposed improvements were implemented, though. For instance, Tupolev refused to introduce an alternating current main electric system on the grounds that most of the equipment used direct current. Thus, today the Tu-134 is the world's last remaining airliner with a DC main electric system. The planned integral airstairs were likewise never fitted to the standard passenger version.

The first prototype, CCCP-65624 (c/n 8350601), was built by pulling a standard 'short' fuselage off the production line, cutting it up and adding a 2.1-m plug to the centre fuselage section. The maiden flight from Khar'kov-Sokol'nikovo with factory test pilots Datsenko and Mikhail Vladimirovich Petlyakov (the son of aircraft designer Vladimir Mikhaĭlovich Petlyakov) at the controls took place on 22nd April 1969. (22nd April just happened to be the birthday of Vladimir I Lenin, the founder of the Soviet state.) The prototype attained a top speed of 920km/h (571mph) and a range of 1,700km (1,055 miles) during manufacturer's tests.

On 23rd May the aircraft was ferried to the OKB's test facility in Zhukovskiy; two days later the Tu-134A made its international debut at the 27th Paris Air Show, wearing the exhibit code 827. Unlike all other 'As, CCCP-65624 wore the same livery as Aeroflot's Tu-134s *sans suffixe*; this may explain the erroneous view held by some Western observers that it was converted from an aircraft *flown* earlier as a 'short' version. (Incidentally, Tu-134 *sans suffixe* CCCP-65617 No 1 (c/n 7350305) was also displayed at Le Bourget in that year – probably for the sake of comparison.) The first prototype was retained by the OKB, serving for many years as a 'dog-ship' for testing new features (more of this later).

The second prototype, CCCP-65626 (c/n 9350704), was apparently a similar conversion – that is, never flown earlier as a Tu-134 *sans suffixe*. This aircraft received a striking new colour scheme which became standard for Aeroflot's Tu-134As for the next five years or so. The bright blue cheatline was heavily outlined in black above, with a blue pinstripe below, widening at the front to wrap around the fuselage nose; there were blue Aeroflot titles above the cheatline and the winged logo below it. The

CCCP-65973, an early-production Tu-134A belonging to the Lithuanian CAD/Vilnius UAD/277th Flight, on short finals to Moscow-Sheremet'yevo in the early 1970s.
Sergey Komissarov

flightdeck glazing frame was painted black, the colour extending aft into Tu-124-style 'feathers'. The lower fuselage and wings were normally natural metal (or light grey on some aircraft). The vertical tail and engine nacelles were the same intense blue colour, with the Soviet flag edged in gold and the registration painted in white on the fin; the thrust reverser assemblies were normally left unpainted.

For initial flight tests CCCP-65626 carried huge calibration markings looking like Maltese crosses on the fuselage near the entry and service doors. After completing its OKB trials programme the aircraft was used for test and development work by GosNII GA until at least 1984, later returning to Zhukovskiy to serve with the Air Transport School.

The first production Tu-134A, CCCP-65646 (c/n 0351001), left the Khar'kov factory in June 1970. This and the two subsequent aircraft had a maximum landing weight restricted to 40 tons (88,180 lb); from the fourth production aircraft (CCCP-65649, c/n 0351004) onwards the MLW was increased to the intended 43 tons (94,800 lb). It may as well be said now that the Tu-134A was to become the most numerous version, with some 400 examples rolling off the production line by late 1983.[3]

Some while earlier, in the spring of 1970, Aeroflot had started evaluation of the Tu-134A with the two prototypes, joined by initial production aircraft as they became available; route proving flights between Moscow and Leningrad continued until late autumn. The first revenue flight took place on 9th November 1970 and the type was formally included into the Aeroflot inventory on 23rd December pursuant to Ministry of Civil Aviation (MGA – *Ministerstvo grazhdahnskoy aviahtsii*) order No 592.

Changes in the window placement kept coming. The first 30 or so production Tu-134As had 16 full-size cabin windows on each side. From Batch 14 onwards (built in 1971) the number of windows on the port side was reduced to 15 (door+7+exit+1+exit+3+1). The idea was to maximise structural commonality between the standard passenger version and the Tu-134AK VIP version which had an extra entry door replacing the original two rearmost windows (that is, door+7+exit+1+exit+3+door).

Also, the prototypes and the first 19 production aircraft (batches 10 and 11 built in 1970) lacked the small galley window immediately aft of the service door, but this was reinstated in Batch 12 the following year. The galley window was deleted in batches 13 and 14 but reappeared from Batch 15 onwards in 1972. Yet again, Tu-134As in batches 46 through 56 (1978-1980), some aircraft in Batch 61 (1981) and the sole Tu-134A in Batch 63 (1984) lack this window! However, the galley window is almost invariably blanked off by the cabin wall trim (looking like a white or grey plug from outside) and therefore useless.

As the Tu-134A entered production and service, the Tupolev OKB set about improving the aircraft. In 1973 the ABSU-134 automatic landing approach system (ALS; *avtomaticheskaya bortovaya sistema oopravleniya* – lit. 'automatic on-board control system') was brought out, enabling ICAO Cat II landings (decision altitude 30m/100ft, horizontal visibility 400m/1,300ft). The system featured an autothrottle with a go-around function and new autopilot servos which were pyrotechnically disengaged from the control cables if they jammed. Stanislav Danilovich Dragoonov was the engineer in charge of the development of the ABSU-134 at OKB-156.

The new ALS was put through its paces at GosNII GA, using Tu-134A CCCP-65966 (c/n 3351902) which belonged to the Tupolev OKB; this was, in effect, an avionics testbed, as the aircraft had actually been built with the ABSU-134 system (with a resulting delay in completion). The test crew consisted of captain Viktor Il'yich Shkatov, first officer Vladimir Vasil'yevich Sevan'kayev, navigator Lev Stepanovich Sikachov, flight engineer Aleksandr Nikitovich Milenin and radio operator S S Ivanov. Viktor Zakharovich Dobrovitskiy was project engineer for the ABSU-134 at the institute.

The trials were quite a protracted affair, lasting from 22nd August 1973 to 20th March 1976. Within this time frame several Tu-134As, including CCCP-65813 (c/n 3352204) and probably CCCP-65800 (c/n 3352009), were laid down with provisions for the ABSU-134; however, due to problems with the new ALS the OKB and the plant decided to play safe, hastily converting these aircraft to take the old ALS.

Despite the long development period, the new system acquitted itself and became a standard fit on all Tu-134s from the end of July 1977 onwards. (The last example to have the old BSU-3P as planned was Tu-134A CCCP-65072 (c/n (73)49972, f/n 4107) manufactured on 30th July; however, the first aircraft to receive the production-standard ABSU-134 was a Tu-134AK (CCCP-65073). Thus, the first regular 'A with a production ABSU-134 was CCCP-65074 (c/n (73)49987, f/n 4110) manufactured on 7th September.)

There was, however, a notable exception. In 1976-77 OKB-156 and the design bureau responsible for the ALS undertook a programme at the request of the East German airline Interflug, upgrading the BSU-3P to an intermediate level between Cat I and II (decision altitude 45m/150ft, horizontal visibility 400m/1,300ft) by replacing some of the avionics modules. Radar-nosed Tu-134A DM-SCM (c/n 3351904) was suitably modified and tested successfully, but crashed on landing on 22nd November 1977 due to pilot error. Now all of Interflug's Tu-134s had the BSU-3P; hence, wishing to maintain fleet-wide equipment commonality, the airline insisted that radar-nosed Tu-134A DM-SCY (c/n (83)60495, f/n 4610) ordered as a replacement and manufactured on 16th June 1978 be completed with the old ALS!

Like the Tu-134 *sans suffixe*, Tu-134As built up to and including late March 1978 featured a large ventral speedbrake under the wing centre section increasing the glideslope angle to 9°. However, the advent of instrument landing systems working with a glideslope angle of just 3° rendered the speedbrake unnecessary – in fact, it became a liability because it increased drag and hence fuel consumption. Hence the speedbrake was eliminated from Tu-134A CCCP-65112 (c/n (83)60350, f/n 4510) onwards and permanently locked in the up position on aircraft built previously. At the same time the maximum flap setting was reduced from 38° to 30° in order to reduce wear and tear on the flap drive screw jacks and reduce aerodynamic noise levels in the rear cabin.

The crews were less than overjoyed about these changes, as flying the aircraft became more complicated (pilots say that with the ventral speedbrake the Tu-134 would land almost by itself). Specifically, in order to maintain the correct approach speed the throttles had to be set at 80% maximum turbine speed (N_1), but the flight manual forbade this mode for some reason. Hence the pilots would set one throttle to 75% N_1 and the other to 85% N_1; this created a yaw which had to be countered.

In 1976 a reinforced wing structure underwent extensive testing on Tu-134As CCCP-65020 (c/n (63)48380, f/n 3503), CCCP-65025 (c/n (63)48450, f/n 3601), CCCP-65033 (c/n (63)48540, f/n 3609) and CCCP-65035 (c/n (63)48590, f/n 3702). From CCCP-65037 (c/n (63)48850, f/n 3704) onwards all Tu-134s were built with the reinforced wings; on existing

aircraft the wing torsion box was beefed up during the nearest overhaul. Tu-134A CCCP-65089 (c/n (73)60180, f/n 4308) became a testbed for the new MSRP-64-2 flight data recorder and Mars-BM cockpit voice recorder which became a standard fit in late 1978.

On domestic routes the Tu-134A was initially operated in a 76-seat tourist-class layout (48 seats in the forward cabin and 28 in the rear cabin). Starting in 1987, however, some Aeroflot divisions increased the seating capacity to 80 by removing the partition between the cabins and installing an extra row of seats in order to increase profitability. This modification was approved by the OKB and earned high profits by the day's standards (an additional 46,000 roubles per aircraft per annum). The first aircraft to be thus modified was CCCP-65840 (c/n (43)18118, f/n 2602) of the Komi CAD/Syktyvkar UAD/75th Flight. Some export aircraft (for instance, the Tu-134As built for Aviogenex) were delivered as 80-seaters.

A 68-seat layout was developed for Aeroflot's Central Directorate of International Services (TsUMVS – *Tsentrahl'noye oopravleniye mezhdunarodnykh vozdooshnykh so'obschcheniy*)/207th Flight. The first cabin had first-class seating for eight, while the second and third cabins had 32 and 28 tourist-class seats respectively. Such aircraft, including CCCP-65777 (c/n (93)62552, f/n 5402) and CCCP-65780 (c/n (93)62622, f/n 5407), featured two 750-litre bag tanks in the wing centre section increasing the total capacity to 18,000 litres (3,960 Imp gals) and the fuel load to 14.4 tons (31,750 lb), with accordingly longer range. In the 1990s many Tu-134As were retrofitted with such tanks. Alternative 68-seat mixed-class arrangements were also possible (16 business-class seats plus 52 tourist-class seats, or 12 business-class/56 tourist-class).

Several Tu-134As were custom-built for the 235th IAD in mixed-class 60-seat (8 first-class and 32+20 tourist-class) or all-tourist 72-seat (44+28) layout with additional wing centre section fuel tanks. These aircraft, including CCCP-65055 (c/n (73)49856, f/n 3906) and CCCP-65867 (c/n (53)28296, f/n 2902), were presumably intended for supporting state visits when a lot of service personnel had to be carried. Another 60-seat layout had four first-class seats and 56 tourist-class seats. Furthermore, export aircraft had cabins furnished with higher-quality materials.

In-flight entertainment (IFE) systems have become quite common on Western airliners since the 1960s, and they have developed ever since; conversely, Soviet airliners are generally known for their rather austere ('no frills') interiors. However, you will be surprised to learn that the concept was known in the Soviet Union, too! As early as March 1971 several Tu-134As flying the popular Moscow-Leningrad service (and apparently belonging to the Leningrad CAD/1st Leningrad UAD/344th Flight) were equipped with an IFE system featuring ten compact TV sets suspended from the overhead

baggage racks on special holders; the screen size was 23cm (9in). Besides playing back videotapes, the system could show local TV channels. However, the idea was not carried further – apparently someone decided the IFE system was dangerous. For one thing, TV sets are a fire hazard; for another, if the TV set breaks loose during a heavy landing (or a crash), it may hit a luckless passenger on the head with sufficient force to kill him!

Tu-134A with Groza-M134 Radar (Export Version)

The standard Tu-134A delivered to Aeroflot (and, initially, to foreign customers as well) had a glazed navigator's station and an ROZ-1 radar in a chin radome. However, in 1971 an export model featuring the Groza-M134 weather radar and a three-man flightdeck was brought out to meet insistent demands from foreign customers. The radar installation was identical to the one used on Tu-134 *sans suffixe* YU-AHS. The modification increased the overall length from 37.1m (121ft 8⅝in) to 37.322m

(122ft 5⅜in), the more pointed nose making the aircraft look somewhat more elegant; yet it was the lower operating costs (due to the elimination of the navigator) that appealed to the operators.

The prototype of the export version (colloquially referred to as the radar-nosed or 'solid-nosed' version – *s radahrnym nosom*) was registered YU-AHX (c/n 1351203), as it was the first of several Tu-134As ordered by Aviogenex. This aircraft was delivered in March 1971, followed by three more during the next month. (Because Yugoslavia was the launch customer for the radar-nosed Tu-134A this version was known in the Eastern Bloc as 'the Yugoslav version'.) Shortly afterwards, wearing the exhibit code 453, the fifth radar-nosed Tu-134A (CCCP-65667, c/n 1351207), a demonstrator owned by the Tupolev OKB, was displayed at the 28th Paris Air Show which opened on 20th May 1971.

On 24th-31st August 1971 CCCP-65667 underwent trials at GosNII GA as Tupolev promoted the new version to Aeroflot – but

received a thumbs-down from the Soviet airline. This was probably a case of mental inertia: Soviet pilots were used to flying with a navigator and were not eager to assume his functions. Thus, excluding the demonstrator, all Tu-134As equipped with the Groza-M134 radar were built for export only (34 were manufactured by 30th January 1981, not counting the new-build Tu-134A-1s – see below), and all Soviet/CIS-registered examples except CCCP-65667 are re-export aircraft. (Despite allegations by some Western authors, all 34 'solid-nosed' 'As were new-build aircraft, *not* converted from standard 'As. This misconception is due to the fact that the first two Tu-134As for East Germany (to be precise, Tu-134AKs, see below) were 'glass-nosed' aircraft while the rest were 'solid-nosed' ones.)

Speaking of which, most radar-nosed Tu-134As operated in the Commonwealth of Independent States have had their flightdecks modified to feature a navigator's station behind the pilots! This is partly because current Russian regulations require the Tu-134A to carry a navigator, regardless of the type of radar, partly due to the need to provide employment for qualified navigators. It was not until the advent of the Tu-134B that a three-man crew version of the *Crusty* entered service with Aeroflot (see below).

Interestingly, export sales of the 'glass-nosed' version continued even after the radar-nosed version came on the scene. As for the company-owned demonstrator (CCCP-65667), this aircraft remained operational until September 1999 as RA-65667.

Several Tu-134As flying the Moscow-Leningrad route were experimentally fitted with an in-flight entertainment system in March 1971. ITAR-TASS

Tu-134A CCCP-65667 was the export version demonstrator and the fifth Tu-134A built with the Groza-M134 radar. It is seen here as RA-65667 at the OKB's flight test facility at Zhukovskiy on 19th September 1999 in the final days of its flying career. Author

Tu-134AK VIP Aircraft

No sooner had the Tu-134A entered production and service than a VIP version was developed in 1970. By analogy with the preceding Tupolev VIP jets the aircraft received the designation Tu-134AK. However, the correct designation is never painted on the actual aircraft; the nose titles invariably read 'Tu-134A' or 'Tu-134A-3', depending on what series of engines is fitted. This has nothing to do with trying to 'conceal' the VIP jets for fear that someone would try to assassinate the passengers; most probably the paint shops were just too lazy to use separate stencils, sticking to a common standard. (This is probably why the operators do not discern between the Tu-134A and the Tu-134AK; the latter designation appears to be used mostly by the OKB itself. Yet this author chooses to call a spade a spade.)

Outwardly the Tu-134AK is readily identifiable by the additional rectangular entry door ahead of the port engine. It is somewhat lower but wider than the quasi-oval forward entry door, measuring 1.42 x 0.87m (56 x 34¼in), and likewise opens inward and forward. (On late-production Tu-134AKs the door incorporates an illuminated sign on the inside, 'Do not open – engine running'.)

Three-section electrically powered airstairs are mounted next to the rear entry door, stowing against the rear vestibule bulkhead when not in use. They are used when the aircraft arrives at a military base or a factory airfield where mobile boarding ramps may be absent (a likely scenario, considering that many Tu-134AKs belonged to the Air Force or MAP). In contrast, the Tu-124K and Tu-134K had no integral airstairs, and sometimes the occupants were forced to use the rickety telescopic ladder with which each aircraft is provided.

Another external recognition feature is that the first full-size cabin window to starboard is blanked off by the cabin wall trim (looking like a white or grey plug from outside) whereas the small galley window aft of the service door remains clear; on the regular Tu-134A it is vice versa. This is because the starboard toilet is relocated to a position opposite the forward entry door on the Tu-134AK and a coat closet occupies its original place at the rear. Speaking of windows, Tu-134AKs normally have this galley window even if Tu-134As in the same production batch lack it. The only known exceptions are CCCP-65907, CCCP-65908 and CCCP-65934, which have no galley window – and no white 'plug' in the first full-size window; unless you *know* they are Tu-134AKs, you'll never guess it when looking at them from starboard!

From Batch 61 (January 1981) onwards many Tu-134AKs had an exceptionally wide unpainted fin leading edge where the de-icer was. Some examples, though, lost this distinguishing feature following a repaint (see also Tu-134A-3 section).

Some of the differences were not so obvious. For instance, the radio operator's workstation

Tu-134AK CCCP-65970 pictured at Khar'kov-Sokol'nikovo during its maiden flight in natural metal condition, with the registration carelessly stencilled on the engine nacelles. The rear entry door is clearly visible. Yefim Gordon archive

RA-65940 of ShaNS-Air (ex-Bulgarian Air Force LZ-TUM), seen here at Moscow/Vnukovo-1 on 18th June 2002, was the first Tu-134AK to be built in radar-nosed export configuration. Author

was reinstated, allowing the pilots to concentrate on flying the aircraft. The wing centre section housed two 750-litre bag tanks bringing fuel capacity to 18,000 litres.

The prototype was apparently registered CCCP-65670 (c/n 0351110) and converted from a stock Tu-134A directly on the production line. The conversion job took rather long and the aircraft, which had been laid down in 1970, was not released by the factory until 31st March 1971. CCCP-65670 was delivered to the Soviet Air Force; unfortunately it crashed on 28th July 1989. (Incidentally, it was common for Tu-134AKs to have a manufacture date a few weeks, or even months, later than ordinary Tu-134As in the same production batch. This was due to the need to make sure all systems were absolutely trouble-free, the higher complexity of the interior outfitting job and so on.)

The Tu-134AK was built in large numbers, ranking second only to the Tu-134A; about 180 were produced for Soviet and foreign government flights, air forces and ministries between

31st March 1971 and 15th December 1986. Known Soviet/CIS-registered examples are: CCCP-63757, -63761, -63775, -63955, -63957, -63960, -63961, -63975, -63976, -63979, -63982, *-64451*, -65005, -65017, -65021, -65028, -65041*, -65042, -65045, -65065, -65073, 65092*, -65093, -65094, -65097, -65099, -65109, -65120, -65140, -65550 through -65557, *-65559*, *-65565*, *RA-65566 through -65568, RA-65570, RA-65571, CCCP-65604 No 2, -65606 No 2 through -65610 No 2, -65612 No 2 through -65616 No 2, -65619 No 2, -65620 No 2, -65623 No 2*, -65663*, -65665, -65666, -65668*, -65670*, -65671*, -65675, -65676, -65679 through -65686, -65687*, -65688 through -65691, -65707, -65718, -65719, -65726, -65733, -65734*, -65735, -65746, -65748, -65749, -65760, -65761, -65764*, -65771, -65773, -65801, -65802, -65821, -65830, -65841*, *EW-65861 No 2*, CCCP-65877, -65880, -65881, -65888, -65900, -65904 through -65908, -65909*, -65910 through -65912, -65913*, -65914 through -65916, -65919, -65920*, -65921, -65926, -65927, -65934, -65935, *RA-65939*, *-65940*, *-65942*, *-65944*, CCCP-65950, -65952*, -65954, -65956, -65957, -65961, -65962, -65964*, -65965, -65970, -65977 through -65997 and Soviet Air Force '01 Red' (later Russian Air Force '01 Blue', c/n (83)60650, f/n 4809). Aircraft marked with an asterisk are unconfirmed; those marked in italic are re-export aircraft.

Most Tu-134AKs were 'glass-nosed' aircraft with the ROZ-1 radar, but 25 examples were built in radar-nosed export configuration; the

first of these was LZ-TUM (c/n 3351906) built in June 1973. A further eight examples built for the East German Air Force between June 1978 and 17th August 1983– DM-SDM, DM-SDN, DM-SDO, DM-SDP, DDR-SDR, '184 Black' (DDR-SDS allocated), DDR-SDT and DDR-SDU – were completed to Tu-134A-1 standard, combining the Groza-M134 radar with large rear emergency exits (see below).

Like the basic passenger version, Tu-134AKs built from mid-1976 onwards featured a reinforced wing torsion box; the first being CCCP-65028 (c/n (63)48490, f/n 3604). As already noted, Tu-134AK CCCP-65073 (c/n (73)49980, f/n 4108) manufactured on 19th December 1977 was the first Tu-134 to be equipped with a production-standard ABSU-134 ALS.

The Tu-134AK had about a dozen different interior layouts to suit the needs of specific customers. The forward part of the cabin ahead of the wings is divided into one, two or three VIP cabins with sofas, tables, swivelling armchairs and coat closets.[4] Moving the toilet to the forward vestibule required the galley to be reconfigured, with an attendant reduction in forward baggage hold capacity to 2.6m³ (91.8ft³). The rear part of the cabin has standard four-abreast tourist-class seating for the VIPs' retinue, followed by the rear vestibule (with a second galley to starboard), a toilet to port and a coat closet across the aisle.

The first variant of the Tu-134AK to enter production was the 37-seat (so-called executive) version, with two VIP cabins (seating six and seven respectively) and two tourist-class cabins (8+16). Such aircraft were built for the 235th Independent Air Detachment, the government flights of the Soviet republics and various ministries (MAP etc). The aircraft had a dry weight of 29.2 tons (64,370 lb), an operating empty weight (OEW) of 30.1 tons (66,360 lb), an MTOW of 47 tons (103,615 lb) and a payload of 2.6 to 4.5 tons (5,730-9,920 lb). Range in 750-km/h (465-mph; 405-kt) cruise at 10,000m (32,810ft) was 3,300-3,510km (2,050-2,180 miles).

Another version for the 235th IAD seated 50, with a single six-seat VIP cabin and two cabins for the retinue (24+20). The Soviet Air Force operated a 44-seat variant with two VIP cabins (5+7) and two cabins for the retinue (12+20). Configurations offered to foreign customers included a 'glass-nosed' 36-seat variant for the East German Air Force with two VIP cabins (5+7) and two tourist-class cabins (8+16); a 'glass-nosed' 37-seater for the Bulgarian Air Force identical to the Soviet executive variant except for the interior trim; a 'glass-nosed' 47-seater for the Czechoslovak Federal Ministry of the Interior with one VIP cabin and two tourist-class cabins; a radar-nosed 34-seat version for East Germany with two VIP cabins (5+7) and two tourist-class cabins (8+14); radar-nosed 36-seat versions for Bulgaria, Hungary and Poland; a radar-nosed 39-seater for East Germany with one VIP cabin and three tourist-class cabins; another radar-nosed version for Poland seating 41 (one VIP cabin plus three tourist-class cabins) and a third radar-nosed version for Poland seating 47 (one VIP cabin plus two for the retinue). Some sources also mention 52- and 55-seat versions, possibly re-equipped from some of the above configurations.

In 1969 the Tupolev OKB started work on versions of the Tu-134AK fitted with VHF secure communications equipment for the 235th IAD and the Soviet Air Force. Five such versions existed; the first of these, equipped with the Tatra VHF comms suite, was built in a handful of examples in 1970-71. The radios and scram-

Tu-134AK RA-65568 of Aeroflot Russian International Airlines is one of examples built to Tu-134A-1 standard for the East German Air Force. Note the enlarged rear emergency exits and the white 'plug' in the first full-size window. Dmitriy Petrochenko

blers/descramblers were installed in a large enclosure (the so-called *spetsotsek* – 'special bay') along the port wall of the rearmost cabin, which required some local structural reinforcement; besides the usual flight crew of five and three flight attendants, there were two communications officers. The aircraft had a 29-seat layout with two VIP cabins (6+7) and two tourist-class cabins (8+8). The special equipment weighed 1,900kg (4,200 lb). Maximum range was 3,160km (1,960 miles).

CCCP-65665 (c/n 1351201) was probably representative of this version. Outwardly it differed from ordinary Tu-134AKs in having a small additional blade aerial atop the centre fuselage. The special communications gear was later removed from this aircraft.

Later, several Tu-134AKs were completed with the upgraded Tatra-M suite (*modernizeerovannaya* – updated) weighing 1,200kg (2,645 lb). They had an identical 29-seat interior layout and a range of 3,500km (2,175 miles). At least three aircraft built for the 235th IAD in 1982 – CCCP-65904 (c/n (23)63953, f/n 6312), CCCP-65905 (c/n (23)63965, f/n 6317) and CCCP-65911 (c/n (23)63972, f/n 6320) – apparently had, and still have, the Tatra-M suite. They are identifiable by single extra blade aerials on the centre fuselage and under the rear fuselage. Another possible candidate is CCCP-65556 (c/n (43)66372, f/n 6364) which is fitted with one blade aerial on the centre fuselage and another atop the fin.

In 1976-77 the Soviet Air Force's 8th ADON (*aviadiveeziya osobovo naznacheniya* – Special Mission Air Division, ≅ air wing) at Chkalovskaya AB took delivery of two Tu-134AKs earmarked for the Soviet Minister of Defence. Initially registered CCCP-65680 (c/n (63)49020, f/n 3706) and CCCP-65681 (c/n (73)49760, f/n 3901), they were equipped with the Karpaty-ST VHF comms suite (*Karpahty* is the Russian name for the Carpathian Mountains); hence some sources refer to these aircraft as Tu-134 *Karpaty*. The new version was readily identifiable by the prominent dorsal fairing housing communications antennas and wiring which ran all the way from the forward emergency exits to the fin fillet, plus a small additional blade aerial atop the fin. (A similar fat spine characterises the Il'yushin IL-62M 'Salon TM-3SUR' VIP variant of the IL-62M *Classic* long-haul airliner operated by the 235th IAD and the Air Force.)

The Tu-134 *Karpaty* had a 27-seat layout similar to the ones described above but with six seats in the first tourist-class cabin. The special equipment was worked by three operators and was exceptionally heavy as compared to the Tatra suite (not to mention the Tatra-M), weighing 2,900kg (6,390 lb); this necessitated a reduction of the fuel load to 13.84 tons (30,510 lb) so as not to exceed the 49-ton MTOW. Maximum range was 3,340km (2,075 miles).

Later, both aircraft received overt military markings and the registrations were abbreviated to three-digit tactical codes, '680 Black' and '681 Black' (a practice not very common in the Soviet Air Force); '681 Black' even made an appearance at London-Heathrow in October 1990 with a Soviet military delegation on board. By late 1995, however, '680 Black' and '681 Black' were stripped of VHF comms equipment and converted to 44-seat VIP configuration (probably because they had lost their 'ministerial jet' status), gaining larger star insignia on the tail and having the codes relocated to the top of the fin.

Also in the late 1970s a version of the Tu-134AK equipped with the Surgut-T VHF comms suite was brought out; this was based on the late-model aircraft featuring the ABSU-134 ALS. The aircraft had a 27-seat layout; the crew included three comms officers. The special equipment weighed 2,600kg (5,730 lb); the MTOW was 49 tons and maximum range 3,200km (1,985 miles).

Soviet Air Force Tu-134AK '681 Black' (ex-CCCP-65681), one of two fitted with Karpaty-ST VHF communications gear for use by the Minister of Defence. This version was readily identifiable by the dorsal fairing housing antennas. Sergey and Dmitriy Komissarov archive

YU-AHX of Aviogenex started life as the first radar-nosed Tu-134A in 1971 but was converted to the Tu-134A-1 prototype in 1975. The enlarged rear emergency exits are clearly visible. Sergey and Dmitriy Komissarov collection

Quasi-civil Tu-134AK CCCP-65830 (c/n (43)12093, f/n 2409) was likewise outfitted with VHF comms gear, as revealed by tandem blade aerials on the upper centre fuselage and on the rear fuselage underside. However, this aircraft hardly had the Surgut-T suite, as it was built in 1974 and still equipped with the old BSU-3P ALS. It was subsequently stripped of special equipment and sold to a civilian owner. (The fifth version, called Tu-134 *Balkany*, is described separately – see below.)

The static park at the MAKS-95 airshow in Zhukovskiy (22nd-27th August 1995) featured all-white Tu-134AK RA-65801 (c/n 3352010) devoid of titles/logos and guarded by some tight-lipped gentlemen. At first this author wondered why the aircraft, which was certainly not new, had been put on display in the first place. However, close inspection showed that RA-65801 was unusual after all. It turned out that the jet had been fitted out with a new VIP interior designed by the British company Diamonite Aircraft Furnishings. The outfitting job had been performed in Ul'yanovsk which was then the aircraft's home base. A characteristic feature of Diamonite interiors is the cabin wall trim panels which make the Tu-134's circular windows appear rectangular from the inside, giving a 'Western biz-jet look' and supposedly adding passenger appeal; these panels are clearly visible from outside.[5]

The Tu-134AK has a few problems unique to it. The aprons on Soviet/CIS airfields are often in less than perfect condition; sometimes the lower end of the integral airstairs gets snagged in a pothole and the thing will not unfold fully. If nobody is at hand to jerk the stubborn airstairs into position, one of the crewmembers has to jump down through the service door to do it. The hinges and locks of the folding handrails (which, incidentally, are erected and folded manually) tend to work loose after several years of operation. Finally, the septic tank of the forward toilet is located in the No 1 equipment bay, hindering access to the fuse box installed there (which the tech staff is unhappy about).

After an average five or six years of service with a government flight or an air force many Tu-134AKs were transferred to an airline and converted to passenger aircraft. This was because government flights and air force VIP flights had a habit of renewing their fleets quite often so as not to put the lives of the high and mighty at risk. On the other hand, it was superfluous for Aeroflot and the other Soviet Bloc airlines to operate VIP-configured aircraft on scheduled services. Hence the luxury of the VIP cabins gave way to a 68-seat mixed-class (for example, RA-65623), 74-seat (CCCP-65910), 76-seat (CCCP-65666) or 80-seat (CCCP-65977) all-tourist layout. This involved removing the airstairs and rear galley, since they were eating up valuable space, and permanently locking the rear entry door. (Quite often this non-functional door is not outlined in colour as all exits are required to be; still, watch for the nickel-plated external handle below the window and the rain gutter above the door.) Some ex-German aircraft owned by Komiinteravia have had the starboard toilet relocated aft *à la* Tu-134A, with a storage rack at its original location; however, when RA-65608 and RA-65620 were subsequently refitted with business class seating in the forward cabin, the forward toilet had to be reinstated, which cost Komiinteravia a bundle!

Some Tu-134AKs (for instance, CCCP-65906 and -65907) were converted to avionics testbeds or research aircraft. This again required the interior to be gutted to make room for the test equipment and operators' workstations; however, the rear entry door and airstairs remained fully functional.

Tu-134A-1 Short/Medium-haul Airliner

This designation is quoted in several sources for a sub-variant of the radar-nosed export version. Developed in 1975 to meet a requirement by Aviogenex, the Tu-134A-1 differs from the regular export model in featuring larger ICAO Type III rear emergency exits measuring 0.916 x 0.6m (36 x 23⅝in). This was because the aircraft had to comply with British Civil Airworthiness Regulations (BCAR) specifying passenger evacuation time after the Yugoslavs had modified their existing Tu-134As to 86-seaters to increase revenue. The issue could not be ignored because Aviogenex was flying a lot of inclusive tour charters from the UK; being banned from flying to the UK on safety grounds would mean the airline would lose a lot of lucrative business.

Thus the Tu-134A-1 is outwardly identical to the later Tu-134B – except for the nose titles. (Speaking of which, again the titles always read either 'Tu-134A' or 'Tu-134A-3', probably for the same reason.) The difference lies within: the Tu-134A-1's flightdeck is identical to that of any radar-nosed 'A, with two pairs of throttles (that is, no central control pedestal) and one centrally mounted radar display; hence there is no provision for flight spoilers. There are also differences in cabin and galley layout.

The prototype was presumably converted in late 1975 from the very first radar-nosed Tu-134A, YU-AHX, at the MGA's Aircraft Overhaul Plant No 407 in Minsk (ARZ No 407; ARZ = *aviaremontnyy zavod*). Three more Aviogenex aircraft (YU-AHY, YU-AJA and YU-AJD) underwent a similar conversion during the winter of 1975-76. Later Tu-134A-1s were new-build aircraft manufactured to order; six such aircraft were built between April 1976 and 13th March 1980 – four for Aviogenex (YU-AJS, YU-AJV, YU-AJW and YU-ANE) and two for ČSA Czechoslovak Airlines (OK-HFM and OK-IFN). Additionally, as recounted earlier, eight Tu-134AKs for East Germany were built to

Tu-134A-1 standard with Type III rear emergency exits between June 1978 and 17th August 1983.

Tu-134A-3 Short/Medium-haul Airliner

To improve the Tu-134A's hot-and-high performance the Solov'yov OKB developed an improved version of the D-30 turbofan designated D-30-III (D-30 Srs III). The new version retained a 6,800-kgp rating at ambient temperatures up to +25°C (+77°F); by comparison, the D-30 and D-30-II delivered only 6,300kgp (13,890 lbst) in these conditions. At +15°C (+59°F) the D-30-III had a take-off rating of 6,930kgp (15,280 lbst).[6] The uprated engine was interchangeable with the D-30-II, requiring no modifications to the airframe. Accordingly the version powered by D-30-IIIs received the designation Tu-134A-3 – this time with appropriate nose titles applied.

The improved engines allowed the maximum TOW to be increased from 47.6 to 49 tons (from 104,940 to 108,025 lb) at a flap setting of 10° and from 42.9 to 45.7 tons (from 94,580 to 100,750 lb) at 20° flap. At a 47.6-ton TOW the required runway length was reduced by 430m (1,410ft). The payload was 8.2-9.0 tons (17,640-19,840 lb) and the service ceiling 11,900-12,000m (39,040-39,370ft).

The prototype was converted in 1981 from the original Tu-134A prototype (CCCP-65624), gaining cruciform photo calibration markings on the fuselage ahead of the wings. A second aircraft was modified shortly afterwards; tests showed that the Tu-134A-3 met the design specifications, and the new version entered production. A Tajik CAD/Leninabad UAD/292nd Flight/1st Squadron aircraft performed the first revenue service from Leninabad to Chelyabinsk on 6th January 1982. As for the prototype, it was retired in Zhukovskiy by 1992.

Early- and mid-production Tu-134As were often upgraded to the new standard during overhauls, and the D-30-IIIs retrofitted to such aircraft were frequently conversions of D-30-IIs, not new engines. Sometimes, however, Tu-134A-3s actually had to be downgraded to Tu-134As due to the unavailability of Srs III engines! One such aircraft was UR-65134 on which an overpainted '-3' was clearly visible aft of the Cyrillic 'Tu-134A' nose titles at one time.

Several Tu-134A-3s received a wide

unpainted fin leading edge in the manner of late-production Tu-134AK after an overhaul, which is unusual for the passenger version. Known examples are RA-65019, RA-65049, RA-65056, RA-65110, CCCP-65717, EK-65731 and CCCP-65932.

Tu-134A 'Salon' (Tu-134A-1 'Salon', Tu-134A-3 'Salon') VIP/Executive Aircraft

Some standard Tu-134As have been refitted with VIP interiors – usually in post-Soviet times; this author calls such aircraft Tu-134A 'Salon' in order to distinguish them from Tu-134AKs built in VIP configuration (*samolyot-'salon'* being the Russian term for VIP aircraft). Unlike the Tu-134AK, the Tu-134A 'Salon' lacks the rear entry door/airstairs and, as a rule, the forward toilet. In other words, the aircraft is outwardly identical to an ordinary Tu-134A – except maybe for the paint job which may give a hint of the VIP role. As a rule, Tu-134A 'Salons' are operated by large enterprises such as major banks or petroleum companies; government flights rarely use such aircraft.

The conversion normally involves installation of an emergency oxygen system with a chemical oxygen generator. Auxiliary bladder tanks in the wing centre section *à la* Tu-134AK are often installed.

Known Tu-134A 'Salons' are registered: RA-65035, RA-65040*, RA-65047, RA-65067, EK-65072, UR-65081, RA-65088*, EX-65119*, RA-65127, RA-65132*, EW-65149*, RA-65560 (Tu-134A-1 'Salon'), RA-65563 (Tu-134A-1 'Salon'), RA-65626 (?), RA-65653, CCCP-65740* (?), RA-65751*, RA-65756, UN 65776, UR-65782, CCCP-65785*, RA-65794, 4L-65798 (to RA-65798), RA-65819*, RA-65823* (?), RA-65903*, RA-65932, RA-65941 (radar-nosed), RA-65943 (radar-nosed), RA-65960, EK-65975 (*?), LY-ASK (to RA-65079), LZ-TUK*, LZ-TUZ (?) and OK-BYT (to LZ-TUG). Aircraft marked with an asterisk have since been reconverted to passenger configuration.

However, at least three aircraft – LZ-TUK (c/n 1351209), OK-BYT (c/n 7349858, f/n 3907) and CCCP-65932 (c/n (33)66405, f/n 6367), and possibly CCCP-65740 (c/n 2351510) as well – were actually built as Tu-134A 'Salons'. The reason is unclear, since the Tu-134AK was in quantity production at the time; possibly someone had mixed things up when processing the orders, with the result that the airframes were built with no rear entry door and had to be hastily refitted with a VIP interior.

The customer's wish is the outfitter's command, and two Tu-134A 'Salons' – RA-65079 and RA-65943 – do feature a forward toilet *à la* Tu-134AK. Hence the former aircraft has white 'plugs' both in the galley window and in the first full-size window to starboard; the sixth and seventh cabin windows to starboard are also blocked, suggesting that a bar or something is located there.

Tu-134A-3 RA-65067 in Voronezhavia colours at Moscow/Sheremet'yevo-1. Mike Kell

Tu-134A (Experimental 96-seat Version)

In April 1983 Tu-134A CCCP-65966 was converted to an experimental 96-seat layout under a joint programme held by the Tupolev OKB, KhAPO and ARZ No 407. The first 16 rows of seats now had five-abreast seating at 75cm (29½in) pitch, with the aisle narrowed from 70 to 40cm (from 27½ to 15¾ in) and offset to port. The last three rows were standard, with four-abreast seating. Two pairs of seats facing each other were installed in the vestibule, requiring the galley to be reconfigured at the expense of the forward baggage hold. The cabin featured enclosed luggage bins.

To facilitate passenger evacuation CCCP-65966 was provided with Type III (0.916 x 0.6m) rear emergency exits and is unique in combining these with a glazed nose. One might be tempted to call this aircraft a 'glass-nosed Tu-134A-1' but it is not, because it has yet another unique feature – a non-standard windowless entry door measuring 1.61 x 1.09m (63⅜ x 43in). This was an ICAO Type Ia exit allowing passengers to 'abandon ship' two at a time. Hence the number of windows on the port side was reduced to 14 (door+6+exit+1+exit+3+1) and a large reinforcement plate of complex shape was riveted on around the entry door.

Service trials yielded good results – seat-mile costs were 18% lower as compared to the standard Tu-134A. Nevertheless, MAP and MGA did not put the 96-seater into airline service; as a result the nation lost 1 billion roubles' net profit in potential earnings over a five-year period. Several Aeroflot directorates, including the Georgian CAD, tried to get Tu-134A CCCP-65966 transferred from the OKB in 1988 but their requests were turned down, as was a request from Balkan Bulgarian Airlines which wanted to try this aircraft on the high-density Sofia-Varna route. (True, in 1990 the OKB did loan this aircraft to the Ukrainian CAD/Khar'kov UAD/87th Flight and later to the Azerbaijan CAD/Baku UAD/339th Flight.)

In post-Soviet times the airliner, now reregistered RA-65966, was used for various support duties (for example, acting as a camera ship during air-to-air photography sorties) and periodically leased to various air carriers. By August 1997 it had been withdrawn form use at the Tupolev Company's flight test facility in Zhukovskiy.

Tu-134B Short/Medium-haul Airliner (Third use of designation)

In 1979 the Tupolev OKB brought out an improved version of the airliner designated Tu-134B. The designation was reused, having been allocated earlier to two stillborn projects (see next chapter). Developed in accordance with a joint MAP/MGA decision dated 6th October 1978, the Tu-134B was a derivative of the Tu-134A-1, featuring the same 'radar nose' housing a Groza-M134 radar and the same Type III (0.916 x 0.6m) rear emergency exits.

As noted earlier, the changes lay within: the B model introduced at long last the central

RA-65653 was one of the Tu-134As outfitted as Tu-134A 'Salon' executive jets; here the absence of a rear entry door is obvious because it is a Batch 10 aircraft with 16 windows to port. Seen here at Moscow/Vnukovo-1 on 5th September 2001 in the anonymous colours of Sirius Aero, it was the oldest operational Tu-134 at the time when the picture was taken; it has been retired since. Author

The Tupolev OKB's unique 96-seat Tu-134A-3 RA-65966, seen at the OKB's flight test facility on 19th September 1999 with a Tu-144D in the background, shows off the enlarged entry door and rear emergency exits. The engines have been removed, hence the dragster-like tail-up attitude. Author

Close-up of the entry door of RA-65966; note the double-layer reinforcement plate around it and the circle of rivets just aft of the door where the second window used to be. Author

A KrAZ-255B 6x6 truck pushes back the prototype Tu-134B CCCP-65146 (updated to 'B-3 standard) on a winter's day at Leningrad-Pulkovo. Aleksey Ivanov

CCCP-65712, a production Tu-134B of the Latvian CAD/Riga UAD/280th Flight, resting between flights. Sergey and Dmitriy Komissarov archive

control pedestal. Mounted in place of the panel where the radar display had been, the central control pedestal carried the single pair of throttles and thrust reverser control levers (which, as distinct from the Tu-134A, allowed the first officer to control reverse thrust), pitch trim handwheels and navigation system controls. Each pilot now had his own radar display mounted on the side console.

The cabin and galley layout were also different. While the Tu-134B had an 80-seat configuration as standard, the increase in capacity was not obtained by removing the inter-cabin partition but by installing two pairs of seats facing each other opposite the entry door. The galley was made more compact and the forward baggage compartment shrank from 6m³ to a mere 2.6m³. (However, you can't put a quart into a pint pot, and one can only guess how they managed to cram more baggage into less space!)

The Tu-134B's service door was equipped with a second inflatable emergency slide replacing the canvas slide of the earlier versions. Unlike the Tu-134A, all Tu-134Bs have the small galley window just aft of this door. Normal TOW was 47.6 tons (104,940 lb).

In keeping with the abovementioned MAP/MGA decision a radar-nosed Tu-134A airframe was earmarked for conversion as the first prototype Tu-134B. Registered CCCP-65146 (c/n (93)61000, f/n 5001), the aircraft was completed in late 1979 and it was not until 31st

March 1980 – roughly a year and two months later than the neighbouring aircraft in the production sequence – that the jet was officially released by the factory. The first production aircraft, CCCP-65799 (c/n (03)63187, f/n 5702), followed on 30th April 1980 – ahead of the second prototype (CCCP-65720, see below) which again was manufactured late. A mere 32 Tu-134Bs were built in regular airline configuration by late August 1984 (that is, not counting the new-build VIP aircraft described separately); they pertained to batches 50, 55, 57-61 and 63. Soviet examples were registered CCCP-65146, -65692 through -65696, -65698 through -65706, -65708 through -65716, -65720 and -65799.

Tu-134B operations were kicked off in May 1980 by MGA order No 72 dated 31st April 1980. The B model was the Soviet Union's first short/medium-haul airliner cleared for operation without a navigator; the navigational tasks were supposed to be performed by the pilots. Nevertheless, Soviet and CIS Tu-134Bs usually carried a navigator – partly due to the crews' ingrained working procedures and habits, partly due to the need to keep people employed.

Tu-134B-3 Short/Medium-haul Airliner

Tu-134Bs manufactured from 1982 onwards were powered by D-30-III engines and designated Tu-134B-3 by analogy with the Tu-134A-3. This version was developed pursuant to MAP

order No 287 dated 3rd July 1980. All previously built examples were retrofitted with the new engines in due course.

It may be said here that 13 Tu-134B-3s in both regular and VIP versions were exported to Bulgaria, North Korea, Syria and Vietnam; the latter two nations operated both sub-types. The Syrian and Vietnamese 'Bs (according to other sources, all export 'Bs) featured flight spoilers/airbrakes; see next entry.

Tu-134B-1 Experimental Short/Medium-haul Airliner

The second prototype Tu-134B with the out-of-sequence registration CCCP-65720 (c/n (03)62820, f/n 5508) was again manufactured a full year 'behind schedule' (compared to the neighbouring aircraft on the production line, that is) – actually later than all other Tu-134Bs for the home market! This was because the aircraft was involved in a multi-aspect development programme aimed at improving the type's operational procedures and operating economics. Hence CCCP-65720 received a separate designation, Tu-134B-1.

The most important change introduced on the Tu-134B-1 was the provision of flight spoilers which could open at any angle up to 40° to slow the jet down in flight. The issue of airbrakes had been a major problem in the USSR for years. With many aircraft in a congested holding area of a major airport, the air traffic controllers would order the pilots to increase or reduce speed in order to maintain safe horizontal separation. While Western jetliners had featured airbrakes since the 1960s, their Soviet counterparts had none, and adjusting the speed by 'playing' with the throttles was inconvenient (the ventral speedbrake could not be used for this, as it served a different role). Thus a Tu-134 would often close in dangerously on the aircraft in front and the approach controller would remove the offender from the holding pattern – which then had to be entered anew, wasting fuel. At times the situation would get pretty nervous when an ATC officer would warn every aircraft in the holding pattern that a 'Russian jet with no brakes' was close at hand; this turned into a political issue.

Flight spoilers could not be fitted to the standard 'glass-nosed' Tu-134 because there was no central control pedestal where the spoiler controls had to be mounted. The advent of the Tu-134B made this possible. Tests of the new feature gave encouraging results; yet MAP and MGA showed no interest, and flight spoilers were installed on export 'Bs only.

To cut seat-mile costs the seating capacity was increased to 84 or 90 at 75cm pitch by installing a new compact galley and new compact toilets; in 90-seat configuration part of the modular galley was removed. Two pairs of seats facing each other with a table in between were installed on the port side immediately ahead of the entry door. This accounted for the Tu-134B-1's sole recognition feature – an extra full-size window ahead of the entry door between frames 12 and 13; this window first appeared on the Tu-134UBL (see below). Strangely enough, the nose titles remained

unchanged (that is, Tu-134B). Finally, a new rack-and-pinion steering mechanism/shimmy damper was installed, increasing the nose-wheel steering angles to ±70° to improve ground manoeuvrability.

CCCP-65720 was reportedly completed in December 1980 (however, the official manufacture date is 19th February 1981) and delivered to the OKB on 17th April 1981. Tests gave good results; the payload was increased from 8.2 to 8.55 tons (18,080 to 18,850 lb) at the expense of a small reduction in maximum-payload range (from 2,000 to 1,950km/1,240 to 1,210 miles), and fuel burn per seat-mile was reduced by 15-17%. Still, the customer (MGA) showed a complete lack of interest and the Tu-134B-1 remained a one-off. It was a year before the Tu-134B finally got flight spoilers.

Tu-134B-1-3 Experimental Short/Medium-haul Airliner
In due course CCCP-65720 was refitted with D-30-III engines and accordingly redesignated Tu-134B-1-3 (the nose titles were amended to Tu-134B-3 in so doing). The aircraft remained with the OKB, gaining the Russian registration prefix in 1993, and operated from Zhukovskiy until it was finally sold to the Ukraine in August 2000 and reregistered UR-BYE.

Tu-134B-3 (VIP version)
A VIP version of the Tu-134B-3 featuring a rear entry door-cum-airstairs, forward toilet and

extra fuel tanks à la Tu-134AK was brought out in 1982. No separate designation is known; this author is sorely tempted to call this version Tu-134BK but no confirmation of this has been found as yet!

Seven Tu-134Bs in Batch 63 were completed as VIP aircraft between late 1982 and early 1984. All of them were export aircraft ordered by Bulgaria (LZ-TUT, the prototype), Vietnam (VN-A114, VN-A116 and VN-A118) and Syria (YK-AYA, YK-AYB and YK-AYD).

Tu-134B-3 'Salon' VIP/Executive Aircraft
Additionally, at least seven ordinary Tu-134Bs were refitted with VIP interiors in the 1990s and at the turn of the century. These are RA-65146, RA-65693, RA-65694, RA-65701, AL-65711 (now 4K-65711), UN-65799 and YL-LBB (now RA-65692). They were mostly outfitted for corporate customers; AL-65711 was an exception, being operated by the Azerbaijan Government. Two of these aircraft (RA-65146 and RA-65693) feature a forward toilet.

Tu-134SKh Agricultural Survey Aircraft
A highly specialised derivative of the Tu-134A-3 was developed for the Soviet Ministry of Agriculture in keeping with Council of Ministers directive No 127-39 dated 28th January 1981. Provisionally designated Tu-134I (*issledovatel'skiy* – research, used attributively) at the ADP stage, the aircraft emerged as the Tu-134SKh (*sel'skokhozyaistvennyy* – agricul-

CCCP-65720, the one-off Tu-134B-1-3 (marked Tu-134B-3 on the nose); the extra window ahead of the entry door is plainly visible. Sergey and Dmitriy Komissarov archive

YK-AYB was one of the seven Tu-134B-3s to be completed as VIP aircraft with a Tu-134AK-style rear entry door. Tupolev JSC

RA-65693, pictured here in Alrosa-Avia colours at Moscow/Vnukovo-1 on 18th June 2002, exemplifies a different kind of Tu-134B-3 'Salon' – a converted regular 'B with no rear entry door. The white 'plugs' in the windows indicate the position of closets or some such. Author

CCCP-65917, the prototype of the Tu-134SKh agricultural research aircraft, during trials in ultimate configuration with Nit'-S-1SKh SLAR pods. Note the wide unpainted fin leading edge, the A-723 LORAN strake aerial and the absence of the Tu-134SKh's characteristic markings. Tupolev JSC

tural). Its mission was to survey agricultural land, measuring soil humidity, detecting pest attacks etc and thus allowing crop yields to be estimated and corrective measures taken if necessary.

The Tu-134SKh (*not* 'Tu-134CX', as it is often called erroneously in Western publications!)[7] was easily identifiable because the airframe incorporated major structural changes. Firstly, the emergency exits and most of the cabin windows were omitted as unnecessary, resulting in a very characteristic arrangement – 1+door+3+1+1+1+1 to port and service door+3+1+1 to starboard. As it were, most of the cabin was occupied by mission equipment, and the two doors were enough for evacuating the flight crew and ten equipment operators.

Secondly, four camera/sensor ports were provided on the fuselage underside; the first three were covered by an optically flat glass panel forming part of the pressure cabin, while the rearmost port was an unpressurised bay. A sliding cover forming a flat-bottomed bulge ahead of the wings protected the camera/sensor ports during take-off and landing; this required the lower anti-collision beacon to be relocated under the rear fuselage.

Thirdly, the aircraft featured a 2-cm waveband Nit' S-1SKh (Thread) side-looking airborne radar (SLAR); the antennas were housed in two cigar-shaped pods 8m (26ft 3in) long carried under the wing roots on short pylons.

The first Tu-134SKh surveyors were built with no SLAR but retrofitted in due course.

Other identification features included a Type AShS L-shaped aerial (identical to those above and below the forward fuselage) further aft and an exceptionally wide unpainted fin leading edge, as on late-production Tu-134AKs. Finally, the Tu-134SKh sported characteristic markings – an ear of wheat was painted on the fuselage aft of the Aeroflot titles and a blue circle outlined in yellow with the white letters 'CX' (SKh in Cyrillic characters) was located on the nose below the 'Tu-134A-3' nose titles.

The mission equipment included three cameras – East German Zeiss Ikon MKF-6M and MSK-4 multi-spectrum cameras on fixed mounts (alternatively, indigenous AFA-41/10 and AFA-TE/35 cameras could be installed) and a TAFA-10 topographic camera on an AFUS-U tilting mount.[8] The Soviet cameras' focal length (f) was 100mm (4in) for the AFA-41/10 and TAFA-10 or 350mm (13¾in) for the AFA-TE/35. A processing lab was located at the rear of the cabin, allowing films to be developed and photos printed on board.

A six-channel infra-red scanner developed by the French company Matra fed images to a magnetic data storage system. In the USSR this scanner was known as *Yashma* (Jasper).

The SLAR offered a field of view 15 or 37.5km (9.31 or 23.29 miles) wide, generating a radar map to 1/100,000th or 1/200,000th scale in the

former case and 1/250,000th or 1/500,000th scale in the latter case. A 'blind spot' 11km (6.83 miles) wide remained directly below the aircraft. Radar mapping was performed at 3,000-6,500m (9,840-21,325ft) and 350-750km/h (217-465mph); an area of up to 10,000km² (3,860 miles²) could be surveyed in a single sortie. Radar data was fed to two screens, one showing the actual radar map and the other displaying the data fed into the storage system. Unlike aerial photography, which in many regions is possible only 25 to 35 days a year, radar imaging is possible day and night, in any weather and season. Radar imagery shows dry, saline and swampy areas (such as rice paddies); the SLAR can even see through a layer of snow, making it possible to check up on winter crops.

A special Mak (Poppy) navigation suite allowed the Tu-134SKh to move in a shuttle pattern during photography/remote sensing, follow a preset route and automatically return along the same route.

OEW was 34.4 tons (75,840 lb) with SLAR or 32.4 tons (71,430 lb) without SLAR, and the MTOW was 47.6 tons (104,940 lb). The fuel supply was 18,000 litres (14.4 tons), providing a range of 3,600km (2,240 miles) and a maximum endurance of 4.5 hours.

The prototype, CCCP-65917 (c/n (33)63991, f/n 6329), entered flight test in April 1983 and was retained by the OKB. Nine production aircraft followed (CCCP-65721 through -65725, -65918 and -65928 through -65930). Contrary to allegations by some Western sources, all Tu-134SKh surveyors were purpose-built aircraft, not converted from Tu-134As. Production was slow because plant No 153 was switching to the Antonov An-72 *Coaler* STOL transport; each aircraft was delivered at least a year later than the next passenger-configured aircraft in Batch 63, the final example leaving the factory in the late summer of 1989.

The Tu-134SKh entered service on 28th September 1984 pursuant to MAP order No 335, MGA order No 210 and Ministry of Agriculture order No 230. All nine production aircraft were delivered to the Central Regions CAD/ Voronezh UAD/243rd Flight but three were later transferred to the Ivanovo UAD/176th Flight. (Both Voronezh and Ivanovo are located in central Russia's bread belt.) Nevertheless, trials at GosNII GA continued for another 18 months, with V Vvedenskiy as project test pilot.

The first major 'operation' in which the type made its mark was the Kursk-85 experiment aimed at studying the condition of crops and developing crop yield prediction methods. Apart from the Tu-134SKh, it involved An-30s, modified An-2 *Colt* biplanes, Meteor and Kosmos satellites and the Salyut-7 space station from which cosmonauts Vladimir Djanibekov and Aleksey Savinykh took pictures of the Earth.

The jet proved much more cost-effective for aerial photography than the An-30 or the Mil'

Mi-8 *Hip* multi-role helicopter, the cost per square kilometre being 2.7 and 4.6 times lower respectively. In mid-1986 an all-Union research centre called Agricultural Resources Automated Info & Control System (AIUS '*Agroresoorsy*') was established within the ministry, making use of several more-or-less specialised aircraft, including the Tu-134SKh.

The aircraft was progressively upgraded. In May 1987 the Nit' S-1SKh SLAR was finally cleared for full-scale operation after rigorous testing. In 1990 the Tu-134SKh received an A-723 long-range navigation system (identified by a new starboard strake aerial atop the fuselage which was twice taller than usual), a VEM-72F electromechanical altimeter, Kama-S/ Kama-F six-channel gamma spectrometers and a *Voolkahn* (Volcano) IR scanner.

On 11th-16th August 1992 the Tu-134SKh made its public debut when CCCP-65917 was in the static park at MosAeroShow-92 in Zhukovskiy, Russia's first major airshow. The prototype was displayed again at the MAKS-93 airshow (31st August – 5th September 1993).

Unfortunately, Tu-134SKh operations were beset by organisational problems and all kinds of bureaucratic snags which kept the aircraft on the ground most of the time. As a result, in the early 1990s the new airlines operating them (Voronezhavia and IGAP) decided to sell them for conversion into freighters or biz-jets. By August 2002 nine out of ten had been converted, leaving RA-65929 as the 'last man standing' (see next two entries).

Tu-134SKh Combi Conversion

In 1995 Voronezhavia's Tu-134SKh RA-65930 (c/n (63)66500, f/n 6374) was converted to combi configuration at ARZ No 407 as the airline had no other use for it. After all, an aircraft should fly and earn revenue, not sit gathering dust and making losses. To facilitate cargo operations the standard entry door gave way to a windowless 1.61 x 1.09m door identical to that of Tu-134A CCCP-65966. This required one window on the port side to be deleted (the new arrangement was 1+door+2+1+1+1+1). The SLAR pods were removed; the ventral camera bay doors remained but were non-functional (replacing that part of the fuselage structure was not worthwhile).

Tu-134A-3M Executive Aircraft

In the above configuration RA-65930 was ill-suited for passenger operations because of the lack of overwing emergency exits (a major safety concern) and the limited number of windows making the cabin uncomfortable. Thus in 1999 the aircraft was further modified at ARZ No 407 during refurbishment, becoming a 40-seat business jet. Additional windows and emergency exits were incorporated, the components coming from time-expired airframes. The resulting window arrangement is still non-standard – 1+door+8+exit+2+1 to port and service door+9+exit+2 to starboard. Oddly enough, the repainted aircraft wore 'Ty-134CX' nose titles – which it never wore while it was a Tu-134SKh!

CCCP-65918, the second Tu-134SKh, with the proper 'ear of wheat' and nose badge. These photos illustrate the characteristic and asymmetric window arrangement. Tupolev JSC

Close-up of the ventral camera window fairing of Tu-134SKh CCCP-65917 with the protective door slid open. Author

Thus the trend was set. In the three years that followed, eight more survey aircraft were converted into biz-jets which received a new designation, Tu-134A-3M (not to be confused with the Tu-134M project, see Chapter 4). In due time RA-65930 also received 'Tu-134A-3M' nose titles.

Interestingly, practically all Tu-134A-3Ms differ in window arrangement! For instance, RA-65721 (c/n (43)66130, f/n 6339) has 1+door+3+3+1+2+1 to port and service door+3+1+1+exit+1+5 to starboard. RA-65723 (c/n (63)66440, f/n 6369) and RA-65724 (c/n (63)66445, f/n 6370) are identical, featuring 1+door+6+2+exit+2+1 to port and service door+6+2+exit+2+1 to starboard. RA-65725 (c/n (63)66472, f/n 6371) and RA-65917 are likewise identical, with 1+door+7+1+exit+2+1 to port and service door+7+1+exit+2 to starboard. Finally, RA-65928 (c/n (63)66491, f/n 6372) has 1+door+5+1+1+exit+2+1 to port and service door+5+1+1+exit+3 to starboard. Most Tu-134A-3Ms were outfitted by Kvand Aircraft Interiors.

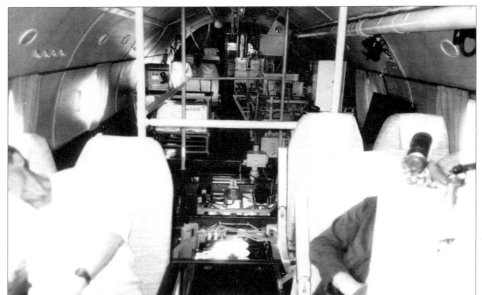

Close-up of SLAR pods of Tu-134SKh CCCP-65917; the one-piece dielectric lower portions swing open outwards. Author

The cabin of Tu-134SKh CCCP-65917 has research crew workstations at the front and rear; the camera window section in the middle is surrounded by a guard rail. Sergey Komissarov

'The first man down'. Voronezhavia Tu-134SKh RA-65930, seen here lifting off from runway 24 at Moscow-Vnukovo past the hangars of ARZ No 400, has been converted to cargo/passenger configuration. Note the non-standard entry door identical to that of Tu-134A-3 RA-65966.
Yuriy Kirsanov

Tu-134TS Military Transport/CASEVAC Aircraft

Until the 1980s all new Soviet civil aircraft were designed to be easily adaptable for military roles, even if it be merely troop transportation in times of war, and the Tu-134 was no exception. In 1968 a single Tu-134 *sans suffixe* was converted into a military transport/casualty evacuation (CASEVAC) aircraft designated Tu-134TS (*trahnsportno-sanitahrtnyy* – transport/medical). Its identity is unknown; however, the *Euromil* handbook lists Tu-134 *sans suffixe* c/n 6350203 (for which no civil registration is known) as '01 Red' and this may be the aircraft in question.

The conversion technology had been tried by the Tupolev OKB earlier with the Tu-104A-TS and Tu-104B-TS which were military transport/CASEVAC versions of the Tu-104A and Tu-104B respectively. In transport configuration the aircraft could carry five to six tons (11,020-13,230 lb) of materiel; in medical configuration several tiers of stretchers were fixed to uprights in the cabin, allowing patients to be carried with a medical attendant.

The Tu-134TS underwent trials at GK NII VVS. The military had one main comment, concerning the small size of the doors preventing the carriage of bulky items. (The Tu-134TS was no match for the McDonnell Douglas C-9A Nightingale with its large cargo door and powered ramp allowing stretchers to be wheeled on and off.) Concurrently Aeroflot's top management ruled that all equipment associated with military transport duties be removed from mainline passenger aircraft, as it was reducing the profits from airline operations. Hence the Tu-134TS remained a one-off.

Tu-134Sh-1 Navigator Trainer (*Crusty-A?*)

Dedicated military versions for the Soviet Air Force (VVS – *Voyenno-vozdooshnyye seely*) were developed as well. The first of these was the Tu-134Sh navigator trainer (*shtoormanskiy* – for navigators); designed in 1969-70 jointly with the Khar'kov aircraft factory, this spinoff of the Tu-134A was a replacement for the 1962-vintage Tu-124Sh. Some Western sources erroneously call this version 'Tu-134BSh' (*bombardirovochno-shtoormanskiy* – for bomber navigators) or 'Tu-134UB' (*oochebno-boyevoy [samolyot]* – combat trainer).

RA-65721, one of the Tu-134A-3M biz-jet conversions of the Tu-134SKh, at Moscow/Vnukovo-1 on 18th June 2002; the altered window arrangement is clearly visible. Author

RA-65930 following its second conversion in early 2002 as a Tu-134A-3M for Kras Air. Curiously, the nose titles read 'Tu-134SKh'. Sergey and Dmitriy Komissarov archive

The well-appointed main cabin of Tu-134A-3M RA-65723, one two operated by Sirius-Aero for S-Air Service (looking aft); note the quasi-rectangular windows. Kvand Aircraft Interiors

Contrary to Western reports, the Tu-134Sh trainers were new-build aircraft, **not** converted Tu-134As and Tu-134s *sans suffixe*. This misconception is due to the fact that, as noted in Chapter 1, for some reason a separate c/n sequence was used for the trainer, creating confusion with early-production civil aircraft (incidentally, this was also the case with the Tu-124Sh). No separate NATO reporting name for the navigator trainer is known to this author, but regarding the name assigned to the Tu-134UBL, it is almost certainly *Crusty-A*. (If there is a B, there has to be an A, after all!)

Like its precursor, the aircraft had two subvariants differing in specialisation and hence equipment. The first of these, designated Tu-134Sh-1, was intended for training navigators for the VVS's strategic bomber arm (DA – **Dahl**'*nyaya aviahtsiya*) – specifically, navigators flying the Tu-22 *Blinder* and, to a certain extent, the Tu-22M2/Tu-22M3 *Backfire-B/C*.

The Tu-134Sh-1 can be recognised first of all by the much larger and deeper chin radome housing an R-1 Rubin-1Sh (Ruby; pronounced *roobin*) panoramic navigation/bomb-aiming radar;[9] the radome is usually painted dark grey,

which makes it even more conspicuous. The radar is linked with an OPB-15 optical bomb sight (*opticheskiy bombardirovochnyy pritsel*).

Two small flat-topped blisters offset to port are installed above the 11th and 13th cabin windows near the wing trailing edge. They mount BTs-63 star trackers (astrosextants) for celestial navigation training.

Two removable BD-360 multiple ejector racks (MERs) are fitted under the inner wings (BD = **bah**lochnyy derzhahtel' – beam-type rack). The racks are faired, looking like large strakes, and can carry four 120-kg (265-lb) PB-120 practice bombs each; the bombs are dropped by means of an ESBR-49AS electric bomb release unit (*elektrosbrahsyvatel'*). In bombed-up condition the extra drag reduces the trainer's top speed from 860 to 800km/h (534 to 496mph).

An AFA-BAF-40R vertical camera (f = 400mm/ 15¾in) is housed in the rear fuselage immediately ahead of the APU bay to record the bombing results; the lens is closed by a small teardrop fairing with clamshell doors. Hence the single ventral APU intake grille is replaced by two smaller grilles flanking the said fairing. A

The Tu-134Sh-1 prototype ('01 Red', c/n 0350001) parked at the Russian Air Force's 929th State Flight Test Centre at Vladimirovka AB, Akhtoobinsk, in 1995. The TWA-style late colour scheme shows considerable weathering. The BD-360 bomb racks are just discernible under the wing roots; note also the dorsal star trackers, large radome and 16 cabin windows to port. Yefim Gordon

'84 Red', a late-production Tu-134Sh-1 (c/n 63550720) of the Russian Air Force's 148th OVTAE (Independent Military Airlift Squadron) parked at Klin-5 AB, its home base. The second galley window to starboard is typical of the 'Sh-1; two cabin windows above the wing are obscured by equipment. The BD-360 bomb racks have been removed. Sergey Panov

wire aerial for an R-802V VHF radio runs from the fin leading edge to a short strut above the wing leading edge. The ventral L-shaped AShS aerial aft of the nose gear associated with the Landysh (Lily of the valley) command link radio on passenger versions was replaced by an AShS-UD blade aerial for an R-832 or R-832M Evkalipt (Eucalyptus) radio. Twin pitot heads are installed on the port side between windows No 4-5 and 10-11, plus a single pitot head between windows 14-15. Most aircraft have the SRO-2M Khrom (Chromium; NATO *Odd Rods*) IFF transponder,[10] aka *izdeliye* 023, with its trademark triple aerials of unequal length replaced by an SRO-1P *Parol'*-2D (Password) transponder, aka *izdeliye* 62-01, with equally characteristic triangular blade aerials.

The cabin features 12 trainee workstations associated with specific groups of equipment. Two shifts of trainees take turns using them during a typical sortie.

The first prototype Tu-134Sh-1 (tactical code '01 Red', c/n 0350001) was manufactured on 29th January 1971. The second prototype (tactical code unknown, c/n 0350002) followed on 17th March; this was possibly the Tu-134Sh-2 prototype (see next entry). The first prototype had 16 cabin windows on the port side, as did Tu-134As in batches 10-12; on production trainers manufactured from December 1971

onwards this was reduced to 15, as on Tu-134As from Batch 13 onwards.

Tu-134Sh-1 trainers were mostly delivered to the Chelyabinsk Military Navigator College (VVAUSh – *Vyssheye voyennoye aviatsionnoye oochilischche shtoormanov*) in the Urals region of central Russia. A few saw service with the 652nd UAP (*oochebnyy aviapolk* – training air regiment, = Training Wing in USAF terminology) forming part of the DA's 43rd TsBP i PLS (*Tsentr boyevoy podgotovki i pere-oochivaniya lyotnovo sostahva* – Combat & Conversion Training Centre) at Dyaghilevo AB near Ryazan'.

Tu-134Sh-2 Navigator Trainer (*Crusty-A?*)

The other navigator trainer version called Tu-134Sh-2 was originally developed for training navigators of the tactical aviation arm (FA – *Frontovaya aviahtsiya*), specifically Yakovlev Yak-28I *Brewer-C* tactical bomber crews. The type is long since retired and replaced by the Sukhoi Su-24 *Fencer* bomber.

The Tu-134Sh-2 is equipped with an Initsia-tiva-1Sh (Initiative; NATO codename *Short Horn*) panoramic navigation/bomb-aiming radar in an identical large radome; this is a centimetre-waveband radar with a detection range of 220km (136 miles). Other changes in equipment include an ESBR-49M bomb release unit, an NVU-VI-1 navigation computer and so on.

Outwardly the Tu-134Sh-2 can be identified mainly by the window arrangement which differs from that of the Tu-134Sh-1. The latter's fuselage is identical to that of a Tu-134A featuring a galley window to starboard (say, batches 15-45), whereas the Tu-134Sh-2 has only the port forward emergency exit and lacks the galley window. The window arrangement is this: entry door+7+exit+1+4+1 to port and service door+1+7+1+6 to starboard (the starboard forward emergency exit is deleted together with the window!). This is because the mission equipment is arranged differently, obstructing the (missing) exits.

The other recognition feature is that the Tu-134Sh-2 is equipped with a different type of MERs (providing they are fitted, of course). These are the rather untidy-looking MBD3-U6-68Sh bomb racks attached by tandem struts; each MER can carry six 50-kg (110-lb) PB-50-75 (P-50T) practice bombs as an alternative to four PB-120s.[11]

Both sub-variants passed their State acceptance trials successfully and were cleared for service entry on 21st January 1972. Full-scale production began later that year and a total of 90 navigator trainers had been reportedly built when production ended in 1980; the proportion of Tu-134Sh-1s and Tu-134Sh-2s within this total is not known. All Tu-134Sh trainers had the old BSU-3P ALS.

Below left: The attachment points for BD-360 bomb racks on Tu-134Sh-1 '84 Red' (c/n 63550720). Sergey Panov

Bottom left and right: The trainee workstations in the cabin of Tu-134Sh-1 '84 Red' (c/n 63550720). Sergey Panov

'40 Blue', a Tu-134Sh-2 (c/n 93550983) of the Russian Air Force's 978th VTAP (Military Airlift Regiment)/2nd Squadron, also based at Klin-5 AB. Note the absence of the second galley window and the different MBD3-U6-68Sh bomb racks, both indicative of the 'Sh-2 version. Sergey Panov

Close-up of the MBD3-U6-68Sh bomb racks on a Tu-134Sh-2. Unlike the Tu-134Sh-1, the attachment points are not faired. Sergey Panov

Tu-134Sh-2 '34 Blue' (c/n 93550970), another 978th VTAP/2nd Squadron aircraft, was first repainted in the blue/white version of the Tu-134Sh livery and then had a replacement tail fitted. Note the overpainted Soviet flag still discernible just above the unusually small red star. Sergey Panov

The Tu-134Sh-2s were mostly delivered to the Voroshilovgrad VVAUSh in the Ukraine.

Originally Tu-134Sh trainers left the factory in a livery almost identical to that of Aeroflot Tu-134s *sans suffixe*, except for the absence of Aeroflot titles/logo and the Tupolev OKB badge on the nose (instead, the red lower pinstripe had a 'lightning bolt' shape). The VVS red star insignia replaced the Soviet flag on the tail, and the tactical code was carried on the engines.

Later, the Tu-134Sh received a smart red/ white colour scheme strongly reminiscent of Trans World Airlines' then-current livery. Soon, however, it turned out that the red paint was not durable enough and the aircraft quickly assumed a very weathered look. Therefore the red colour of the double cheatline, pinstripe and fin was substituted by dark blue on some Tu-134Sh-2s. One such blue-painted example coded '34 Blue' (c/n 93550970, f/n unknown) and belonging to the 978th Airlift Regiment/2nd Squadron based at Klin-5 AB north of Moscow was unusual in having an all-white tail with a smaller-than-usual red star; to top it all, *an over-painted Soviet flag was plainly visible above the star*! Apparently the original fin was damaged in a ground accident and replaced by a unit sourced from a cannibalised civil airframe.

Tu-134Sh VIP Conversions

Several Tu-134Sh-1s were converted to VIP aircraft – mostly for use as air army or fleet air arm commanders' 'hacks'. For instance, a Tu-134Sh-1 in old colours coded '01 Red' (c/n unknown) was used by the Cosmonaut Detachment for carrying cosmonauts from Chkalovskaya AB to the Baikonur Space Centre and back until replaced by a Tu-134AK with the same tactical code (c/n (83)60650, f/n 4809) in late 1978.

By 1998 a Tu-134Sh-1 coded '07 Blue' (c/n 73550795?, f/n unknown) was converted into a VIP jet for the Russian Navy. The aircraft wore basic Aeroflot colours and 'Tu-134A' nose titles; the MERs and even the port side blisters for the star trackers were removed, but the large radome, the blade aerial aft of the nose gear and the strike camera fairing spoke for themselves, of course. The tactical code was carried only on the nose gear doors; the aircraft sported a Russian flag on the tail (augmented by the Navy's St Andrew's flag on the fuselage) and 'Rossiya' (Russia) titles in stylised Old Russian script.

A similarly painted aircraft (except for the 'Tu-134' nose titles and the absence of the Navy flag) with the unusual registration RA-19 (c/n unknown) is a converted Tu-134Sh-2 – the least likely aircraft for a VIP conversion, since it has just one emergency exit!

Interestingly, some perfectly standard examples were occasionally used as VIP transports; thus, red-painted Tu-134Sh-2 '19 Red' (possibly the same aircraft!) complete with MERs brought some of the high-ranking guests to the Kubinka-92 air fest on 11th April 1992. As no airstairs were available, the portly generals had to use the flimsy telescopic ladder, which certainly did not make for a dignified arrival.

Tu-134UBL *Crusty-B* pilot trainer

The second major military version was the Tu-134UBL (*oochebno-boyevoy dlya lyotchikov* = combat trainer for pilots). The designation is sometimes rendered as Tu-134UB-L; the aircraft has also been misidentified in the foreign press as the 'Tu-134UT' (*oochebno-trenirovochnyy* [*samolyot*] – trainer) and 'Tu-134BU' (that is, Tu-134B-*oochebnyy*). The NATO codename is *Crusty-B*.

Derived from the Tu-134B, the Tu-134UBL is a crew trainer for the Tu-22M2/Tu-22M3 and Tu-160 *Blackjack*. Its *raison d'être* is that, unlike the earlier Tu-22 *Blinder*, they do not have specialised trainer versions, and using them for conversion training would be a waste of their service life. The Tu-134 was selected for this role because it is similar to the bombers in thrust-to-weight ratio and low-speed handling. Development proceeded in parallel with the civilian 'donor' and was triggered by joint MAP/Air Force resolution No 3659 of 6th-7th August 1979.

The Tu-134UBL's appearance is unmistakable. First of all, the aircraft has a long pointed nose borrowed from the Tu-22M3 which increases overall length to 41.918m (137ft 6¼in); the lower half of this 'beak' is a huge dielectric radome. However, instead of the *Backfire*'s PNA (NATO codename *Down Beat*) navigation/target illumination radar the nose houses an ROZ-1 weather radar, since the aircraft is intended for flight training only (including formation flying). Originally the nose was to incorporate a telescopic in-flight refuelling probe but this was never installed because the *Backfire* was stripped of IFR capability under the terms of the SALT II strategic arms limitation treaty signed on 19th July 1979.

Secondly, half the cabin windows, the galley window and the forward emergency exits are omitted as unnecessary; the remaining two exits are large (Tu-134B-style), measuring 0.916 x 0.6m. The window arrangement is 1+door+1+1+1+1+exit+1+1 to port and service door+1+1+1+1+1+exit+1+1 to starboard. The extra window ahead of the entry door (frames 12-13) was necessary because the navigator's station is located there.

(It should be noted at this point that again, contrary to allegations by some Western authors that Tu-134UBLs were converted from Tu-134Sh trainers and Tu-134As, all Tu-134UBL trainers were purpose-built aircraft, *not* conversions. Consider the difference in window placement; eliminating the windows and emergency exits and then enlarging the remaining exits was pointless and the huge amount of work involved would not be worth the effort anyway.)

Other detail changes include AShS-UD blade aerials for the R-832M Evkalipt command link radio above and below the forward fuselage. The fin incorporates slot aerials for the *Backfire*'s RSBN-PKV short-range radio navigation system (RSBN = *rahdiotekhnicheskaya sistema blizhney navigahtsii* – SHORAN); they are located one above the other, not in a stepped arrangement as on other Tu-134 versions featuring the RSBN-2S Svod (Dome) SHORAN. As on the Tu-22M, a light is built into the fin leading edge for unknown purposes. All Tu-134UBLs have the late SRO-1P IFF transponder. Finally, the *Crusty-B* has a characteristic overall grey colour scheme with huge red/white 'go faster' lightning side flashes; this, together with the long pointed nose, gives it a lean and predatory look. The tip of the nose is painted Dayglo orange to prevent damage by ground vehicles.

A Tu-134Sh coded '01 Red' in the original colour scheme was used as a VIP transport by the Soviet Cosmonaut Detachment. On 26th October 1976 it brought the crew of the Soyuz-23 spacecraft – Lt Col Vyacheslav Zoodov (left) and Lt Col Valeriy Rozhdestvenskiy (centre) to Chkalovskaya AB after a space mission.
ITAR-TASS

The Tu-134UBL is powered by D-30-II engines and equipped for ICAO Cat II operations. OEW is 28.5 tons (62,830 lb) and maximum take-off weight 44.25 tons (97,550 lb); auxiliary tanks in the wing centre section give a fuel capacity of 18,000 litres. The aircraft has a top speed of 890km/h (552mph) and a range of 3,400km (2,110 miles).

The instrument panels are modified to emulate those of the Tu-22M. The aircraft has a crew of four. Three rows of seats are installed in the forward part of the cabin, allowing 12 trainees to take turns flying the aircraft from the right-hand seat. The cabin also features a rack for breathing apparatus near the entry door, a rack for the crew's parachutes opposite this door and a rack for the trainees' parachutes at the rear; the rear baggage door is opened by a pneumatic ram to permit bailing out in an emergency.

The first prototype (CCCP-64010, c/n (13)64010, f/n 6401) was manufactured in January 1981. This and several more aircraft completed by early spring participated in manufacturer's flight tests coinciding with Stage A of the State acceptance trials which were held at Khar'kov-Sokol'nikovo (the KhAPO factory airfield) in May-June 1981. On 24th-29th July GK NII VVS issued a preliminary report recommending the Tu-134UBL for service.

Stage B of the State acceptance trials began in October 1981, using the second prototype (CCCP-64020, c/n (13)64020, f/n 6402) outfitted with a test equipment suite; the trials were completed in June 1982. The longer nose and hence increased area forward of the CG affected handling at high angles of attack to such an extent that spinning trials had to be held. To this end a Tu-134UBL coded '02 Red' (c/n unknown) was fitted with a spin recovery parachute container on a massive tubular adapter supplanting the standard tailcone.[12] The trials were held at GK NII VVS in Akhtoobinsk in 1983, with the first prototype Tu-134Sh-1 acting as chase plane; later the *Crusty-B* was reconverted to standard and delivered to one of the Air Force's flying schools.

Ninety (some sources say 77) examples had been completed when production ended in late 1983; the Tu-134UBL made up the lion's share of *Crusty* production in 1982-83, no fewer than 35 being completed in 1982 alone. For pre-delivery flight tests all Tu-134UBLs all were given temporary civil registrations matching the c/n (CCCP-64073, CCCP-64585 and so on).

Tu-134UBL '37 Red' operated by the Tambov Military Pilot College takes off past a line of retired IL-28U trainers undergoing scrapping.
ITAR-TASS

Close-up of a Tu-134UBL's characteristic nose.
Yefim Gordon archive

The Tu-134UBL's nose with the radome removed, showing the LTs-2-12 antenna of the ROZ-1 radar. Yefim Gordon archive

Tu-134UBL '16 Red' shows off the type's characteristic colour scheme. Vyacheslav Martynyuk

A poor-quality but interesting shot of Tu-134UBL CCCP-64585 on a pre-delivery test flight from Khar'kov-Sokol'nikovo. Yefim Gordon archive

'72 Red' (c/n (23)64728), the sole Tu-134UBK naval trainer, during trials; the tactical code is carried on the nose gear doors only. The I-098 fixed acquisition round emulating a Kh-22M missile is visible under the centre fuselage; note also the tall LORAN strake aerial. Tupolev JSC

These remained assigned to the aircraft even after they received overt military markings and are etched on plates in the flightdeck, just like on passenger versions.[13]

Actually deliveries commenced in April 1981 – before the trials had ended, which was fairly common practice in the Soviet Air Force; a training regiment at Engels-2 AB was reportedly the first unit to receive the type. The Tambov Military Pilot College (VVAUL – *Vyssheye voyennoye aviatsionnoye oochilischche lyotchikov*) named after Marina Raskova at

Tambov-Yoozhnyy AB started re-equipping with the Tu-134UBL in August 1981; there the *Crusty-B* superseded the Tu-124Sh-1 and the last remaining Il'yushin IL-28U *Mascot* bomber trainers of 1950s vintage. The Orsk VVAUL near Orenburg followed suit.

In early 1991 a few Tu-134UBLs were delivered to Squadron 3 of the 184th GvTBAP (*Gvardeyskiy tyazhelobombardirovochnyy aviapolk* – Guards heavy bomber regiment, = Bomber Wing (Heavy) in USAF terminology) stationed at Priluki airbase in the Chernigov

Region, the Ukraine. These aircraft were used for proficiency training, saving the service life of the unit's Tu-22M3s and Tu-160s. Several *Crusty-Bs* were operated by the 652nd UAP at Dyaghilevo AB.

The type had its public debut on 11th April 1992 when an example coded '16 Red' (possibly c/n (13)64073; f/n 6407?) was in the static display during the open doors day at Kubinka AB. Other public appearances include an air fest at Shaykovka AB in late 1994 on occasion of the resident 52nd GvTBAP's gold jubilee and the open doors day at Kubinka AB on 8th August 2002 to celebrate the 60th anniversary of the 16th Air Army when Tu-134UBL '18 Red' (RA-64800, c/n (33)64800, f/n unknown) was on display.

Occasionally the *Crusty-B* acted as a VIP transport. For instance, at the 1992 Kubinka event some of the invited guests arrived in Tu-134UBLs '26 Red' (possibly c/n (23)64392, f/n unknown) and '37 Red'.

Tu-134UBK *Crusty-B*
Weapons Systems Trainer

Although the Tu-22M2/Tu-22M3 has a conventional bombing capability, its main weapon is the Kh-22M (NATO AS-4 *Kitchen*) air-to-surface missile used mostly against large surface ships. Therefore the need arose to train *Backfire* crews in bombing and missile launch techniques. For a while this mission was performed by the two Tu-104Sh-2 trainers, CCCP-42342

(c/n 7350502) and CCCP-42347 (c/n 76600301), operated by the Soviet Naval Air Arm since 1964 and 1966 respectively. However, by the early 1980s these aircraft built in 1957 were due for retirement as time-expired and a replacement was needed urgently.

To fill this need the OKB of the Soviet Navy's ARZ No 20 in Pushkin, Leningrad Region, developed a derivative of the Tu-134UBL designated Tu-134UBK (alternatively rendered as Tu-134UB-K). Unlike the Tu-134K and Tu-134AK, in this case the K denoted **kom**pleks [*vo'orouzheniya*] – weapons system. (By comparison, the Soviet Air Force's/Soviet Navy's missile strike aircraft were designated Tu-16K-26 *Badger-G Mod*, Tu-95K *Bear-B* etc)

By arrangement with KhAPO the last Tu-134UBL manufactured in 1982 ('72 Red', c/n (23)64728, f/n unknown) was completed with specially reinforced wings. In 1983 it was converted to the Tu-134UBK prototype at ARZ

No 20 by transferring most of the mission equipment from Tu-104Sh-2 CCCP-42342 to the new airframe.

The Tu-134UBK differed a lot from the standard *Crusty-B* inside and out. Now the nose radome indeed housed a PNA target illumination radar while the ROZ-1 weather radar was

The flightdeck of Tu-134UBKM '25 Red'. Note the registration 64630 (matching the c/n) on the plates attached to the instrument panel shrouds. Pyotr Batuyev

The weapons systems operator trainee's workstation of the Tu-134UBKM, with radar displays, a moving map display above them and a map table. Pyotr Batuyev

moved to a Tu-134A-style chin radome. A similar twin-antenna arrangement characterised the Tu-104Sh-2 and the Tu-16K-10 *Badger-C*; the Tu-134UBK's nose was identical to that of the Tu-134SL avionics testbed (see below).

A detachable I-098 fixed acquisition round emulating a Kh-22M ASM was carried under the centre fuselage on four streamlined struts; alternatively, two MBD3-U6-68Sh MERs could be fitted. Accordingly an AFA-BAF-40R strike camera was fitted in identical fashion to the Tu-134Sh. The *Backfire*'s OPB-15T electro-optical bomb sight was fitted, with an identical fairing incorporating an optically flat window aft of the nose gear. As on the Tu-134SKh, the starboard ADF strike aerial was twice as tall than usual.

Other new equipment included a TV-18 radio altimeter, a DISS-7 Doppler speed/drift sensor (*doplerovskiy izmeritel' skorosti i snosa*) in a small ventral fairing replacing the *Crusty-B*'s DISS-013-134 and the Vakhta (Watch, or Vigil) navigation suite. The trainee workstations emulating the Tu-22M's rear cockpit (navigator's and weapons systems operator's stations) were placed amidships, with more workstations for the Vakhta and OPB-15T and equipment racks further aft. Four AC converters were installed in the rear baggage compartment for powering the mission equipment.

The Tu-134UBK remained a one-off. Upon completion of trials in 1984 the aircraft was delivered to the Naval Air Arm's 33rd TsBP i PLS named after Ye N Preobrazhenskiy at Kool'bakino AB in Nikolayev. It was retained by the Ukrainian Naval Air Arm after the break-up of the USSR.

Tu-134UBKM *Crusty-B*
Weapons Systems Trainer

Interest in a weapons systems trainer for Tu-22M3 crews revived in Russia in the mid-1990s and the Tu-134UBK programme was dusted off. Enough changes were made warrant a new designation, Tu-134UBKM (M = *modernizeerovannyy* – upgraded).

The mission equipment was housed inside the fuselage, obviating the need for the draggy I-098 acquisition round; this meant the MERs could be fitted whenever necessary. The strike camera was moved forward to a position just aft of the wing trailing edge, obviating the need to modify the APU's lower intake.

Coded '25 Red', the Tu-134UBKM prototype (RA-64630, c/n (23)64630, f/n unknown) was rolled out after conversion at ARZ No 20 in 1996. In the spring of 1999 the pant began

upgrading several more Tu-134UBLs. 'Production' aircraft were intended for the 240th GvOSAP (*Gvardeyskiy otdel'nyy smeshannyy aviapolk* – Guards Independent Composite Air Regiment) forming part of the Russian Navy's 33rd TsBP i PLS, now home-based at Ostrov AB located 40km (25 miles) from Pskov.

Tu-134UBL Passenger
and Business Jet Conversions

In 1999 several Russian companies specialising in aircraft interior outfitting proposed converting Tu-134UBL trainers being withdrawn by the Russian Air Force (*sic*) into passenger, combi or executive aircraft. The *Crusty-B* was an attractive option for such conversions, as the trainers were low-time airframes and were equipped with a central control pedestal as fitted to the Tu-134B.

Thus in early 2002 an as-yet unidentified Russian bank purchased the eighth production Tu-134UBL (tactical code and c/n unknown, f/n 6410)[14] for conversion into a biz-jet in similar

fashion to the Tu-134A-3M. The job was performed by ARZ No 407. By May 2002 conversion of the airframe was almost complete, involving removal of the trademark 'beak' (which is a two-piece structure riveted onto a Tu-134B flightdeck section) and installation of extra windows. No further details are known as of this writing.

During 2002 the first prototype Tu-134UBL ('11 Red', c/n (13)64010, f/n 6401), which had been used as an avionics testbed (see below), was sold to the Roos' Leasing Co and converted into a 'Tu-134B-3'. (It is not known whether the window arrangement now matches that of the standard airliner, but even if it does, this is a false Tu-134B anyway!) Registered RA-65945 on 25th September 2002, the aircraft was leased to Avcom in 2003.

The author believes this practice will not be widespread. The Russian Air Force has come to its senses and is trying to stop further disposals of *Crusty-Bs* which it needs for training *Backfire* and *Blackjack* crews.

Tu-134 *Balkany* VIP Aircraft/
Tactical Airborne Command Post

In the mid-1980s a special sub-variant of the 'glass-nosed' Tu-134AK featuring a *Bal**kany*** (Balkans) secure HF communications suite was developed for the Soviet Armed Forces. This was effectively a tactical airborne command post (ABCP) to be used by the commanders of Defence Districts (entities into which the Soviet Union's territory was divided form an order of battle standpoint), the VVS's air armies (= air forces, in USAF terminology) and the Soviet Navy's fleets. The *Balkany* suite ensured command and control no matter if the aircraft was on the ground or in the air.

In Western sources this aircraft is obstinately misidentified as the 'Tu-135'. In reality, however, the Tu-135 was a strategic bomber project of 1963 outwardly similar to the North American XB-70 Valkyrie.

The Tu-134 *Balkany* is readily identifiable by the HF aerial 'sting' under the APU exhaust; this is identical to the forward-pointing aerial installed at the top of the fin on all Tu-134As *et seq*. The bulged mounting for this aerial incorporates the APU cowling doors. Additionally, the aircraft sports four small blade aerials – one on the upper fuselage, one atop the fin and two in tandem under the rear fuselage. The traditional white 'plug' in the first full-size cabin window to starboard is augmented by four more in the last two windows to starboard and the tenth and 14th windows to port (some aircraft have a 'plug' in the 11th window to port which is the rear emergency exit). This is because the HF

comms gear and operators' stations are located in large enclosures ('special bays') along the cabin walls at the rear, which reduces the seating capacity to 26; some examples have a single long enclosure to port and seat 31. Finally, almost all Tu-134 *Balkany* ABCPs have the SRO-1P IFF transponder.

The prototype, CCCP-65980 (c/n (03)63207, f/n 5704), first flew on 20th February 1986; the State acceptance trials were completed successfully on 30th October. By the early 1990s about 40 Soviet Air Force and Soviet Navy Tu-134AKs in batches 50-63 built in 1979-82 had been converted to Tu-134 *Balkany* ABCPs at ARZ No 407 in Minsk. Most aircraft ostensibly wore Aeroflot colours and were registered CCCP-63757, -63955, -63957, -63975, -65682 through -65684, -65686, -65688 through -65690, -65979 through -65993, -65996 and -65997 (although CCCP-65990 needs confirmation – see end of entry). CCCP-65996 is one of very few examples to have the old SRO-2M IFF transponder. CCCP-65989 and -65991 through -65993 have a wide unpainted fin leading edge.

Some *Balkany*s, however, wear overt military markings, a red cheatline with a 'lightning bolt' pinstripe and a while-outlined red stripe along the engine nacelles; this colour scheme inspired by East German Air Force Tu-134AKs appeared back in 1982. Known examples were coded '01 Red', '01 Black', '05 Red' (RA-63976, c/n (23)63976, f/n 6322), '10 Red', '25 Red' (c/n 1363761, f/n 6207), '35 Red', '50 Black' (ex-CCCP-65996/to RA-65996?), '100 Red' and '101 Blue'. '35 Red' has an SRO-2M IFF

transponder, while '100 Red' is unusual in having a red-striped rudder.[15]

The red-painted ABCPs ran into the same problem as the Tu-134Sh trainers: the red cheatline became very weathered in no time at all, giving the aircraft an untidy look. It was obviously unbecoming for an air army or fleet commander to go on his inspection trips in a shabby aircraft. Like priest, like people. Therefore at least one Russian Air Force Tu-134 *Balkany* coded '10 Black' (c/n (23)63961, f/n 6316) had a similar livery but with the red colour substituted by blue; the blue paint was more weather-resistant. This aircraft is unusual in having three white 'plugs' on the port side (in both emergency exits and the 14th window); '10 Red' has the same arrangement but is a different aircraft. Quasi-civil RA 63757 (c/n (13)63757, f/n 6206) and RA-63975/'01 Blue' (c/n (23)63975, f/n 6321) have a similar blue/white livery with a 'lightning bolt' pinstripe and nacelle stripes;[16] so do Ukrainian Air Force

Tu-134 *Balkany* CCCP-65688 sports a blue/white tail and a different 'plug' arrangement to port; note the open rear entry door and extended airstairs. It is seen here with Tu-134Sh-2 '19 Red' and Tu-134UBL '25 Red' at Kubinka AB on 11th April 1992; all three aircraft brought visiting VIPs to the base's first open day. Sergey Komissarov

Standing on a snowbound ramp at Klin-5 AB, visiting Tu-134 *Balkany* '35 Red' (c/n (23)63775?) illustrates the livery in full military markings. It is the aircraft of the Leningrad Defence District's Commander. Sergey Panov

Several Tu-134 *Balkany* ABCPs, including RA-65682, have been sold to civilian owners and stripped of the *Balkany* HF comms suite. The hole in the adapter for the tail 'stinger' is closed by a hemispherical fairing. Author

'01 Yellow' (c/n (23)63957, f/n 6314) which later became UAF 63957, '02 Yellow' (UR-63960, c/n (23)63960, f/n 6315) and '03 Yellow' (UR-63982, c/n (23)63982, f/n 6324).

Tu-134 *Balkany* ABCPs were assigned to various Armed Forces formations throughout the country. These included the Baltic DD ('10 Red' at Riga-Skul'te, pulled out on 31st August 1994), the Belorussian Defence District (CCCP-63955, 50th OSAP at Lipki AB and later at Machoolischchi AB), the Central Asian DD (CCCP-65683), the Carpathian DD (CCCP-63960, 243rd OSAP/L'vov-Sknilov AB, the Ukraine and CCCP-65686 based Tiraspol', Moldavia), the Kiev DD (CCCP-63957, 16th OSAP/Kiev-Borispol' airport), the Leningrad DD ('35 Red'), the Moscow DD (CCCP-65682 at Kubinka AB; CCCP-65980, -65981 and '10 Black' at Klin-5 AB), the Transcaucasian DD (CCCP-65985), the North Fleet ('100 Red', Severomorsk-1 AB), the Pacific Fleet (CCCP-63757, Artyom AB) and so on. A few served with Soviet/Russian Armed Forces contingents deployed in Eastern Europe, including '25 Red' with the Group of Soviet Forces in Germany (16th Air Army/226th OSAP, Sperenberg AB) and '50 Black' with the Southern Group of Forces (36th Air Army, Tökol AB, Hungary). Most aircraft, however, belonged to the 8th ADON at Chkalovskaya AB.

CCCP-65682 was displayed at the open doors days at Kubinka AB on 11th April 1992, 29th May 1993 and 14th May 1994. (Incidentally, some quasi-civil Russian Air Force aircraft retained the old CCCP- prefix and Soviet flag as late as 1999!) The 226th OSAP's new Tu-134 *Balkany*, '05 Red', was on show at the same base on 8th August 1997 when the 16th Air Army celebrated its 55th anniversary. On 18th August 2002 RA-65989 was on display during the air fest at Chkalovskaya AB on the occasion of the Russian Air Force's 90th anniversary; surprisingly, the visitors were allowed inside.

At least seven aircraft were stripped of the *Balkany* suite at the turn of the century; these are EW-63955 (became RA-65571), Ukrainian Air Force 63982 (ex-'03 Yellow'), RA-65682,

ER-AAZ (ex-Moldovan Air Force ER-65686), RA-65979, RA-65983 and 4L-65993 (became 4L-AAJ). All of these except 63982 and 4L-AAJ have been converted to passenger configuration and are now in airline service. During reconversion the characteristic 'sting' of the rear HF aerial is removed (as are the blade aerials) but the adapter for it remains and the hole is closed by a hemispherical fairing; the triangular aerials of the SRO-1P IFF transponder remain, too. One more aircraft, CCCP-65990, has been reported as a Tu-134 *Balkany*, but TV footage of RA-65990 did not appear to show any traces of the famous 'sting' and it is doubtful if it had ever been there.

As a point of interest, it may be said that… the Americans have their own 'Tu-134 *Balkany*'! Quite simply, the US Air Force operates a number of Gulfstream Aerospace C-20A, C-20B and C-20C staff transports based on the G.1159 Gulfstream III biz-jet and C-20Hs based on the G.1159C Gulfstream IVSP. These aircraft look like a 'baby Tu-134 *Balkany*', featuring a similar antenna fit; only the rear entry door and the white window 'plugs' are missing.

Tu-134LK and Tu-134LK-2 Astronaut Trainers

The Soviet Cosmonaut Group operated a large number of assorted aircraft from Chkalovskaya AB for training the cosmonauts for their missions. These were first of all the Tu-104AK zero gravity trainers; later they were superseded in their 'Vomit Comet' role by the IL-76K and IL-76MDK/IL-76MDK-2 zero-G trainers whose capacious freight hold can accommodate mock-ups of spacecraft modules or test rigs weighing up to 6 tons (13,230 lb) for verifying the operation of the spacecraft's systems in zero-G conditions.

However, zero-G training was not the only aspect of the programme; the cosmonauts also had to be trained in observation and photography techniques, as pictures taken from the orbit could yield valuable information. Hence on 11th April 1974 MAP issued order No 150 tasking the Tupolev OKB with developing the Tu-134LK trainer. The suffix letters denoted [*dlya podgotovki*] *lyotchikov-kosmonahvtov* – 'for pilot-cosmonaut training'. (This *lyotchik-kosmonahvt* appellation was quite logical, since you have to qualify as a pilot before becoming an astronaut!)

Derived from the Tu-134AK, the Tu-134LK featured two additional windows with special high-quality glass were provided in the cabin roof immediately aft of the forward emergency exits (between the ninth and tenth cabin window on each side), 'looking up' at 45° to port

The Tu-134LK-2 zero-gravity/observation trainer, '03 Red' (c/n (13)63620, f/n 6105), over the Moscow Region near Chkalovskaya AB in mid-1989. Note the absence of the fifth cabin window. Sergey Komissarov

The Tu-134LK, '02 Red' (c/n (93)62732, f/n 5503), at Chkalovskaya AB in the spring of 1998. Unfortunately all that remains of the original blue/white colours is the cheatline; the tail has been painted grey with the Russian flag and the RA prefix. The window arrangement is clearly visible. Yuriy Kirsanov

and starboard. (Later, these windows were faired over for some reason.) Conversely, the fifth cabin window on each side is riveted over by a round metal plate because test and recording equipment racks are located in that part of the cabin. Thus the window arrangement is door+3+3+exit+[upper window]+1+exit+3+door to port and door+1+3+3+exit+[upper window]+1+exit+5 to starboard. There is no galley window, nor a white 'plug' in the first full-size window to starboard.

A largish fairing, triangular in side view, was originally located under the wing centre section, accommodating a device of unknown purpose called K01-7034-01. As on the Tu-134Sh, an AFA-BAF-40R camera is housed in the rear fuselage, with appropriate modifications to the ventral APU intake. An SRO-1P IFF transponder is fitted.

Coded '02 Red', the one-off Tu-134LK (c/n (93)62732, f/n 5503) was manufactured on 8th May 1980 and delivered to the 70th Independent Special Test and Training Air Regiment named after Vladimir S Seryogin[17] at Chkalovskaya AB a few days later. In early 1981 it was joined by a second aircraft, '03 Red' (c/n (13)63620, f/n 6105); developed in accordance with a joint MAP/Air Force decision of 24th September 1979; it differed from the first aircraft in equipment fit and was designated Tu-134LK-2. Outwardly the Tu-134LK-2 differed in lacking the ventral fairing; this was later removed from the Tu-134LK as well.

The Tu-134LK and Tu-134LK-2 were used to train Soviet and foreign cosmonauts who flew missions to the Salyut-6, Salyut-7 and Mir space stations. For many years the jets wore a stylish dark blue/white colour scheme patterned on that of the Tu-134Sh. Unfortunately both aircraft were repainted in 1995, the colour of the tactical codes changing to blue at the same time. '02 Blue' got a grey fin on which the Russian flag and the RA registration prefix (but no registration digits!) were painted, while '03 Blue' now wears basic Aeroflot colours, 'Y A Gagarin Cosmonauts Training Center' titles (in Russian to port and in English to starboard) and logo, and again the RA- prefix but no registration. The tactical code is carried on the nose gear doors only.

Tu-134IK (Tu-134A-IK)

In 1983 a one-off custom-built aircraft designated Tu-134IK (sometimes called Tu-134A-IK) was manufactured for the Soviet Ministry of Defence. Its exact role remains unclear to this day; the letters IK may stand for *izmeritel'nyy* **kom***pleks* (measurement suite) and it has been suggested that the aircraft was used in some areas of the Soviet space programme. The Tu-134IK was developed jointly with the Khar'kov aircraft factory and the Leningrad-based VNIIRA, aka LNPO[18] Leninets (Leninist), which was one of the Soviet Union's leading avionics houses.

The aircraft, which received the non-standard registration CCCP-64454 (c/n (33)66140, f/n 6341), is a unique hybrid between the Tu-134A and the Tu-134UBL, combining the former version's glazed nose and ROZ-1 radar in a chin radome with the *Crusty-B*'s centre

fuselage featuring eight windows and one Type III emergency exit on each side. (The Tu-134IK's window arrangement is almost identical to that of the Tu-134UBL, save for the absence of the window ahead of the door.)[19]

The aircraft bristles with all manner of non-standard antennas. Two oval fairings incorporating dielectric panels are mounted on the fuselage sides just of the entry door, with a slightly larger third fairing mounted ventrally a bit further forward. The result is not dissimilar to the Embraer EMB-145.RS/MP electronic intelligence (ELINT) aircraft, and this may indicate CCCP-64454 could have been an ELINT platform. A blade aerial is fitted dorsally just of the entry door. Two additional slot aerials are built into the fin on each side below the usual three serving the RSBN-2S SHORAN and the ATC transponder; another pair of slot aerials is built into the sides of the nose immediately forward

The Tu-134BV is again a 'cross-breed' – this time between the Tu-134B-1 and the Tu-134UBL, combining the 'head' of the former aircraft with the 'body' of the latter (with modifications in both cases). This accounts for the window arrangement unique to this aircraft – 1+door+1+3+1+exit+1+1 to port and service door+galley window+1+1+3+2+exit+3 to starboard. The additional windows cut in a stock *Crusty-B* centre fuselage section are positioned to provide adequate natural lighting for the many test equipment operators' stations; the extra window ahead of the entry door is for the navigator's station.

The fuselage nose features two prominent bulges immediately aft of the radome incorporating slot aerials. A third, flat-bottomed fairing under the nose houses a retractable high-powered light for photo theodolite measurements. L-shaped AShS aerials are installed above the wing leading edge, above the wing trailing edge and atop the fin; the latter has a Tu-134SKh-style leading edge treatment.

Once again the Tu-134BV was publicly unveiled at the Aviation Day air fest at Pushkin on 18th August 1991. Later, reregistered RA-65931, it was displayed there on 14th June 1997 at an air fest marking the 60th anniversary of Valeriy P Chkalov's cross-Polar flight from Moscow to Vancouver. On 2nd-5th August 2001 the aircraft was in the static park at the Business Aviation-2001 airshow at Pushkin.

of the service door. The fin has a wide unpainted leading edge. The aircraft wears full Aeroflot colours and 'Tu-134A' nose titles, hence the alternative Tu-134A-IK designation.

The Tu-134IK was unveiled at the open doors day at Pushkin, LNPO Leninets's flight test facility, on 18th August 1991 during the annual Aviation Day air fest. On 15th August 1999 the aircraft was noted as RA-64454 at Chkalovskaya AB where it was probably undergoing trials at the 929th GLITs (*Gosoodarstvennyy lyotno-ispytahtel'nyy tsentr* – State Flight Test Centre), formerly GK NII VVS. It is now based at Levashovo AB near St Petersburg and reportedly stripped of all mission equipment for use as a transport.

Tu-134BV Automatic Landing System Calibrator/Testbed

On 2nd December 1983 the Khar'kov aircraft factory manufactured another unique Tu-134 custom-built for LNPO Leninets. Designated Tu-134BV and registered CCCP-65931 (c/n (33)66185, f/n 6347), it was one of several assorted aircraft involved in the development of the Buran (Snowstorm) space shuttle. Its mission was to verify the *Vympel* (Pennant) automatic approach and landing system designed for the Buran (hence the V suffix to the designation); development of this system had been under way since 1979. Thus to all intents and purposes CCCP-65931 was both an avionics testbed and a navaids calibration aircraft.

TEST AND RESEARCH AIRCRAFT

Airliners and transports are often modified for various test and research work, both civil and military, and the Tu-134 was no exception. The *Crusty*'s fairly high performance and pressurised cabin made it a good candidate for the testbed role. Known examples are listed below; however, dividing them into classes according to the nature of the research work is not always easy, as some aircraft fall into several categories at once. No attempt is made to arrange the testbeds chronologically; instead, the aircraft are listed in registration order within their respective class.

1. Avionics testbeds (and more)
A dozen Tu-134s was operated by various divisions of the Ministry of Electronics Industry (MRP – *Ministerstvo rahdioelektronnoy promyshlennosti*) as avionics testbeds. While not formally Air Force aircraft, they were mostly used to test military avionics.

a) Sometime before 1992 the Moscow-based NPO Vzlyot (Takeoff) converted Tu-134AK CCCP-65604 No 2 (c/n (93)62561, f/n 5403) into an avionics testbed for testing some sort of navigation equipment. Three dielectric panels

of unequal size were incorporated on each side of the extreme nose; as in the case of the Tu-134IK, two additional slot aerials were built into the fin on each side below the normal three. The rear fuselage underside featured tandem camera windows in flat-bottomed fairings, with a round dielectric blister further forward; the cameras were probably fitted to verify navigation accuracy by capturing landmarks as the aircraft overflew them! The traditional white 'plug' in the first full-size window to starboard was missing, probably because a test engineer's workstation was installed in lieu of the forward toilet.

CCCP-65604 No 2 was first seen at Zhukovskiy on 11th August 1992, the opening day of MosAeroShow '92. By June 1993 the aircraft had been reconverted to standard and seconded to the United Nations Peace Forces.

b) According to the Czech magazine *Létectvi + Kosmonautika* (Aviation and Spaceflight), Tu-134K CCCP-65669 (c/n 0350916) served as a testbed for the N-019 Rubin (RP-29; NATO codename Slot Back) fire control radar[20] developed for the initial production version of the Mikoyan MiG-29 tactical fighter (*izdeliye 9.12*/NATO *Fulcrum-A*). This pulse-Doppler radar was a product of the Moscow-based NPO

Phazotron (aka NII Radio). However, the aircraft itself was possibly owned by LNPO Leninets and designated SL-134K (for *samolyot-laboratoriya* – laboratory aircraft), which is in line with Leninets's system of designating its avionics testbeds.

No proof of this has been found to date, but if it is true, CCCP-65669 was later reconverted to standard and transferred to the Perm' aero engine factory, an MAP enterprise.

Below left: **Tu-134AK CCCP-65907, a testbed for the MiG-29M's Phazotron N-010 Zhuk radar, at Zhukovskiy during MosAeroShow '92. The radome supplanting the nose glazing is barely visible.** Author

Below right: **The nose of Tu-134UBL '11 Red', showing the adapter with the development radar replacing the standard 'beak'. The green paint on the radome has weathered away completely.** Pyotr Batuyev

Bottom: **The Tu-134UBL prototype, used by LNPO Leninets as a testbed for the Tu-95MS's Obzor target illumination radar, at Pushkin in the mid-1990s. The tactical code '11 Red' is almost gone and the test registration CCCP-64010 is bleeding through the paint on the engine nacelles.** Sergey and Dmitriy Komissarov archive

c), d) According to Tupolev OKB sources, an avionics testbed designated SL-134K was converted in 1976 from a Tu-134K VIP jet for testing first the Tu-22M3's PNA (*Down Beat*) navigation/target illumination radar and later the *Taïfoon* (Typhoon) fire control radar. These were installed on adapters supplanting the nose glazing. The aircraft's identity is not known.[21]

e) In 1981 or 1982 Tu-134AK CCCP-65687 (c/n (93)62400, f/n 5302) was transferred from the Soviet Air Force to MRP (possibly to NPO Vzlyot) and converted into a testbed for a unique system designed for detecting nuclear submarines in submerged condition. No details of the aircraft's appearance are available. Tragically, the aircraft crashed near Severomorsk-1 AB on 17th June 1982 during Stage B of the State acceptance trials, killing the designers of the system; this loss prevented the system from entering service.

f) Tu-134AK CCCP-65907 (c/n (33)63996, f/n 6333) became a testbed in 1987 for the Phazotron N-010 Zhook (Beetle) fire control radar developed for the MiG-29K shipboard fighter (*izdeliye* 9.31) and the MiG-29M advanced tactical fighter (*izdeliye* 9.15). The ogival radome was mounted on a slightly downward-angled adapter with angular bulges on the sides sup-

planting the nose glazing (the standard ROZ-1 weather radar was retained). As on CCCP-65604 No 2, there was no white 'plug' in the first full-size window to starboard – possibly because the navigator's station was relocated there. Some Russian publications call this aircraft Tu-134LL (*letayuschchaya laboratoriya* – lit. 'flying laboratory')[22] – but see below!

Again, the aircraft was first seen at Zhukovskiy on 11th August 1992. In January 1994 it was reconverted to standard and sold to Alrosa-Avia as RA-65907.[23]

g) Tu-134AK CCCP-65908 (c/n (23)63870, f/n 6307) owned by NPO Vzlyot was a navigation systems testbed at one time, featuring the same ventral tandem cameras/dielectric blister as on CCCP-65604 No 2, plus L-shaped aerials at the wingtips. This equipment was removed before 1995.

h) An unidentified Tu-134A or Tu-134AK in Aeroflot colours (possibly CCCP-65604 No 1 or CCCP-65908) owned by NPO Vzlyot served as a testbed for a cruise missile's radar seeker head. In similar fashion to CCCP-65907 the long ogival radome (albeit of smaller diameter) was mounted on a metal adapter supplanting the nose glazing; it had three small round sensors mounted in T fashion below the radome

and two more side by side above the radome. A 'Devil's pitchfork' ILS aerial was installed ahead of the weather radar's radome between the standard pitots.

i) In 1982 or 1983 the first prototype Tu-134UBL, '11 Red' (c/n (13)64010, f/n 6401) was transferred from GK NII VVS to LNPO Leninets. Soon afterwards the main portion of the 'bill' was removed at the production break in line with the forward pressure bulkhead and replaced by an adapter mounting what looked like the *Obzor* (Perspective) navigation/target illumination radar of the Tu-95MS *Bear-H* missile strike aircraft. The new blunt and flattened radome gave the aircraft a really weird look.

In this guise the aircraft was first seen in the summer of 1990 when somehow accidentally-on-purpose a group of American hot air balloons flew over Pushkin airfield. After standing idle for several years '11 Red' had become so weathered that the tactical code almost vanished, assuming a nondescript colour, and the original registration CCCP-64010 was showing through the grey paint on the engine nacelles; this fooled some Western observers into thinking the aircraft was coded '100 Blue'! Eventually, as recounted earlier, the aircraft was sold to a civilian owner in 2002 and converted to a Tu-134B-3 (more or less) as RA-65945.

j) In 1984 an uncoded Tu-134UBL (reportedly ex-'21 Red'; c/n (33)64740, f/n unknown) operated by the Flight Research Institute (LII) became a testbed for the Phazotron N-007 *Zaslon* (Shield; NATO codename *Flash Dance*) fire control radar developed for the MiG-31 *Foxhound* interceptor. This powerful phased-array radar has an antenna array of 1.1m (3ft 7¼in) diameter, necessitating the use of a special adapter. It has also been referred to as the RP-31, SBI-16 and S-800.

k) Later, the same aircraft was used to test the Phazotron N-019M Topaz radar developed for the MiG-29S (*izdeliye* 9.12S/*Fulcrum-A* and *izdeliye* 9.13S/*Fulcrum-C*), or possibly the N-019ME for the MiG-29SE export version. Once again the radar was mounted on a special adapter with a hemispherical projection on top resembling the *Fulcrum*'s OEPS-29 infrared search and track unit/laser rangefinder (IRST/LR).

l) By June 1994 Tu-134UBL c/n (33)64740 was re-equipped for testing the N-011 fire control radar developed for the Sukhoi Su-27M (Su-35) multi-role fighter by the Moscow Research Institute of Instrument Engineering named after Vladimir V Tikhomirov (MNIIP – *Moskovskiy naoochno-issledovatel'skiy institoot priborostroyeniya*), aka NPO Vega-M. The large white-painted radome immediately caught your attention. Trials were completed in 1997.

m) Sometime before 1993 Tu-134UBL '30 Red' (possibly ex-'42 Red'; c/n (33)64845, f/n unknown) operated by GK NII VVS was converted into an avionics testbed of unknown purpose. Two small teardrop fairings were mounted under the forward and rear fuselage on short pylons; their front and rear portions respectively were dielectric. Wiring conduits ran along the upper rear fuselage sides from the emergency exits to the engine nacelles.

The aircraft was first seen as such at Zhukovskiy in September 1993 during the MAKS-93 airshow. Seven years later, on 21st September 2000, the freshly painted aircraft wearing red ROSSIYA titles made a formation flypast with Su-27UB *Flanker-C* '80 Red' during the air fest at Vladimirovka AB, Akhtoobinsk, marking the 80th anniversary of GK NII VVS.

n) Pursuant to an MAP/VVS joint decision of 21st July 1977 several Tu-134Sh navigator trainers were converted into avionics testbeds designated Tu-134Sh-SL or SL-134Sh. Interestingly, not all of them belonged to LNPO Leninets, despite the SL designator.

The first of these aircraft was probably converted from Tu-134Sh-1 '10 Red' (c/n 3350303) which became a testbed for missile guidance systems. The nose glazing was replaced by a conical metal fairing tipped by a dielectric radome. The guidance system avionics occupied all of the former navigator's station, with an access hatch provided on the starboard side of the extreme nose. The navigator now sat opposite the service door, and a full-size window was added ahead of the entry door to admit daylight to his workstation (just as on the later Tu-134UBL, Tu-134B-1, Tu-134SKh and Tu-134BV). Unusually, the c/n was actually painted on the port side of the nose.

o) In the late 1980s NPO Vzlyot converted Tu-134Sh-1 '01 Red' (c/n 63550705, f/n unknown)[24] into a testbed for the *Bagration* ELINT suite. (General P I Bagration was a hero of the Patriotic War of 1810-12; perhaps the

Tu-134Sh-1 '10 Red' (c/n 3350303) was one of the SL-134Sh avionics testbeds, featuring missile guidance systems equipment in a conical fairing supplanting the nose glazing. Tupolev JSC

The nose of Tu-134Sh-1 '10 Red' seen at Minsk-2, with the hangars of ARZ No 407 and stripped-down Yak-40s in the background. Note the forward-looking cine camera above the nose radome, the equipment fairing above the flightdeck and the extra window where the navigator now sits. It was unusual for Tu-134Sh trainers to carry the c/n like this. Tupolev JSC

Tu-134Sh-1 '01 Red' (c/n 63550705), another SL-134Sh which served for testing the *Bagration* ELINT suite, at Zhukovskiy during MosAeroShow '92, showing the lateral antenna farms, the ventral equipment pod (covered by a tarpaulin) and the absence of star tracker prisms. Author

Do not believe the 'Tu-134A' nose titles – Tu-134SL CCCP-65098, seen here in its original configuration with a Tu-22M3 style nose, is a converted Tu-134Sh-1. Tupolev JSC

The Tu-134SL – now with 'Tu-134A-3' nose titles – after being refitted with the Su-27's Phazotron N-001 Mech fire control radar. Note the ventral test equipment pod. Ghennadiy Petrov collection

The Tu-134SL in its latest guise (known as the L17-10V) with the navigation/attack radar for the Su-34 fighter-bomber in the static park of the MAKS-2001 airshow on 21st August 2001. Note that the registration is painted on without a prefix. The titles read 'KhK Leninets – NPP Mir' (Leninets Holding Co – Mir Scientific & Production Enterprise). Author

system was named after him as a tribute to his efficiency in reconnoitring the disposition of Bonaparte's troops! Just guessing.)

The aircraft featured two largish raised metal panels wrapped around the fuselage sides ahead of the wings (beneath the fourth, fifth and sixth cabin windows). Each panel was faceted and mounted eight square-shaped white antenna plates (four large ones and four smaller ones), and the whole assembly was very prominent indeed. The star tracker prisms were removed, leaving only the mounting blisters.

The standard BD-360 MERs were replaced by a special frame mounting two different equipment pods. The first of these was cylindrical and unpainted, with a conical front end sprouting four probe aerials and a cut-off rear end; the aircraft was last noted with this external store at Zhukovskiy on 11th-16th August 1992 during MosAeroShow '92. The other pod was substituted sometime between August 1992 and August 1993; it was grey, looking like an outsize drop tank with horizontal fins equipped with endplates (in reality these were probably aerials). By August 1995 Tu-134Sh-1 c/n 63550705 had been withdrawn from use.

p) In early 1978 LNPO Leninets took delivery of a Tu-134Sh-1 (c/n 73550815; f/n 0805?) which

was registered CCCP-65098 and converted into the Tu-134SL avionics testbed; this aircraft, too, has been referred to as a Tu-134Sh-SL or SL-134Sh. The aircraft was painted in full Aeroflot colours and wore 'Tu-134A' nose titles. The star tracker mounting blisters were deleted; so was the strike camera and the associated fairing, but the characteristic design of the APU's lower intake was the giveaway that this was not a Tu-134A after all. Quite possibly the aircraft had been earmarked for conversion from the start and was never delivered to the Air Force.

CCCP-65098 had three distinct configurations. Originally the aircraft featured a long Tu-22M3 nose grafted on instead of the normal nose glazing; accordingly overall length was 41.918m. Since this 'beak' was incompatible with the Tu-134Sh's deep chin radome, the latter was replaced by a stock Tu-134A radome housing an ROZ-1 weather radar. Hence the Tu-134SL was commonly misidentified as either the Tu-134UBL prototype or Tu-134UBK. Since the *Backfire-C*'s PNA radar had been tested back in 1976 on another aircraft, the nose of CCCP-65098 apparently housed a different version of this radar – possibly the PNA-D. A pylon was fitted under the fuselage ahead of the wings, offset to port, for carrying a cylindrical test equipment pod housing what

appeared to be a long-range camera. Pilots are quick to give nicknames to the aircraft they fly, and the original configuration of the Tu-134SL earned the sobriquet *Booratino* (the Russian equivalent of Pinocchio).

q) Later the *Backfire* nose was removed. Instead, CCCP-65098 was fitted with a short adapter mounting the N-001 Mech (Sword) fire control radar for the Su-27 *Flanker-B* (*izdeliye* T-10S) interceptor. This is a coherent pulse-Doppler radar with an antenna diameter of 1.076m (3ft 6⅜in). Interestingly, it was not an LNPO Leninets product but was developed by MNIIP (NPO Vega-M) which probably had no aircraft available for conversion at the time. Equally interestingly, like the MiG-29's N-019 radar, the N-001 appears to have the same NATO codename, *Slot Back*.

A smaller pod on a shorter centreline pylon was added ahead of the existing one; this appears to house a laser ranger. In this guise the aircraft was dubbed *Booratino II*.

r) In late 2000 CCCP-65098 was refitted again, receiving a navigation/attack radar of undisclosed type developed by the Leninets Holding Co for the Su-34 (aka Su-32FN or *izdeliye* T-10V) multi-role combat aircraft. This radar is set to replace the Su-34's current radar with which the Russian Air Force is dissatisfied. The phased-array radar is enclosed by the Su-34's characteristic downward-angled 'duck bill' radome with sharp chines – a feature which has earned Sukhoi's new combat jet the nickname *Ootkonos* (Platypus); this required a new adapter to be manufactured and installed.

Sporting the registration 65098 (with no prefix) and 'KhK Leninets – NPP Mir' (Leninets Holding Co – Mir Scientific & Production Enterprise) titles instead of Aeroflot markings, the freshly overhauled and refitted Tu-134SL was unveiled at the Business Aviation-2001 airshow at Pushkin on 5th-8th August. Surprisingly, it now wore 'Tu-134Sh' nose titles. Less than a week later the aircraft was displayed at the MAKS-2001 airshow, albeit on the trade days only (13th-17th August). The placard in front of the aircraft identified it as the L17-10V testbed (which probably means *laboratoriya* (testbed) No 17 under the T-10V development programme. 65098 was displayed again on the trade days of the MAKS-2003 airshow (18th-22nd August).

s) In 1991 the State Research Institute of Aircraft Systems (GosNII AS – *Gosoodarstvennyy naoochno-issledovatel'skiy institoot aviatsionnykh sistem*) in Zhukovskiy received a second-hand Tu-134Sh-1 (tactical code unknown, c/n 2350201)[25] which was registered CCCP-65562 and extensively modified for research and development work. This aircraft has been called Tu-134LL in some publications; yet again Tupolev OKB sources call it Tu-134Sh-SL or SL-134Sh.

Its original mission was to test the guidance systems of TV- and laser-guided 'smart weapons'. Later, with the onset of *konversiya* (the adaptation of defence industry assets for civilian needs), the Tu-134LL was magically transformed into a geophysical survey and environmental monitoring aircraft. Its peaceful uses included photo mapping, thermal imaging, ecological survey and assessment of the damage in the wake of natural and man-made disasters.

The Tu-134LL was readily identifiable by the large square-section ventral canoe fairing stretching all the way from the third full-size window on each side to the rear emergency exits. The front portion of this gondola housing cameras and sensors was additionally secured to the fuselage by five prominent metal hoops. A small cylindrical pod with conical ends was pylon-mounted low on the starboard side of the fuselage immediately ahead of the service door. An angular fairing with three ventral sen-

sor windows was located aft of this door, with a long rod aerial further aft. Two more rod aerials were mounted dorsally fore and aft of the wings, with an L-shaped aerial in between. The star tracker mounting blisters were deleted.

The aircraft was painted in full Aeroflot colours and wore 'Tu-134' nose titles – yes, Tu-134 *sans suffixe*, although 'Tu-134A' would be more appropriate. Since the manufacturer's plate in the nosewheel well is only marked 0201, some people could be misled to believe this was ex-Tu-134 *sans suffixe* CCCP-65609 No 1 (c/n 6350201), converted and reregistered! Once again, however, the deep chin radome and the APU intake treatment revealed what it really was.

The front end of the ventral canoe fairing accommodated a T-2 TV system used for target tracking and image recording; it was mounted in a revolving turret with a traversing angle of ±75° and a depression angle of 90° (that is, the camera could shoot anywhere from straight ahead to straight down). The TV camera's field of view could be selected between 16° and 2.8°. An AFA-BAF-40 oblique camera and an LDI-3 laser rangefinder were slaved to the TV system. The camera lenses were protected from foreign object damage by a movable shutter on take-off and landing.

The canoe fairing also accommodated five vertical cameras on two AFUS-U tilting mounts and three GUT-3 and GUT-8 gyrostabilised mounts. Camera options included: the Soviet TK-10, TAFA-10 or East German Zeiss Ikon LMK (f = 100mm/4in), the AFA-41/20 (f = 200mm/7⅞in), the Soviet TEA-35 (f = 350mm/13¾in), the AFA-42/100 (f = 1,000mm/39⅜in) and the AS-707 four-spectrum camera (f = 140mm/5½in).

The mission equipment included an OD-4M optical seeker (f = 1,000mm) with 80x zoom for locating and tracking the 'targets', a TV scanner with a 156 x 40° field of view and a laser scanner with a 120° field of view having a passive day mode and an active night mode. For thermal imaging the Tu-134LL was fitted with an IR line scanner with a 120°/60° field of view, a two-mode IR line scanner with a 120° field of view, and an IKR4-2 four-channel IR radiometer with a 3° field of view. The experiment was controlled by a 66-MHz Compaq 486 computer. The data furnished by the various mission systems was stored by a Schlumberger 27-chan-

nel digital data recorder and a Soviet Gamma recorder. The latter captured flight and navigation parameters, as well as the time when cameras etc were activated, and could inscribe this information into the TV image.

The aircraft featured an I-21 inertial navigation system, a Global Positioning System (GPS) kit and the Soviet equivalent of GPS called GLONASS (*globahl'naya navigatsionnaya spootnikovaya sistema*), plus a programmable device enabling the jet to automatically fly a shuttle pattern. Missions were flown at up to 10,000m (32,800ft) and 650km/h (403mph); the drag generated by the various appendages reduced top speed to 800km/h (496mph). Maximum range was 3,000km (1,860 miles) and endurance 3.5 hours. The crew included ten mission equipment operators.

CCCP-65562 was first noted at Zhukovskiy, its home base, on 11th August 1992. During the MAKS-95 airshow the aircraft was displayed statically as RA-65562 and minus Aeroflot markings. By then the pod on the starboard side of the nose had been altered to feature a TV seeker head of an air-to-surface missile; this was removed in 1997. By August 1999 the Tu-134LL had been retired.

2. Propulsion Testbeds (and more)

a) In 1968 the second pre-production Tu-134 *sans suffixe*, CCCP-65601 (c/n 6350003), was re-engined for the second time, becoming a testbed for Tu-134A's intended powerplant. The D-30 turbofans were replaced by reverser-equipped D-30-IIs in extended nacelles, and a TA-8 APU was installed in the tailcone, making a unique combination with the short fuselage and square forward baggage door.

b) The first prototype Tu-134A, CCCP-65624 (c/n 8350601), a company-owned 'dogship' which became the Tu-134A-3 prototype in 1981, may be regarded as a testbed for the D-30-III engine if you wish.

c) In 1987 the Flight Research Institute's Tu-134A CCCP-65740 (c/n 2351510), a former Tu-134A 'Salon' VIP aircraft obtained from the Air Force,[26] was converted into a multi-role testbed/research aircraft known as the Tu-134A-1510.

The Tu-134LL avionics testbed/survey aircraft (RA-65562) on display at the MAKS-95 airshow. The ventral camera/sensor fairing with external reinforcing hoops around the fuselage and the sensor packs fore and aft of the service door are clearly visible. The 'Tu-134 *sans suffixe*' nose titles are not to be believed either!
Sergey Komissarov

The aircraft's equipment fit and hence appearance changed over the years. By 1992 the original development engine had been replaced by a different model in a larger nacelle (type unknown in both cases), while the cigar-shaped pod gave place to two shorter pods mounted side by side, each of which had a hemispherical front end. A small sensor turret was added at the front of the ventral platform.

The dorsal IR sensor cupola was modified by grafting on a cylindrical fairing at the rear. Two IR spectrometers and a gamma spectrometer were installed at the second, third and fifth cabin windows to starboard and the glazing was replaced by special filters. The glazing of the galley window gave place to an external metal plug mounting a temperature probe, an aerosol particle counter and an ozone sensor. The mission equipment included gas analysers for measuring hydrocarbon (CH), ozone, nitrogen oxide (NOx), carbon oxide and sulphur dioxide (SO_2) concentrations. Measurement results were processed in real time by a computerised system.

CCCP-65740 was usually captained by the late Yuriy Pavlovich Sheffer, one of LII's best pilots who held the Distinguished Test Pilot grade for expertise and experience. Flying the Tu-134A-1510 had a few quirks. Firstly, wake turbulence during measurement missions could be quite severe, the aircraft vibrating violently and tending to roll. For instance, it was impossible to get closer than 700m (2,300ft) to a Su-24 tactical bomber – the heavy Tu-134 was kicked out of the wake with up to 60° bank, and normal flight could only be restored after the airliner had lost some 500m (1,640ft) of altitude. Secondly, the mission equipment was troublesome, and some modules which functioned beautifully on the ground simply refused to work in flight!

Reregistered RA-65740, the Tu-134A-1510 was also in the static park at the MAKS-95 airshow. By late 1996 the aircraft had been withdrawn from use, as the prescribed time between overhauls had run out; LII's management was still debating whether to overhaul the aircraft and keep it flying a little longer or to strike it off charge, transferring the equipment to a newer Tu-134.

Its primary mission was to test small expendable or short-life turbofan engines developed for cruise missiles and unmanned aerial vehicles, such as the 350-kgp (770-lbst) Tumanskiy RDK-300 and the 450-kgp (990-lbst) Saturn 36MT turbofan developed for the Kh-59M air-to-surface missile. Concurrently, however – or rather between engine tests – the Tu-134A-1510 was used for aerothermophysical and environmental research, such as measuring the heat signature and air pollution levels in the wake of other aircraft. Thus it is hard to say which 'bumps and bulges' pertained to which programme.

In accordance with its engine testbed role the aircraft gained a large flat-bottomed bulge under the wing centre section which mounted three pylons of different shape. The forward-swept port pylon carried the development engine in a small nacelle, with a sensor shaped like an inverted T immediately aft, while the centre pylon carried a cigar-shaped pod housing unknown equipment.

A hemispherical fairing enclosing heat sensors was mounted dorsally just ahead of the entry door. The tenth cabin window on each side (the one between the emergency exits) had the glazing replaced by emergency decompression valves with air outlet grilles. These allowed the cabin to be depressurised within two or three seconds prior to bailing out, should the need arise; otherwise the pressure differential would make it impossible to open the doors, all of which open inwards.

3. Geophysical Survey Aircraft

In 1991 MNIIP (NPO Vega-M), the All-Union Research Institute of Cosmoaerological Methods and LII converted Tu-134AK CCCP-65906 (c/n (33)66175, f/n 6345) into a geophysical survey aircraft equipped with the IMARK all-weather high-resolution polarimetric scanning suite (*izmeritel'nyy mnogochastotnyy aviatsionnyy rahdiolokatsionnyy kompleks* – multi-frequency airborne radar measuring suite).

The range of tasks this aircraft performed was truly vast. In geology it could be used for surface and subsurface mapping of geological formations, oil/natural gas and ore prospecting, searching for ground waters (this included tracing ground water migration which can carry pollutants and locating swamped areas). In oceanology it was detection of surface pollution and tracing the movement of icefields in Polar regions. In agriculture and forestry it was measurement of soil humidity, detection of deforestation etc and specifying the land evaluation cadaster.

Once again the aircraft was readily identifiable by its unique combination of tell-tale 'bumps and bulges'. Originally CCCP-65906 sported a natural metal fairing wrapped around the starboard side of the fuselage; it ran from the service door to the third full-size window, incorporating two yellow cruciform antennas of a synthetic aperture SLAR one above the other, and the top was level with the door. A large boxy fairing housing more SLAR antennas was located beneath the wing centre section; most of it was dielectric. Two forward-pointing probes ('roach antennae') were located on the sides of the extreme nose just aft of the navigator's glazing. The rear fuselage underside featured tandem fairings enclosing vertical cameras.

In 1993 the aircraft was modified: the lateral SAR fairing became longer and wider, terminating ahead of the seventh window; it now incorporated two pairs of 'crosses', with a large square dielectric panel consisting of small squares further aft. The enlarged fairing obstructed the Aeroflot titles, and these were painted out untidily. A blade aerial was added at the top of the fin, Tu-134 *Balkany* style. A further upgrade in 1995 saw the addition of a smaller square dielectric panel aft of the large one.

The SLAR worked in four wavebands – 3.9cm (1⅓in), 23cm (9in), 68cm (26¾in) and 2.54m (100in), with a resolution of 4-6m (13-20ft),

8-10m (26-33ft), 10-15m (33-50ft) and 15-25m (50-80ft) respectively. The radar 'looked' both sides in 3.9cm wavelength mode and to starboard only in all other modes, scanning a strip 24km (15 miles) wide. Scanning was performed with the aircraft flying at 500-5,000m (1,640-16,400ft) and 500-600km/h (310-370mph). The mission equipment also included IR radiometers and a microwave radiometer. The aircraft was provided with a GPS kit.

Reregistered RA-65906, the IMARK survey aircraft was used to monitor the ecology of the Volga River estuary near Astrakhan' in the summer of 1993. During that year it was on show at the MAKS-93 and two years later it was displayed again at the MAKS-95. In late 1997 RA-65906 was stripped of all mission equipment, refurbished and sold to Nefteyugansk Airlines as an 80-seater.

4. Aerodynamics Testbeds

As already noted, after fitment of D-30 engines and a large horizontal tail the first -production Tu-134 *sans suffixe*, CCCP-65600 (c/n 5350002), was modified for high-alpha/low-speed tests by fitting a spin recovery parachute etc, so it can be regarded as an aerodynamics testbed if you please. In fact, some Western sources have listed this aircraft under such improbable designations as 'Tu-134LLShP' (which supposedly means *letayuschchaya laboratoriya s protivoshtopornym parashootom* – testbed with an anti-spin 'chute) and even 'Tu-134LLChR'.[27]

5. Miscellaneous Testbeds and Research Aircraft

a) GosNII GA used Tu-134A CCCP-65047 (c/n (73)49600, f/n 3805) as a 'dogship' for studying aerodynamics, developing new piloting tech-

The Tu-134A-1510 in the static park at the MAKS-95 airshow as RA-65740. Note the modified dorsal IR sensor 'turret' and the LII logo ahead of service door. Author

The Tu-134A-1510's ventral platform as of mid-1995, with a different engine and new test equipment pods. Note the video camera aimed at the development engine. Author

The cabin of RA-65740, looking towards the nose. Note emergency air pressure relief vents (port and starboard) nearest to camera. Author

The IMARK geophysical survey aircraft (CCCP-65906) in its original configuration.
Yefim Gordon archive

The same aircraft after two upgrades, shown here in the static park at the MAKS-95 airshow as RA-65906; note the much larger SLAR fairing.
Author

The cabin of RA-65906, looking aft, showing research equipment racks. Author

niques and investigating flight safety issues. Among other things, it was used to study the propagation of smoke via the cabin ventilation system in the event of a fire in the rear baggage compartment or the No 3 equipment bay when the crash of Tu-134AK CCCP-65120 on 2nd July 1986 was being investigated (see Appendix 2). To this end the aircraft was fitted with a GD-1M smoke generator (*ghenerahtor dyma*); two test flights were made on 12th and 20th August 1986.

b) In 1983 GosNII GA converted the second prototype Tu-134A, CCCP-65626 (c/n 9350704), was converted into a testbed for an active

static electricity neutralisation system designed to replace the traditional static discharge wicks. Two static dischargers were mounted at the wingtips, two at the tips of the main gear fairings and two more under the APU exhaust; each discharger was a pointed rod 8mm (⁵⁄₁₆in) thick with inner and outer contacts and a Teflon insulator in between.

c) In 1971 the abovementioned Tu-134 *sans suffixe* CCCP-65600 was converted into a testbed for some unspecified 'special equipment'.

d) In the early 1970s the ninth production Tu-134A, CCCP-65653 (c/n 0351009), was out-

fitted by the Tupolev OKB and the Siberian Aviation Research Institute (SibNIA – *Sibeerskiy naoochno-issledovatel'skiy institoot aviahtsii*) in Novosibirsk for measuring the structural loads applied to the landing gear on different types of runways. This instrumented test aircraft made a round of all Soviet airports where the Tu-134 could land. As a result, the main gear bogies were reinforced and the original KT-81/3 wheels replaced by lighter KT-153 wheels to preclude cracking of the bogies.

e) In early 1978 the Soviet Cosmonaut Group (or, to be precise, the 70th Independent Special Test and Training Air Regiment named after V S Seryogin) operated a Tu-134 (identity unknown) as a 'flying laboratory' for training spacemen in observation and photography techniques. Cosmonauts Vladimir Kovalyonok and Aleksandr Ivanchenkov took a training course on this aircraft in May 1978 before starting on their space mission to the Salyut-6 space station in June.

This aircraft is a real mystery. A photo in the Soviet *Aviatsiya i Kosmonavtika* (Aviation and Spaceflight) monthly shows the aircraft had an ROZ-1 radar and a colour scheme identical to the Tu-134LK/Tu-134LK-2 space trainers, but these did not yet exist in May 1978. Nor can the aircraft in question be the Cosmonaut Group's Tu-134AK '01 Red' (c/n (83)60650, f/n 4809) because this did not yet exist either, being manufactured in October 1978 at the earliest!

Chapter Four

Unrealised Projects

Regrettably, some versions of the Tu-134 – versions that would have improved the type's capabilities considerably – never got off the drawing board. The projects are listed in chronological order insofar as possible.

Tu-134B Short/Medium-haul Airliner (first use of designation, aka Tu-164)

This aircraft was different enough from the *Crusty* to warrant a new designation. It had a new fuselage of 3.3m (10ft 10in) diameter featuring underfloor baggage compartments and Yak-40 (or DC-9) style ventral airstairs. Overall length was 32.5m (106ft 7½in), wing span 29.3m (96ft 1½in), stabiliser span 9.2m (30ft 2¼in), height on ground 8.7m (28ft 6½in) and wheel track 9.85m (32ft 3¾in). The powerplant consisted of two D-30s. The Tu-134B (Tu-164) was to have a 42-ton (92,590-lb) TOW and an 8.5-ton (18,740-lb) payload, a maximum/economic cruising speed of 870-900km/h (540-560mph)/800km/h (497mph) respectively, a maximum-fuel range of 3,000km (1,860 miles) and a maximum-payload range of 1,500km (930 miles). The airliner had a crew of two and seated 73 or 83 four/five-abreast.

The prototype was to begin certification trials in the fourth quarter of 1967 but the aircraft was never built.

Tu-134M Short/Medium-haul Airliner (first use of designation)

Again, this project developed in 1969 was to be an altogether new aircraft. The fuselage of 3.8m (12ft 6½in) diameter incorporated a Tu-154 three-crew flightdeck and two underfloor baggage compartments with a volume of 18.5 and 11.0m³ (653.3 and 388.4ft³) respectively and a container handling system. There was a rear entry door-cum-airstairs as later fitted to the Tu-134AK. The aft fuselage/tail unit assembly was borrowed from the Tu-134A. The wings featured new (possibly supercritical) airfoils, full-span leading edge slats and no main gear fairings, as the main gear units (incidentally, borrowed from the Tu-154!) retracted inwards into the fuselage. All-new wings of reduced sweepback (25° at quarter-chord) were also considered.

A three-view drawing of the Tu-134D, showing the oval-section fuselage, the two entry doors ahead of the wings, the underfloor baggage hold doors and the D-30A engines with clamshell thrust reversers. Tupolev JSC

The Tu-134M was to be powered by either two Solov'yov D-30M-1 turbofans rated at 6,800kgp (14,990 lbst) or two Solov'yov D-60M-2 turbofans rated at 8,200kgp (18,080 lbst).

The baseline aircraft seating 122 or 134 passengers was to begin certification trials in 1971 and enter service in 1973. Other versions included a cargo variant carrying up to 13.5 tons (29,760 lb) of cargo over a range of 1,700-2,100km (1,055-1,300 miles); a 152-seat short-range version; a stretched 144/159-seat version with a payload of 14.5-15 tons (31,970-33,070 lb) and 33m³ (1,165ft³) of baggage hold space, and military transport/medevac versions.

The basic Tu-134M was to be 39.1 or 37.5m* (128ft 3⅜in or 123ft ⅜in*) long, with a wing span of 30.6 or 31.2m* (100ft 4¾in or 102ft 4⅜in*) and a wing area of 122 or 106m²* (1,311 or 1,140ft²*). Maximum TOW was 53.8 or 52.4 tons* (118,600 or 115,520 lb*), OEW 30.2 or 29.12 tons* (66,580 or 64,200 lb*) and the payload 12-13.5 tons (26,455-29,760 lb). Cruising speed was 920 or 870km/h* (571 or 540mph* and range 1,700km. The figures marked with an asterisk apply to the version with 25° wing sweep.

Tu-134B Short/Medium-haul Airliner (second use of designation)

This project of the mid-1970s was nothing more than a Tu-134 *sans suffixe* with a seating capacity increased to 76 thanks to a more compact galley, which cut seat-mile costs by 5%; otherwise the performance was unchanged. Con-

version to this standard was to take place at ARZ No 400 at Moscow-Vnukovo and ARZ No 407 but never occurred, and the designation Tu-134B was reused again in 1979 (see Chapter 3).

Tu-134V Short/Medium-haul Airliner (first use of designation)

Designated in Russian alphabetical order (V is the third letter of the Cyrillic alphabet), this version of the Tu-134A proposed in 1974 was to carry 78 passengers; the galley was redesigned to permit installation of two more seats in the forward vestibule to starboard.

Tu-134V Short/Medium-haul Airliner (second use of designation)

Developed concurrently with the first Tu-134V, this derivative of the Tu-134A featured new D-30M turbofans, a 'radar nose' and a three-man flightdeck with centrally mounted throttles. The wings were reinforced and equipped with two-section flight spoilers; the APU had aft-opening air intakes permitting in-flight starting by windmilling. Production was to begin in 1975.

Tu-134V Short/Medium-haul Airliner (third use of designation)

This proposed upgrade of the Tu-134A seating 80 at 75cm pitch featured plug-type doors opening outwards through 180° and equipped with inflatable escape slides. Developed by Boeing, this type of door had been first used on the Boeing 707; the Soviet Union had bought a

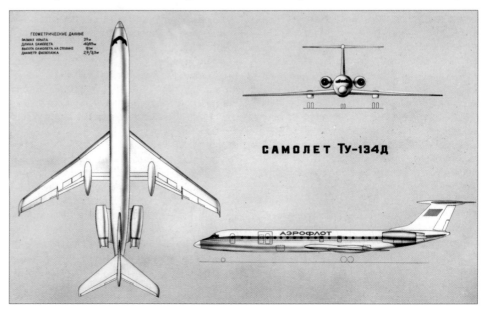

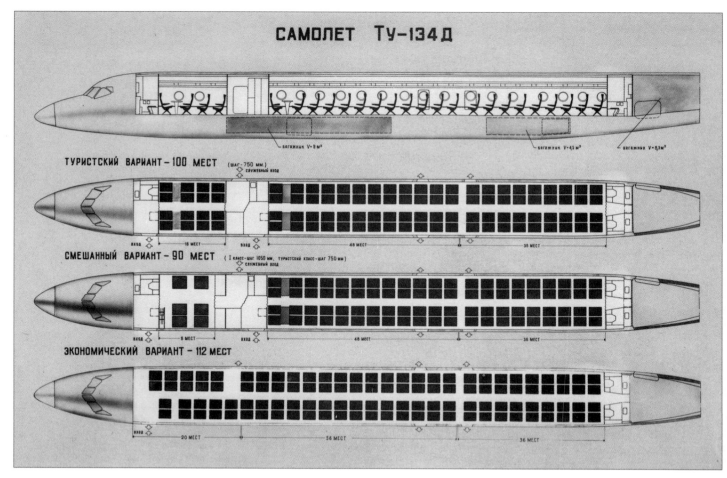

САМОЛЕТ ТУ-134Д

ТУРИСТСКИЙ ВАРИАНТ – 100 МЕСТ

СМЕШАННЫЙ ВАРИАНТ – 90 МЕСТ

ЭКОНОМИЧЕСКИЙ ВАРИАНТ – 112 МЕСТ

licence to use this design.[1] Integral airstairs were fitted as standard and the emergency exits were enlarged. The landing gear was reinforced; flight spoilers were introduced and the ventral speedbrake deleted. A Groza-M134 radar and a three-crew flightdeck were optional.

Other changes included hushkitting the D-30-II engines, fitting updated avionics (including an ABSU-134 ALS) and provisions for APU starting by windmilling. The first Tu-134Vs were to be converted from Tu-134As during overhauls; new-build 'Vs were to be manufactured from 1977 onwards.

Tu-134G Short/Medium-haul Airliner

This derivative of the Tu-134V (again designated in alphabetical order) differed only in having an 86-seat cabin. This was achieved by reducing the seat pitch to 72cm and shrinking the galley and the forward baggage compartment (total baggage hold volume was reduced to 12m³/423ft³). Again, the first Tu-134Gs were to be converted from Tu-134As and new production was to begin in 1977.

Tu-134D Short/Medium-haul Airliner

In 1973 the Tupolev OKB began studying ways of radically rectifying the Tu-134's 'hereditary' drawbacks and improving the type's operating economics. In December 1974 the concept crystallised as the Tu-134D, the next in alphabetical sequence after the Tu-134G; this was a competitor to Yakovlev's 120-seat Yak-42 short-haul trijet.

The fuselage was stretched by inserting a 2.25-m (7ft 4⅛in) plug forward and a 1.5-m (4ft 11in) plug aft of the wings. The forward and centre sections were completely new, featuring an elliptical cross-section of 2.9 x 3.3m (9ft 6⅛in x 10ft 10in); this allowed underfloor baggage compartments with doors on the starboard side and hermetically sealed equipment bays to be incorporated. Total baggage hold space was increased to 22.5m³ (794.5ft³), that is, 9.5+4.5+8.5m³ (335.4+158.9+300.1ft³). The galley was repositioned amidships and a third toilet added in the forward cabin.

There were two 1.7 x 0.75m (5ft 7 in x 2ft 5½in) entry doors to port ahead of the wings, with a 1.5 x 0.75m (4ft 11 in x 2ft 5½in) service door to starboard; all doors were Boeing-type. All four emergency exits were enlarged to 0.965 x 0.5m (3ft 2 in x 1ft 7⅝in).

While having the same planform and 35° sweep, the wings received a more efficient airfoil. Full-span leading-edge slats deflected 27°, new double-slotted flaps (set 10°, 20° or 35°) and flight spoilers deflected up to 45° were fitted and the ventral speedbrake deleted. The draggy slots on the control surfaces were sealed, and the airframe was generally 'cleaned up' aerodynamically.

The Tu-134D was powered by 8,400-kgp (18,520-lbst) Solov'yov D-30A turbofans. This engine had little in common with the D-30-II,

being based on the core of the very different and much bigger D-30KU/D-30KP; like the latter engines, the D-30A had a clamshell thrust reverser. The new engines offered 23% more thrust in ISA conditions and 38% more thrust at +30°C; they were also 7-10dB quieter and 8% more fuel-efficient in cruise mode. A more powerful TA-6A APU was fitted.

The landing gear was basically similar but featured two-chamber oleo struts; the nose gear steering angle was increased to ±60° and the main bogies were rotated hydraulically during retraction, not mechanically. The Tu-134D had an all-new 115/200V AC main electric system. The control system was revised, making use of many Tu-154 components. The fuel supply of 16,500 litres (3,630 Imp gals) was accommodated in six wing tanks, with provisions for a 5,000-litre (1,100-Imp gal) centre section integral tank. There was hot air (rather than electric) de-icing on the stabilisers, no de-icing on the fin, and hot air de-icing on the wing root portions only. Changes were also made to the hydraulics and air conditioning systems.

The Tu-134D had a Groza-M134 radar with two displays and a central control pedestal. Normally the crew would comprise two pilots and a flight engineer, but a navigator could also be carried on routes with few or no ground navaids.

On 24th January 1975 MAP issued order No 16 concerning construction of three Tu-134D development aircraft in Khar'kov. Pursuant to this document all preparations for production were to be completed by July 1976; the first prototype was to be rolled out in February 1977, with construction of a static test airframe proceeding in parallel. According to MGA plans the Tu-134D was to enter service not later than 1978-79; chief project engineer Leonid L Selyakov gave a more realistic date (1981).

The ADP was completed in April 1975. Three configurations were envisaged: a tourist class layout seating 100 four-abreast (16+84) at 75cm pitch, a 90-seat mixed-class layout (with a first class cabin for six, three-abreast) and a 108-seat all-economy layout with a smaller galley and no forward toilet. A 114-seat version was added later. Enclosed overhead luggage bins and indirect lighting gave 'wide-body looks'.

A partial full-scale mock-up was built at MMZ No 156 and reviewed on 23rd-30th August 1976. The review commission reacted favourably, noting that the Tu-134D was superior to the Tu-134A in capacity, payload, field performance and powerplant. It was described as

A cutaway drawing of the projected Tu-134DOL mobile eye surgery lab. Tupolev JSC

a cheaper and more reliable alternative to the Yak-42, providing service entry took place in 1978. The OKB issued a full set of manufacturing drawings and completed a forward fuselage section with Boeing-type doors. Meanwhile, KhAPO was tooling up to build the type and several D-30A prototype engines were undergoing bench testing in Perm'.

In 1978, however, the Soviet leader Leonid I Brezhnev expressed his preference for the Yak-42. This was the turning point: interest in the Tu-134D waned quickly. Finally, on 28th August 1978 General Designer Andrey A Tupolev pulled the plug on the programme with the vague explanation that 'Tupolev aircraft carried most of Aeroflot's passengers and the share of Antonov, Il'yushin and Yakovlev aircraft was minor'. In reality he was probably pressured into terminating the Tu-134D by MAP – both because *ipse dixit* that the Yak-42 was the better aircraft and because the OKB was overburdened with military programmes.

As of 1976 the Tu-134D had the following specifications: length 41.0m (134ft 6⅛in), wing span 29.46m (96ft 7⅞in), height on ground 9.15m (30ft ¼in), wing area 130.0m² (1,397ft²); OEW 32 tons (70,550 lb), MTOW 52 tons (114,640 lb), maximum landing weight 47 tons (103,615 lb). Maximum cruising speed was 950km/h (590mph) and economic cruising speed 850km/h (530mph); range with an 11-ton (24,250-lb) maximum payload was 1,500km (930 miles) and maximum-fuel range 2,750km

(1,700 miles). At 2,000m (6,560ft), the required runway length was 20% less than for the Tu-134A.

Tu-134GM Short/Medium-haul Airliner

To ensure engine and systems commonality with the Tu-134D, from 1979 onwards Tu-134As, Tu-134Vs and Tu-134Gs were to be converted to a new standard called Tu-134GM (*modernizeerovannyy*). This was basically an 86-seat Tu-134G re-engined with D-30A turbofans and a TA-6A APU. Described in one sources as 'a Tu-134V version with D-30A engines', this was to feature a 1.5-m (4ft 11in) fuselage stretch increasing seating capacity to 88-90 at 75cm pitch; the aircraft was to feature a 'radar nose' and an ABSU-134 ALS. TOW was to be 49 tons (108,025 lb), payload 11 tons (24,250 lb) and OEW 31 tons (68,340 lb); range with an 8-ton (17,640-lb) payload was to be 1,850km (1,150 miles).

Tu-134DOL Flying Hospital

A mobile ophthalmic surgery lab designated Tu-134DOL (Tu-134D – *oftal'mologicheskaya laboratoriya*) was designed in 1975-76 at the request of the famous eye surgeon Dr Sviatoslav F Fyodorov (tragically, he was killed in a helicopter crash on 2nd July 2000). It was based on the Tu-134D and featured a diagnostics room, an operating room, a recuperating room with three cots, a treatment room and a cinema room.

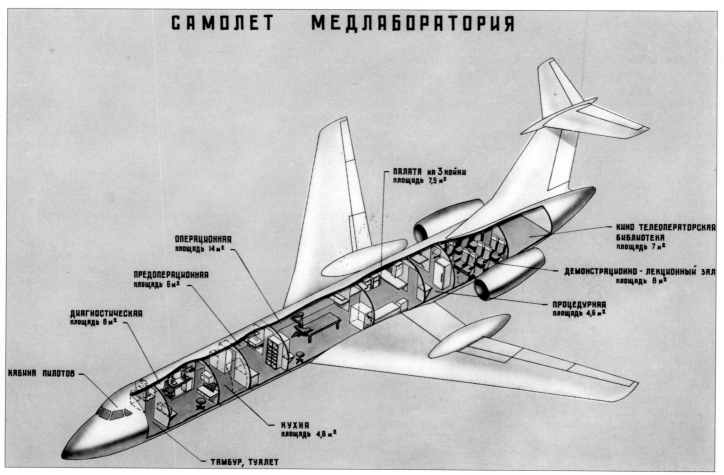

The project was presented to G I Petrovskiy, the then Minister of Health Care, who axed it; he was not convinced even by the fact that similar Orbis ophthalmic surgery labs based on the Douglas DC-8-21 and McDonnell Douglas DC-10-10 were successful in the USA.

Tu-134A-2 Short/Medium-haul Airliner

This project of 1977 was the last of the versions to be powered by D-30A turbofans. To preserve the CG position the fuselage was stretched 0.75m (2ft 5½in) ahead of the wings; this and the new compact galley increased seating capacity to 84. The avionics and equipment were identical to the Tu-134GM. Maximum TOW was 49 tons, the payload was 9-10 tons (19,840-22,045 lb); cruising speed as 850km/h and maximum-payload range 1,850km (1,150 miles). The termination of the Tu-134D killed off this project as well.

Tu-134A Cargo Conversion

In 1977 the Tupolev OKB proposed a cargo modification of the Tu-134A. The conversion involved installation of a 1.41 x 1.6m (55½ x 63in) cargo door replacing the entry door; this was opened manually by pushing inward and sliding forward. The seats and galley were removed; the cabin floor was protected by special panels and the cabin windows by bars.

Up to 9.5 tons (20,940 lb) of cargo were accommodated in the existing baggage compartments and the cabin. Removable roller conveyors were used for cargo handling; the cargo was tied down by nylon nets and straps to transverse beams secured to the seat tracks. Maximum floor loading was 250kg/m² (51 lb/ft²). The new door weighed 240kg (530 lb), the cargo handling and protective equipment adding another 500kg (1,100 lb); on the other hand, removing the seats and galley saved 1,100kg (2,425 lb). MTOW was 49 tons (108,025 lb) and OEW 28.5 tons (62,830 lb); the performance and CG range were unchanged. The project was cut, becoming a stepping stone towards the Tu-134C (see below).

Tu-134C Convertible Short-haul Airliner

In cargo configuration the standard Tu-134 only took small packaged goods because of the narrow doors. Therefore in 1978 the Yugoslav charter carrier Pan-Adria approached the Tupolev OKB with a request to develop a fully-fledged convertible version with a large cargo door. The aircraft was designated Tu-134C for 'cargo' ('convertible' is also applicable, as will be seen from the following); in Russian documents, it was called Tu-134S (because the Cyrillic S is identical to the Roman C!).

The Tu-134C was based on the radar-nosed version of the Tu-134AK (some sources say Tu-134B!). The port side cargo door was similar to that of the above project but larger, measuring 1.41 x 1.85m (55½ x 72⅞in). Cargo handling equipment was also similar but included a 'ball mat' near the cargo door. The cabin floor was stressed to 400kg/m² (82 lb/ft²).

Three configurations were possible: an 86-seat layout, an all-cargo layout and a combi configuration with 5 tons (11,020 lb) of cargo in the forward cabin and 24 seats in the rear cabin. A change of configuration required no more than three hours. The cargo was carried on nine pallets measuring 1.5 x 1.9m (4ft 11 in x 6ft 2¾in), with up to 2.82m³ (99.5ft³) and 1,000kg (2,204 lb) per pallet. If the cargo weighed more than 300kg/m³ (18.72 lb/ft³), eight pallets were loaded for CG reasons; in that case 1,000kg of cargo was carried in the rear baggage compartment.

Passenger access was via a Tu-134AK-style rear entry door with airstairs. The forward baggage compartment was deleted, the galley reduced and the starboard toilet moved forward à la Tu-134AK; a small rear galley was fitted in passenger/combi layout. The Tu-134C featured a three-man flightdeck with a central control pedestal and flight spoilers. The TOW was 49 tons, OEW 29 tons (63,930 lb) in cargo configuration or 30 tons (66,140 lb) in passenger configuration; maximum-payload range was 2,000 or 2,150km (1,240 or 1,335 miles) respectively. Alas, Pan-Adria cancelled the order when the project was well advanced. Aeroflot had no requirement for such aircraft at the time and the Tu-134C never materialised.

Tu-134L Photo Mapping Aircraft

Work on a photo survey version of the Tu-134 designated Tu-134L (laboratoriya) was initiated in the 1970s to meet an order from East Germany. No further information is available.

Tu-134R Communications Relay Aircraft

In the late 1970s/early 1980s a communications relay version of the Tu-134A designated Tu-134R (retranslyator – relay installation) was developed for the Soviet Navy to ensure radio communications between ships at sea and shore-based command centres. The project did not materialise because the Tu-142MK Bear-F Mod anti-submarine warfare aircraft was developed into a more capable communications relay platform called Tu-142MR Bear-J.

Tu-134B-2, Tu-134B-2-3 Short/Medium-haul Airliners

The Tu-134B-2 was a proposed 100-seat version of the real Tu-134B featuring lightweight seats five-abreast, as on Tu-134A CCCP-65966 (and probably a similar 1.61 x 1.09m entry door). If powered by D-30-III engines, the aircraft was designated Tu-134B-2-3.

Tu-134OK Short/Medium-haul Airliner

Interest in cryogenic aviation fuel – liquefied petroleum gas (LPG) – rose appreciably when the Tu-155 technology demonstrator (CCCP-85035, a highly modified Tu-154 sans suffixe) flew on 15th April 1988, proving the viability of the concept. Cryogenic fuels are much more environmentally friendly than kerosene; besides, the world's petroleum gas deposits are much richer than oil deposits.

Hence in 1990 the Tupolev OKB developed a version of the Tu-134A running on LPG. ČSA Czechoslovak Airlines was the motive power behind this project; since the Czech registration prefix (and the airline's flight code) is OK, the aircraft was designated Tu-134OK (some Western sources misquoted the designation as 'Tu-135OK'). Two cryogenic tanks strongly resembling the SLAR pods of the Tu-134SKh were pylon-mounted under the inner wings; the normal fuel system was retained so that the aircraft could operate on jet fuel if necessary. The Soviet Union was to build an LPG filling station at Bratislava-Ivanka airport as part of the programme. The economic chaos that followed the demise of the Soviet Union prevented the Tu-134OK from materialising.

Tu-134M Upgrade (Second use of designation)

In 1993 Leonid L Selyakov proposed re-engining the Tu-134A/B with 7,500-kgp (16,534 lbst) D-436T1 turbofans developed at the 'Progress' Zaporozhye Engine Design Bureau (ZMKB) led by Fyodor M Muravchenko. Designed for the Tu-334-100 airliner, the engine has a high bypass ratio (5.6), a low SFC (0.608 lb/lbst·hr) and a cascade thrust reverser. The D-436T1-134 version adapted for the Tu-134 features a DC generator, a different hydraulic pump and additional bleed valves for the de-icing system. The new version inherited the Tu-134M designation of an earlier project, though some Western writers referred to this aircraft as the 'Tu-134RE' (re-engined).

Fitting D-436T1-134 engines allows the Tu-134 to meet current ICAO noise and emission regulations. Additionally, it improves fuel efficiency by 17-20%, increasing range by 750-1,000km (465-620 miles), and reduces runway length requirements by 250-300m (820-980ft). A VIP version with extra fuel would have a range of 6,000km (3,730 miles). The conversion involves installing new pylons, a more powerful Aerosila TA-12A or TA-14 APU and an electronic engine control system. The aircraft is also to receive a 'wide-body look' interior with an emergency oxygen system and an updated avionics fit, including satellite navigation and traffic collision avoidance systems. The upgrade enables a low-time Tu-134 with at least 15,000 hours remaining to stay in service until 2010.

The prototype was originally due to fly in 1999, but the first flight date has been slipping continually due to funding shortages. The Tupolev JSC, ARZ No 407, Belavia Belorussian Airlines, ZMKB Progress and the Motor Sich company manufacturing the engine formed the Interavia[2] consortium to promote the Tu-134M, but the future of the project is still uncertain. Curiously, the original plans of 1997 called for the modification of some 200 aircraft, with a fly-away price of US$4.5 to 5 million; by December 1999 the scope had shrunk to 60 aircraft and the conversion cost to US$ 2.8 million.

Chapter Five

Service as Usual

On 26th August 1967, the trials stage finally complete, Tu-134 CCCP-65600 performed the type's first passenger service, carrying 23 passengers from Moscow-Sheremet'yevo to Murmansk-Murmashi on a route-proving flight. The first scheduled domestic flight took place on 9th September 1967 on the Moscow/Vnukovo-1-Adler route. Three days later the Central Directorate of International Services joined in when one of its Tu-134s flew the inaugural Moscow-Stockholm service. Four years and one month had passed from first flight to service entry.

Shortly before that, production Tu-134 *sans suffixe* CCCP-65610 No 1 (c/n 6350202) was displayed at the 26th Paris Air Show in June 1967, wearing the exhibit code 232. Immediately after the show the Aviaexport All-Union Agency launched an 'offensive', offering the Tu-134 with a US$ 2 million price tag. In the hope of attracting orders Tu-134 *sans suffixe* CCCP-65601 made a demonstration tour of Japan (21st-26th October), Hungary (21st-24th November) and Czechoslovakia (24-30th November).

Curiously, Aviaexport was not the only promoter of the type. The Tu-134 is probably the world's only aircraft to have its own… brand of cigarettes! Yes! In the early 1970s the Bulgartabac company launched a new product – the 'Tu-134' filter cigarettes. The packaging featured a photo of the second prototype as originally flown and the slogan: 'Offered by Aeroflot'. (Incidentally, nowadays Aeroflot's flights are strictly non-smoking.)

After this, the introduction of the new jet on Aeroflot's routes proceeded at a brisk pace. On 14th September 1967 Tu-134 *sans suffixe* CCCP-65606 No 1 flew the first service from Moscow-Sheremet'yevo to Vienna via Kiev-Borispol; the Moscow-Belgrade service was inaugurated two days later. On 2nd October 1967 Tu-134 *sans suffixe* CCCP-65611 No 1 made the type's first visit to Warsaw; on 19th October CCCP-65606 flew the inaugural service to Helsinki, and on 18th December CCCP-65610 No 1 was introduced on the Moscow-Zurich route.

Meanwhile, production gradually gained pace at Khar'kov. Thirteen aircraft were delivered in 1966, with only six following in 1967 (mostly Tu-134Ks for the Soviet government flight) but 20 aircraft in 1968 and 28 aircraft in 1969. (These figures are based on actual manufacture dates, not the first digit of the c/n which not necessarily coincides with the actual year of production.) For a while the Tu-134

Tu-134 *sans suffixe* CCCP-65610 No 1, in front of the old control tower at Moscow-Shermet'yevo, with a Civil Aviation Administration of China IL-18V in the background. This aircraft operated by TsUMVS had the distinction of opening the type's service on the Moscow-Zurich route.
Boris Vdovenko

A typical scene at Moscow-Shermet'yevo as Tu-134K CCCP-65615 No 1 (by then probably converted to tourist class configuration) rests between missions while Tu-134 *sans suffixe* CCCP-65643 is refuelled for the next flight. Apart from illustrating the type's early livery, this view shows the difference in equipment and hence in fin top shape between early and late Tu-134s.
Sergey Komissarov

The changing of the guard: The last-but-one Tu-134 *sans suffixe*, CCCP-65643 (c/n 0350927), and a Tu-124V share the apron at Moscow-Shermet'yevo. Sergey Komissarov

shared the production line with the Tu-124 until the latter was terminated in 1969 after 165 had been built, including 40 Tu-124Sh trainers.

The Tu-134 introduced new manufacturing technologies, such as automatic riveting, chemical milling of wing skins (for the first time in the Soviet Union; there goes commonality with the Tu-124...) and subassembly of wiring runs outside the aircraft to facilitate installation – no small thing, as the overall length of the wiring was 60km (37.25 miles). Production aircraft were rolled out unpainted, with the registration sloppily applied on the engine nacelles instead of the tail (in the case of Soviet examples), and made their first pre-delivery test flight in this guise before going to the paint shop.

Speaking of registrations, Soviet/CIS Tu-134s were registered CCCP-65000 through -65149, 4K-65496, CCCP-65550 through -65557, -65559 through -65565, RA-65566 through -65571, RA-65575, RA-65579, CCCP-65600 through -65935, RA-65939 through -65945 and CCCP-65950 through -65997.[1] As already mentioned,

the registrations CCCP-65604 through -65623 have been used twice. RA-65156, CCCP-65232, -65282, RA-65534, CCCP-65570 (sic), -65587, -65594, -65597, -65937, -65944, -65949, -65998 and -65999 were also reported in the Western press, but these are probably mis-sightings.

Non-standard registrations (apart from the two prototypes, CCCP-45075 and CCCP-45076) include RA-14, RA-19, CCCP-63757, -63775, -63955, -63957, -63960, -63975, -63976, -63979, -63982, -64010, -64020, -64035, -64065, -64073, -64083, -64095, -64105, -64121, -64140, -64148, -64175, -64182, -64188, -64235, -64245, -64270, -64277, -64310, -64315, -64325, -64350, -64365, -64375, -64392, -64400, -64435, -64451, -64454, -64505, -64585, -64630, -64640, -64650, -64670, -64678, -64728, -64740, -64753, -64775, -64800, -64830, -65835, -64845, -93926, -93927, -93929 and -93930. These are mostly military aircraft, except for the latter three and CCCP-64451 which were MAP aircraft.

The new jet soon grew popular with the passengers, offering quiet comfort (especially in comparison with the noisy turboprops) and a smooth ride. Cabin noise and vibration levels were the lowest among Soviet airliners of the day, and the semi-levered-suspension main landing gear catered for a very smooth touchdown. The cabin wall trim was made of a new synthetic material which was good-looking and hygienic (but emitted a pungent and persistent odour). The new lightweight seats were upholstered in different colours with printed decorative patterns and incorporated folding meal trays. For the first time on a Soviet airliner the overhead luggage racks incorporates passenger service units (PSUs) with individual ventilation nozzles, reading lights and flight attendant call buttons. The Tu-134 sans suffixe came in three configurations: a 64-seat mixed-class version for TsUMVS and foreign customers, the baseline 72-seater used on domestic routes and the so-called tourist version seating 68.

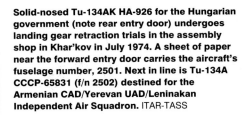

Solid-nosed Tu-134AK HA-926 for the Hungarian government (note rear entry door) undergoes landing gear retraction trials in the assembly shop in Khar'kov in July 1974. A sheet of paper near the forward entry door carries the aircraft's fuselage number, 2501. Next in line is Tu-134A CCCP-65831 (f/n 2502) destined for the Armenian CAD/Yerevan UAD/Leninakan Independent Air Squadron. ITAR-TASS

Tu-134A CCCP-65658 at Copenhagen-Kastrup on a nasty, sleety December day in 1970 after arriving from Moscow on flight SU215 – the stretched version's first international service. Note the ground power cart near the tail and the absence of the galley window in Batch 11. This aircraft later went to the Armenian CAD/Yerevan UAD/279th Flight. Sergey Komissarov

Compared with the Tu-124, the aircraft proved to have 25% lower seat-mile costs and earned 12% greater revenue; it was best suited for routes with a typical load of 70 passengers per flight. Aviaexport claimed that 30 passengers (that is, a load factor of about 42%) were enough for break-even and that the figure would be even lower in the West where airline fares were higher. In the Soviet Union, however, load factors consistently approached 100%, especially in the summer season.

The Tu-134 was soon nicknamed *mahlen'kiy Tu* ('little Tu', as compared with its larger stablemates), later replaced by the somewhat demotic *tooshka*. The latter is derived from the Tu brand but coincides with the diminutive form of *toosha* (animal carcass) used for fowl or game, evoking unwelcome associations with chicken drumsticks!

Because of their low bypass ratio the D-30 turbofans emitted a high-pitched screech, which earned the Tu-134 another nickname, *svistok* (whistle). The four-engined IL-62M and IL-76 powered by D-30KU/D-30KP turbofans with a BPR of 2.42 produce a much more agreeable sound; believe it or not, they appear less noisy than the twinjet Tu-134 (not to mention the din which it produces on take-off)! To be perfectly honest, however, cabin noise levels are quite acceptable.

The other major drawback of the engines was their sooty efflux; a Tu-134 coming in to land leaves a smoke trail that can be seen for miles. Worse, looking from behind at a Tu-134 poised for take-off can give you quite a shock, as the cloud of black smoke rising when the engines go to full power creates the impression that the aircraft is on fire! None of this was regarded as a problem back in the 1960s, but it certainly is a problem now with all those ICAO annexes concerning noise and emissions. (Perhaps the aforementioned cigarettes were meant as a hint at this aspect of the Tu-134…)

Export deliveries commenced in September 1968, with Balkan Bulgarian Airlines as the first foreign customer. Export aircraft had a slightly different avionics fit and better cabin trim. The Tu-134 proved to have far better export potential than the Tu-124, even if this was clearly helped by the Berlin Agreement of 27th October 1965. Under this agreement Bulgaria, Czechoslovakia, Hungary, East Germany, Mongolia, Poland, Romania and the USSR were to cooperate in establishing air traffic between their respective capitals and to Western Europe; this presumably included equipment commonality between the airlines.

Romania, however, refused to toe the line and ordered the BAC 111 Srs 400 and 500 (later built under licence as the Rombac 111-561RC). Mongolia and China probably did not order the Tu-134 because of underdeveloped infrastructure; Cuba lacked suitable routes for the Tu-134, while Albania was in self-imposed political isolation since 1962.

The Tu-134 was the first Soviet airliner certified to British Civil Aviation Requirements (BCAR). Poland did the certification testing, issuing Type Certificate BB 051/1 on 9th November 1968. True, the USSR had introduced its first common airworthiness regulations for fixed-wing aircraft in 1967, but starting certification trials at that point would have delayed service entry unacceptably.

Production of the short-fuselage versions ended in June 1970 after 80 had been built. They were superseded by the stretched 76-seat Tu-134A which entered service on 9th November 1970 after six months' evaluation on the busy Moscow-Leningrad route. International flights started in December when CCCP-65658 (c/n 0351104) flew to Copenhagen on flight SU215.

Grievances and Merits

Foreign operators of the Tu-134 noted several serious shortcomings. For instance, LOT Polish Airlines were unhappy with the small baggage compartments; to aggravate the problem, Western travellers seemed to prefer soft valises (which, unlike suitcases, cannot be stacked on top of one another for fear of crushing the contents), and the baggage space was not used to the full. In an example of air transport lunacy, sometimes a Tu-134 carrying a load of passengers from A to B had to be *supplemented with an IL-18V turboprop carrying their baggage!* (In their latter days, LOT IL-18s were relegated to the cargo role.)

Unfortunately little could be done to correct this: the Tu-134's extremely narrow fuselage precluded underfloor baggage stowage. Main deck stowage was adequate for the 56-seat Tu-124V but no good for the 72-seat Tu-134; incidentally, the floor was 2.33m (7ft 7in) above ground level, which also gave cause for complaint. The late Leonid L Selaykov recalls how he and GosNII GVF Director Nikita Alekseyevich Zakharov tried to persuade Andrey N Tupolev to increase the fuselage diameter to 3.4m (11ft 1⅞in): *'When we entered his study, he was alone. I outlined our request to increase the fuselage diameter; the reply was a squeaky "f**k you". We shrugged and left.'*

The narrow fuselage and the resulting limitation in capacity increased the airframe weight per passenger, reducing economic efficiency – an issue hardly considered in Soviet times. The high fuel consumption caused by aerodynamic imperfections added to this; compared to the BAC 111-200, direct operating costs (DOC) were an overwhelming 35.3% higher!

Yugoslavia's civil aviation authority further pointed out the lack of an automatic oxygen system, a sprinkler system to keep the windscreen clear in heavy rain and electric exit signs (the latter were eventually introduced on late-production Tu-134A/Bs). The oxygen system had been deleted on Aeroflot's aircraft in 1962 because Yevgeniy F Loginov, the then Minister of Civil Aviation, called it 'unnecessary and a fire hazard'! This myopic approach not only crippled the export potential of Soviet airliners (the oxygen system was by then mandatory in

the West) but endangered human lives in the late 1980s when several Aeroflot aircraft decompressed at high altitude. (The fact that Tu-134AK VIP jets *did* have this system speaks for itself.)

Under international standards engine thrust should remain constant up to +30°C (86°F). The D-30 could not meet this requirement: at +30°C take-off thrust dropped from 6,800 to 6,300kgp (14,990 to 13,890 lbst); this problem was not overcome until the advent of the D-30-III in 1981.

Inevitably, the Tu-134 had its share of teething troubles. Fatigue cracking of the aileron mounting brackets manifested itself because the big, heavy ailerons 'wobbled' up and down on uneven runways. Spring-loading the mass balances took care of the problem, and the feature was introduced on the production line after trials on an instrumented test aircraft. The original mainwheels borrowed from the IL-18 proved too heavy, causing excessive wear on the main gear bogies, which sometimes failed. The OKB and SibNIA fitted the ninth production Tu-134A (CCCP-65653) with sensors, flying it from virtually every suitable runway in the USSR, and a reinforced landing gear was soon developed.

Typical defects included breakage of the wing de-icers' internal structure, loose rivets in the upper fuselage (near frame 15) and stabiliser/wing lower skins, cracking of heated windscreens, failure of flap drives and carriages. There were cases of rear fuselage skin corrosion near the toilets, pressurisation system ducts coming undone, damaged door seals and buckling of the rear baggage hold floor (the latter two resulted from careless operation).

These defects were dealt with as they came by reinforcing the structure and changing operational procedures. For instance, on Tu-134As with more than 30,000 hours' total time fatigue cracks appeared in the corners of the service door and emergency exits due to pressurisation loads (the oval entry door was not affected by this problem). The remedy was to stop drill the cracks and rivet on external U-shaped reinforcing plates above and below the aperture. Aircraft operating from uneven runways had a similar problem, cracks appearing near the nose gear fulcrum due to repeated shock loads, and the solution was the same.

Operational difficulties included engine starting problems at ambient temperatures above +30°C and in extremely cold weather when the fuel filters tended to freeze (they had to be heated before flight). Another unpleasant surprise was that the filters could not be completely emptied of fuel before a change, and the technician performing the change would get doused in kerosene! Sharp changes of ambient temperature sometimes ruined the rubber gaskets in the nose gear steering mechanism and wheel brakes, causing hydraulic leaks. Oil constantly seeped from the engines' accessory gearboxes, decomposing on the hot engine casing, with the result that characteristic smutty streaks appeared on the nacelles along the cowling hinge line.

On the plus side, the Tu-134 was very much a 'pilot's airplane', pleasing to fly, forgiving of pilot errors and easy to service. The aircraft demonstrated high survivability (if the word is applicable to an airliner!), flying well with a failed de-icing system, yaw damper or stabiliser trim mechanism (sufficient elevator authority remained).

Taking off in the event of an engine failure was no problem if the TOW was within prescribed limits; with the gear up and flaps down the aircraft had adequate thrust reserves. There was almost no yaw in the direction of the dead engine but there was a tendency to roll in that direction which had to be swiftly countered, otherwise the bank would reach 20° in five seconds.

An incident which testifies to the Tu-134's 'willingness to fly' – and to good airmanship – occurred at Moscow-Sheremet'yevo on 25th July 1995. As Komiavia Tu-134A-3 RA-65069 sped along runway 07R, taking off on flight OG2279 to Syktyvkar, the crew saw a Douglas DC-8-55F of Aéronaves del Peru just 150-200m (490-660ft) ahead; the freighter's crew had begun crossing the active runway without clearance. At 230km/h (142mph), the Tu-134 was past V_1 (decision speed); the aircraft's captain Sergey M Knyazhev kept his head and continued the take-off. Getting unstuck at 246km/h (153mph), RA-65069 cleared the obstacle with an AOA of 13.5° – virtually in stall mode.

The Tu-134 was one of Aeroflot's most dependable aircraft (a reputation it shared with the IL-18), thanks in no small part to the OKB, the Khar'kov aircraft factory, the overhaul plants and the operators working in close cooperation. Overall mean time between failures was 9,000 hours in 1977, rising to 11,700

hours by 1980. Dispatch reliability was higher than on most other types; one flight delay exceeding 15 minutes occurred in 834 flights.

To illustrate the type's high reliability it may be said that foreign (notably Bulgarian and Yugoslav) Tu-134s withstood a daily utilisation of up to 15-16 hours without major problems. A record of sorts was set on 22nd July 1976 when Aviogenex Tu-134A-1 YU-AHX made six flights with load factors of 100%, carrying a total of 516 passengers; the aircraft was airborne for 19 hours 9 minutes, covering a distance of 13,469km (8,365 miles).

On 4th November 1972 the group of aviation industry specialists involved with the Tu-134 was awarded the prestigious State Prize for services rendered. These were Andrey N Tupolev (posthumously), Leonid L Selyakov, Vladimir M Vool', V P Nikolayev, Khar'kov factory General Director Boris A Khokhlov, Minister of Civil Aviation Boris P Boogayev, S D Dragoonov, N N Kashtanov and N T Belyayev.

Airline Workhorse

During the first five years the Tu-134 served alongside the Antonov An-10, one of the first-generation turbine-powered airliners designed for short/medium-haul routes. The An-10 did not enjoy a good reputation; there were 23 fatal and non-fatal accidents with the type which occurred between April 1958 and February 1963, more than half of them due to airframe and engine defects.

By 1967 the An-10's longitudinal stability problems caused by tailplane icing had long since been cured, and everything seemed to be going very well when disaster struck again. On 18th May 1972 a Ukrainian CAD An-10A, CCCP-11215 (c/n 0402502?), crashed close to Khar'kov-Sokol'nikovo airport, killing all 114 passengers and eight crew. The cause of the crash, which provoked a huge public outcry,

was quickly traced to fatigue failure of the wing centre-section. As a result, on 27th August 1973 MGA issued order No 032 withdrawing the An-10 from Aeroflot service.[2] The knock-on effect was that the Tupolev twinjet's workload grew appreciably.

Until the mid-1970s Aeroflot's colour schemes were as disparate as the aircraft it operated. Each type had its own livery – or, in the case of such aircraft as the An-10 and the An-24, several liveries. As already mentioned, Aeroflot's Tu-134As received an eye-catching colour scheme that was totally different from the one applied to the carrier's Tu-134s *sans suffixe*.

Then MAP and MGA put an end to this 'identity crisis'. A fleet-wide standard livery was developed and duly endorsed by the ministries in March 1973, but it was a while before the now-familiar blue/white livery with bold 'Aeroflot' titles began appearing on actual aircraft. For each type, the first aircraft to be repainted was duly inspected and approved by a ministerial panel. Still, in the first few years curious hybrids of old and new liveries (with non-standard titles etc) appeared from time to time. The Tu-134 was no exception; for instance, Leningrad-based Tu-134A CCCP-65815 (c/n 4352209) had natural metal undersurfaces instead of the prescribed light grey colour. Additionally,

different production batches had the registration applied in two different type faces (rounded or angular); it was the same story with most other Aeroflot types: An-12, An-24, IL-62, IL-76, Tu-154 and so on.

Conversion training of both Soviet and foreign flight and ground crews took place at the Ul'yanovsk Higher Civil Aviation Flying School (UVAU GA – *Ool'yahnovskoye* **vyss**heye **lyot**noye *oochilischche grazhdahnskoy aviahtsii*) which was within the framework of the Training Establishments Directorate (UUZ – *Oopravleniye oochebnykh zavedeniy*). This establishment, which handled all Soviet civil types larger than the 50-seat Antonov An-24, was known as the COMECON Civil Aviation Centre (*Tsentr GA SEV*) in the 1970s and early 1980s but then reverted to its original name. (The COMECON, or Council for Mutual Economic Assistance (SEV – *Sovet ekonomicheskoy vzaimopomoschchi*), was the Eastern Bloc's counterpart of the EEC.) Before flying the real thing the trainees would 'fly' the KTS-Tu-134 (*kompleksnyy trena*zhor *samolyo*ta – integrated aircraft simulator). Such simulators are also found at some military bases with lots of Tu-134s, including Chkalovskaya AB.

By the end of the 1970s the Tu-134 equipped 25 of Aeroflot's 33 directorates in all Soviet republics except Turkmenia. On 21st January 1980 MGA issued order No 13 phasing out the Tu-124 as uneconomical to operate (military Tu-124Ks and Tu-124Sh trainers soldiered on at least until mid-1983). This left the Tu-134 as Aeroflot's only short/medium-haul jet for a while; the Yak-40 was strictly a feederliner, while the newly-introduced Yak-42 was grounded after the crash of CCCP-42529 near Mozyr' on 29th June 1982, returning to service in October 1984 after the variable incidence tailplane actuator had been redesigned). Known operators are detailed in the table on this page.

The Komi CAD deserves a detailed account. The introduction of the Tu-134A in the Syktyvkar UAD, the directorate's main air enterprise, was a crash programme (no pun intended) necessitated by the enforced retirement of the An-10 in the wake of the 1972 Khar'kov tragedy. The 75th Flight had seven An-10As which shouldered the entire workload on the unit's high-density routes, and their premature withdrawal left the Syktyvkar UAD with almost nothing.

Taking delivery of its first Tu-134A (CCCP-65958) in March 1973, the Syktyvkar UAD effectively had to rebuild its route network from scratch as the fleet grew. The new hardware brought about heightened requirements concerning the airports; the runways at Syktyvkar, Vorkuta and Ukhta had to be reconstructed and extended, and a whole new runway built at Usinsk – all for the Tu-134A. (In contrast, the An-10 could operate from unpaved airstrips if necessary, having been designed with maximum commonality with the future An-12 military transport in mind for which rough-field capability was a must.)

Civil Aviation Directorate	United Air Detachment/constituent Flight	Home base
Arkhangel'sk CAD	1st Arkhangel'sk UAD/312th Flight/2nd Sqn	Arkhangel'sk-Talagi
Armenian CAD	Yerevan UAD/279th Flight/4th Sqn	Yerevan-Zvartnots
	Yerevan UAD/Leninakan Independent Air Sqn	Leninakan
Azerbaijan CAD	Baku UAD/339th Flight/1st and 2nd Sqns	Baku-Bina
Belorussian CAD	Gomel' UAD/105th Flight	Gomel'
	Kaliningrad UAD/380th Flight*	Kaliningrad-Khrabrovo
	2nd Minsk UAD/104th Flight	Minsk-2 (Velikiy Dvor)
Central Directorate of International Services (TsUMVS)	207th Flight	Moscow-Sheremet'yevo†
Central Regions CAD	Ivanovo UAD/176th Flight	Ivanovo-Yoozhnyy (Zhukovka)
	Voronezh UAD/243rd Flight	Voronezh-Chertovitskoye
Estonian CAD	Tallinn UAD/141st Flight/?? Sqn	Tallinn-Ylemiste
Georgian CAD	Sukhumi UAD/297th Flight/1st Sqn	Sukhumi-Babushara
	Tbilisi UAD/347th Flight	Tbilisi-International (Lochini)
Kazakh CAD	Alma-Ata UAD/240th Flight/3rd Sqn	Alma-Ata
Kirghiz CAD	Frunze UAD/250th Flight/?? Sqn	Frunze-Manas
Komi CAD	Syktyvkar UAD/75th Flight	Syktyvkar
Latvian CAD‡	Riga UAD/280th Flight/3rd and 4th Sqns	Riga-Skulte
Leningrad CAD	1st Leningrad UAD/344th Flight	Leningrad-Pulkovo
Lithuanian CAD	Vilnius UAD/277th Flight/2nd and 3rd Sqns	Vilnius
Moldavian CAD‡	Kishinyov UAD/269th Flight	Kishinyov
North Caucasian CAD	Astrakhan' UAD/110th Flight	Astrakhan'-Narimanovo
	Groznyy UAD/82nd Flight	Groznyy-Severnyy
	Mineral'nyye Vody CAPA/209th Flight/?? Sqn	Mineral'nyye Vody
	Rostov UAD/78th and 336th Flights §	Rostov-on-Don
	Volgograd UAD/231st Flight	Volgograd-Goomrak
Tajik CAD	Leninabad UAD/292nd Flight/1st Sqn	Leninabad
Tyumen' CAD	2nd Tyumen' UAD/259th Flight	Tyumen'-Roschchino
Ukrainian CAD	Borispol' UAD/208th Flight	Kiev-Borispol'
	Chernovtsy UAD	Chernovtsy
	Khar'kov UAD/10th and 87th Flights	Khar'kov-Osnova
Urals CAD	Chelyabinsk UAD/6th Flight (124th Flight?)	Chelyabinsk-Balandino
	Izhevsk UAD	Izhevsk
	Kirov UAD/12th Flight	Kirov-Pobedilovo
	Perm' UAD/8th Flight (311th Flight?)	Perm'-Bol'shoye Savino
Uzbek CAD	Tashkent UAD/219th Flight/?? Sqn ¶	Tashkent-Yoozhnyy
235th Independent Air Detachment		Moscow/Vnukovo-2
Volga CAD	Cheboksary UAD	Cheboksary
	Gor'kiy UAD/220th Flight	Gor'kiy-Strigino
	1st Kazan' UAD/261st Flight ‖	Kazan'-Osnovnoy
	1st Kuibyshev UAD/173rd Flight	Kuibyshev-1 (Kurumoch)
	Orenburg UAD/195th Flight	Orenburg-Tsentral'nyy
	Ufa UAD/282nd Flight	Ufa
	Ul'yanovsk UAD (occasional 'leases' only?)	Ul'yanovsk-Vostochnyy
Training Establishments Directorate	Leningrad Civil Aviation Academy (OLAGA)	Leningrad-Pulkovo
	Ul'yanovsk Higher Civil Aviation Flying School	Ul'yanovsk-Baratayevka
GosNII GA		Moscow-Sheremet'yevo

* Of course the Kaliningrad Region is part of the Russian Federation, not Belorussia; nevertheless, the Kaliningrad UAD was assigned to the Belorussian CAD – simply because the region was too small to warrant the establishment of a separate directorate. Nowadays Kaliningrad-Avia (the former Kaliningrad UAD) is assigned to the North-Western Regional Air Transport Directorate (the former Leningrad CAD).

† International operations moved to the south side of the airport when the Sheremet'yevo-2 terminal was opened in 1980, the old terminal on the north side (henceforth called Sheremet'yevo-1) becoming the domestic terminal.

‡ The Latvian and Moldavian divisions were called Republican Civil Aviation Production Associations (RCAPA) in the late 1970s but were later renamed Civil Aviation Directorates.

§ The Tu-134s were probably transferred to the newly formed 336th Flight after 1987, the 78th Flight re-equipping entirely with Yak-40s.

¶ All aircraft transferred to Komi CAD between 1985 and April 1988.

‖ All Tu-134 except one crashed aircraft were disposed of and replaced by Yak-42s around 1984.

Gradually the Komi CAD not only resumed the services which the An-10As had flown but added new ones, including some quite long routes. These included flights from Syktyvkar to Moscow-Sheremet'yevo and Leningrad, from Syktyvkar to Sofia, Varna or Bourgas via Kiev, flights to the resort cities of Sochi, Krasnodar, Mineral'nyye Vody and Anapa, eastbound flights to Irkutsk via Sverdlovsk and Novosibirsk, southbound routes to Kazakhstan (to Semipalatinsk via Kustanay and to Ust'-Kamenogorsk via Kokchetav). Non-stop flights were made from Ukhta and Vorkuta to Moscow and Leningrad, as well as to Sochi and Simferopol' via Gor'kiy. When the Volga CAD reconstructed the runways at Saransk, Yoshkar-Ola, Cheboksary and Penza, enabling Tu-134 operations, the jets from Syktyvkar linked these cities with the Black Sea resorts by making stopovers there.

By April 1988 the Syktyvkar UAD had increased its Tu-134A/AK fleet to 25 – the largest number in any Aeroflot division. Less than half of them had been delivered new from the factory; the others, including all of the Tu-134AKs, were second-hand aircraft transferred from other directorates. It should be noted that the Komi CAD also consistently ranked first among Tu-134 operators in the Soviet Union as far as utilisation was concerned, with an average yearly utilisation of up to 2,400 hours per aircraft; some aircraft logged as many as 380 hours per month in the summer season! Hence, using support from the head office in Moscow, the Komi CAD habitually took aircraft away from other CADs, leaving a lot of hard feelings in the industry. For instance, between 1985, when Karim Rashidov, the leader of the Uzbek SSR, was arrested and convicted for large-scale corruption, and April 1988 the Syk-

tyvkar UAD laid hands on all five Tu-134s operated by the Uzbek CAD – four 'As and one 'AK which was Rashidov's personal aircraft.

In 1990-91 the fleet was further expanded by the acquisition of 18 ex-Interflug Tu-134As/AKs, bringing the total to 43 and making what was now the Komiavia concern (soon to be an independent airline) the largest single operator of the type in the (ex-) USSR. Curiously, in Soviet times civil aircraft registrations were issued and approved by the Air Force's General Headquarters – another 'side effect' of the militarisation of the Soviet society. In this case the purchase had to be made urgently and MGA, not managing to obtain new registrations from the GHQ in time for the deal, chose to reuse the registrations of retired Tu-134s *sans suffixe*/ Tu-134Ks (CCCP-65605 through -65622). This ran contrary to traditions, but the offending registrations were never changed.

Opposite page, top: **Almost new Tu-134A CCCP-65820 of the Tajik CAD/Leninabad UAD/292nd Flight/1st Squadron during a turnaround at the brand-new airport in Aktyubinsk, Kazakhstan, in February 1975. Note the angular presentation of the registration characters. A standard SPT-104 electrically-powered gangway stands at the entry door; a TZ-22 fuel bowser (KrAZ-258 with semitrailer) and a UPG-300 power cart on a ZiL-131 6x6 truck chassis are hooked up to the aircraft.** ITAR-TASS

Opposite page, bottom: **'Triple seven', a Komi CAD/Syktyvkar UAD/75th Flight Tu-134A-3 at Leningrad-Pulkovo. The Komi CAD was the largest operator of the type in the Soviet Union, and subsequently Russia.** Aleksey Ivanov

Photographs on this page:

Below: **Dead bird? Not at all. This tailless and nacelle-less Tu-134 is seen at the opening stage of refurbishment at ARZ No 400 at Moscow-Vnukovo. Judging by the single emergency exit and the six windows ahead of it, this is CCCP-65604 No 1, -65605 No 1 or -65606 No 1.** RART

Bottom: **During the XXII Olympic Games in Moscow the aircraft of Aeroflot's International Services Directorate, including Tu-134A CCCP-65038 here, wore Official Olympic Carrier titles.** Aeroflot

The purchase itself was not altogether without incident, too. The first three aircraft (paid for by MGA) included Tu-134AK DDR-SDI, the former aircraft of Erich Mielke, head of the infamous StaSi. On 17th December 1990 the Komi CAD team which was to accept the aircraft was informed that Flugtechnik (the maintenance department of Interflug) refused to perform the required and contractually agreed maintenance on this aircraft. The hatred towards *das Mielke-Ministerium* was somehow targeted at the aircraft itself. Having recovered from the initial shock, the Russians got in touch with the head office. In those days the ministerial machinery still worked efficiently when it had to, and the gears were set in motion. On 23rd December an entire shift of technicians arrived at Berlin-Schönefeld from Syktyvkar and, having received the keys for the hangar (the Germans were having their Christmas holidays at the time!), set to work. On 28th December the serviced aircraft was reflown; the crew was ill at ease, being well aware of the malicious glances from the many onlookers. Then, after eliminating a few more malfunctions discovered during the flight, the Russians flew the jet to Minsk for refurbishment – and barely made it home in time for the New Year celebrations.

In 1992 Komiavia's Tu-134s logged 50,000 hours between them – a record figure for a single operator (consider that many of the ex-German aircraft were still grounded then, awaiting upgrades and certificate of airworthiness renewal). As of March 2002, the aggregate time logged by the Tu-134s in the Komi Republic since 1973 was about 900,000 hours – another record.

Now we have to go back in time a little. Mass production of the Tu-134 ended in September 1984; however, production of special-mission versions continued at a trickle for another five years. The highest c/n is (63)66550 (f/n 6375), a radar-nosed Tu-134AK registered XU-102 which was manufactured on 15th December 1986 as the final passenger-configured example. The last aircraft off the line, however, was probably Tu-134SKh CCCP-65723 (c/n (63)66440, f/n 6369) released by the factory on 30th June 1989. Total production was 852 aircraft of all models – not an overwhelming figure, considering that the Boeing 737 Classic (Srs 100/200/300/400/500) was manufactured in 3,132 copies, with the 737 New Generation (Srs 600/700/800/900) now approaching 1,000 copies, and the DC-9/MD-80/Boeing 717 family approaching 2,500.

In 1985 KhAPO was tasked with building the An-72/An-74 transport. Originally it was due to enter production in Kiev, but the local aircraft factory No 473 had no spare capacity, being busy manufacturing the An-32 *Cline* transport which enjoyed considerable export success; hence General Designer Oleg Konstantinovich Antonov picked the Khar'kov factory. Being a long-standing Tupolev partner, the plant was dead set against this because a transition to Antonov aircraft meant a total change of technology, but the MAP decision could not be overruled.

According to Soviet practice a single aircraft overhaul plant would handle all aircraft of a given type, regardless of where they were based; if the aircraft was produced in large numbers, several plants would be assigned. The Tu-134 was initially overhauled by ARZ No 400 at Moscow-Vnukovo but this switched to the Tu-154 when this type entered service on 9th February 1972. From then on, Tu-134s – civil and military alike – were refurbished by ARZ No 407 in Minsk, later joined by ARZ No 412 in Rostov-on-Don. Minor repairs of export aircraft, however, were carried out abroad; for instance, the maintenance facility at Prague-Ruzyne handled both Czech and East German aircraft.

Since the early 1990s some paint jobs are done by ARZ No 402 at Moscow-Bykovo[3] which repairs D-30 engines; the first engine was redelivered on 11th January 1974. Some repair work on Tu-134Sh trainers is performed by the Russian Air Force's ARZ No 712 in Chelyabinsk.

Originally the Tu-134 had a service life of 30,000 hours, 20,000 landings and 25 years; measures developed by the OKB and overhaul plants have extended it to 35,000 hours from 2nd February 1988 onwards and then to 40,000 hours. Early aircraft had a 5,000-hour mean time between overhauls (MTBO) but this was doubled by 1979. Currently overhauls are performed every 10,000 hours, 4,000 cycles or 4.5 years of service, with heavy maintenance every 330, 1,000 and 2,000 hours. The Solov'yov OKB kept working in the same direction, increasing the D-30's MTBO from 1,500 to 3,000 hours by 1976. In 1989 the *Vozdooshnyy Trahnsport* (Air Transport) gazette wrote that the D-30 engines were *'coming apart'*; yet, when questioned on the subject of engine reliability in 1997, Maj Aleksandr A Kotyukha who headed the maintenance department of the Russian Air Force's 226th OSAP at Kubinka AB said that 'the man who created the D-30 deserves a monument'.

All Sorts of Missions

The Tu-134's service career includes a wealth of interesting facts. During the XXII Summer Olympic Games held in Moscow in 1980 the TsUMVS aircraft fleet, including the Tu-134As of the 207th Flight, sported red 'Official Olympic Carrier' titles and the stylised Kremlin emblem of the Moscow Olympics. Such aircraft included CCCP-65027, -65035 and -65038 which were later transferred to the Belorussian CAD/Kaliningrad UAD, Urals CAD/Perm' UAD and Tyumen' CAD respectively.

Besides scheduled services, Aeroflot Tu-134As were habitually chartered by the Soviet oil and natural gas industry for carrying shifts of workers to and from airports located close to major oilfields in the Tyumen' Region. This practice was continued by major Russian oil companies, such as Yukos, in post-Soviet times.

Occasionally Tu-134s were adapted for carrying cargo by the simple expedient of removing the seats; however, just like the IL-18Gr, it could only carry items small enough to go through the entry/service doors. Tu-134 cargo operations were practised both in the USSR and abroad – notably by Aviogenex which used its aircraft as freighters in the winter season. In another example, on 17th June – 1st July 1978 ČSA Czechoslovak Airlines performed what was jocularly referred to as Operation *Wild Berry*: each afternoon a cargo-configured Tu-134A delivered 8 tons (17,640 lb) of fresh berries from Prague to Warsaw.

Other noteworthy special flights by ČSA aircraft include 18th November 1980 when an aircraft captained by B Rydl brought the prestigious Davis Cup tennis trophy from Zurich to Prague. In December of that year another ČSA Tu-134A brought the earthly remains of Johannes of Luxembourg, one of the ancient kings of Czechia, to Prague for anthropological examination, carrying them back to Luxembourg in February 1981.

Originally conceived as a short-haul airliner, the Tu-134 sometimes performed quite long flights (true enough, usually involving one or several intermediate stops). For example, Komiavia Tu-134As flew 'kiddie charters' for several years, carrying children non-stop from Syktyvkar to Bourgas. Charter flights took them all over Europe; in Asia, Komiavia Tu-134As ventured as far as New Delhi and Beijing. On 11th January 1992 Lithuanian Airlines Tu-134A LY-ABH took a Lithuanian government delegation to the USA via Shannon and Reykjavik. Possibly the longest mission flown by the type, however, was in December 1995 when Lat-Charter Tu-134B-3 YL-LBB carried a 55-man relief crew for a Russian cruise liner from Riga to Durban, South Africa, via Damascus, Djibouti and Dar-es-Salaam and then flew back along the same route with 53 passengers.

The 243rd Flight of the Voronezh UAD was special, operating almost the entire fleet of the specialised Tu-134SKh surveyers (though three aircraft were later transferred to Ivanovo). Their range of missions was soon extended beyond crop survey. In 1987 one aircraft participated in the Polish Telegeo-87 geophysical experiment; a similar experiment was held on 4th June 1988. On 31st August – 22nd September 1988 the Tu-134SKh was used to locate ground water supplies in Mongolia.

A line-up of six Voronezh UAD/243rd Flight Tu-134SKh surveyers (with CCCP-65929 nearest to the camera) at Voronezh-Chertovitskoye in the late 1980s, with a regular Tu-134A sandwiched in between. The surveyers' noses are covered with tarpaulins; bureaucratic snags kept these aircraft on the ground most of the time. Via Aleksandr Melikhov

The Tu-134 was operated by many MAP divisions. Here, Tu-214 prototype RA-64501, still in primer finish, takes off on its first flight at Kazan'-Borisoglebskoye on 21st March 1996 with the Tupolev OKB's unique 96-seat Tu-134A-3 RA-65966 flying chase. ITAR-TASS

In late August 1988 the Soviet State Committee for Nature Protection (Goskomprirody) launched the Aral-88 expedition to survey the rapidly shrinking Aral Sea (now dead and gone). Cotton growers who took most of the water from the Amudar'ya and Syrdar'ya rivers feeding the Aral Sea for irrigation purposes were to blame for the disaster. From 27th October to 4th November a 243rd Flight Tu-134SKh was seconded to the expedition, surveying the Kara-Kum, Amu-Bukhara and Karshi Canals, the mouth of the Amudar'ya and the polluted Lake Sary-Kamysh. The specialists of the Leningrad Institute of Agriculture established that the walls of the canals, which had been dug in the 1960s without any form of water-proofing, were leaking huge amounts of water, with the result that bogs formed up to 2km (1.25 miles) from the banks! Recommendations were given to surface the canal beds and walls with concrete.

On 15th February 1989 the Tu-134SKh was used to assess the damage caused by the disastrous earthquake of 7th December 1988 which destroyed the Armenian cities of Kirovakan and Spitak, killing 25,000. The aircraft surveyed an area of 4,600km^2 (1,776 miles^2) near the epicentre containing 180 towns and villages, detecting potential landslide areas and damaged irrigation facilities which could cause floods if ruptured.

On 10th January 1990 the Tu-134SKh participated in the **Nevskaya guba** (Neva Bight) environmental research programme. Back in 1983 an earthen flood protection dam had been built in Leningrad. From the start there had been serious misgivings as to the ecological impact of the dam, but the city's Executive Committee had ignored them. Now it became clear that the proverb about good intentions is valid. The dam had created stagnant areas where industrial waste dumped into the Neva River and the Gulf of Finland accumulated; by 1986 more than 40% of the Neva Bight had been polluted. It was recommended that the dam be demolished to restore normal water circulation.

In August 1992 the aircraft took part in the Russian/US PRECHERI hydrological experiment alongside modified Douglas DC-8 and Lockheed P-3A Orion aircraft, the Russian oceanographic vessel M/V *Akademik Ioffe* and the ERS-1 satellite (Earth Resources Satellite). The Tu-134SKh also found use as a fishery surveyer on the Kamchatka Peninsula, an ice reconnaissance aircraft in the High North, a forestry inspection aircraft and an ore finder.

Unfortunately, as noted earlier, Tu-134SKh operations were beset by organisational problems. Only four aircraft were delivered initially, whereas the Voronezh UAD had enough crews to operate ten. Cutting through the red tape to get the version's research aircraft status took a maximum of effort. Yuriy P Sergevnin, a justifiably annoyed Tu-134SKh captain, expounded in an interview to *Vozdooshnyy Trahnsport*: '*There was even a case when we were to photograph a tract of land 16km* [10 miles] *from the airport. At 850km/h* [530mph] *it takes us 40 minutes to reach the required altitude* (10,000m/32,810ft – Auth.). *Then an MGA offi-

cial tells me I have exceeded the fuel usage limits! I tell him that the aircraft climbs in a spiral, and he tells me that's rubbish: aeroplanes should fly in a straight line…'*

The crews' hourly pay rates, too, were two to three times lower than on ordinary passenger/cargo aircraft due to bureaucratic subtleties. Also, when Mikhail S Gorbachov's new policy of *perestroika* introduced self-accounting of industrial enterprises, the airmen ran into problems with maintenance, board and lodging and the like, when operating off-base. The crews had to go half hungry – no small thing, considering that missions lasted up to ten hours.

To top it all, the local authorities often threw a spanner in the works because pollution and other mischief would be uncovered during Tu-134SKh missions, whereupon the local authorities would get it in the neck from the 'higher command' – which of course they would rather not.

By 1987 (during the first 20 years of service) Aeroflot Tu-134s had carried 367 million passengers. By November 1990 the figure rose to 475 million, and by 1st April 1991 the Tu-134 had carried more than 550 million passengers in the Soviet Union alone! If you place that many people shoulder to shoulder, the line will run around the equator five times!

Unfortunately, the Tu-134 has a rather high accident rate. As of 1st January 2003, 126 accidents of varying seriousness involving the type had occurred, resulting in the loss of 58 aircraft. However, as the reader will see from Appendix 2, the tell-tale human factor was the cause in most cases – namely pilot or ATC error, and sometimes even illegal interference or acts of war.

Also, no aircraft type is immune against aerial terrorism, and the Tu-134 is no exception. Nineteen hijackings involving Tu-134s operated by Aeroflot, ČSA and LOT Polish Airlines were recorded between 10th July 1977 and 15th September 1993. Quite often the hijackers were deranged people, but this was not always the case.

Apart from the 'true Aeroflot', Tu-134s in Aeroflot colours were operated by various branches and twigs of MAP, MRP and the Ministry of General Machinery (MOM – *Ministerstvo* **ob***schchevo* **ma***shinostroyeniya*, or Minobschchemash), the industry responsible for the Soviet space and missile programmes. Numerous Tu-134s – both quasi-civil and in full military markings – were in service with the Soviet Air Force and Naval Air Arm.

An Airliner at War

As mentioned in Chapter 3, VIP and ABCP versions of the Tu-134 were stationed all over the USSR and abroad but the greatest concentration was around Moscow. Sometimes the 'stinger tail' Tu-134 *Balkany*s were used by Soviet military leaders on their foreign trips; for example, in October 1989 CCCP-65992 paid a visit to Oslo-Fornebu airport, carrying Army General (that is, four-star general) Valentin I Varennikov. There were some unusual missions, too; some sources claim that on 13th March 1991 former East German leader Erich Honecker used Russian Air Force Tu-134 *Balkany* '25 Red' for his escape to Moscow (Honecker was declared a wanted man after German reunification for executing East Germans who had attempted to 'go over the wall').

Most of the VVS's Tu-134s, however, were Tu-134UBL pilot trainers (operated by the Tambov and Orsk Military Pilot Colleges) and Tu-134Sh-1/-2 navigator trainers operated by the Chelyabinsk and Voroshilovgrad Military Navigator Colleges. The cadets flew the Tu-134Sh during the fourth and final year of training, which was preceded by numerous 'flights' in a simulator. Live weapons training involved flying over three target ranges with different approach conditions; the entire regiment participated in such sessions, the aircraft making their bombing runs consecutively.

Inevitably, spills occurred. Sometimes trainees dumped all bombs at once instead of just one and the training session had to be cut short. Occasionally the crew would lose their way en route; as a result, the grain processing units and vehicle depots of nearby collective farms could get bombed, since their image on the radar display was similar to the practice targets. Fortunately the damage was usually minimal because practice bomblets are filled mostly with soot to produce 'smoke'. There was a joke at the Chelyabinsk VVAUSh: if chicken is served at the officers' canteen, this means another poultry farm has had it…

In 1982 a single Tu-134UBL starred in the motion picture *Tenderness for the Roaring Beast* based on a novel by Aleksandr A Bakhvalov, portraying a fictitious aircraft – the S-14 bomber designed by Nikolay S Sokolov. Accordingly the cabin windows were disguised and all markings obliterated.

Additionally, the Ministry of Defence periodically 'chartered' Aeroflot Tu-134s for carrying military personnel. For instance, starting in the mid-1970s, they were used alongside IL-62s and Tu-154s for troop rotation in the Group of Soviet Forces in Germany (GSVG – **Grooppa** *sovetskikh voysk v Ghermahnii*).[4] Such missions for were flown under Aeroflot flight codes ranging from SU6000 to SU6999; standard Aeroflot gangways had to be specially delivered to East German airbases to facilitate boarding.

Unfortunately the Tu-134s has been involved in several armed conflicts – although their use was nearly always directed at stopping the war or dealing with its consequences. The first such case was probably in 1993 when two Elf Air Tu-134AKs, RA-65097 and RA-65604, were seconded to the United Nations Peacekeeping Forces in ex-Yugoslavia. The aircraft were duly painted in all-white UNPF colours and used to carry UN representatives to the sites of various negotiations.

Tu-134s have been involved in both Chechen Wars (1994-96 and 1999-2001) – in various ways. On 28th July 1995 Tu-134 *Balkany* RA-65988 took a Russian government delegation to Groznyy to negotiate a ceasefire in Chechnya. Later, Transaero Express Tu-134AK RA-65926 brought another delegation to Khasavyurt, Daghestan; the talks that followed culminated in a peace accord being signed on 30th August 1996.

Tu-134Sh-2 trainers on the flight line at the Chelyabinsk Military Navigator College, 28th March 1996. ITAR-TASS

An impressive line-up of ten Tambov VVAUL Tu-134UBL trainers at Tambov-Yoozhnyy AB; another one is taxying out for take-off. Sergey and Dmitriy Komissarov archive

One peculiarity of the Chechen conflict was the ongoing and indiscriminate kidnapping of people by the separatists – usually for ransom, though sometimes the kidnappers placed political demands. Usually the Russian special forces succeeded in liberating the hostages which were then carried to Moscow by assorted Tu-134s. Thus, on 20th October 1998 Kosmos Aircompany Tu-134AK RA-65956 delivered 14 Russian Army servicemen from Mozdok, Ingushetia, to Moscow/Vnukovo-3. On 12th November Transaero Express Tu-134AK RA-65830 arrived at Sheremet'yevo-1, carrying Presidential Representative Valentin Vlasov who had spent six months in captivity. Exactly one month later Rusair Tu-134AK RA-65005 delivered the Frenchman Vincent Cochetel, a UN High Commission for Refugees representative who had been a hostage for almost a year (he had been kidnapped in Groznyy on 25th January 1998). On 28th May 1999 RA-65830 brought a whole group of ex-hostages – Russian Orthodox priests Pyotr Markov and Sergey Potapov, Russian Police Maj Vitaliy Khapov, Russian AF Capt Valeriy Korotin and four more servicemen. Finally, on 29 June the same aircraft brought US citizen Jonathan Gregg who had likewise been abducted by the Chechens.

On 25th January 1998 Askhab Air Tu-134A RA-65124 brought an Organisation for Security and Co-operation in Europe (OSCE) delegation to Groznyy for monitoring the peace process in Chechnya. On 3rd March 1999, however, the same aircraft was involved in the outrageous kidnapping of Maj Gen Ghennadiy Shpigoon, the Russian Minister of the Interior's Representative in the republic. As the general boarded the aircraft at Groznyy-Severnyy, he was ambushed by four terrorists sitting in the rear baggage compartment; pushing him out of the aircraft, they thrust him into a waiting car and were off. This time there was no happy end; after several months of imprisonment Shpigoon managed to escape from his captors but died of exposure before he could reach friendly forces.

On 4th July 2000 a Tu-134UBL coded '33 Red' delivered a load of medicines from Chelyabinsk to Mozdok. On the return trip it carried the bodies of Chelyabinsk SWAT policemen killed in a suicide attack by a Chechen terrorist in Argun, Chechnya.

Thrills and Spills
Tu-134 operations involved some amusing episodes. One day a Russian Air Force Tu-134AK was carrying 'big brass' from one airbase to another; it was winter and the cabin heating was turned all the way up, so that some of the passengers soon dozed off, as snug as a bug in a rug. Everything was normal until suddenly a passenger burst into the flightdeck, wild-eyed, and yelled, 'FIRE!'

Reacting instantly, the flight engineer grabbed a portable fire extinguisher and ran to the cabin. Sure enough, the air was filled with

Resplendent in Rusair colours, Tu-134AK RA-65005 sits on the GosNII GA apron at Moscow/Sheremet'yevo-1, its home base. On 12th December 1998 this aircraft brought the Frenchman Vincent Cochetel, who had been held hostage by Chechen separatists for almost a year, to Moscow. Mike Kell

smoke… which, upon close examination, turned out to be no smoke at all: another fire extinguisher hanging on a bulkhead above the luckless passenger's head had self-discharged. Awakened by the loud pop, the passenger saw a 'cloud of smoke' and immediately assumed the worst; it took nearly 20 minutes to calm him down…

The next one is probably a fish story. An Aeroflot Tu-134A of the Kaliningrad UAD/380th Flight was flying the twice-daily Kaliningrad-Moscow service. The passengers (or baggage?) included… a Himalayan bear cub destined for the Moscow Zoo. The bear cage was placed in the forward baggage compartment after the accompanying handler had assured everyone the cage was 100% secure.

No sooner had the aircraft climbed to 7,000m (22,965ft) than the stewardess called on the intercom, 'I have a problem here! There's a leak in the galley!' The leak was quickly traced to the baggage compartment; unaccustomed to air travel, the furry passenger had… well, *wet his pants*. That was not all. Soon curiosity got the better of the bear; somehow he managed to break out of his cage and poked his nose out into the galley, scaring the stewardess (fortunately not to *that* degree). The crew had to summon the handler who 'arrested and detained' the inquisitive bear before he had a chance to explore the cabin.

There have been lesser 'animals' aboard, too. A TsUMVS Tu-134A serving an African destination (probably as a stand-in for a Tu-154) brought back stowaways – giant tropical cockroaches. These horrible insects infested the entire aircraft, and getting rid of them turned into a major problem, as they proved to be immune to aerosols. One such mega-roach insolently strolled into the flightdeck one day; the flight engineer promptly took off a shoe and killed the beast!

A curious incident occurred at Moscow/Sheremet'yevo-2 on 10th January 2001. Aeroflot Russian Airlines Tu-134A-3 RA-65770 was due to fly to Ljubljana on flight SU163 departing at 09:10, while sister ship RA-65783 was bound for Zagreb on flight SU166 departing at 08:50. The aircraft were parked next to each other, some distance away from the terminal and out of reach of the boarding fingers, which meant the passengers had to be taken to the aircraft by shuttle bus. Somebody mixed things up at the gates and the passengers of the Ljubljana flight were ushered into the wrong aircraft.

Imagine the consternation of the apron personnel when a second bus carrying the legitimate passengers of the Zagreb flight rolled up to RA-65783. The passengers for Ljubljana had to climb out and walk the short distance to RA-65770. However, as '770 taxied out for take-off a malfunction occurred and the flight was aborted. After spending several hours at the airport due to lack of a substitute aircraft the passengers of SU163 eventually departed for Ljubljana in… RA-65783 which had by then returned from Zagreb. You cannot dodge fate!

Wrecks and Relics
Most aircraft find their way to museums sooner or later. The Central Russian Air Force Museum in Monino near Moscow is the most well-known; it has a number of civil aircraft but no Tu-134. However, the Civil Air Fleet Museum in Ul'yanovsk has the third production Tu-134A CCCP-65648 (c/n 0351003). An unidentified Tu-134 *sans suffixe* is preserved at the museum of the Ul'yanovsk Higher Civil Aviation Flying School. Tu-134A CCCP-65655 (c/n 0351101) is preserved at the factory museum of the Khar'kov aircraft factory (KhGAPP) at Khar'kov-Sokol'nikovo. The Long-Range Aviation (= strategic bomber arm) Museum at Engels-2 AB boasts Tu-134UBL '34 Red' (c/n unknown) and Tu-134Sh-1 '76 Blue' (c/n 3350302). Another Tu-134UBL coded '34 Red' (c/n (13)64182) is preserved in the Victory Park in Saratov; possibly it is the same one which was at Engels. Other aircraft are preserved abroad (see Chapter 7).

Additionally, several examples were preserved in cities around the former Soviet Union. As already mentioned, the first prototype is a

Sic transit gloria mundi. Volga CAD/Gor'kiy UAD/220th Flight Tu-134A CCCP-65662 retired in 1982 sits derelict at Samara-Kurumoch. Judging by the savagely mauled fuselage, it had been used as a crash rescue trainer for a while. The missing port engine nacelle was used to repair Tu-134AK CCCP-65045 which had suffered an engine explosion on 10th February 1985. Dmitriy Petrochenko

Tu-134K CCCP-65615 No 1 survives as an instructional airframe at the tech school in Krivoy Rog. Peter Davison

'gate guard' in Moscow. The first pre-production Tu-134 *sans suffixe*, CCCP-65600, was preserved in Urgench, Uzbekistan, in October 1985. Tu-134 *sans suffixe* CCCP-65922 (c/n 9350805) was preserved in Omsk; Tu-134 *sans suffixe* CCCP-65634 (c/n 9350908) was mounted on a plinth at Murmansk-Murmashi. Tu-134K CCCP-65618 No 1 (c/n 8350301) was placed in a children's playground in Ul'yanovsk until burned by local vandals in 1997 or 1998.

Most early production aircraft, however, sat derelict in airports until finally scrapped. In Soviet days airframe life limits were observed strictly; thus in January 1987, when aircraft which had reached the critical limit of 15,000 cycles were undergoing checks, a lot of high-time Tu-134s were written off (the service life extension programme based on additional static tests had not yet been implemented).

Some Tu-134s were destined to find 'life after death'. Thus, Tu-134 *sans suffixe* CCCP-65601 and Tu-134A CCCP-65743 (c/n 2351605) became instructional airframes at the Kiev Institute of Civil Aviation Engineers (KIIGA – *Kiyevskiy institoot inzhenerov grazhdahnskoy aviahtsii*) at Kiev-Zhulyany airport. Tu-134 *sans suffixe* CCCP-65605 No 1 (c/n 6350102) served

the same purpose at the Leningrad Civil Aviation Academy decorated with the Order of Lenin (OLAGA – *Ordena Lenina Akademiya grazhdahnskoy aviahtsii*). Other instructional airframes included Tu-134As CCCP-65645 (c/n 0351005) at Riga-Spilve and CCCP-65654 (c/n 0351010) at Riga-Skul'te (unfortunately both were scrapped in 1997), Tu-134K CCCP-65614 No 1 (c/n 7350302) and Tu-134A CCCP-65663 (c/n 1351109) at Minsk-Chizhovka,[5] Tu-134As CCCP-65737 (c/n 2351506), CCCP-65739 (c/n 2351509) and CCCP-65883 (c/n (53)35300, f/n 3010) in the Kirsanov Technical School (the town of Kirsanov, Tambov Region) and, finally, Tu-134 *sans suffixe* CCCP-65613 No 1 (c/n 8350403) and Tu-134K CCCP-65615 No 1 (c/n 7350303) at the tech school in Krivoy Rog, the Ukraine.

Gor'kiy UAD/220th Flight Tu-134 *sans suffixe* CCCP-65609 No 1 (c/n 6350201) retired in 1982 was outfitted as a movie theatre at a pioneer camp near Mogilyov at the orders of MGA head Boris P Boogayev. An unidentified Tu-134A served a similar purpose at a pioneer camp in Věciki near Riga.

Tu-134 *sans suffixe* CCCP-65607 No 1, which had been written off after a ditching, was

used as an evacuation trainer by the Moscow Institute of Civil Aviation Engineers (MIIGA – *Moskovskiy institoot inzhenerov grazhdahnskoy aviahtsii*); the fuselage lay on the bank of the Moscow Canal not far from Sheremet'yevo until some scrap metal hunters stole it! Tu-134 *sans suffixe* CCCP-65643 (c/n 0350927) served as a cabin trainer at Leningrad-Pulkovo until 1991.

Retired Tu-134A CCCP-65745 (c/n 2351607) was delivered to Wartin, East Germany, in 1984 for use as an anti-terrorist trainer by StaSi; after German reunification the aircraft became a café in Grünz. Similarly, on 18th September 1997 LOT Polish Airlines Tu-134A SP-LHA (c/n 2351808) was delivered to a training centre near Warsaw for use by the Polish Ministry of the Interior's GROM anti-terrorist squad. ('Grom' is the Polish word for 'thunder', but here it is also an acronym for *Grupa reagowania operacyjno-mobilnego* – mobile rapid reaction group.) The dismantled aircraft was trucked to the site by Radom-based company Zakład Transportu Energetyki specialising in outsize cargo haulage.

In 1966 or 1967 the fuselage of a Tu-134 *sans suffixe* (probably the static test airframe) was

converted into a test rig for the dynamic heat insulation system of the Tu-144 *Charger* supersonic transport. The fuselage skin was double, and cooling air from the cabin was forced between the layers to protect the cabin against the kinetic heating during supersonic cruise. The appropriately modified fuselage with a metal fairing replacing the nose glazing was placed in a chamber with foam plastic insulated walls into which hot air was blown to heat the outer skin to the anticipated temperature of 160°C (320°F). The Tu-144's air conditioning system was installed in a special hyperbaric chamber imitating flight at up to 20,000m (65,620ft) and connected to the fuselage by ducts. The dynamic heat insulation worked perfectly, as later corroborated by the tests of the Tu-144.

Gor'kiy UAD/220th Flight Tu-134 *sans suffixe* CCCP-65963 (c/n 0350921) was used as a rescue trainer at Gor'kiy (later Nizhniy Novgorod)-Strigino until broken up in 1994. Tu-134A-3 65624 was donated to the Russian Ministry of Emergency Control (EMERCOM) for use as a rescue trainer at the training range in Noginsk north-east of Moscow.

Tu-134A CCCP-65729 (c/n 1351309), yet another Gor'kiy UAD/220th Flight aircraft retired in 1982 or 1983, was transferred to the Riga Institute of Civil Aviation Engineers (RKI-IGA – *Rizhskiy krasnoznamyonnyy institoot inzhenerov grazhdahnskoy aviahtsii*) and used for fatigue tests. Tu-134A CCCP-65744 (c/n 2351606?) retired with 24,500 hours' total time was tested to destruction at SibNIA in 1987; these static tests allowed the Tu-134's designated service life to be increased to 35,000 hours. Radar-nosed Tu-134A OK-AFA retired by ČSA with 22,185 hours and 19,987 cycles was ferried to the Soviet Union on 30th November 1988 and tested to destruction because no Aeroflot Tu-134 had that many cycles.

Tu-134A CCCP-65657 (c/n 0351103) written off at Yerevan-Zvartnots was used in 1986 for fire resistance tests as the crash of Tu-134AK CCCP-65120 was being investigated.[6] Flammable liquid was poured on the floor of the rear baggage compartment and ignited; the burning fluid quickly seeped through into the No 3 equipment bay, burning through the fuselage structure within five minutes. (The last six cases, however, are not 'life after death' but sooner 'death after death'!)

35 Years of Service: The Road Goes On

In Soviet times, Aeroflot Tu-134s averaged some 1,100 flights per year with an average load factor of 80%. However, the demise of the USSR triggered rampant inflation; the cost of an airline ticket from Moscow to Kiev rose from 19 roubles (an average two days' wages) in 1990 to 350,000 roubles (an average two weeks' wages) in late 1995. Traffic volumes plummeted, and yearly utilisation dropped from its 1989 high of 1,692 hours per aircraft to 900 hours in 1994; former Aeroflot units simply curtailed flights rather than try to attract pas-

Life after death. The nose section of Interflug Tu-134A DM-SCM, which had crashed at Berlin-Schönefeld on 22nd November 1977, escaped the breaker's torch to become an evacuation trainer and was later preserved in Aeropark Diepensee. Helmut Walther

A stewardess slides down the canvas escape slide of Chernomorskie Airlines Tu-134A RA-65575 during a passenger evacuation drill at Sochi/Adler airport in September 1997. It takes two strong men to hold the thing in position! The TN-3 inflatable escape slide at the entry door can be seen on the other side of the aircraft. ITAR-TASS

sengers by advertising and improving service standards.

Still, this crisis served to prolong the Tu-134's career as no replacement was in sight (the Tu-134D and other growth projects never materialised). First flown in 1974, the Yak-42 complemented the Tu-134 rather than replace it as originally intended; besides, its service introduction was lengthy and troubled. The

aptly-designated Tu-334 was eventually chosen as the successor, but the programme was plagued by funding shortfalls. The prototype (RA-94001) rolled out on 25th August 1995 did not make its maiden flight until 8th February 1999 (!) because the OKB could not purchase some critical components. Production is only just getting under way at the Aviant factory in Kiev, with LAPIK in Lookhovitsy near Moscow due to follow soon. The chase plane during the Tu-334's first flight was a Tu-134A (RA-65667), and the result was a classic 'changing of the guard' scene!

Consider also that the new airlines of the CIS could not afford to buy new hardware and were stuck with what they had inherited from Aeroflot. (True, some have resorted to leasing Western hardware, and the government is now promoting leasing as a way of furthering the service introduction of the Tu-334-100.)

Foreseeing the difficulties with the Yak-42 and the Tu-334, the Tupolev OKB wisely developed a service life extension programme which

The successor is in sight but takes a long time coming... The Tu-334-100 was unveiled in August 1995 but did not fly until 8th February 1999. Here the prototype (94001, c/n 01001) performs a demonstration flight at the MAKS-2001 airshow; the RA- prefix worn originally has been removed. Yefim Gordon

has now brought the Tu-134's design life to 45,000 hours. For instance, as of 25th August 2002 Astrakhan' Airlines Tu-134A-3 RA-65828 manufactured in June 1974 – one of the oldest examples as of this writing – had accumulated 41,913 hours and 25,075 cycles, having undergone seven overhauls – and consider that it is an aircraft with the original (not reinforced) wings! Of course, people are wary of geriatric airliners, but these figures testify that the Tu-134 turned out to be a sturdy airliner.

Still, aircraft don't last forever. In 1996 Russia's civil Tu-134 fleet amounted to 267 aircraft; this number decreased to 208 in 1997, 191 in 1998, 176 in 1999, 159 in Y2K and 136 (that is, 51% of the 1996 figure!) in 2001. According to recent forecasts, however, 16 aircraft will be retired in 2003 and 18 each in 2004-05, leaving 126 operational Tu-134s in Russia by that date. Though the arithmetic does not tally, one thing is clear: in spite of earlier forecasts, 2005 will *not* be the end of the line for the Tu-134.

Components of obscure origin compromising flight safety added another twist to the matter; the Russian CAA (GSGA – *Gosoodarstvennaya sloozhba grazhdahnskoy aviahtsiï*, State Civil Aviation Service) began large-scale inspections after the issue had been dragged into public view by a fraud-hunting gadfly. For example, out of 62 hydraulic pumps checked at Aeroflot Russian Airlines, 19 had forged documents. Tu-134A-3 RA-65783 was equipped with two counterfeit hydraulic pumps. As the Tu-134 has only two of them, were was not a single proper pump aboard left...

Noise and emissions are a major problem affecting Tu-134 operations. In the late 1990s the airlines operating the type into Western Europe had to pay big fines, and from 1st January 2001 Tu-134 flights into Europe were banned altogether (except in special cases). The last scheduled flight into Western Europe was performed by Aeroflot Russian Airlines Tu-134A-3 RA-65717 which flew to Venice on 31st December 2000.

Also, even though the Tu-134's fuel burn has been reduced from 55 to 34-39 g/seat-km, it is still twice that of modern airliners in the same class; more fuel-efficient engines are required if operations are to continue. Hence the Tu-134M re-engining programme is still on the agenda – though little progress has been made after Leonid L Selyakov's death.

Another problem is that airliners lacking a traffic collision avoidance system (TCAS) are banned from operating over Europe from 1st April 2001. ARZ No 412 is offering the installation of TCAS at the customer's request since 2002; however, imported systems built by Honeywell or Rockwell Collins are expensive and only a few CIS airlines can afford them. To remedy the situation Moscow-based Intechavia has developed the Acrobat-1 TCAS which will be more affordable. Some aircraft have been equipped for reduced vertical separation minima (RVSM).

A further area requiring attention is the cabin. Here there's plenty of room for upgrades – first and foremost installation of an oxygen system. Such systems are offered by ARZ No 407, ARZ No 412 and Intechavia. The latter installs AKB-17UM units (*avtonomnyy kislorodnyy blok* – self-contained oxygen module) developed by NPP Zvezda (Star), a company based in Lyubertsy east of Moscow and better known for its ejection seats. Many aircraft have had their interiors refurbished, with modern imported materials, enclosed baggage bins, new PSUs borrowed from the Tu-204, indirect lighting and quasi-rectangular windows for better passenger appeal.

In Soviet times, when aircraft were supplied to Aeroflot free of charge and fuel was cheap, the Tu-134 was considered to be efficient enough. Today, its shortcomings notwithstanding, it is still a valuable asset for the airlines operating it – especially since many aircraft have been retrofitted with the No 1A wing centre section tanks to extend range. At a time when passenger numbers dwindled due to the financial crisis, the extended-range Tu-134 proved to be just the right format on routes where operating the 160-180-seat Tu-154, to say nothing of the IL-86 *Camber* widebody, was uneconomical.

The Tu-134 is set to stay in service until 2007. And when it finally does retire, it will be after a long period of sterling service.

Chapter Six

Playing on Home Ground
Tu-134 Operators in the CIS

After the break-up of the Soviet Union and the dissolution of Aeroflot into hundreds of new airlines, ex-Aeroflot and ex-Soviet Air Force Tu-134s were operated by most of the new CIS republics. True, many of these air carriers retained Aeroflot colours (with or without titles) for a long time before adopting their own liveries.

For each republic, operators are listed in alphabetical order, with each airline's two-letter International Air Transport Association (IATA) designator and three-letter International Civil Aviation Organisation (ICAO) designator where applicable.

Aircraft no longer operated by the respective carrier are shown in italics in the fleet lists (except when the airline itself no longer exists or *all* of its Tu-134s have been sold or retired). For aircraft leased to other carriers, only the last known lease is indicated for reasons of space. 'Tu-134AK*' (with an asterisk) means the aircraft is converted to passenger configuration. 'r.n.' denotes 'radar nose' (Groza-M134 radar).

RUSSIA

TsUMVS, the international division of the old Aeroflot based at Moscow/Sheremet'yevo-2, became **AEROFLOT RUSSIAN INTERNATIONAL AIRLINES** (*Aeroflot – Rosseeyskiye mezhdunarodnyye avialinii*) [SU/AFL] and was renamed **AEROFLOT RUSSIAN AIRLINES** in July 2000. Russia's new flag carrier operated 17 Tu-134s.

Registration	Version	C/n	F/n	Notes
RA-65148	Tu-134A-3	(93)61025	5003	Leased from Komiinteravia ?-02 to ?-??
RA-65559	Tu-134AK/r.n.	7349909	4103	Ex-CCCP-65559, ex-Polish AF '101 Red' No 2. D/D ?-03; grey tail. To Aeroflot Plus 3-99
RA-65566	Tu-134AK/r.n.*	(23)63952	6311	Tu-134A-1 standard. Ex-9A-ADL, ex-Luftwaffe 11+11, ex-EGAF '184 Black'; D/D 7-93; grey tail
RA-65567	Tu-134AK/r.n.*	(23)63967	6318	Tu-134A-1 standard. Ex-9A-ADP, ex-Luftwaffe 11+10, ex-DDR-SDR; D/D 7-93; grey tail
RA-65568	Tu-134AK/r.n.*	(33)66135	6340	Tu-134A-1 standard. Ex-9A-ADR, ex-Luftwaffe 11+12, ex-DDR-SDU; D/D 7-93; grey tail
RA-65612	Tu-134AK/r.n.*	3352102		Leased from Komiinteravia 2-01 to ?-03
RA-65618	Tu-134A-3/r.n.	4312095	2410	Leased from Komiinteravia by 10-02; returned by 8-03
RA-65623	Tu-134AK/r.n.*	7349985	4109	Ex-CCCP-65623 No 2, ex-Polish AF '102 Red' No 2. D/D ?-03; grey tail. Occasionally opb Aeroflot Plus?
RA-65697	Tu-134A-3	(03)63307	5803	
RA-65717	Tu-134A-3	(13)63657	6107	
RA-65769	Tu-134A-3	(93)62415	5303	
RA-65770	Tu-134A-3	(93)62430	5304	Grey tail
RA-65777	Tu-134A-3	(93)62552	5402	Leased from Komiaviatrans ?-99 to ?-??
RA-65780	Tu-134A	(93)62622	5407	Leased from Komiaviatrans ?-99 to ?-00
RA-65781	Tu-134A-3	(93)62645	5408	
RA-65783	Tu-134A-3	(93)62708	5501	
RA-65784	Tu-134A-3	(93)62715	5502	
RA-65785	Tu-134A-3	(93)62750	5504	Grey tail. SOC by 1998 after ground accident
RA-65793	Tu-134A-3	(03)63128	5604	Leased from Komiinteravia ?-00 to ?-??

Most aircraft have a 68-seat configuration with eight first class seats. Tu-134AKs CCCP-65559 and CCCP-65623 No 2 wore Air Ukraine colours before being RA- registered.

In March 1997 Aeroflot announced a decision to streamline its fleet; the Tu-134s were to be retired and replaced by ten Boeing 737-4M0s. In fact, however, the aircraft were simply transferred to domestic routes. Moreover, when they could no longer cope the own Tu-134s were augmented by leased examples that wore basic Komiavia colours (with or without tail logo) and small Aeroflot (or 'FROM AEROFLOT') titles.

In late 2003 Aeroflot Russian Airlines started taking delivery of Airbus Industrie A319-111 and A320-214 short-haul narrowbody twinjets. Concurrently the airline introduced an all-new livery in an effort to enhance its customer appeal (the Aeroflot titles and the well-known winged logo were the only items remaining unchanged). The stylish new colour scheme with a largely silver fuselage, a dark blue belly, tail and engine nacelles, and an orange stripe blending into a Russian flag flying across the tail is now being introduced fleetwide; RA-65783 was the first Tu-134A-3 to be thus repainted.

A branch called **AEROFLOT PLUS** was formed in 1996 for flying business charters with two Tu-134AKs, performing the first service to Shannon in June 1997. Initially the jets were operated when available; flights had to be booked five days in advance, which was inconvenient. In March 1999 RA-65559 was permanently assigned to Aeroflot Plus after refurbishment with a new 32-seat interior. By January 2001 the fleet was bolstered by Tu-134B-3 'Salon' RA-65694 (ex-Latavio YL-LBD, c/n (03)63235, f/n 5707). The aircraft wear standard Aeroflot colours.

AEROFREIGHT AIRLINES (Aerofrakht) [RS/FRT] based at Moscow-Vnukovo occasionally leased Tu-134AKs RA-65719, -65726 and -65956 from Kosmos (see below) in the owner's colours. In March 2001 it reportedly leased radar-nosed Tu-134AK RA-65570 (c/n (63)66550, f/n 6375) from Tatneft'aero – again in the owner's colours but with overpainted titles. In 2003 the airline's operating licence was withdrawn for grave breaches affecting flight safety.

Moscow/Vnukovo-1 based **AERO RENT** [–/NRO] bought Tu-134AK RA-65557 from the Rossiya State Transport Co in March 2000; sister ship RA-65919 was purchased from the same carrier by February 2001. The aircraft were operated for the Russian/Kazakh **ITERA HOLDING CO** (a petroleum company), though only RA-65557 wore full colours. RA-65919 gained a small Aero Rent logo by May 2003.

By July 1999 the charter carrier **AEROTEX** [–] based at Moscow/Sheremet'yevo-1 leased Tu-134AK RA-65934 from the Irkutsk aircraft factory (IAPO; see MAP). Tu-134A 'Salon' RA-65756 purchased from the Ivanovo Air Enterprise was added in late 2000. Unlike RA-65934, which retains blue/white/black IAPO house colours with an AT logo, it wore the grey/white/black AeroTex livery based on that of the defunct airline Trans Charter.

Above: **Aeroflot Russian International Airlines announced the retirement of its Tu-134s in March 1997; seven years later, they are still going strong. Here, ARIA Tu-134A-3 RA-65769 starts up its engines on a rain-soaked apron at Moscow-Domodedovo on 3rd November 1998 – presumably for the short hop to Sheremet'yevo which had shut down due to foul weather, forcing a diversion.** Author

Below: **Tu-134AK RA-65557 of Aero-Rent (operated for the Itera petroleum company) rests between flights at Moscow/Vnukovo-1 on 22nd March 2001. The aircraft was purchased from the Russian government flight.** Author

Bottom: **Seen landing on runway 30 at Zhukovskiy in mid-1998, Air Vita Tu-134B-3 'Salon' RA-65693 has been chartered for singer Alla Pugachova's road tour; hence the aircraft is bedecked with 'Alla' titles and the logos of Nescafe, the *Argumenty i Fakty* (Arguments and Facts) weekly newspaper, Radio *Serebryanyy Dozhd'* (Silver Rain) and other sponsors.** Yefim Gordon

AEROTRANSSERVICE [–/AAS], a now-defunct charter airline based at Moscow-Vnukovo, leased Tu-134s as required. These included Tu-134A-3 RA-65148, radar-nosed Tu-134AK RA-65619 (December 1995) and radar-nosed Tu-134AK RA-65614 (July 1997, all Komiavia), Tu-134A-3 RA-65059 (Perm' Airlines, July 1999) and radar-nosed Tu-134AK RA-65608 (Komiinteravia, late 1999).

The **AIR TRANSPORT SCHOOL** (*Shkola vozdooshnovo trahnsporta*) [–/AIS] operated Tu-134A RA-65626 (c/n 9350704) and Tu-134A-3 RA-65855 (c/n (53)23252, f/n 2710) from Zhukovskiy. The former aircraft was in basic Aeroflot colours without titles, while the other machine retained Aeroflot titles. In 1996 the Air Transport School began doing business as **AIS AIRLINES**, while RA-65626 was sold to Vaynakhavia. In 1997, however, the airline ceased operations and the other aircraft was retired.

In mid-1997 Zhukovskiy-based **AIR VITA** [–/SEV] leased Tu-134B-3 'Salon' RA-65693 from Aviaenergo. In early 1998 the aircraft was chartered for pop star Alla Pugachova's road tour; accordingly the airline titles were removed (only the 'AV' tail logo remained) and replaced by bold 'Alla' titles and sponsors' logos (Nescafe etc). The aircraft returned to its owner at the end of the year.

ALANIA AIRCOMPANY [–/OST] of Vladikavkaz (Alania is the native name of North Ossetia) operated five Tu-134s. The first of them, RA-65616, originally flew in ex-Interflug red colours with 'Alania' titles on the nose; a restrained but attractive livery was introduced in mid-1998.

Registration	Version	C/n	F/n	Notes
RA-65613	Tu-134AK/r.n.*	3352106		D-30-III engines. Bought from Karat 9-00
RA-65614	Tu-134AK/r.n.*	4352207		D-30-III engines. Lsf Komiinteravia circa 6-99 to 1-02
RA-65616	Tu-134AK/r.n.*	4352206		Leased from Komi[inter]avia 11-97 to ?-??
RA-65622	Tu-134A	(83)60495	4610	Bought from Komiavia 9-98, named 'Gheorgiy'
RA-65970	Tu-134AK*	3351910		Leased from ARZ No 412 ?-00 to ?-02

ALLIANCE AVIA [–/NZP] based at Zhukovskiy leases several aircraft from Yamal Airlines. These include Tu-134AK RA-65554 in 54-seat configuration leased in 2000; the airliner is in basic Yamal livery with 'ALLIANCE AVIA' titles and tail logo.

Shortly after adopting a new corporate image as **ALROSA** [–/DRU], the airline formerly known as *Almazy Rossiï – Sakha* (Diamonds of Russia – Sakha, a subsidiary of the identically named mining company based in Mirnyy, Yakutia) leased Tu-134A-3 RA-65847 from Orenburg Airlines. By mid-2000 it was returned. In the meantime, Alrosa had bought ex-Latavio Tu-134B-3 YL-LBA (c/n (93)61000, f/n 5001) which had been grounded at Moscow/Sheremet'yevo-1 since 1995; after refurbishment as a Tu-134B-3 'Salon' the aircraft was registered RA-65146, receiving Alrosa's stylish green/white colour scheme and 'two gems' tail logo. The Alrosa titles were removed by August 2002. A second Tu-134B-3 (ex-4L-AAC, c/n (13)63536, f/n 6009) was acquired from Sukhumi Airlines in 2001, becoming RA-65715.

ALROSA-AVIA [–/LRO], the Moscow subsidiary of Almazy Rossiï – Sakha, acquired Tu-134AK RA-65907 (c/n (33)63996, f/n 6333), a former avionics testbed, in January 1994. A second example, Tu-134B-3 'Salon' RA-65693, was purchased from Aviaenergo in May 2001; it received a hybrid colour scheme, combining the green cheatline of the parent company with Alrosa-Avia titles (Russian to port and English to starboard) and 'AA' tail logo. The former aircraft was repainted in this fashion by May 2003.

ASA AMERICAN ST PETERSBURG AIRLINES [–/SPB] leased Tu-134s as required until it went broke in 1997.

ANTARES AIR [–/ANH] leased Tu-134AK RA-65097 (c/n (83)60540, f/n 4704) from Elf Air in 1997. The anonymous-looking aircraft was returned to the lessor after a landing mishap in 1998.

ANTEX-POLUS [–/AKP] based at Yermolino industrial airfield near Moscow bought Tu-134AK RA-65908 (c/n (23)63870, f/n 6307) from the defunct Yermolino Airlines in 2002. The aircraft is white with purple, blue and green zigzag stripes all over and a small Antex-Polus badge.

AVIAKOMPANIYA ARKHANGEL'SK [–] (Arkhangel'sk Airlines; not to be confused with AVL!) leased radar-nosed Tu-134A RA-65667 (c/n 1351207) and Tu-134B-1-3 RA-65720 (c/n (03)62820, f/n 5508) from Tupolev-Aerotrans in 1995-96.

ASKHAB AIR[1] [–/HAB] was established in 1997 as Chechnya's second 'inter-war' air carrier, purchasing Tu-134A RA-65124 (ex-Estonian Air ES-AAN, c/n (83)60560, f/n 4705) in February 1997. The aircraft wore full colours with an 'Islamic green' cheatline, galloping horse logo and Ashab Air (*sic*) titles. Additionally, Tu-134AK RA-65939 configured as a 72-seater was leased from the Flight Research Institute in 1997-98 in basic Aeroflot colours without titles.

On 3rd March 1999 RA-65124 was involved in the kidnapping of police general Ghennadiy Shpigoon. Consequently flights to Groznyy were suspended; nevertheless, RA-65124 continued flying to Moscow-Vnukovo from Mozdok, Ingushetia, until the outbreak of the Second Chechen War in September 1999. Then the aircraft was impounded and has been stored at Zhukovskiy ever since.

ASTRAKHAN AIRLINES [OB/ASZ] has five Tu-134A-3s.

Registration	Version	C/n	F/n	Notes
RA-65055	(73)49856	3906		Leased to Kolavia 11-01
RA-65080	(73)60065	4207		Leased to Kolavia 3-03
RA-65102	(83)60267	4408		Leased to Bashkirian Airlines ?-01
RA-65825	(43)09078	2404		
RA-65828	(43)12086	2407		

ATLANT-SOYUZ AIRLINES [3G/AYZ], a scheduled and charter passenger and cargo operator based at Moscow (Sheremet'yevo-2 and Domodedovo) and Chkalovskaya AB, leased Tu-134AK RA-65681 from and the Russian Air Force (see below) in late 1995. It was later joined by two more Russian AF Tu-134AKs – RA-65679 and -65680; all three have been returned since. Additionally, Tu-134AK RA-65956 was reportedly briefly leased from Kosmos Aircompany in August 1996. None of these aircraft wore 'Atlant-Soyuz' titles or logo.

Atlant-Soyuz is called 'the Moscow Government airline' – for more than one reason. Firstly, the Moscow Government has a stake in it; secondly, government officials often made use of the airline's aircraft. For example, on 6th-10th July 1998 RA-65681 brought a delegation of Russian MPs headed by Ghennadiy N Seleznyov, the then Chairman of the State Duma (the lower house of the Russian Parliament), to Copenhagen. In November 1998 Moscow Mayor Yuriy M Luzhkov made a tour of Russia's regions on the same aircraft.

In 1997 the airline **AVCOM** [J6/AOC] based at Moscow/Sheremet'yevo-1 and specialising in business charters ('Avcom' means 'aviation, commercial') operated four Tu-134s.

Registration	Version	C/n	F/n	Notes
RA-65079	Tu-134A-3 'Salon'	(73)60054	4206	Ex-LY-ASK; bought from Tulpar ?-01. White/red/blue 'biz-jet' c/s
RA-65701	Tu-134B-3 'Salon'	(03)63365	5710	Ex-Baltic Express Line YL-LBI, regd 16-11-01. White fuselage, curved red/blue cheatline
RA-65940	Tu-134AK/r.n.	3351906		Ex-LZ-TUM; 28 seats, basic Aeroflot c/s, no titles. Bought from Tupolev-Aerotrans ?-97, opf ShaNS; sold to ShaNS-Air ?-99
RA-65945†	'Tu-134B-3'	(13)64010	6401	Converted Tu-134UBL '11 Red' [RA-64010], regd 25-9-02. Leased from Roos' Leasing Company

† Some sources say RA-65945 was operated by Orenburg Airlines.

AVIAENERGO [–/ERG], the Zhukovskiy-based flying division of the United Energy System of Russia JSC (*RAO Yedinaya energheticheskaya sistema Rossii*, the electric power monopoly), bought Tu-134B-3 YL-LBC (c/n (03)63221, f/n 5706) from Latavio in 1996. Reregistered RA-65693, the aircraft was outfitted as a 36-seat Tu-134B-3 'Salon'. In mid-1997 it was leased to Air Vita, returning to the lessor a year later; unfortunately the bright yellow/red/green band characteristic of Aviaenergo's first livery was not reinstated and the 'Electric Eagle' tail logo became rather duller.

In March 2001 Aviaenergo bought Tu-134AK RA-65962 from the Russian Air Force; this aircraft wears the airline's current livery with a stylised 'A' logo. In May 2001 RA-65693 was sold to Alrosa-Avia.

The charter carrier **AVIAEXPRESSCRUISE** [E6/BKS][2] based at Moscow-Vnukovo operated four Tu-134s. All have now been disposed of.

Registration	Version	C/n	F/n	Notes
4L-65061	Tu-134A	(73)49874	4003	Leased from Abavia ?-02, no titles/logo
RA-65117	Tu-134A-3	(83)60450	4606	Lsf Orenburg Airlines 4-00 to ?-??; Orenburg c/s, Aviaexpresscruise titles
RA-65144	Tu-134A	(93)60977	4909	Ex-Orient Avia, bought ?-98; white with twin red cheatline, titles/logo. Sold to Pulkovo by 10-00
RA-65569†	Tu-134B-3	(03)63340	5807	Ex-Sukhumi Airlines 4L-AAB, D/D 2-00; dark blue/white c/s, titles only. Sold to Daghestan Airlines 9-01

† Logically 4L-AAB should have become RA-65700 (it is ex-YL-LBH, ex-CCCP-65700).

AVIALINII CHETYRESTO (Airlines 400) [–/VAZ], the flying division of Aircraft Overhaul Plant No 400 at Moscow-Vnukovo, bought Tu-134AK RA-65935 (c/n (33)66180, f/n 6346) from TsSKB Progress in 2003.

Troitsk-based **AVIAOBSHCHEMASH** [–/OBM], also known as **AOM AIR COMPANY** (not to be confused with the French AOM – Air Outre Mer), operated Tu-134AK RA-65935 in Aeroflot colours. Aviaobshchemash is not really an airline but the flying division of the former Ministry of General Machinery (MOM, or Minobshchemash). Later RA-65935 was transferred to TsSKB Progress, another MOM enterprise.

AVIAPRIMA SOCHI AIRLINES [J5/PRL] leased Tu-134s as required until it went bankrupt in 1998. Known cases are Chelyabinsk Air Entareprise Tu-134As RA-65131 and -65786 (1995), plus radar-nosed Tu-134AKs RA-65614 and -65620 of Komiavia (1997) which carried Aviaprima titles.

The **AVIAZAPCHAST'** (= Air Spares) trading company wet-leased Tu-134AK RA-65908 from Yermolino Airlines in 1999-2002. The aircraft properly wore Aviazapchast titles and logo.

AVL ARKHANGEL'SK AIRLINES (*Arkhangel'skiye vozdooshnyye linii*) [5N/AUL] had 16 Tu-134As.

Registration	Version	C/n	F/n	Notes
RA-65052	Tu-134A-3	(73)49825	3902	Leased to UTair ?-02
RA-65066	Tu-134A	(73)49898	4008	Colour scheme 3-A
RA-65083	Tu-134A-3	(73)60090	4210	Lst Tyumen'AviaTrans by 6-02
RA-65084	Tu-134A-3	(73)60115	4302	Colour scheme 1, later 2.
RA-65096	Tu-134A	(83)60257	4405	Colour scheme 1, later 3-A
RA-65103	Tu-134A-3	(83)60297	4410	Colour scheme 2, later c/s 3-A, named 'Nar'yan-Mar'
RA-65116	Tu-134A-3	(83)60420	4604	Colour scheme 2, later 3-B
RA-65132	Tu-134A-3 'Salon'	(83)60639	4804	Later reconverted to standard. Sold to Yamal ?-99
RA-65143	Tu-134A-3	(93)60967	4908	Sold to Yamal ?-98
RA-65811	Tu-134A	4352202		WFU Arkhangel'sk-Talagi 7-94?
RA-65819	Tu-134A 'Salon'?	4352304		Later reconverted to standard. SOC
RA-65827	Tu-134A	(43)12084	2406	SOC and scrapped Riga-Spilve 9-94
RA-65846	Tu-134A	(43)23132	2610	SOC
RA-65898	Tu-134A-3	(53)42220	3207	SOC
RA-65955	Tu-134A-3	2351708		SOC
RA-65976	Tu-134A-3	3352007		WFU Arkhangel'sk-Talagi after accident 7-5-94

At first they wore Aeroflot colours, sometimes with a round *Arkhangel'skiye vozdooshnyye linii* badge on the nose (c/s 1). Later the fin was painted blue with white Cyrillic letters 'AVL' but no titles (c/s 2); RA-65084 was the only aircraft to combine this with the old badge.

A smart new livery appeared in 1997, featuring a dark blue belly and tail, 'Northern lights' tail trim and red titles. Usually the colour division line rises gently towards the tail (c/s 3-A); on some aircraft, however, it is horizontal and the *Arkhangel'skiye vozdooshnyye linii* titles are bolder (c/s 3-B).

BASHKIRIAN AIRLINES (*Bashkirskiye avialinii*) [V9/BTC] operated nine Tu-134s.

Registration	Version	C/n	F/n	Notes
RA-65026	Tu-134A-3	(63)48470	3602	Sold or retired by 2003
RA-65028	Tu-134AK*	(63)48490	3604	D-30-III engines
RA-65040	Tu-134A-3 'Salon'	6349100	3708	Ex-Lithuanian Airlines LY-ABC, D/D 9-94; reconverted to standard by 2002
RA-65046	Tu-134A-3	(63)49550	3804	Leased from Perm' Airlines 7-99 to ?-02; basic PAL c/s
RA-65102	Tu-134A-3	(83)60267	4408	Leased from Astrakhan' Airlines by 10-01; Astrakhan' cheatline, BAL tail colours/titles
RA-65671	Tu-134AK?	1351208		D-30-III engines. SOC by 1998
RA-65843	Tu-134A-3	(43)18123	2605	SOC by 1998
RA-65853	Tu-134A	(53)23245	2707	SOC by 1995
RA-65961	Tu-134AK	3351807		D-30-III engines. SOC by 2003

RA-65040 originally was a 39-seat VIP aircraft used by Bashkirian President Murtaza Rakhimov – probably because it was the airline's newest Tu-134. It had basic BAL colours but 'Bashkortostan' titles (by 2001 these were replaced by *Bashkirskiye avialinii* titles).

Tu-134AK RA-65970 in Alania colours taxies in at Moscow/Vnukovo-1 after arriving from Vladikavkaz on 5th September 2001. The aircraft was leased from ARZ No 412 whose badge is visible ahead of the forward entry door; the tail logo represents the North Ossetian flag. Author

Askhab Air Tu-134A-3 RA-65124 on runway 24 at Moscow-Vnukovo. This aircraft was involved in a kidnapping on 3rd March 1999. Dmitriy Petrochenko

Astrakhan' Airlines Tu-134A-3 RA-65080 seen immediately after touching down on runway 14L at Moscow-Domodedovo in April 1998. The anti-glare panel on the nose has been entirely removed by rain. Yuriy Kirsanov

The **CHEBOKSARY AIR ENTERPRISE** (*Cheboksarskoye avia-predpriyatiye*) [–/CBK] had five Tu-134s.

Registration	Version	C/n	F/n	Notes
RA-65007	Tu-134A-3	(63)46100	3306	
RA-65015	Tu-134A	(63)48325	3407	
RA-65021	Tu-134AK*	(63)48390	3504	Full c/s, D-30-III engines
RA-65024	Tu-134A	(63)48420	3509	C/n also rep. as (63)48428. Stored Rostov as CCCP-65024 by 7-02 (RA- prefix faded); leased to Karat by 7-02 as RA-65024!
RA-65033	Tu-134A-3	(63)48540	3609	No titles. Leased to Tatarstan Air by 7-02

The **CHELYABINSK AIR ENTERPRISE** (*Chelyabinskoye aviapred-priyatiye*) [H6/CHB], aka **CHELAL** (Chelyabinsk Airlines), had three Tu-134A-3s – RA-65118 (c/n (83)60462, f/n 4607), RA-65131 (c/n (83)60637, f/n 4803) and RA-65786 (c/n (93)62775, f/n 5505). Initially flown in basic Aeroflot colours with a Chelal 'bird' on the nose, they later received a smart livery with a white bird on a blue tail and Cyrillic titles; RA-65786 was the first to be repainted in 1998.

In 1997 Chelal formed a charter subsidiary called **ENKOR** [5Z/ENK]. In 2001 a reorganisation saw the parent company vanish, and the entire fleet is now operated by Enkor [H6/ENK].

CHERNOMORSKIYE AVIALINIÏ [–/CMK] (Black Sea Airlines, a Russian-Armenian joint venture based in Sochi) operated five Tu-134s. Some had a pleasing livery with a 'stormy sea' cheatline, 'Chernomorskie Airlines' titles and a 'Cheral' tail logo. In 1998 the airline was renamed **CHERNOMOR-AVIA**, abandoning this livery in favour of basic Aeroflot colours; it now has three Tu-134AKs.

Registration	Version	C/n	F/n	Notes
RA-65560	Tu-134A-1	(83)60321	4504	Lsf Ulan-Ude Aircraft Factory ?-98 to ?-99, full c/s
RA-65565	Tu-134AK*	(33)63998	6335	Tu-134A-1 standard. Ex-Belair EW-65565, lsf ARZ No 407 ?-95, basic Belair c/s, no titles. To Chernomor Soyuz 1996-98; returned as Chernomor-Avia
RA-65604	Tu-134AK*	(93)62561	5403	Lsf Elf Air ?-97 to ?-98; all-white, Cheral nose badge. Leased again by 8-00, basic Aeroflot c/s, Chernomor-Avia titles
RA-65605	Tu-134A/r.n.	(43)09070	2310	Ex-Belair EW-65605, lsf ARZ No 407 ?-95, full c/s. To Chernomor Soyuz ?-96
RA-65575†	Tu-134A	(93)62350	5209	Ex-Estonian Air ES-AAL, bought ?-97; full c/s. Sold to Armavia ?-01 as EK-65575
RA-65939	Tu-134AK*	1351409		Ex-VTS-Trans, bought 3-01; no titles

† Logically ES-AAL should have become RA-65768 (it is ex-CCCP-65768).

With aft trim very much in evidence, Tu-134AK RA-65962 comes in to land at Moscow-Vnukovo in the latest colours of Aviaenergo. Dmitriy Petrochenko

Aviaexpresscruise Tu-134B-3 RA-65569 soaks in the sun at Moscow/Vnukovo-1 on 22nd March 2001. The livery is that of Sukhumi Airlines, with which this aircraft had served as 4L-AAD; Sukhumi Airlines Tu-134B-3 4L-AAB is visible beyond. Author

A pleasing shot of Tu-134A RA-65144 in the colours of its second Russian operator, Aviaexpresscruise. The aircraft was resold to Pulkovo Air Enterprise in 1999 or 2000. Yuriy Kirsanov

Tu-134A RA-65084 in the old livery of AVL Arkhangel'sk Airlines; the overpainted '-3' on the nose reveals it had D-30-III engines at one time. Western magazines remarked scathingly that 'there was probably not enough paint for the titles'! Via Ghennadiy Petrov

CHERNOMOR SOYUZ [–/CHZ], likewise based in Sochi, received RA-65565 and RA-65605 from Chernomorskiye Avialiniï in 1996. Only the former aircraft wore Chernomor Soyuz titles. The airline ceased operations in 1998; RA-65565 was returned to what was now Chernomor-Avia and RA-65605 to ARZ No 407.

In September 2001 **DAGHESTAN AIRLINES** [–/DAG] bought Sukhumi Airlines' last remaining Tu-134B-3, 4L-AAD which was reregistered RA-65579, though it really should have been RA-65696. Concurrently Tu-134B-3 RA-65569 was purchased from Aviaexpresscruise. Both have had the livery of their ex-owners amended with Daghestani flag colours and the airline's titles/logo.

The fleet of **DONAVIA** (*Donskiye avialiniï* – Don Airlines) [D9/DNV] based in Rostov-on-Don included eight Tu-134As in 68-seat configuration. In 1998 the debt-ridden airline succumbed to the 17th August bank crisis and filed for bankruptcy protection. After a period of negotiations with Aeroflot Russian Airlines it was absorbed, changing its name to **AEROFLOT-DON** in April 2000.

Registration	Version	C/n	F/n	Notes
RA-65016	Tu-134A-3	(63)48340	3408	SOC by 2003
RA-65100	Tu-134A-3	(83)60258	4406	
RA-65104	Tu-134A-3	(83)60301	4501	SOC 3-02
RA-65666	Tu-134AK*	1351202		D-30-III engines. SOC by 2003
RA-65771	Tu-134AK*	(93)62445	5305	D-30-III engines
RA-65796	Tu-134A-3	(03)63150	5607	First Tu-134 to get Aeroflot-Don titles
RA-65834	Tu-134A-3	(43)17109	2506	SOC by 2003
RA-65863	Tu-134A	(53)28283	2808	

Established in 1993 as a cargo charter carrier, Moscow-Domodedovo based **EAST LINE** [P7/ESL] has since grown into a major airline with both cargo and passenger services. The impressive and constantly changing fleet includes a single Tu-134A-3, RA-65798 (ex-Georgian International Airlines 4L-65798, c/n (03)63179, c/n 5701). Bought in early 2001, it originally wore East Line's smart green/white livery as applied to some of the airline's IL-76TDs. In the autumn of 2002 the refurbished aircraft was outfitted as a Tu-134A-3 'Salon' by Kvand Aircraft Interiors, receiving a non-standard paint job.

ELF AIR [E6/EFR],[3] the commercial flying division of avionics designer NPO Vzlyot, operated a mixed bag of passenger and cargo aircraft from Zhukovskiy, including four Tu-134AKs – RA-65097, -65099, -65604 and -65908 (see Ministry of Electronics Industry). These were leased far and wide, including United Nations operations. In 2002 Elf Air suspended operations; some sources, however, report it has been renamed *Aviakompaniya imeni Grizodoobovoy* (Airline named after Valentina Grizodoobova, a famous Soviet aviatrix who undertook a transcontinental record-breaking flight in the 1930s).

In 1996 the airline **FLIGHT** [–/FLV] based at Astrakhan'-Narimanovo leased Tu-134AK RA-65962 from the Russian Air Force, returning it in 1999. Currently Flight operates Tu-134A-1 'Salon' RA-65563 leased from NAPO-Aviatrans and Tu-134AK RA-65682 (a former Russian AF Tu-134 *Balkany*); both are operated for the Astrakhan'gazprom natural gas company. The airline's operating licence was withdrawn on 1st September 2003; the fate of the aircraft is unknown.

The **FLIGHT RESEARCH INSTITUTE** named after Mikhail M Gromov (LII) in Zhukovskiy operated several Tu-134s for test and research purposes, mostly in full Aeroflot colours.

In 1992 LII established its first commercial division, **VOLARE AIR TRANSPORT CO** [OP/VLR],[4] for performing support operations (carrying delegations to airshows etc) and business charters. RA-65926 was the only aircraft to wear full Volare colours. By May 1997 the airline was dissolved and replaced by a new airline, **GROMOV AIR** [–/LII, later –/GAI].[5]

Registration	Version	C/n	F/n	Notes
RA-65047	Tu-134A	(73)49600	3805	Gromov Air, full c/s (version B), bought from GosNII GA by 8-01
RA-65067	Tu-134A-3 'Salon'	(73)49905	4010	C/s No 1. Bought from Voronezhavia ?-03; Voronezhavia cheatline, Gromov Air titles
A-65740	Tu-134A-1510	2351510		Testbed. WFU by 8-01
CCCP-65742	Tu-134A	2351604		Testbed? SOC by 8-95, scrapped Zhukovskiy
RA-65760	Tu-134AK	(93)62187	5105	Crashed near Yegor'yevsk 9-9-94
RA-65926	Tu-134AK	(33)66101	6336	Volare (full c/s), later Gromov Air (Volare cheatline)
RA-65927	Tu-134AK	(43)66198	6350	Volare, later Gromov Air (Volare c/l; later full c/s, version A)
RA-65932	Tu-134A-3 'Salon'	(43)66405	6367	Gromov Air, lsf Sukhoi OKB 8-01 to 4-02 (basic Aeroflot c/s, old titles) and from 4-03 (full c/s, version B plus Sukhoi badge)
RA-65939	Tu-134AK*	1351409		Gromov Air, 72-seater, bought ?-97; basic Aeroflot c/s, no titles. Sold to Chernomor-Avia by 2-02

By September 2000 RA-65927 had exchanged its blue/red cheatline and 'GROMOV AIR' titles for a smart new livery with a bright blue belly and wings, a dark blue cheatline and LII's stylised aeroplane logo on the fin. Soon afterwards it was named 'Yuriy Sheffer' in memory of a Distinguished Test Pilot who had worked for LII. Newly-acquired Tu-134A 'Salon' RA-65047 introduced an even smarter version with Cyrillic 'Громов Эйр' titles above the windows, small 'Gromov Air' titles in white on the cheatline (which is outlined in white), a blue anti-glare panel and a new logo consisting of the stylised letters GA.

GAZPROMAVIA LTD [–/GZP], the flying division of the powerful Gazprom corporation controlling Russia's natural gas industry, acquired Tu-134AK RA-65045 from Nizhegorodskiye Airlines in March 1998. Refitted again with a VIP interior, it was repainted in full Gazpromavia livery in 2001. Tu-134AK RA-65983 (a former Russian AF Tu-134 *Balkany*) was bought from Perm'transavia-PM in April 1998. This retains the ex-owner's 70-seat layout and livery, with Gazprom's logo on the tail (a G with a small tongue of flame, dubbed 'lighter'). The aircraft are based at Ostaf'yevo, a Naval Aviation base just south of Moscow. By July 2003 RA-65045 was leased to Kolavia.

GOSNII GA (the State Civil Aviation Research Institute) [–/ISP] at Moscow/Sheremet'yevo-1 had a single Tu-134A, RA-65047 (c/n (73)49600, f/n 3805). The aircraft was operated jointly with the **FLIGHT-CHERNOBYL ASSOCIATION** (*Polyot-Chernobyl'*) [–/FCH] in Aeroflot colours. By August 2001 it was sold to Gromov Air.

GOTVIL ENTERPRISES leased Tu-134A-3 'Salon' RA-65819 from AVL Arkhangel'sk Airlines in August 1993, returning it by August 1994. Earlier the company had leased Tu-134A-3 'Salon' RA-65132 from the same carrier.

INGUSHETIA AIRLINES [–/ING] with a registered office in Moscow operated two Tu-134As. Some sources quoted them as RA-65835 and RA-65876 but these aircraft are owned by Tajikistan Airlines and accordingly EY- registered! Also, there is no documentary evidence they were even leased by Ingushetia Airlines.

According to press reports, in 2003 the airline was to receive two Tu-134AKs from the Russian Air Force. One of them was probably RA-65979, a former Tu-134 *Balkany* seen in February 2003.

Moscow/Vnukovo-1 based **INSAT-AERO** leased Tu-134B-3 'Salon' RA-65692 from ShaNS-Air in late 2000. Like the two Yak-40 'Salons' operated by Insat-Aero, it is all-white with light/dark blue trim and a tail logo resembling the intertwined letters ALT.

The **IVANOVO STATE AIR ENTERPRISE** (IGAP – *Ivanovskoye gosoodarstvennoye aviapredpriyatiye*) [–/IGP] had five Tu-134s. The airline went bankrupt in 2000.

Registration	Version	C/n	F/n	Notes
RA-65550	Tu-134AK	(43)66200	6351	Sold to Tret'yakovo Aircompany ?-00
RA-65722	Tu-134SKh	(63)66420	6368	Sold to Sirius-Aero and converted to Tu-134A-3M
RA-65725	Tu-134SKh	(63)66472	6371	Sold to Sibur JSC and converted to Tu-134A-3M
RA-65756	Tu-134A-3	(93)62179	5104	Sold to AeroTex by 9-00
RA-65928	Tu-134SKh	(63)66491	6372	Sold to Sirius-Aero and converted to Tu-134A-3M

In September 1997 RA-65550 was chartered for pop star Filipp Kirkorov's road tour. The aircraft was bedecked with a huge portrait of the singer and 'Supertour – Filipp Kirkorov' titles.

IZHAVIA [–/IZA] (the Izhevsk Air Enterprise) operated four Tu-134As. For many years they wore Aeroflot colours without titles; it was not until March 2002 that RA-65056 received a new livery, RA-65141 following suit in 2003. Curiously, like the airline's sole Yak-42D (RA-42451), they wear 'Udmurtiya' titles, though neither aircraft is a VIP jet operated for the republican government.

Registration	Version	C/n	F/n	Notes
RA-65002	Tu-134A-3	(53)44020	3301	SOC ?-00
RA-65056	Tu-134A-3	(73)49860	3908	
RA-65141	Tu-134A-3	(83)60945	4906	
RA-65842	Tu-134A	(43)18121	2604	SOC ?-00

KALININGRAD-AVIA [K8/KLN] had ten 76-seat Tu-134As.

Registration	Version	C/n	F/n	Notes
RA-65010	Tu-134A	(63)46130	3309	Full c/s
RA-65011	Tu-134A-3	(63)46140	3310	Full c/s
RA-65019	Tu-134A	(63)48375	3502	
RA-65027	Tu-134A	(63)48485	3603	Full c/s
RA-65054	Tu-134A-3	(73)49840	3905	Full c/s
RA-65087	Tu-134A-3	(73)60155	4306	Full c/s
RA-65090	Tu-134A	(73)60185	4309	Full c/s
RA-65824	Tu-134A-3	(43)09074	2403	Lst Air Service Hungary 5-93 to 1-95 as HA-LBS
RA-65845	Tu-134A	(43)23131	2609	Leased to Sibaviatrans by 9-01
RA-65870	Tu-134A-3	(53)28310	2905	

For a while the airline operated foreign services jointly with Aeroflot. This arrangement is no longer valid, but aircraft in full Kaliningrad-Avia colours still carry small 'Aeroflot Russian International Airlines' titles aft of the flightdeck.

The charter carrier **KARAT** [2U/AKT, later V2/AKT] based at Moscow-Vnukovo operated nine Tu-134s.

Opposite page, bottom two photographs:

Chernomorskie Airlines Tu-134A RA-65575 (ex-ES-AAL, ex-CCCP-65768) completes its landing run on Moscow-Vnukovo's runway 24, approaching the intersection with runway 20. Dmitriy Petrochenko

Tu-134A-3 RA-65796 of Aeroflot-Don, formerly Donavia, caught by the camera on final approach to Moscow-Vnukovo. This was the airline's first Tu-134 to gain the new titles in 2000. Dmitriy Petrochenko

Right: **BAL Bashkirian Airlines Tu-134A-3 RA-65026 at Moscow-Domodedovo on 20th November 1998. The tail emblem represents a stylised bee, since Bashkiria is renowned as a producer of high-quality honey.** Author

Below: **Seen here on short finals to Moscow-Domodedovo, Tu-134A-3 RA-65786 was the first to receive the new livery of the Chelyabinsk Air Enterprise.** Yuriy Kirsanov

Registration	Version	C/n	F/n	Notes
RA-65021	Tu-134AK*	(63)48390	3504	D-30-III engines. Lsf Cheboksary AE by 9-01, CAE cheatline, Karat titles/logo, returned after 3-02
RA-65024	Tu-134A	(63)48420	3509	Lsf Cheboksary AE by 7-02, full white c/s
RA-65055	Tu-134A-3	(73)49856	3906	Leased from Astrakhan' Airlines 10-99 to ?-?? without repaint
RA-65102	Tu-134A-3	(83)60267	4408	Leased from Astrakhan' Airlines ?-00 to 1-01 without repaint
RA-65137	Tu-134A-3	(83)60890	4901	Lsf Kirov AE by 1-01, full white c/s
RA-65825	Tu-134A-3	(43)09078	2404	Leased from Astrakhan' Airlines 4-00 to ?-?? without repaint
RA-65613	Tu-134AK/r.n.*	3352106		D-30-III engines. Bought from Komiinteravia 5-99, basic Yamal c/s, Karat titles/logo; sold to Alania 9-00
RA-65830	Tu-134AK*	(43)12093	2409	Bought from Transaero Express 7-99, red/blue cheatline
RA-65930	Tu-134A-3M	(63)66500	6374	Bought from Kras Air, red/blue cheatline

Charter carrier **KAVKAZSKIYE AVIATRASSY** (Caucasian Air Routes) [–/KAV] which vanished in 1999 leased Tu-134s as required. For instance, Tu-134A-3 EY-65876 was leased from Tajikistan Airlines in mid-1998, retaining basic Tajikistan colours without titles and with a new logo (a seagull on a blue circle).

The **KIROV AIR ENTERPRISE** (*Kirovskoye aviapredpriyatiye*) [–/KTA] has three Tu-134A-3s.

Registration	Version	C/n	F/n	Notes
RA-65035	(63)48590		3702	Ex-Perm' Airlines. Leased to Rusline by 8-03
RA-65060	(73)49872		4002	
RA-65137	(83)60890		4901	Leased to Karat by 1-01

KMV (Kavminvodyavia) [KV/MVD] has five Tu-134As. The carrier is based in Mineral'nyye Vody, a popular health resort (KMV = *Kavkazskiye minerahl'nyye vody*, Caucasian Mineral Waters).

Registration	Version	C/n	F/n	Notes
RA-65074	Tu-134A-3	(73)49987	4110	Full c/s (red titles) by 6-02
RA-65101	Tu-134A-3	(83)60260	4407	Leased from Orenburg Airlines 2-00 to ?-??
RA-65126	Tu-134A-3	(83)60588	4707	Full c/s (black titles) by 2-93; red titles by 3-01)
RA-65139	Tu-134A	(83)60915	4903	Full c/s (red titles) by 5-00
RA-65797	Tu-134A-3	(03)63173	5610	Leased from Samara Airlines 5-98 to ?-??
RA-65844	Tu-134A	(43)18125	2606	
RA-65887	Tu-134A	(53)36170	3104	

Flight Tu-134AK RA-65682 with additional Astrakhan'gazprom titles awaits its next flight at Moscow/Vnukovo-1 on 18th June 2002. The bulge underneath the APU exhaust identifies it as a former Tu-134 *Balkany*. Author

Tu-134A 'Salon' RA-65047 displays the latest livery of Gromov Air with Cyrillic titles and GA tail logo at Moscow/Vnukovo-1 on 18th June 2002. Author

Former Tu-134 *Balkany*, RA-65983, on short finals to Moscow-Vnukovo's runway 24 on 6th June 1999. The aircraft wears basic Perm'transavia-PM colours with the 'lighter' tail logo of its current owner, Gazpromavia. Author

Despite the additional 'Udmurtiya' titles, Izhavia Tu-134A-3 RA-65056 seen parked at Moscow-Domodedovo on 15th August 2002 is not a government VIP aircraft. The aircraft was repainted in this restrained but nevertheless attractive livery only a few months earlier, having flown in basic Aeroflot colours without titles for many years. Note the pavilions of the Civil Aviation-2002 airshow in the background. Author

KOENIGSBERG INTER-TRADE based in Kaliningrad reportedly leased Tu-134AK RA-65934 from MAP in 1994-95.

KOGALYMAVIA [7K/KGL], an airline operating from Kogalym and Surgut and doing business as **KOLAVIA**, operated eight Tu-134s.

Registration	Version	C/n	F/n	Notes
RA-65045	Tu-134AK	(63)49500	3803	Lsf Gazpromavia by 6-03, basic Gazpromavia c/s, Kolavia titles/logo
RA-65148	Tu-134A-3	(93)61025	5003	Leased from Komiinteravia ?-01 to ?-??
RA-65611	Tu-134A/r.n.	3351903		Leased from Komiinteravia, basic Komiavia c/s, Kolavia titles/logo
RA-65618	Tu-134A-3/r.n.	4312095	2410	Leased from Komiinteravia by 8-03
RA-65861	Tu-134AK	1351407		Ex-Techaviaservice EW-65861 No 2 (see Belair!), ex-Czech AF '1407 White', D/D 4-99
RA-65942	Tu-134AK/r.n.*	(43)17103	2503	D-30-III engines. Ex-Malév HA-LBO, D/D 5-99
RA-65943	Tu-134A-3/r.n.	(13)63580	6102	Ex-Malév HA-LBR, D/D 4-99; refitted as Tu-134A-3 'Salon' 5-01
RA-65944	Tu-134AK/r.n.*	(43)12096	2501	D-30-III engines. Ex-Malév HA-LBN, D/D 5-99

The three ex-Hungarian examples were bought from LUKoil as 68-seaters, but RA-65942 and -65943 were refitted locally as 76-seaters. RA-65943 was later converted into a Tu-134A-3 'Salon' because it is the newest in the fleet.

KOMIAVIA [–/KMA] was the largest Russian Tu-134 operator, the main division in Syktyvkar (capital of the Komi Republic) operating 42 of the type.

Registration	Version	C/n	F/n	Notes
RA-65000	Tu-134A-3	(53)42230	3209	SOC Syktyvkar 11-94, scrapped
RA-65005	Tu-134AK*	(63)44065	3304	D-30-III engines. To Komiinteravia 11-96 **(see below); leased to Rusair ?-98**
RA-65006	Tu-134A-3	(63)44080	3305	WFU Syktyvkar 6-94
RA-65029	Tu-134A	(63)48500	3605	WFU Syktyvkar
RA-65069	Tu-134A-3	(73)49908	4102	Sold to Atyrau Air Ways ?-98 as UN-65069
RA-65070	Tu-134A-3	(73)49912	4104	Sold to Atyrau Air Ways ?-97 as UN-65070
RA-65148	Tu-134A-3	(93)61025	5003	Leased to UTair ?-02
RA-65606	Tu-134AK/r.n.	(63)46300	3405	Ex-CCCP-65606 No 2, ex-Interflug D-AOBR, ex-DDR-SDH; D/D 21-12-90
RA-65607	Tu-134AK/r.n.*	(63)48560	3610	Ex-CCCP-65607 No 2, ex-Interflug D-AOBS, ex-DDR-SDI; D/D 30-12-90
RA-65608	Tu-134AK/r.n.*	5338040	3109	Ex-CCCP-65608 No 2, ex-Interflug D-AOBO, ex-DDR-SDE. **Sold to UTair ?-02**
RA 65609	Tu-134AK/r.n.*	(63)46155	3401	Ex-CCCP-65609 No 2, ex-Interflug D-AOBQ, ex-DDR-SDG; D/D 21-8-91. **Leased to UTair by 6-03**
RA-65610	Tu-134AK/r.n.*	(53)40150	3204	Ex-CCCP-65610 No 2, ex-Interflug D-AOBP, ex-DDR-SDF. **Sold to Atyrau Air Ways ?-00 as UN-65610**
RA-65611	Tu-134A/r.n.	3351903		Ex-CCCP-65611 No 2, ex-Interflug D-AOBA, ex-DDR-SCI. **Leased to Kolavia 12-01**
RA-65612	Tu-134AK/r.n.*	3352102		Ex-CCCP-65612 No 2, ex-Interflug D-AOBC, ex-DDR-SCN. **Leased to UTair by 8-03**
RA 65613	Tu-134AK/r.n.*	3352106		Ex-CCCP-65613 No 2, ex-Interflug D-AOBD, ex-DDR-SCO. **Sold to Karat 5-99**
RA-65614	Tu-134AK/r.n.*	4352207		Ex-CCCP-65614 No 2, ex-Interflug D-AOBG, ex-DDR-SCS, D-30-III engines. **Lst Tyumen'AviaTrans (UTair) by 2-02**
RA 65615	Tu-134AK/r.n.*	4352205		Ex-CCCP-65615 No 2, ex-Interflug D-AOBE, ex-DDR-SCP. **Sold to Sibaviatrans ?-99**
RA 65616	Tu-134AK/r.n.*	4352206		Ex-CCCP-65616 No 2, ex-Interflug D-AOBF, ex-DDR-SCR; D/D 15-10-91. **Leased to UTair ?-02**

Registration	Type	C/n	F/n	Notes
RA 65617	Tu-134A/r.n.	4308068	2309	Ex-CCCP-65617 No 2, ex-Interflug D-AOBH, ex-DDR-SCT; D/D 27-8-91. Lst Harka Air ?-95; crashed Lagos 24-6-95
RA-65618	Tu-134A-3/r.n.	4312095	2410	Ex-CCCP-65618 No 2, ex-Interflug D-AOBJ, ex-DDR-SCV. **Leased to Kolavia by 8-03**
RA-65619	Tu-134AK/r.n.*	(53)31218	3001	Ex-CCCP-65619 No 2, ex-Interflug D-AOBK, ex-DDR-SCW. **Sold to Atyrau Air Ways 1-02 as UN-65619**
RA-65620	Tu-134AK/r.n.*	(53)35180	3006	Ex-CCCP-65620 No 2, ex-Interflug D-AOBN, ex-DDR-SDC, D-30-III engines
RA-65621	Tu-134A-3/r.n.	6348320	3406	Ex-CCCP-65621 No 2, ex-Interflug D-AOBL, ex-DDR-SCX. Leased to Tyumen'AviaTrans by 2-02
RA-65622	Tu-134A/r.n.	(83)60495	4610	Ex-CCCP-65622 No 2, ex-Interflug D-AOBM, ex-DDR-SCY. **Sold to Alania 9-98**
RA-65716	Tu-134B-3	(13)63595	6103	To Komiinteravia 12-97 (see below)
RA-65755	Tu-134A-3	(93)62165	5103	**Leased to UTair ?-02**
RA-65777	Tu-134A-3	(93)62552	5402	**Leased to UTair ?-02**
RA-65780	Tu-134A	(93)62622	5407	
RA-65793	Tu-134A-3	(03)63128	5604	**Leased to UTair ?-02**
RA-65805	Tu-134A-3	3352105		SOC Syktyvkar 3-96, scrapped
RA-65813	Tu-134A-3	4352204		WFU Syktyvkar 6-94, **SOC 8-99, scrapped**
RA-65840	Tu-134A	(43)18118	2602	SOC Syktyvkar 3-97, scrapped
RA-65866	Tu-134A-3	(53)28292	2901	**SOC Syktyvkar 1-00, scrapped**
RA-65891	Tu-134A-3	(53)38030	3108	**SOC Syktyvkar 1-00, scrapped**
RA-65901	Tu-134A-3	(13)63731	6203	
RA-65902	Tu-134A-3	(13)63742	6204	**Leased to UTair ?-03**
RA-65954	Tu-134AK*	2351707		D-30-III engines. **SOC Syktyvkar 2-99, scrapped**
RA-65958	Tu-134A	3351804		WFU Syktyvkar 6-94, **SOC 8-99, scrapped**
RA-65969	Tu-134A-3	3351909		**SOC Syktyvkar 8-99, scrapped**
RA-65971	Tu-134A-3	3352001		**SOC Syktyvkar 1-00, scrapped** (see Air Moldova ER-65791!)
RA-65972	Tu-134A-3	3352002		SOC Syktyvkar 4-97, scrapped
RA-65977	Tu-134AK*	(03)63245	5708	D-30-III engines. To Komiinteravia 11-96 (see below); **leased from UTair ?-03**

The delivery dates for CCCP-65606 No 2 and -65607 No 2 are the dates when the aircraft were ferried from Berlin-Schönefeld to Minsk-2 (ARZ No 407), as the prescribed time between overhauls had expired. The Komi CAD/Syktyvkar UAD also acquired radar-nosed Tu-134A CCCP-65605 No 2 (ex-D-AOBI, c/n (43)09070, f/n 2310) delivered on 6th December 1990, but this was transferred to ARZ No 407 on 8th December 1992 to pay for the overhaul of the former two aircraft and thus never entered service with Komiavia. Some ex-German aircraft originally had the RA- registration applied with no dash but reverted to a normal presentation later.

Originally most of the fleet wore full Aeroflot livery, except for the 17 ex-German aircraft (CCCP-65606 No 2 through -65622 No 2) which retained the basic red/white colours of their ex-owner, Interflug, looking remarkably similar to Aeroflot's Polar colours. (Imagine a Polar Aviation Tu-134A!) The Soviet flag and registration were positioned 'East German style' on the rudder and aft fuselage respectively instead of the fin; some aircraft carried Aeroflot titles in red (!), while others had only the winged hammer and sickle logo (irreverently referred to by some people as *kooritsa*, 'chicken'!). Nine of the eleven Tu-134AKs were imported as 80-seaters; only CCCP-65606 No 2 and -65607 No 2 retained their original interior. Most of the radar-nosed examples later received Aeroflot colours, but a few stuck to the red/white version up to 1996; one aircraft even *wore the Soviet and Russian flags simultaneously!*

In 1996 Komiavia introduced its own livery featuring the Komi national colours of green and blue and a leaping stag tail logo (an allusion to that used by the Komi CAD in the 1960s); RA-65608 was one of the first to be repainted. Two years later the name was changed to **KOMIAVIA-TRANS** but the old Komiavia titles remained. The airline also eagerly leased its Tu-134s to other carriers. But… see next entry.

KOMIINTERAVIA [8J/KMV], another Syktyvkar-based airline founded in 1996 as an affiliate of Komiaviatrans, started on a small scale with two Tu-134AKs (RA-65005 and -65977) joined in December 1997 by Tu-134B-3 RA-65716. They wore a striking 'Northern Lights' livery with stripes in three shades of blue on a pale blue background.

In September 1998, however, the Komi Regional Air Transport Directorate underwent a major reorganisation which resulted in Komiinteravia taking over all of Komiaviatrans's heavy fixed-wing aircraft, leaving the latter carrier with only ten An-2 utility biplanes and assorted helicopters. (Note: as there is no point in repeating the ex-Komiavia fleet list, post-takeover changes of status for Komiinteravia Tu-134s are marked in the previous table in bold type.)

Throughout 1999 the newly-acquired Tu-134s retained ex-Komiavia colours with or without titles, repainting taking place as each aircraft was due for overhaul; RA-65901 was the first to be repainted by March 2000.

In May-June 1994 the now-defunct airline **KONVEYER** [EC/TUG] based at Moscow-Vnukovo leased the one-off 96-seat Tu-134A-3 RA-65966 from Tupolev-Aerotrans. No titles were applied.

Generally *konveyer* means 'conveyor belt' or 'assembly line' in Russian; when used as an aviation term, however, it means 'touch and go', hence the airline's other name, **TOUCH & GO LTD**. Obviously whoever picked the English name wanted to hint at the carrier's efficiency, with excellent turnaround times ('we barely touch down at all', that is) and was unaware of the expression's *other* meaning. (Incidentally, the Russian name isn't the best choice either, implying the passengers are routinely whisked from A to B without the 'personal touch'.)

The charter airline **KORSAR** [6K/KRS] based at Moscow/Vnukovo-3 leased two Tu-134AKs from the 235th Independent Air Detachment. Later, when relations with the government flight were soured, it leased two other Tu-134AKs from the NPO Energiya space corporation (an MOM enterprise responsible, among other things, for the world's biggest space launch vehicle). These aircraft were upgraded with an IFE system in Minsk. *Korsar* is Russian for 'corsair', but the name has nothing to do with pirates; it derives from the names of the airline's founders, Korovin and Sarzhveladze.

Western businesspeople (notably oil company executives) were the first passengers; hence early flights were mostly to Siberia and the Russian Far East. Inclusive tour flights and even scheduled services to Cyprus were added later.

Registration	C/n	F/n	Notes
CCCP-65553	(33)66300	6359	Aeroflot c/s. Became RA-65553 during lease; returned 2-93
RA-65719	(13)63637	6106	Full c/s plus NPO Energiya logo. Returned late 1996
RA-65726	(13)63720	6202	Aeroflot c/s plus NPO Energiya logo. Returned late 1996
RA-65915	(33)66120	6338	Basic ex-Greenair c/s, Korsar titles/logo; returned 2-93

In late 1996 Tu-134AKs RA-65719, RA-65726 and RA-65956 (c/n 2351709), another NPO Energiya aircraft, were transferred to **KOSMOS AIRCOMPANY** [–/KSM], Energiya's house airline. Two of them were

Kavminvodyavia Tu-134A RA-65139 shares the apron at Moscow/Vnukovo-1 with a USAF/89th Air Wing Gulfstream Aviation C-37A (97-0401) after arriving from Mineral'nyye Vody on 29th May 2000. Like most of the airline's aircraft, it has red KMV titles. Author

Radar-nosed Tu-134A 'Salon' RA-65943 parked at Moscow-Domodedovo on 15th August 2002 displays the stylish livery of Kogalymavia, doing business as Kolavia. Author

Komiavia Tu-134AK RA 65613 in basic Interflug colours is seen here landing at Moscow-Sheremet'yevo. Yuriy Kirsanov

Tu-134AK RA-65608 in full Komiavia colours at Ghelendjik in September 2000. Yefim Gordon

immediately given a stylish new livery with a red/white/blue cheatline and a blue tail with a Planet-Earth-cum-orbiting-satellite logo; RA-65726 retained full Aeroflot colours until 1999. A fourth aircraft, radar-nosed Tu-134A-3 'Salon' RA-65941 (ex-LZ-TUS, c/n (83)60642, f/n 4805), was acquired from Menatep Bank in 1998; it still carries basic Menatep colours without titles.

KRAS AIR (Krasnoyarsk Airlines/*Krasnoyarskiye avialinii*) [7B/KJC] based at Krasnoyarsk-Yemel'yanovo operated eight Tu-134s.

Registration	Version	C/n	F/n	Notes
RA-65560	Tu-134A-1	(83)60321	4504	Lsf Ulan-Ude Aircraft Factory 18-6-02, basic Barguzin c/s, Kras Air titles
RA-65605	Tu-134A/r.n.	(43)09070	2310	Leased from ARZ No 407, full c/s. Damaged Irkutsk-1 16-7-02 and returned
RA-65608	Tu-134AK/r.n.*	5338040	3109	Leased from Komiinteravia by 6-00, returned by 12-01; basic Komiavia c/s, Kras Air titles
RA-65616	Tu-134AK/r.n.*	4352206		Leased from Komiinteravia 11-01 to ?-02
RA-65618	Tu-134A-3/r.n.	4312095	2410	Leased from Komiinteravia ?-01 to ?-02
RA-65780	Tu-134A	(93)62622	5407	Leased from Komiinteravia by 6-00, returned by 12-01; basic Komiavia c/s, Kras Air titles
RA-65930	Tu-134A-3M	(73)66500	6374	Bought from Voronezhavia by 2-00. Red/blue cheatline, Kras Air titles/logo. Sold to Karat
RA-65960	Tu-134A 'Salon'	3351806		Lsf SibNIA ?-01; corporate c/s, no titles

RA-65930 was purchased as a passenger/cargo conversion of a Tu-134SKh with an enlarged entry door, immediately undergoing further conversion to a 40-seat executive jet. Interestingly, it wears 'Tu-134SKh' nose titles, which it never did when it *was* one!

By September 2001 **KUMERTAU AIRLINES**, the flying division of the Kumertau Aircraft Production Enterprise manufacturing Kamov helicopters, leased Tu-134A 'Salon' RA-65960 from SibNIA. The anonymous aircraft had a white top, a grey belly and a thin turquoise cheatline.

In January 1999 **LUKOIL**, one of the leading Russian petroleum companies, bought radar-nosed Tu-134AKs HA-LBN, HA-LBO and Tu-134A-3 HA-LBR from Malév Hungarian Airlines; these were reregistered RA-65944, -65942 and -65943 respectively. Concurrently 'glass-nosed' Tu-134AK EW-65861 No 2 was leased from Techaviaservice. However, as early as April-May 1999 all four aircraft were sold to Kogalymavia.

MADINA AIRLINES [–/MND] of Makhachkala, Daghestan, leases Tu-134s from Voronezhavia as required. For instance, in 1997 it operated Tu-134A RA-65062 and Tu-134A-3 RA-65067; Tu-134A-3 RA-65762 was also leased at an unknown date.

Tu-134AK RA-65005, the first to be transferred to Komiinteravia, displays the airline's striking livery at Moscow/Sheremet'yevo-1.
Dmitriy Petrochenko

Kras Air Tu-134A RA-65780 at Krasnoyarsk-Yemel'yanovo on 16th February 2001. Being leased from Komiinteravia, the aircraft retains basic ex-Komiavia colours. The 'East German style' placement of the registration on the extreme rear fuselage instead of the fin is noteworthy.
Dmitriy Petrochenko

Madina Airlines Tu-134A-3 RA-65762 takes off at Moscow-Vnukovo.
Yuriy Kirsanov

Resplendent in this green/grey/white colour scheme, Meridian Airlines Tu-134A-3M RA-65725 still retains the stylised S tail logo of its previous owner, the Sibur Group (later replaced by the Meridian logo). The airline's other Tu-134A-3M, RA-65917, had a striking red/yellow/white colour scheme following the same pattern but with a 'sun d'or' tail logo.
Sergey and Dmitriy Komissarov archive

MENATEP BANK of Moscow purchased radar-nosed Tu-134A-3 RA-65941 from Tupolev-Aerotrans in the spring of 1996 and had it outfitted as a Tu-134A-3 'Salon' by Diamonite, operating it from Moscow/Vnukovo-3 as a corporate jet. The 32-seat aircraft was painted in Menatep's house colours of maroon and white, which rendered the registration on the tail (applied in black on maroon) all but illegible. In 1998, however, the bank got into serious financial difficulties and was forced to sell the aircraft to Kosmos Aircompany.

Business charter operator **MERIDIAN AIR** [–/MMM] based at Moscow/Vnukovo-1 had two Tu-134A-3M executive jets – RA-65725 (c/n (63)66472, f/n 6371) and RA-65917 (c/n (33)63991, f/n 6329). Both were apparently purchased in 2001 from another company; the basic livery is identical but the colours are different (RA-65725 has green and grey trim while RA-65917 was red and yellow). RA-65725, which is confirmed as being second-hand, retained the tail logo of its ex-owner, Sibur JSC – a stylised S with a green leaf, at least until February 2002 (it was later replaced by the Meridian logo). Conversely, RA-65917 had a stylised 'golden sun' tail logo (by May 2003 it was applied to the fuselage of the other aircraft as well). By December 2003 RA-65917 was sold to an unknown Ukrainian owner as UR-65917.

About 20 Tu-134s were operated by various divisions of the **MINISTRY OF AIRCRAFT INDUSTRY** (MAP). This was liquidated in 1996, but a successor was formed in 1999 in the shape of the Russian Aerospace Agency (RAKA – *Rosseeyskoye aviatsionno-kosmicheskoye aghentstvo*); thus it makes sense to describe all the factories together. MAP Tu-134s were usually operated in Aeroflot colours with or without titles; in post-Soviet times several aircraft wore Rossiya (Russia) titles in stylised Old Russian script, although they had nothing in common with the Rossiya State Transport Company (see below).

Registration	Version	C/n	F/n	Notes
CCCP-65109	Tu-134AK	(83)60339	4507	KhAPO? To Ukrainian CAD/Khar'kov UAD
RA-65560	Tu-134A-1 'Salon'	(83)60321	4504	Ex-CCCP-65560, ex-Aviogenex YU-AJW, D/D 1985, D-30-III engines; Rossiya titles. U-UAPO[6]. Later to 76-seater
RA-65563	Tu-134A-1 'Salon'	(73)60035	4204	Ex-CCCP-65563, ex-Aviogenex YU-AJV, D/D 1985, D-30-III engines. NAPO[6]. Leased to Flight ?-02
RA-65564	Tu-134A-1	(03)63165	5609	Ex-CCCP-65564, ex-Aviogenex YU-ANE, D/D 1985, D-30-III engines. KnAAPO[6]
RA-65653	Tu-134A	0351009		SibNIA. Leased to Sirius-Aero by 5-00, SOC ?-03
RA-65669	Tu-134K	9350916		Ex-CCCP-65669, ex-Iraqi Airways YI-AED. Perm' Engine Factory (Perm'transavia-PM), bought from LNPO Leninets? SOC 1998
RA-65738	Tu-134A	2351507		SibNIA. Lst Tyumen' Airlines; SOC ?-03?
RA-65739	Tu-134A	2351509		Operator unknown
CCCP-65855	Tu-134A	(53)23252	2710	Myasishchev Experimental Machinery Plant (EMZ); to Air Transport School as RA-65855
CCCP-65922	Tu-134	9350805		Ex-LOT SP-LGD, D/D by 1983; OAPO?[6] SOC 1995, preserved Omsk
CCCP-65924	Tu-134	9350806		Ex-LOT SP-LGE, D/D by 1983; KnAAPO. SOC by 1995
RA-65932	Tu-134A-3 'Salon'	(43)66405	6367	Sukhoi OKB, Rossiya titles. Leased to Gromov Air by 4-03
CCCP-65933	Tu-134	8350602		Ex-LOT SP-LGA, D/D by 1983; Myasishchev EMZ? SOC by 1995
RA-65934	Tu-134AK	(33)66143	6342	D-30-III engines. IAPO[6] (Irkut JSC). Leased to AeroTex by 7-99
RA-65960	Tu-134A 'Salon'	3351806		SibNIA. Leased to Kras Air ?-01
RA-65983	Tu-134AK	(03)63350	5808	Ex-Russian AF Tu-134 Balkany, D-30-III engines. Perm' Engine Factory (Perm'transavia-PM); sold to Gazpromavia 4-98

RA-93926	Tu-134A-1	1351204		Ex-CCCP-93926 No 2†, ex-Aviogenex YU-AHY, D/D 28-12-90, D-30-III engines. AAPO[6]
RA-93927	Tu-134A-1	2351508		Ex-CCCP-93927, ex-Aviogenex YU-AJD, D/D 24-12-90, D-30-III engines. KnAAPO
RA-93929	Tu-134A-1	1351206		Ex-CCCP-93929 No 2†, ex-Aviogenex YU-AJA, D/D 28-12-90, D-30-III engines. IAPO; SOC by 2003
CCCP-93930	Tu-134A-1	1351203		Ex-Aviogenex YU-AHX, D/D 24-12-90, D-30-III engines. Sold to Aero Tumi as OB-1489

† CCCP-93926 No 1 was an MAP-operated IL-14; CCCP-93929 No 1 was an An-26 c/n 10704 which was reregistered CCCP-26216.

In 1998 the **RUSSIAN MINISTRY OF THE INTERIOR** took delivery of Tu-134AK RA-65990, a former Tu-134 *Balkany* ABCP transferred from the Russian Air Force. This was the ministerial aircraft of Vadim B Rushaylo and later his successor Boris Gryzlov. The anonymous-looking aircraft has a white top, a grey belly and a thin cheatline in the Russian flag colours running beneath the windows and curving downwards to the radome.

The **MINISTRY OF ELECTRONICS INDUSTRY** (MRP), now likewise liquidated, operated numerous Tu-134s assigned to the ministry's research institutes and used mostly as avionics testbeds. Many of them were later reconverted to standard and operated by the commercial divisions of the respective institutes.

Regn / Code	Version	C/n	F/n	Notes
RA-65097	Tu-134AK	(83)60540	4704	NPO Vzlyot (Elf Air). Leased to Primair by 6-99
65098	Tu-134SL (SL-134Sh)	73550815	0805?	Converted Tu-134Sh-1. Leninets Holding Co (NPP Mir), radar testbed. Ex-'Tu-134A' CCCP-65098 (LNPO Leninets)
RA-65099	Tu-134AK	(13)63700	6201	NPO Vzlyot (Elf Air). Sold to Trans-Charter ?-97
RA-65562	Tu-134LL	2350201		Converted Tu-134Sh-1. GosNII AS; testbed/ surveyer. C/n also reported as 2350104 or 2350204. WFU Zhukovskiy by 8-99
RA-65604	Tu-134AK	(93)62561	5403	Ex-CCCP-65604 No 2; ex-avionics testbed, NPO Vzlyot (Elf Air). Leased to Chernomor-Avia by 8-00
CCCP-65669	Tu-134K	9350916		Ex-Iraqi Airways YI-AED; transferred from Soviet AF. LNPO Leninets (SL-134K testbed)? To MAP/Perm' Engine Factory
CCCP-65687	Tu-134AK	(93)62400	5302	NPO Vzlyot? Avionics testbed; crashed Severomorsk 17-6-82
RA-65906	Tu-134AK	(33)66175	6345	NPO Vega-M, IMARK geophysical survey aircraft. Reconverted and sold to Nefteyugansk Airlines ?-97
CCCP-65907	Tu-134AK	(33)63996	6333	NPO Fazotron, radar testbed. Reconverted and sold to Alrosa-Avia as RA-65907 1-94
RA-65908	Tu-134AK	(13)63870	6307	NPO Vzlyot (Elf Air), ex-avionics testbed. Sold to Yermolino Airlines ?-97
RA-65931	Tu-134BV	(33)66185	6347	Leninets Holding Co, Aeroflot colours
01 Red	Tu-134Sh-1	63550705	?	NPO Vzlyot, avionics testbed. WFU Zhukovskiy by 8-95; scrapped by 8-01? C/n also reported as 3350705 or 6350705
11 Red	Tu-134UBL	(13)64010	6401	[RA-64010]† Leninets Holding Co, radar testbed. Often reported in error as '100 Blue'. Sold to Roos' Leasing Co ?-02 and converted to 'Tu-134B-3' RA-65945
30 Red	Tu-134UBL	(33)64845	?	Ex-'42 Red'? [RA-64845]. NPO Fazotron, avionics testbed
no code	Tu-134UBL	(33)64740	?	Ex-'21 Red' [RA-64740]. NPO Vega-M, radar testbed

† The registration RA-64010 was used in 1993 for an Ul'yanovsk-built Tu-204 which later became the prototype of the Tu-204S cargo version.

RA-65931 and Tu-134UBL '11 Red' were also reported for **NPP MIR** [–/NPP], the commercial division of the Leninets Holding Co based at Pushkin. (NPP = na**ooch**no-proiz**vod**stvennoye predpri**ya**tiye – Scientific & Production Enterprise.)

MOSCOW AIRWAYS [M8/MSC] based at Sheremet'yevo-2 briefly leased Tu-134A-3 RA-65966 from Tupolev-Aerotrans; some sources report Tu-134AK RA-65939 was briefly leased from the same company in April 1995. Only the former aircraft wore red Moscow Airways titles.

MOSTRANSGAZ, one of the natural gas industry's (initially) many flying divisions, operated an unidentified Tu-134AK or Tu-134A 'Salon' in 1995. In April 1997 the airline was integrated into Gazpromavia.

MURMANSK AIRLINES (*Moormanskiye avialinii*) [–/MNK] based at Murmansk-Murmashi leased Tu-134A RA-65083 from AVL Arkhangel'sk Airlines in early 1997, returning it by early 1998.

Starting in March 1998, **NEFTEYUGANSK AIRLINES** [–/NGT] based at Nefteyugansk (Tyumen' Region) operated three Tu-134AKs – RA-65097 and RA-65604 (leased from Elf Air) and RA-65906 (the former IMARK survey aircraft) equipped to Tu-134A-3 standard. The latter two aircraft were outfitted as 80-seaters.

In 1999 the name was changed to **PRIMAIR** [–/PMM], probably because foreigners had trouble pronouncing 'Nefteyugansk'. While RA-65097 initially retained the old tail logo, RA-65604 introduced a new three-legged horse logo. RA-65097 is operated for the Moscow City Department of Construction since 1999, with an appropriate badge on the port side. In 1999 RA-65906 was sold to Tulpar, RA-65604 returning to the lessor in Y2K. In turn, Tu-134A-3 RA-65035 was leased from the Kirov Air Enterprise by May 2000 but returned in 2003.

NIZHEGORODSKIYE AVIALINIÏ [–/NGL] (that is, Nizhniy Novgorod Airlines, formerly the Gor'kiy UAD of the Volga CAD) had eight Tu-134s. They wore basic Aeroflot colours with a red 'HH' (that is, Cyrillic 'NN' for Nizhniy Novgorod) tail logo, Russian titles to port and 'Nizhegorodsky Airlines' titles to starboard! Indeed, *'a mix of tongues, the French and Nizhniy dialect'*, as 19th century Russian poet Aleksandr S Griboyedov wrote in his comedy *Wit Works Woe*.

In the late 1990s the airline's financial position was shaky, with RUR 50 million (US\$ 1.89 million) of debts as of mid-1999. Aeroflot Russian International Airlines considered taking over the ailing carrier as a way of expanding its route network, and in May 1999 a memorandum of understanding was signed with the Nizhniy Novgorod Region administration concerning the establishment of Aeroflot Nizhniy Novgorod JSC. Later, however, Aeroflot dropped these plans; eventually Nizhegorodskiye Avialiniï went bankrupt in 2002.

Tu-134A-1 RA-65563 (equipped to Tu-134A-3 standard) in the full colours of NAPO-Aviatrans, the flying division of the Novosibirsk aircraft factory, at Novosibirsk-Yel'tsovka. Dmitriy Petrochenko

Primair Tu-134AK RA-65097 at Moscow-Domodedovo on 15th August 2002. Note the open service panel of the forward toilet just visible under the fuselage in line with the blanked-off first full-size window. Author

Lit by the setting sun, Orenburg Airlines Tu-134A RA-65860 is serviced at Moscow-Domodedovo on 20th November 1998 (note the water wagon behind the aircraft). Author

Still in the colours of defunct Orient Avia, Tu-134A RA-65144 'Kishinev' languishes on the GosNII GA ramp at Moscow/Sheremet'yevo-1 in mid-1998 in company with Transaero Express Tu-134AK RA-65830 and LUKoil Yak-142 RA-42424, awaiting sale to a new owner. Mikhail Yevdokimov

Permskiye Avialinïï (Perm' Airlines) Tu-134A-3 RA-65064 during a turnaround at Moscow/Vnukovo-1 on 29th May 2000. Author

RA-65004 was the first Tu-134A to be painted in Pulkovo Air Enterprise colours and the only one to wear the light-coloured version. It is seen here at St Petersburg-Pulkovo in April 1997. Yuriy Yelookov

Yet another 'incarnation' of Tu-134A RA-65144 – this time in the colours of the Pulkovo Air Enterprise. All of the airline's Tu-134s in full livery use this dark shade of blue, except Tu-134A RA-65004 which has a lighter shade. Dmitriy Petrochenko

Registration	Version	C/n	F/n	Notes
RA-64451	Tu-134AK/r.n.*	(63)66550	6375	Ex-Kampuchea Airlines XU-102; D-30-III engines, basic Kampuchea Airlines c/s, Aeroflot titles. D/D 8-95; never operated, stored Nizhniy Novgorod-Strigino until sold to Tatneft'aero 2-01 as RA-65570
RA-65043	Tu-134A	(63)49400	3801	Sold to ARZ No 412 ?-00
RA-65045	Tu-134AK	(63)49500	3803	Sold to Gazpromavia 3-98
RA-65065	Tu-134AK*	(73)49890	4007	Ex-Kampuchea Airlines XU-101, D/D 8-95, D-30-III engines. Sold to Tatarstan Air 1-02
RA-65823	Tu-134A	(43)09073	2402	Possibly Tu-134A 'Salon'. WFU Nizhniy Novgorod-Strigino ?-98, SOC ?-00/used for spares
RA-65829	Tu-134A-3	(43)12087	2408	WFU Nizhniy Novgorod-Strigino ?-95, SOC ?-00/used for spares
RA-65867	Tu-134A	(53)28296	2902	WFU Nizhniy Novgorod-Strigino ?-98, SOC 4-01/used for spares
RA-65970	Tu-134AK*	3351910		Sold to ARZ No 412 ?-00

NOVOROSSIYSK AIRLINES (*Novorosseeyskiye avialinii*) [–/NRL] leased Tu-134s from other carriers as required.

NOVOSIBIRSK AIRLINES (*Novosibeerskiye avialinii*) [L8/NLB] based at Tolmachovo airport leased Tu-134AK RA-65935 from Aviaobshchemash in 1996. In 1997 it was returned and replaced by Tu-134A-3 RA-65057 leased from Voronezhavia; additionally, radar-nosed Tu-134AK RA-65609 was leased from Komiaviatrans in 1998-2000.

ORENBURG AIRLINES [R2/ORB] operated seven Tu-134A-3s.

Registration	Version	C/n	F/n	Notes
RA-65049	Tu-134A-3	(73)49755	3808	Ex-Gomel'avia EW-65049, bought by 9-02. Leased to UTair by 12-02
RA-65101	Tu-134A-3	(83)60260	4407	
RA-65110	Tu-134A-3	(83)60343	4508	
RA-65117	Tu-134A-3	(83)60450	4606	Leased to Tyumen'AviaTrans ?-02
RA-65136	Tu-134A-3	(83)60885	4810	
RA-65847	Tu-134A-3	(43)23135	2701	Leased to Tyumen'AviaTrans by 8-01. SOC ?-02
RA-65860	Tu-134A-3	(53)28265	2805	Leased to Tyumen'AviaTrans by 8-01. SOC ?-03

ORIENT AVIA [V6/ORT] based at Moscow/Sheremet'yevo-1 served mostly destinations in the Russian Far East (hence the name). Wishing to expand its route network, in 1996 the airline bought a pair of Tu-134A-3s – RA-65091 (ex-Lithuanian Airlines LY-ABG, c/n 8360195, f/n 4310) and RA-65144 (ex-Estonian Air ES-AAK, c/n (93)60977, f/n 4909). The latter aircraft was named 'Kishinyov', probably after its usual destination.

The airline was suffering serious financial troubles. In an attempt to resolve them Orient Avia approached East Line (then a pure cargo airline), trying to negotiate a merger. Yet the deal fell through and on 10th July 1997 Orient Avia filed for bankruptcy. After prolonged storage RA-65091 was sold to ELK Estonian Airways in 1998 as ES-LTA while RA-65144 was bought by Aviaexpresscruise.

PERM AIRLINES (*Permskiye avialinii*) [UP/PGP, later 9D/PGP][7] based at Perm'-Bol'shoye Savino had seven Tu-134As

Registration	Version	C/n	F/n	Notes
RA-65035	Tu-134A-3	(63)48590	3702	Sold to Kirov Air Enterprise
RA-65046	Tu-134A-3	(63)49550	3804	C/n sometimes rep. in error as (63)49700. Lsf Bashkirian Airlines 8-99; Permskiye avialinii titles but BAL tail logo
RA-65059	Tu-134A-3	(73)49870	4001	
RA-65064	Tu-134A-3	(73)49886	4006	
RA-65751	Tu-134A-3 'Salon'	(93)61066	5007	Perm Airlines titles; later reconverted to 76-seater and Permskiye avialinii titles applied
RA-65775	Tu-134A-3	(93)62530	5310	Aeroflot cheatline (later painted out)
RA-65869	Tu-134A	(53)28306	2904	Sold to Volga Airlines

PERM'TRANSAVIA-PM [–/PMT], the flying division of the Perm' Engine Factory (hence the PM for *Permskiye motory*), operated Tu-134K RA-65669 (c/n 9350916). This was the sole 'short' Tu-134 to survive the break-up of the Soviet Union and gain a new prefix – and the oldest flying Tu-134 as of 1998, thanks no doubt to low flying hours accumulated during its career as a VIP jet and a testbed. In February 1997 it was joined by Tu-134AK RA-65983, a former Russian Air Force Tu-134 *Balkany* (c/n (03)63350, f/n 5808). It was the only aircraft to wear the airline's full colours. Yet, as early as April 1998 RA-65983 was sold to Gazpromavia, the other aircraft being retired by mid-1998.

Moscow/Sheremet'yevo-1 based **PHOENIX AIRLINES** [–/FNH], a subsidiary of Inkombank, bought Tu-134AK RA-65801 from the Ul'yanovsk Higher Flying School in 1998. In February 2000 the airline leased Tu-134A-3 'Salon' RA-65067 from Voronezhavia. Unlike the former aircraft which had an attractive colour scheme (and the registration applied just aft of the flightdeck), RA-65067 retained basic Voronezhavia colours without titles. The airline ceased operations in June 2001; RA-65801 was apparently retired while RA-65067 returned to the lessor, regaining full colours.

In 1993-94 **POLIS AIR** [–/PMR] based at Arkhangel'sk-Talagi leased Tu-134A-3 RA-65084 from AVL Arkhangel'sk Airlines. Repainted in a beige/white livery, the aircraft was sub-leased to Air Guinée.

POLYARNYYE AVIALINII (Polar Airlines) based in Polyarnyy, Yakutia, leased Tu-134As from Voronezhavia as required.

The **PULKOVO AIR ENTERPRISE** (formerly **ST PETERSBURG AIR ENTERPRISE**) [Z8/PLK] operated a total of 21 Tu-134s. For years the entire fleet wore Aeroflot colours with or without titles. It was not until 1997 that Pulkovo introduced its own livery, by which time it was too late for some of the aircraft!

Registration	Version	C/n	F/n	Notes
RA-65004	Tu-134A-3	(63)44060	3303	Full c/s (light), first Tu-134 repainted
RA-65020	Tu-134A-3	(63)48380	3503	
RA-65042	Tu-134AK*	(63)49350	3710	D-30-III engines; full c/s (dark)
RA-65068	Tu-134A-3	(73)49907	4101	Ex-Estonian Air ES-AAG, D/D 8-95; full c/s (dark)
RA-65088	Tu-134A-3	(73)60172	4307	Ex-Clintondale Tu-134A-3 'Salon', D/D 12-98; ex-Lithuanian Airlines LY-ABF. Full c/s (dark)
RA-65093	Tu-134AK*	(83)60215	4402	Ex-Air Ukraine UR-65093, D/D ?-97, D-30-III engines; full c/s (dark)
RA-65109	Tu-134AK*	(83)60339	4507	Ex-Air Ukraine UR-65109, D/D ?-98, D-30-III engines; full c/s (dark)
RA-65112	Tu-134A-3	(83)60350	4510	Ex-Estonian Air ES-AAI, D/D 5-96; full c/s (dark)
RA-65113	Tu-134A-3	(83)60380	4601	Ex-Estonian Air ES-AAM, D/D 8-95; later to Tu-134A?
RA-65128	Tu-134A-3	(83)60628	4710	Ex-Lithuanian Airlines LY-ABI, D/D 3-97
RA-65144	Tu-134A	(93)60977	4909	Bought from Aviaexpresscruise by 10-00, ex-Estonian Air ES-AAK; full c/s (dark)
RA-65759	Tu-134A	(93)62239	5110	Ex-Estonian Air ES-AAO, D/D 8-95; full c/s (dark)
RA-65815	Tu-134A-3	4352209		SOC by 1996

Registration	Type	C/n	F/n	Notes
RA-65837	Tu-134A-3	(43)17114	2509	Ex-Tu-134A-3 'Salon'. SOC by 1998
RA-65851	Tu-134A-3	(43)23241	2705	SOC by 1997
RA-65854	Tu-134A-3	(53)23248	2708	SOC by 1997
RA-65862	Tu-134A-3	(53)28270	2807	SOC by 1998
RA-65872	Tu-134A-3	(53)29312	2907	SOC by 1998
RA-65885	Tu-134A-3	(53)36160	3102	SOC by 1997
RA-65894	Tu-134A-3	(53)40130	3202	SOC by 1997
RA-65967	Tu-134A-3	3351905		SOC by 1997

The re-export and ex-Ukrainian aircraft all have four business class seats and 56 tourist class seats (except RA-65088, which is an 80-seater). The aircraft inherited from the 1st Leningrad UAD originally retained their 76-seat layout, but in 1998 the surviving examples were reconfigured with 16 business class seats and 52 tourist class seats.

Over the years the 235th Independent Air Detachment (the Soviet Federal Government flight) based at Moscow-Vnukovo operated a steady succession of Tu-134s, not all of which were VIP-configured (indeed, some weren't even Tu-134AKs!). On 3rd December 1993 the 235th IAD became **GTK ROSSIYA** (*Gosoodarstvennaya trahnsportnaya kompaniya 'Rossiya'* – Russia State Transport Co) [R4/SDM]. This operated 17 Tu-134AKs equipped to Tu-134A-3 standard.

Registration	C/n	F/n	Notes
RA-65552†	(43)66270	6358	C/s No 1. Jointly opw Aeroflot; sold to Yamal ?-99
RA-65553†	(43)66300	6359	C/s No 3, later No 4
RA-65554†	(43)66320	6360	C/s No 1. Jointly opw Aeroflot; sold to Yamal by 5-00
RA-65555	(43)66350	6361	C/s No 3, later No 4
RA-65557	(43)66380	6365	C/s No 1. Sold to Aero Rent 3-2000
RA-65904	(23)63953	6312	C/s No 1, later No 4; Tatra-M HF comms gear
RA-65905	(23)63965	6317	C/s No 2, later No 4; Tatra-M HF comms gear
RA-65911	(23)63972	6320	C/s No 2, later No 4; Tatra-M HF comms gear
RA-65912†	(23)63985	6325	C/s No 1, later No 4
RA-65914†	(33)66109	6337	Ex-Greenair TC-GRD, c/s No 1/no titles, later No 4. Sold to Yamal 8-99
RA-65915†	(33)66120	6338	Ex-Greenair TC-GRE, c/s No 1, later No 4. Sold to Yamal ?-00
RA-65916†	(33)66152	6343	C/s No 1, later No 4. Sold to Yamal by 8-01
RA-65919	(33)66168	6344	C/s No 3, later No 4. Sold to Aero Rent by 2-01
RA-65921†	(33)63997	6334	C/s No 1, later No 4
RA-65978	(03)63357	5809	C/s No 4. Opf Russian Federal Border Guards
RA-65994	(43)66207	6352	C/s No 1, later No 4. Opf Russian Federal Border Guards
RA-65995	(43)66400	6366	C/s No 4. Opf Russian Federal Border Guards

The aircraft came in 27-, 29- and 37-seat configuration; the former two were equipped with HF comms gear identifiable by the extra blade aerials above the wing centre section and under the aft fuselage.

In Soviet times the 235th IAD's Tu-134s wore standard Aeroflot colours, except for Tu-134AK CCCP-65904 which had a fancy blue/white tail. Shortly after the demise of the USSR most of the government Tu-134AKs had the tails painted grey to make the white stripe of the Russian flag stand out, but 'Aeroflot' titles were retained for the time being. (The normal practice is to highlight this stripe with a grey 'shadow'; incidentally, many aircraft operated by the 'new' Aeroflot and some other carriers got these horrid grey tails.)

Regrettably the white livery with a blue/red cheatline, red 'Rossiya' titles in Old Russian script and the Russian coat of arms on the fin was never applied to the Tu-134AKs. On most grey-tailed examples the pinstripe below the Aeroflot cheatline was broken on the extreme nose and small blue РОССИЯ (Rossiya) titles in italics applied there (colour scheme No 1). RA-65905 wore large 'РОССИЯ' titles in gold in the same typeface above the windows (c/s No 2). RA-65553, -65555 and -65919 had small titles on the nose but the tail was white (c/s No 3).

A new fleetwide standard livery was finally introduced in July 1997 (No 4), and yours truly was disgusted when he saw it. The aircraft is grey overall with a white/blue/red cheatline and red 'Rossiya' titles in plain script. This livery has earned the disdainful nickname **seryy oozhas** ('grey horror'), though Grey Ghost would sound better perhaps. RA-65912 was the first to be repainted at Shannon (the others were resprayed at Bykovo). By 2002 some aircraft had the doors and exits outlined in blue (RA-65553) or white (RA-65555). Furthermore, three aircraft wear the badge of the Russian Federal Border Guards for which they are operated.

Since you cannot make much of a living carrying government officials alone, in 1998 GTK Rossiya started flying passenger charters, later launching scheduled services to several destinations, including the Black Sea resorts of Sochi and Anapa. Hence a major portion of the airline's fleet, including some Tu-134AKs, has been delivered in (or converted to) tourist class configuration; in the table such aircraft are marked with †. Many of GTK Rossiya's Tu-134s have been sold off as surplus.

On 6th December 2000 the **ROOS'[8] AIR TRANSPORT COMPANY** [–/RUR] based in Zhukovskiy bought the last remaining aircraft of former Georgian flag carrier ORBI, namely Tu-134A-1 4L-AAE (c/n 8360282, f/n 4409). Since the aircraft had been cannibalised for spares, it was bought for just US$ 30,000. (Yes, thirty thousand.) On the other hand, it took three months to restore it to airworthy condition; the formal handover took place on 21st February 2001. Five days later a major fuel system malfunction during the ferry flight from Kutaisi to Zhukovskiy forced the aircraft to land at Rostov. Interestingly, it was using the callsign RA-65979 at the time (see Russian Air Force).

On 14th July 2001 a Roos' Air Transport Co IL-76TD freighter (RA-76588) crashed fatally on take-off from Chkalovskaya AB. The ensuing investigation resulted in the airline's operating licence being withdrawn. In August 2003 the former 4L-AAE was still stored at Zhukovskiy in bare metal condition; its ultimate fate is unknown.

The **ROSNEFT'** (= Russian Oil) **COMPANY** operated Tu-134A-3 'Salon' RA-65088 (ex-Lithuanian Airlines LY-ABF, c/n (73)60172, f/n 4307) leased from the Avialeasing Company. The aircraft was smartly painted with a gold cheatline edged in black and the black/gold Rosneft' logo on the tail; small Cyrillic 'Avializing' titles were carried below the cheatline. In 1996 the aircraft was returned to the lessor and promptly leased to Transaero Express.

RUSAIR (formerly CGI Aero) [–/CGI][9] based at Moscow/Sheremet'yevo-1 leased Tu-134AK RA-65005 from newly-formed Komiinteravia in October 1998. The aircraft has a stylish red/white/black livery and a mixed layout with 16 business class seats and 52 tourist class seats. Another Tu-134AK, RA-65908, was leased from Yermolino Airlines by July 2000; the return date is unknown.

'Triple Nickel', Tu-134AK RA-65555 in the original livery of the Russia State Transport Co (formerly 235th Independent Flight Detachment) climbs away from runway 24 at Moscow-Vnukovo past the hangars of ARZ No 400. The grey tail was initially a 'trademark' of the government flight but was later adopted by some other Russian airlines. Note the wide unpainted fin leading edge typical of late production Tu-134AKs. Yuriy Kirsanov

Russia State Transport Co Tu-134AK RA-65912, one of several configured as 68-seaters, taxies out at Moscow/Vnukovo-1 on 29th May 2000 on a scheduled flight to Sochi. The aircraft displays the airline's current 'Grey Ghost' livery; it was another two years before the doors and emergency exits on this particular aircraft were outlined in blue. Author

Russian Air Force/978th VTAP Tu-134 Balkany '10 Black' (c/n (23)63961, f/n 6316) based at Klin-5 AB is one of very few examples in overt military markings to wear a blue/white colour scheme instead of the usual red/white one; it was repainted because the blue paint was more weather-resistant. Note the nose titles applied in the characteristic 'Tupolev typeface' of the 1950s/1960s. Sergey Panov

Russian Air Force/16th VA/226th OSAP/Special Mission Squadron Tu-134 Balkany '05 Red' (c/n (23)63976, f/n 6322) at Kubinka AB, its home base, on 8th August 1997 during the open doors day on occasion of the 16th Air Army's 55th anniversary. The very weathered finish is evident. Sergey Komissarov

By 2003 Tu-134A-3 'Salon' RA-65756 and Tu-134AK RA-65934 of Aero-Tex were sold to **RUSLINE** [–/CGI] (yes, it has the same ICAO code!) based at Moscow/Sheremet'yevo-1. Tu-134A-3 'Salon' RA-65035 joined the fleet by August 2003.

More than 200 Tu-134s were delivered to the Soviet Air Force and the Soviet Naval Aviation. Today the **RUSSIAN AIR FORCE** (VVS RF) continues to operate the Tu-134 in substantial numbers. Known first-line units are the 8th ADON/223rd OSAP (Chkalovskaya AB), 16th VA (*vozdooshnaya armiya* – air army, ≅ air force)/226th OSAP (Sperenberg AB, [East] Germany; later Kubinka AB), 4th VA/535th OSAP (Rostov-on-Don), a 23rd VA unit based at Ulan-Ude/Vostochnyy and the 148th OVTAE (*otdel'naya voyenno-trahnsportnaya aviaeskadril'ya* – independent military airlift squadron) and 978th VTAP (*voyenno-trahnsportnyy aviapolk* – military airlift regiment, ≅ Military Airlift Wing), both at Klin-5 AB, Moscow DD. Training units include the Tambov and Orsk Military Pilot Colleges, the Chelyabinsk Military Navigator College, the 652nd UAP of the DA's 43rd TsBP i PLS at Dyaghilevo AB near Ryazan' and a training air regiment at Engels-2 AB.

Due to the Soviet/Russian system of tactical codes the c/n is the only positive way of identifying aircraft in overt military markings. Hence only aircraft positively identified by c/n or location are listed below. Some Soviet Air Force examples are also included for the sake of completeness.

Regn / Code	Version	C/n	F/n	Notes
RA-14	Tu-134Sh-...?	?	?	Ex-'14'? VIP conversion
RA-19	Tu-134Sh-2	?	?	Ex-'19 Red'? VIP conversion, 43rd TsBP i PLS; basic AFL c/s, 'Tu-134' nose titles, 'Rossiya' titles in Old Russian script
RA-63775	Tu-134AK	(13)63775	6209	'St Petersburg' titles; possibly (ex) Tu-134 *Balkany* and may be ex-'35 Red' (see below)
RA-63975/ 01 Blue	Tu-134 *Balkany*	(23)63975	6321	Blue c/s with lightning bolt pinstripe; ex-'01 Black', registered by 8-01
64121	Tu-134UBL	(13)64121	?	Non-standard c/s with blue lightning bolt, blue/grey tail and 'Baikal' titles; no prefix
RA-64454	Tu-134IK	(33)66140	6341	Based Levashovo AB, Leningrad DD
CCCP-65669	*Tu-134K*	9350916		Ex-Iraqi Airways YI-AED, D/D 1970. 8th ADON, Chkalovskaya AB. To MRP (LNPO Leninets)
CCCP-65670	*Tu-134AK*	0351110		Crashed Ulan-Ude/Vostochnyy 28-7-89
CCCP-65675	*Tu-134AK*	2351705		GK NII VVS. Transferred to Belorussian CAD by 1988
CCCP-65676	*Tu-134AK*	1351502		Belorussian DD? Transferred to Belorussian CAD by 1988
CCCP-65677	?	?		Possibly Tu-134A 'Salon' c/n 2351510/ to CCCP-65740!
CCCP-65678	?	?		Possibly Tu-134A 'Salon' c/n 2351510/ to CCCP-65740!
RA-65679	Tu-134AK	(53)23249	2709	D-30-III engines, 44-seater. 8th ADON; to 223rd Flight Unit
RA-65680	Tu-134AK	(63)49020	3706	Ex-'680 Black', D-30-III engines, 44-seater. 8th ADON; to 223rd Flight Unit
RA-65681	Tu-134AK	(73)49760	3901	Ex-'681 Black', D-30-III engines, 44-seater. 8th ADON; to 223rd Flight Unit
RA-65682	Tu-134 Balkany	(93)62120	5010	Was CCCP-65682 until 1994! Based Kubinka AB until 1995, then to Chkalovskaya AB; 'Rossiya' titles in Old Russian script. Reconverted and sold to Flight ?-00
RA-65684†	Tu-134 *Balkany*	(93)62205	5107	
RA-65685†	Tu-134AK	(93)62375	5210	Ex-'685 Black'; based Domna AB, Chita, non-standard c/s
CCCP-65687	*Tu-134AK*	(93)62400	5302	Transferred to MRP (NPO Vzlyot?) ?-82
RA-65688†	Tu-134 *Balkany*	(93)62575	5404	'Rossiya' titles in Old Russian script
RA-65689	Tu-134 *Balkany*	(93)62655	5409	8th ADON; to 223rd Flight Unit
RA-65690	Tu-134 *Balkany*	(03)62805	5507	8th ADON; to 223rd Flight Unit
CCCP-65740?	*Tu-134A 'Salon'*	2351510		Had other registration when Air Force operated? Transferred to MAP (LII) ?-87

CCCP-65785	Tu-134A 'Salon'	(03)62750	5504	Moscow DD? Transferred to TsUMVS by 1988
CCCP-65830	Tu-134AK	(43)12093	2409	978th VTAP, HF comms gear. Stripped of HF comms and transferred to MGA, to RA-65830
CCCP-65888	Tu-134AK	(53)36175	3105	D-30-III engines. Northern Group of Forces (Poland)/245th OSAP? Transferred to Ukrainian CAD by 1988
CCCP-65913?	Tu-134AK?	?	?	Converted to Tu-134 Balkany in overt military markings?
RA-65962	Tu-134AK	3351901		Ex-'16 Blue'? D-30-III engines. 8th ADON; to 223rd Flight Unit. Sold to Aviaenergo 3-01
CCCP-65964	Tu-134AK?	?		Possibly Tu-134A 'Salon'
RA-65965	Tu-134AK	2351803		978th VTAP; later transferred to another unit
RA-65979	Tu-134 Balkany	(03)63158	5608	8th ADON; to 223rd Flight Unit. Reconverted and sold to Ingushetia Airlines 2-03
RA-65980	Tu-134 *Balkany*	(03)63207	5704	Ex-'980 Black'? 978th VTAP
RA-65981	Tu-134 *Balkany*	(03)63250	5709	978th VTAP
RA-65982	Tu-134 *Balkany*	(03)63315	5804	D-30-III engines; 8th ADON; to 223rd Flight Unit. Stored Chkalovskaya AB since 23-4-98
RA-65983	Tu-134 Balkany	(03)63350	5808	D-30-III engines. 8th ADON; to 223rd Flight Unit. Reconverted and sold to Perm'transavia-PM 2-97
RA-65984	Tu-134 Balkany	(03)63400	5903	D-30-III engines; 8th ADON; to 223rd Flight Unit
RA-65986	Tu-134 *Balkany*	(03)63475	6001	8th ADON; to 223rd Flight Unit
RA-65987	Tu-134 *Balkany*	(13)63505	6005	D-30-III engines; 8th ADON; to 223rd Flight Unit
RA-65988	Tu-134 *Balkany*	(13)63550	6010	8th ADON; to 223rd Flight Unit
RA-65989	Tu-134 *Balkany*	(13)63605	6104	8th ADON; to 223rd Flight Unit
RA-65990	Tu-134 Balkany	(13)63690	6110	8th ADON; to 223rd Flight Unit. Reconverted and transferred to MoI late 1998
RA-65991	Tu-134 *Balkany*	(13)63845	6304	8th ADON; to 223rd Flight Unit
RA-65992	Tu-134 *Balkany*	(13)63850	6305	8th ADON; to 223rd Flight Unit
RA-65993	Tu-134 *Balkany*	(13)63860	6306	Ex-'993 Black'. 8th ADON; to 223rd Flight Unit. Sold to Georgian AF 7-97 as 4L-65993
RA-65996	Tu-134 *Balkany*	(13)63832?	6303?	Ex-Southern Group of Forces '50 Black'/ ex-CCCP-65996? D-30-III engines; 8th ADON; to 223rd Flight Unit
CCCP-65997	*Tu-134 Balkany*	?	?	Later received overt military markings?
RA/02 Blue	Tu-134LK	(93)62732	5503	Ex-'02 Red', Yuriy A Gagarin Cosmonaut Training Centre, Chkalovskaya AB
RA-/03 Blue	Tu-134LK-2	(13)63620	6105	Ex-'03 Red', D-30-III engines; Yuriy A Gagarin Cosmonaut Training Centre, Chkalovskaya AB
01 Blue	Tu-134AK	(83)60650	4809	Ex-'01 Red', Yuriy A Gagarin Cosmonaut Training Centre, Chkalovskaya AB
02 Blue?	*Tu-134AK*	(43)08060	2306	Ex/to CCCP-65821, transferred to Belorussian CAD by 1988? Unconfirmed!

Russian Air Force/978th VTAP/2nd Squadron Tu-134Sh-2 '38 Blue' wears the blue/white version of the navigator trainer's livery (also applied initially to a Tu-134AK and the Tu-134LK/Tu-134LK-2 trainers of the Soviet Cosmonaut Group). Here it is due to undergo landing gear operation checks at Klin-5 AB. Two jacks have been installed under the front ends of the main gear fairings and a third jack under fuselage frame 60, while the forward pair of jacks and transverse frame fitting under frame 15 have yet to be installed. Sergey Panov

A standard Tu-134UBL coded '16 Red'. Note the orange-painted tip of the nose to prevent damage by ground vehicles. Vyacheslav Martynyuk

Russian Navy Tu-134Sh-1 '07 Blue' (c/n 73550795?) in basic Aeroflot colours with 'Tu-134A' nose titles, 'Rossiya' titles and Russian Navy flag on the nose visiting Klin-5 AB in 1998. The tactical code is carried on the nose gear doors only. Sergey Panov

05 Red	Tu-134 *Balkany* (23)63976	6322	[RA-63976] 226th OSAP/Special Mission Sqn, Kubinka AB; red c/s
10 Red	Tu-134 *Balkany* ?	?	Ex-Baltic DD? Seen Klin-5 AB cca. 1998
10 Blue?	*Tu-134AK*	*2351704*	*Ex/to CCCP-65952, transferred to Belorussian CAD by 1988? Unconfirmed!*
10 Black	Tu-134 *Balkany* (23)63961	6316	[RA-63961] 978th VTAP/Command & Control Sqn, Klin-5 AB; blue c/s
25 Red	Tu-134 *Balkany* 1363761	6206	[RA-63761] 226th OSAP, Sperenberg AB; to 535th OSAP, Rostov-on-Don, 1994, and possibly recoded
35 Red	Tu-134 *Balkany* ?	?	Leningrad DD (1998), red c/s; possibly c/n (13)63775, f/n 6206, to RA-63775
77 Blue	*Tu-134K*	*7350304*	*Ex-CCCP-65616 No 1/235th Independent Air Detachment; to CCCP-65616 No 1/Ukrainian CAD*
101 Blue	Tu-134 *Balkany* ?	?	Red c/s
01 Red	Tu-134Sh-1 0350001		First prototype. 929th GLITs, Akhtoobinsk
21 Blue	Tu-134Sh-2 93553016	?	978th VTAP/2nd Sqn, Klin-5 AB; red c/s. To 929th GLITs, Chkalovskaya AB, ?-01
31 Red	Tu-134Sh-2 93551050	?	
34 Blue	Tu-134Sh-2 93550970	?	978th VTAP/2nd Sqn, Klin-5 AB; blue c/s, white tail/small star
38 Blue	Tu-134Sh-2 83550968	?	978th VTAP/2nd Sqn, Klin-5 AB; blue c/s
40 Blue	Tu-134Sh-2 93550983	?	978th VTAP/2nd Sqn, Klin-5 AB; red c/s
40 Red	Tu-134Sh-1 93551120	1201?	
52 Red	Tu-134Sh-1 93550999	?	Chelyabinsk VVAUSh
57 Red	Tu-134Sh-1 73550752	?	Chelyabinsk VVAUSh
63 Blue	Tu-134Sh-1 2350104?		Red c/s; based Orsk
74 Blue	Tu-134Sh-... 53550550	0501?	
76 Blue	Tu-134Sh-1 3350302		Preserved Long-Range Aviation Museum, Engels-2 AB
78 Blue	Tu-134Sh-... 53550580	0503?	Ex-'86 Blue'
82 Red	Tu-134Sh-1 53550650	0505?	148th OVTAE. Klin-5 AB; red c/s. Later to another unit
84 Red	Tu-134Sh-1 63550720	?	148th OVTAE. Klin-5 AB; red c/s
11 Red	Tu-134UBL (*3)64245		[RA-64245]
12 Red	Tu-134UBL (13)64065		[RA-64065]
15 Red	Tu-134UBL (23)64270		[RA-64270] Orsk VVAUL
16 Red	Tu-134UBL (13)64073		[RA-64073]
17 Red	Tu-134UBL (33)64753		[RA-64753]; to Russian AF '17 Blue'?
18 Red	Tu-134UBL (33)64800		[RA-64800]
21 Red (a)	Tu-134UBL (13)64035	6403?	[RA-64035]
21 Red (b)	*Tu-134UBL*	*(33)64740*	*[RA-64740] To MRP/NPO Vega-M with no tactical code*
26 Red	Tu-134UBL (23)64392		[RA-64392]
27 Red	Tu-134UBL (23)64400		[RA-64400]
30 Red (a)	Tu-134UBL (33)64835		[RA-64835]
30 Red (b)	Tu-134UBL (33)64845		[RA-64845] Ex-Soviet AF '42 Red'? Opb 929th GLITs, Akhtoobinsk; red 'Rossiya' titles
34 Red	Tu-134UBL (13)64182		[RA-64182] Preserved Long-Range Aviation Museum, Engels-2 AB? Later to Saratov Victory Park
48 Red	Tu-134UBL (33)64830		[RA-64830] 43rd TsBP i PLS/652nd UAP, Dyaghilevo AB
not known	Tu-134UBL (13)64175		[RA-64175]

† RA-65684, -65685 and -65688 were also reported for the 223rd Flight Unit.

CCCP-65680 and -65681 (later '680 Black' and '681 Black' respectively) equipped with the Karpaty-ST VHF comms suite were used by the Soviet (Russian) Minister of Defence. Quasi-civil aircraft usually wore standard Aeroflot livery, and still do; CCCP-65684 and -65688 were an exception, sporting blue/white tails.

In the late 1990s at least three Tu-134UBLs switched from a 'Red Lightning' to a 'Blue Lightning' scheme. One such aircraft coded '17 Blue'

(presumably ex-'17 Red'; c/n (33)64753?) sports a Russian flag on the tail instead of star insignia, the new Russian Air Force badge aft of the flightdeck and large blue 'Meschchera' titles (the name of a town in central Russia) in stylised Old Russian script.

The Russian Air Force also has commercial divisions. The 223rd OSAP at Chkalovskaya AB was transformed into an 'airline' called **223RD FLIGHT UNIT STATE AIRLINE** [–/CHD]. The aircraft it operated are marked in the table.

The **RUSSIAN NAVAL AIR ARM** also operates a few Tu-134s in the VIP/ABCP and training roles.

Regn / Code	Version	C/n	F/n	Notes
RA 63757	Tu-134 *Balkany* (13)63757	6206	Pacific Fleet, based Artyom. Blue c/s with lightning bolt pinstripe, Tikho'okeanskiy flot Rossiï titles and Russian Navy flag; former tactical code unknown
07 Blue†	Tu-134Sh-1	73550795?	?	VIP conversion; basic Aeroflot c/s
14 Red	Tu-134UBL	?	?	33rd TsBP i PLS/240th GvOSAP, Ostrov AB; to be converted to Tu-134UBKM
25 Red	Tu-134UBKM	(23)64630	?	[RA-64630] First Tu-134UBL converted; 240th GvOSAP

† 07 Blue and c/n 73550795 are confirmed as operated by the Russian Navy, but it is not confirmed that they are the same aircraft.

SAAK (*Stavropol'skaya aktsionernaya aviakompaniya* – Stavropol' Joint-Stock Airline) [–/SVL] leased Tu-134A RA-65047 from GosNII GA and Tu-134AK RA-65935 from TsSKB Progress. Both were subsequently returned.

SAMARA AIRLINES [E5/BRZ], one of the biggest Russian regional carriers based at Samara-Kurumoch airport, operated 15 Tu-134s. Initially they wore basic Aeroflot colours with 'SAMARA' titles and globe logo on the fuselage. A smart red/white/blue livery was introduced in 1996; two years later the huge red 'SAMARA' titles were augmented with small 'AIRLINES' subtitles.

Registration	Version	C/n	F/n	Notes
RA-65105	Tu-134A	(83)60308	4502	Ex-Lithuanian Airlines LY-ABH, D/D 1995; basic 1994-standard LAL c/s with Samara titles/logo; full c/s by 6-99
RA-65122	Tu-134A-3	(83)60519	4702	C/n also reported as (83)60518. Full c/s
RA-65612	Tu-134AK/r.n. *	3352102		*Lsf Komiinteravia ?-00 to ?-01, full Komiavia c/s, small Samara titles on nose*
RA-65753	Tu-134A-3	(93)61099	5009	Full c/s
RA-65758	Tu-134A	(93)62230	5109	Full c/s, all-red nacelles
RA-65780	Tu-134A	(93)62622	5407	*Lsf Komiinteravia by 3-00, returned by 6-00; basic Komiavia c/s*
RA-65792	Tu-134A-3	(03)63121	5603	Full c/s
RA-65797	Tu-134A-3	(03)63173	5610	Full c/s
RA-65800	Tu-134A-3	3352009		Full c/s
RA-65889	Tu-134A	(53)38010	3106	Full c/s
RA-65902	Tu-134A-3	(13)63742	6204	*Lsf Komiinteravia by 5-00, returned?-02, basic Komiavia c/s*
RA-65926	Tu-134AK	(33)66101	6336	*Lsf Gromov Air 2-98 to ?-99; ex-Volare cheatline, Samara titles*
RA-65932	Tu-134A-3 'Salon'	(43)66405	6367	*Leased from Sukhoi OKB 11-97 to ?-??, full colour scheme*
RA-65935	Tu-134AK	(33)66180	6346	Leased from TsSKB Progress 1-01 to ?-??; basic Aeroflot c/s, TsSKB Progress titles, small Samara logo
RA-65970	Tu-134AK*	3351910		Leased from ARZ No 412 ?-02, full c/s

Above: **Russian Navy Tu-134UBL '14 Red' (c/n unknown) sits in the pouring rain at Ostrov AB, seat of the Navy's Combat & Conversion Training Centre, in 2000 with two of the Centre's Tu-22M3 bombers in the background. Though not visible here, a small Russian Navy flag is carried on the nose gear doors. Note the blue-outlined doors and exits. This aircraft** earmarked for conversion as the second Tu-134UBKM was already non-standard at the time, featuring a 'devil's pitchfork' ILS aerial under the extreme nose. Yefim Gordon

Below: **Tu-134A RA-65105 in full Samara Airlines colours at Samara-Kurumoch, with a sister ship visible beyond.** Dmitriy Petrochenko

Bottom: **With a cap of snow on the nose created by a blizzard a few days earlier, Sibaviatrans Tu-134AK RA-65615 sits at Moscow/Vnukovo-1 on 22nd March 2001. The non-functional and hence unmarked rear entry door is almost invisible in this view.** Author

SEVERAERO (= Northaero) [–/NOT] of Noril'sk briefly operated radar-nosed Tu-134A RA-65605 in 1998.

SHANS AIR [–/SNF] based at Moscow/Vnukovo-1 has three Tu-134s. 'Shans' is Russian for 'chance' or 'opportunity', but the name is an acronym referring to the company's head, **Sha**bulidze **N**ana **S**ergeyevna, hence the spelling (ShaNS)!

Registration	Version	C/n	F/n	Notes
RA-65570	Tu-134AK/r.n.	(63)66550	6375	Bought from Tatneft'aero ?-02; biz-jet c/s, no titles
RA-65692	Tu-134B-3 'Salon'	(03)63215	5705	Bought from Skyfield 5-01; opf Insat-Aero in Insat-Aero c/s
RA-65940	Tu-134AK/r.n.	3351906		Basic Aeroflot c/s, no titles. Bought from Avcom ?-99

SIBAVIATRANS (aka **SIAT**) [5M/SIB] incorporated on 1st February 1995 and based at Krasnoyarsk-Yemel'yanovo operated seven Tu-134s.

Registration	Version	C/n	F/n	Notes
UR-65076	Tu-134A-3	(73)60001	4202	Leased from UM Air by 9-01, returned by 9-02; basic Air Ukraine c/s, red Sibaviatrans titles, UM Air logo
RA-65571	Tu-134AK*	(23)63955	6313	Ex-Belorussian AF Tu-134 Balkany EW-63955; regd 18-7-02
RA-65605	Tu-134A/r.n.	(43)09070	2310	Leased from ARZ No 407 ?-99 to 3-00; basic Aeroflot c/s, blue Sibaviatrans titles
RA-65615	Tu-134AK/r.n.*	4352205		Bought from Komiinteravia ?-99, full c/s
RA-65771	Tu-134AK*	(93)62445	5305	D-30-III engines. Leased from Aeroflot-Don ?-02 to ?-03
RA-65845	Tu-134A	(43)23131	2609	Leased from Kaliningrad-Avia by 9-01
RA-65881	Tu-134AK*	(53)35220	3008	D-30-III engines. Bought from Voronezhavia by 5-00, full c/s

In 2000 the newly-acquired Tu-134AK RA-65881 wore the inscription '5 ЛЕТ' (pyat' let – five years) on the nose to mark the fifth anniversary of the airline's existence.

In 1998 **SIBIR' AIRLINES** [S7/SBI], whose main base is at Novosibirsk-Tolmachovo, leased Tu-134A-1 RA-65563 from NAPO-Aviatrans (see MAP). The aircraft was configured with 12 first class and 46 tourist class seats.

Moscow-based **SIBUR JOINT-STOCK CO**, a consortium which owns the car tyre factories in Omsk (Omskshina), Volzhskiy (Voltyre), Yekaterinburg (Uralshina) and Yaroslavl', operated Tu-134A-3M RA-65725 (a former Ivanovo Air Enterprise Tu-134SKh) in 2001. The white/green/grey aircraft wore Sibur titles and tail logo (the latter was retained after sale to Meridian Air in 2001). 'Sibur' is a contraction of 'Siberia' and 'Urals' – the regions where most of the consortium's plants are located, though Yaroslavl' is in the European part of Russia

SIRIUS AERO [–/CIG] based at Moscow/Vnukovo-1 operated seven Tu-134.

Registration	Version	C/n	F/n	Notes
RA-65099	Tu-134AK	(13)63700	6201	Bought from Yermolino Airlines 11-02, all-white with thin emerald green cheatline, no titles
RA-65550	Tu-134AK	(43)66200	6351	Leased from Ivanovo AE by 6-99, returned ?-00. Basic Aeroflot c/s, English titles and 'wing' logo
RA-65653	Tu-134A	0351009		Lsf SibNIA by 5-00. Basic AFL c/s, small Cyrillic titles, no flag; white with triple blue cheatline/no titles by 8-01. SOC by 2003

RA-65723	Tu-134A-3M	(63)66440	6369	Bought from Voronezhavia 5-02, ex-Tu-134SKh. Opf S-Air Service in all-blue c/s, no titles
RA-65724	Tu-134A-3M	(63)66445	6370	Bought from Voronezhavia 5-02, ex-Tu-134SKh. Opf S-Air Service in all-blue c/s, no titles
RA-65794	Tu-134A-3 'Salon'	(03)63135	5605	Lsf Voronezhavia by 6-00. Voronezhavia cheatline, Cyrillic titles, Russian flag on tail
RA-65880	Tu-134AK	(53)35200	3007	D-30-III engines. Lsf Voronezhavia by 5-00, all-white, no titles; triple blue cheatline added by 2-02
RA-65928	Tu-134A-3M	(63)66491	6372	Bought from Ivanovo AE 1-02, ex-Tu-134SKh, all-white with triple blue cheatline/no titles

Moscow/Sheremet'yevo-1 based **SKYFIELD** [–/SFD] bought Tu-134B-3 'Salon' YL-LBB (c/n (03)63215, f/n 5705) from Lat-Charter in November 1996. After sitting at Zhukovskiy totally devoid of markings until the spring of 1997 it was registered RA-65692, retaining the red/white colour scheme of the ex-owner with SkyField titles in Russian to port and English to starboard.

In the spring of 1998 SkyField leased Tu-134AK RA-65550 for Filipp Kirkorov's new road tour. Hence his portrait and 'Filipp Kirkorov' titles were again applied, along with a SkyField sticker. In 1999, however, the airline went bankrupt and the Tu-134AK was returned; the other aircraft sat at Moscow/Sheremet'yevo-1 until sold to ShaNS-Air in late 2000.

SPAIR AIR TRANSPORT CORPORATION [–/PAR][10] based at Yekaterinburg-Kol'tsovo, mainly concerned with cargo operations briefly leased Tu-134A-3 RA-65786 from Chelal in September 1994. The letters SP in the carrier's name are the initials of its director, Valeriy Spoornov.

STIGL ('sky' in Chechenian) was formed in September 1992 as the first Chechen airline, operating a total of eight Tu-134As. One of them was the presidential aircraft of Gen Djokhar Dudayev. Most aircraft had no registration prefix, since the self-proclaimed 'Chechen Republic of Ichkeria' was not recognised by ICAO.

At least two aircraft had a green cheatline with a yellow pinstripe above and a red pinstripe below, red 'STIGL' titles, a red/yellow spiral tail logo and a Chechen flag; the others retained the Aeroflot cheatline, carrying only the logo.

Almost the entire fleet was destroyed at Groznyy-Severnyy, its home base, by a Russian Air Force raid on 11th December 1994 as the First Chechen War broke out.

Registration	Version	C/n	F/n	Notes
65003	Tu-134A-3	(53)44040	3302	Loaned from Tajik CAD; returned ?-94, to EY-65003
65014	Tu-134A-3	(63)46200	3404	Full c/s. Destroyed Groznyy-Severnyy 11-12-94
65030	Tu-134A-3	(63)48520	3606	Reported as presidential aircraft; full c/s? Destroyed Groznyy-Severnyy 11-12-94
65039	Tu-134A-3	(63)49080	3707	Reported in error as to RA-65039. Escaped to Sudan; last noted dumped Khartoum 2-02
65075	Tu-134A-3	(73)49998	4201	Destroyed Groznyy-Severnyy 11-12-94
CCCP-65858	Tu-134A-3	(53)23256	2803	Aeroflot c/s, no flag. Probably destroyed Groznyy-Severnyy 11-12-94
CCCP-65868	Tu-134A	(53)28305	2903	Aeroflot c/s, no flag. Probably destroyed Groznyy-Severnyy 11-12-94 (see also Chapter 7/Sudan!)
65896	Tu-134A-3	(53)42200	3205	Destroyed Groznyy-Severnyy 11-12-94

Some sources claim Stigl also operated Tu-134 sans suffixe CCCP-65631 (c/n 9350902) in full Aeroflot colours until it was retired at Groznyy-Severnyy in 1994. (The hulk of this aircraft was also destroyed.) Even more improbably, other sources list **RA-65858** and **RA-65868** as operated by Donavia!

Top: **Unfortunately the only available photo of Tu-134A 65014, one of two which wore the full colours of the Chechen airline Stigl, shows the aircraft in the form of wreckage after it had been destroyed at Groznyy-Severnyy airport on 11th December 1994.** ITAR-TASS

Above: **Despite the 'Rossiya' titles, Tu-134A 'Salon' RA-65932 seen here being refuelled at St Petersburg-Pulkovo in the mid-1990s is not a Russia State Transport Co Aircraft but belongs to MAP – specifically, the Sukhoi OKB. This was the last example built as a Tu-134A with no rear entry door. Note the wide unpainted fin leading edge usually found on late-production Tu-134AKs.** Pyotr Batuyev

Below: **Tatarstan Airlines Tu-134AK RA-65691, a former Russian Air Force aircraft, takes off at Moscow-Domodedovo.** Yuriy Kirsanov

Moscow-based **STOLICHNY BANK OF SAVINGS** (SBS-Bank; *'stolichnyy'* means 'located in, or pertaining to, the capital') operated Tu-134AK RA-65099 on lease from Elf Air (later from Trans-Charter and Yermolino Airlines). Unlike most corporate aircraft in Russia, it wore full titles in Russian and English.

The Sukhoi OKB, a world famous designer of combat and competition aerobatic aircraft (see MAP), has a division called **SUKHOI DESIGN BUREAU AIR TRANSPORT COMPANY** [–/SDB]. This owns Tu-134A-3 'Salon' RA-65932 which is periodically leased out, the most recent lessee as of May 2003 being Gromov Air.

TATARSTAN AIR (*AviakompaniyaTatarstan*) [U9/KAZ] operated six Tu-134s from Kazan'-International.

Registration	Version	C/n	F/n	Notes
RA-65021	Tu-134AK*	(63)48390	3504	Full c/s, D-30-III engines. Lsf Cheboksary Air Enterprise 3-99 to ?-01; CAE cheatline, TATARSTAN titles, Russian flag on tail
RA-65023	Tu-134A-3	(63)48415	3508	Ex-Prestige-Avia UR-65023, D/D ?-03; red/blue cheatline
RA-65033	Tu-134A-3	(63)48540	3609	No titles. Lsf Cheboksary Air Enterprise by 7-02; CAE cheatline, TATARSTAN titles/logo
RA-65065	Tu-134AK*	(73)49890	4007	Bought from Nizhegorodskiye Avialinii 1-02
RA-65691	Tu-134AK*	(03)63195	5703	Leased from Volga-Aviaexpress 12-2000, later bought; full c/s
RA-65973	Tu-134A-3	3352003		Ex-Lietuva LY-ABA, D/D 10-99; full c/s

In January 2001 **TATNEFT'AERO** [–/TNF], the airline of the Tatneft' (Tatarstan Oil Co) corporation, bought radar-nosed Tu-134AK RA-64451 from Nizhegorodskiye Avialinii. Reregistered RA-65570, the aircraft received Tatneft'aero's pleasing livery with a cheatline in the Tatarstan flag colours of green, white and red. In March the aircraft was leased to Aerofreight Airlines and the 'TAT*NEFT*AERO' titles were removed. In February 2002 Tatneft'aero suspended operations and the aircraft was sold to ShaNS-Air.

Moscow/Sheremet'yevo-1 based **TRANSAERO EXPRESS** operated three Tu-134s.

Registration	Version	C/n	F/n	Notes
RA-65088	Tu-134A-3 'Salon'	(73)60172	4307	Ex-Lithuanian Airlines LY-ABF, lsf Aeroleasing; Rosneft' Oil Co c/s with additional large Transaero Express titles
RA-65830	Tu-134AK	(43)12093	2409	Ex-Russian Air Force. Red/blue cheatline and tail stripe, large Transaero Express titles. Sold to Karat 7-99
RA-65926	Tu-134AK	(33)66101	6336	Lsf Volare ?-95; full Volare c/s with additional small Transaero Express titles, later white with double dark blue cheatline, Russian flag on tail and large Transaero Express titles

In 1997 Moscow-based **TRANS-CHARTER** [–/TCH] bought Tu-134AK RA-65099 from Elf Air; this did not affect operations of the aircraft which was still leased to SBS-Bank, operating from Vnukovo-1. By August 1999 Trans-Charter went out of business, selling the aircraft to Yermolino Airlines.

The **TRET'YAKOVO AIR TRANSPORT COMPANY** [–/TKO] operated three Tu-134s from Moscow-Domodedovo and Lookhovitsy-Tret'yakovo, the factory airfield of the Moscow Aircraft Production Association (MAPO). The aircraft wore basic Aeroflot colours with large Cyrillic 'TRET'YAKOVO' titles.

Unfortunately, one of Tret'yakovo's aircraft (IL-62M RA-86452) crashed on landing at Bishkek-Manas airport on 23rd October 2002. The investigation that followed resulted in the airline's operating licence being revoked on 30th January 2003.

Registration	Version	C/n	F/n	Notes
RA-65057	Tu-134A-3	(73)49865	3909	Leased from Voronezhavia ?-01, Voronezhavia cheatline; returned
RA-65065	Tu-134AK*	(73)49890	4007	Leased from Nizhegorodskiye Avialinii ?-01; returned
RA-65550	Tu-134AK	(43)66200	6351	Bought from Ivanovo State AE ?-00; fate unknown

The flying division of **TsSKB PROGRESS** [–/PSS] (*Tsentrahl'noye spetsiahl'noye konstrooktorskoye byuro* – Central Special Design Bureau) based at the industrial airfield of Samara-Bezymyanka operated ex-Aviaobshchemash Tu-134AK RA-65935 in basic Aeroflot colours with red titles. This is an MOM enterprise which created, among other things, the Proton SLV. The 'airline' ceased operationson 9th January 2003; the aircraft was sold to Avialinii 400.

Kazan'-based **TULPAR** [–/TUL] (the name means 'winged steed' in Tatarian) bought Tu-134AK RA-65906 from Nefteyugansk Airlines in 1999. In late 2000 it was joined by Tu-134A 'Salon' RA-65079 (ex-Aurela Co LY-ASK, c/n (73)60054, f/n 4206) which retained the ex-owner's white/grey/red colours. Both aircraft were sold in January 2001 to Avcom and Yamal respectively.

Like most Russian aviation design bureaux, ANTK Tupolev established its own airline, **TUPOLEV-AEROTRANS** [–/TUP], in 1996. It operated six Tu-134s, mostly in Aeroflot colours without titles; these were mostly leased to other carriers. In mid-2000 the airline ceased operations.

Registration	Version	C/n	F/n	Notes
RA-65667	Tu-134A/r.n.	1351207		WFU Zhukovskiy 9-99
RA-65720	Tu-134B-1-3	(03)62820	5508	Tupolev-Aerotrans titles/Tupolev logo applied ?-97. Sold to ISD-Avia 8-00 as UR-BYY
RA-65939	Tu-134AK*	1351409		Ex-Bulgarian Air Force LZ-TUU, bought by 8-95; D-30-III engines, 72-seater. Sold to Gromov Air ?-97
RA-65940	Tu-134AK/r.n.	3351906		Ex-Bulgarian Air Force LZ-TUM, D-30-III engines, bought 8-95. Sold to Avcom ?-97
RA-65941	Tu-134A-3/r.n.	(83)60642	4805	Ex-Balkan LZ-TUS, bought by 8-95. Sold to Menatep Bank 4-96
RA-65966	Tu-134A-3	3351902		Enlarged entry door and emergency exits. WFU Zhukovskiy by 8-97

ANTK Tupolev also owned two prototypes which were not part of the Tupolev-Aerotrans fleet – Tu-134A-3 CCCP-65624 (c/n 8350601) and Tu-134SKh CCCP-65917 (c/n (33)63991, f/n 6329) which were withdrawn from use/stored at Zhukovskiy by 1993. The former aircraft was eventually delivered to EMERCOM of Russia as a ground trainer in 1997, while CCCP-65917 was sold on 3rd March 2001 (apparently to Meridian Air) to become Tu-134A-3M RA-65917.

TYUMEN' AIRLINES/TYUMENSKIYE AVIALINIÏ [7M/TYM] based at Tyumen'-Roschchino operated 17 Tu-134s. However, the airline's financial state went from bad to worse after the 1998 Russian bank crisis and eventually the carrier was declared bankrupt, ceasing operations on 1st November 2003 when no buyer could be found. The fate of the fleet (including the nine surviving Tu-134s) remains to be seen.

Registration	Version	C/n	F/n	Notes
RA-65009	Tu-134A	(63)46120	3308	
RA-65012	Tu-134A	(63)46175	3402	
RA-65017	Tu-134AK*	(63)48360	3409	
RA-65025	Tu-134A	(63)48450	3601	Basic Aeroflot c/s, Tyumen' Airlines titles/ logo. Sold to Kazakstan AF as 65025 by 8-02
RA-65038	Tu-134A	(63)48950	3705	
RA-65063	Tu-134A	(73)49880	4005	
RA-65127	Tu-134A-3 'Salon'	(83)60627	4709	Ex-Tajikistan Airlines EY-65127, ex-Estonian Air ES-AAJ, D/D 11-93; opf Zapsibgazprom, full colour scheme with additional Zapsibgazprom titles
RA-65651	Tu-134A-3	0351007		SOC by 1998
RA-65653	Tu-134A	0351009		Lsf SibNIA ?-94, returned by 5-00; basic Aeroflot c/s, Tyumen' Airlines titles/logo
RA-65661	Tu-134A	0351107		SOC by 2000
RA-65738	Tu-134A	2351507		Leased from SibNIA ?-97 to ?-??; basic Aeroflot c/s, Tyumen' Airlines titles/logo
RA-65802	Tu-134AK	3352101		
RA-65838	Tu-134A	(43)18116	2510	SOC by 2003
RA-65859	Tu-134A-3	(53)23264	2804	SOC by 2003
RA-65899	Tu-134A-3	(53)42225	3208	
RA-65902	Tu-134A-3	(13)63742	6204	Leased from Komiinteravia ?-03
RA-65950	Tu-134AK*	2351702		SOC by 2003
RA-65960	Tu-134A	3351806		Leased from SibNIA in 1997-2001
RA-65977	Tu-134AK*	(03)63245	5708	Leased from Komiinteravia ?-03

TYUMEN'AVIATRANS [P2/TMN] based at Tyumen'-Plekhanovo was the other major airline in the Tyumen' Region of Siberia. On 1st October 2002 (some sources say May 2002!) the airline was rebranded **UTAIR** – partly because its activities were not limited to the Tyumen' Region, partly because foreigners had trouble pronouncing the old name. Yet it was not until May 2003 that the new titles began appearing on the actual aircraft. All in all 'Dr Jekyll and Mr Hyde' operated 22 Tu-134s.

Registration	Version	C/n	F/n	Notes
RA-65049	Tu-134A	(73)49755	3808	Leased from Orenburg Airlines by 12-02, basic Aeroflot c/s, Tyumen'AviaTrans titles; UTair titles by 6-03
RA-65052	Tu-134A-3	(73)49825	3902	Leased from AVL Arkhangel'sk Airlines ?-02
RA-65083	Tu-134A-3	(73)60090	4210	Leased from AVL Arkhangel'sk Airlines by 6-02, full TAT c/s; white UTair c/s by 5-03 (first Tu-134 with new titles)
RA-65084	Tu-134A-3	(73)60115	4302	Leased from AVL Arkhangel'sk Airlines by 6-02, basic old AVL c/s, Tyumen'AviaTrans titles; returned by 8-03
RA-65110	Tu-134A-3	(83)60343	4508	Leased from Orenburg Airlines by 7-02, returned by 8-03
RA-65117	Tu-134A-3	(83)60450	4606	Leased from Orenburg Airlines by 7-02
RA-65148	Tu-134A-3	(93)61025	5003	Lsf Komiinteravia by 3-01, returned by 7-01; leased again ?-02
RA-65608	Tu-134AK/r.n.	5338040	3109	Bought from Komiinteravia ?-02; 42-seat VIP layout
RA-65609	Tu-134AK/r.n.*	(63)46155	3401	Lsf Komiinteravia by 10-00, basic Komiavia c/s, Tyumen'AviaTrans titles. Leased again as UTair by 6-03
RA-65612	Tu-134AK/r.n.*	3352102		Leased from Komiinteravia by 8-03
RA-65614	Tu-134AK/r.n.*	4352207		Lsf Komiinteravia by 2-02, basic Alania c/s, Tyumen'AviaTrans titles; full UTair c/s by 10-03
RA 65616	Tu-134AK/r.n.*	4352206		Leased from Komiinteravia ?-02
RA-65618	Tu-134A-3/r.n.	4312095	2410	Leased from Komiinteravia by 2-01, returned ?-??; basic Komiavia c/s, Tyumen'AviaTrans titles
RA-65621	Tu-134A-3/r.n.	6348320	3406	Leased from Komiinteravia by 2-02

RA-65755	Tu-134A-3	(93)62165	5103	Leased from Komiinteravia ?-02
RA-65777	Tu-134A-3	(93)62552	5402	Leased from Komiinteravia ?-02
RA-65793	Tu-134A-3	(03)63128	5604	Leased from Komiinteravia ?-02
RA-65847	Tu-134A-3	(43)23135	2701	Leased from Orenburg Airlines by 8-01, basic Orenburg Airlines colour scheme, Tyumen'AviaTrans titles
RA-65860	Tu-134A-3	(53)28265	2805	Lsf Orenburg Airlines by 8-01, basic Orenburg Airlines c/s, Tyumen'AviaTrans titles. SOC ?-03
RA-65916	Tu-134AK*	(33)66152	6343	D-30-III engines. Leased from Yamal by 8-03, full colour scheme
RA-65932	Tu-134A-3 'Salon'	(43)66405	6367	Lsf Sukhoi by 5-02, full c/s; returned by 5-03

The fleet of the **UL'YANOVSK HIGHER CIVIL AVIATION FLYING SCHOOL**[11] (UVAU GA – *Ool'yahnovskoye vyssheye aviatsionnoye oochilischche grazhdahnskoy aviahtsii*) [–/UHS] included Tu-134As RA-65018 (c/n (63)48365, f/n 3410) and CCCP-65078 (c/n (73)60043, f/n 4205), both retired by 2003, and Tu-134AK RA-65801 (c/n 3352010); the latter was sold to Phoenix Airlines by 1998. The establishment possibly also operated Tu-134AKs CCCP-65665 (c/n 1351201) and CCCP-65748 (c/n 2351610) which were WFU at Ul'yanovsk by 1993.

The now-defunct airline **URALINTERAVIA** [U3/URA] based at Yeka-terinburg-Kol'tsovo briefly leased radar-nosed Tu-134AK RA-65607 from Komiavia in August 1995.

VAYNAKHAVIA[12] was formed in Groznyy in 1996 as the first post-war Chechen airline. Its fleet included two Tu-134As, one of which was RA-65626 bought from the Air Transport School.[13] Some sources claim it was outfitted as a Tu-134A 'Salon' for President Aslan Maskhadov. On 23rd September 1999 the aircraft was damaged at Groznyy-Severnyy (or, as the Chechens prefer to call it, Sheikh Mansur International airport) by a Russian Air Force bomb raid during the Second Chechen War.

VAP GROUP operated Tu-134AK RA-65908 leased from Elf Air in 1993-99. Wits commented that if VIP means 'very important person', then VAP must mean 'very annoying person'!

Some sources say **VNUKOVO AIRLINES/VNOOKOVSKIYE AVI-ALINIÏ** [V5/VKO] leased a single Tu-134 from Alania in late 2000. This was probably radar-nosed Tu-134AK RA-65613 which was seen at Vnukovo Airlines' maintenance base in October 2000.

VOLGA AIRLINES [G6/VLA] based at Volgograd-Goomrak had five Tu-134s. The airline adopted a new corporate identity in 1998, changing its name to **VOLGA AVIAEXPRESS** [–/WLG] and introducing a strik-ing new all-blue star-spangled livery; the two remaining Tu-134s, how-ever, serve on in the old colours.

Registration	Version	C/n	F/n	Notes
RA-65008	Tu-134A-3	(63)46105	3307	SOC by 2003
RA-65086	Tu-134A-3	(73)60130	4304	
RA-65691	Tu-134AK*	(03)63195	5703	Leased to Tatarstan Air by 12-00, later sold
RA-65869	Tu-134A-3	(53)28306	2904	Bought from Perm' Airlines; SOC by 2003
RA-65903	Tu-134A-3 'Salon'	(13)63750	6205	Later reconverted to 76-seater. C/n sometimes reported in error as (13)63780

VOLGA-AVIA was established at Nizhniy Novgorod in early 2003 as the successor of the defunct Nizhegorodskiye Avialinii. It operates Tu-134A RA-65043 leased from ARZ No 412.

VORONEZHAVIA [ZT/VRN] based at Voronezh-Chertovitskoye was one of the largest carriers based in Russia's bread belt. Its fleet originally included 13 Tu-134s. The airline suspended operations in late 2003.

Registration	Version	C/n	F/n	Notes
RA-65057	Tu-134A-3	(73)49865	3909	C/s No 2
RA-65062	Tu-134A	(73)49875	4004	C/s No 1
RA-65067	Tu-134A-3 'Salon'	(73)49905	4010	C/s No 1. Sold to Gromov Air ?-03
RA-65721	Tu-134SKh	(43)66130	6339	Sold to private owner by 2-02 and converted to Tu-134A-3M
RA-65723	Tu-134SKh	(63)66440	6369	Sold to Sirius Aero 5-02 and converted to Tu-134A-3M
RA-65724	Tu-134SKh	(63)66445	6370	Sold to Sirius Aero 5-02 and converted to Tu-134A-3M
RA-65762	Tu-134A-3	(93)62279	5203	C/s No 1
RA-65794	Tu-134A-3	(03)63135	5605	C/s No 1. Lst Sirius Aero by 5-00 as Tu-134A 'Salon'
RA-65880	Tu-134AK*	(53)35200	3007	D-30-III engines, 76-seater; c/s No 1. Lst Sirius Aero by 10-00 as VIP aircraft!
RA-65881	Tu-134AK*	(53)35220	3008	D-30-III engines, c/s No 2. Sold to Sibaviatrans by 5-00
RA-65918	Tu-134SKh	(33)63995	6332	Reported sold and converted to Tu-134A-3M
RA-65929	Tu-134SKh	(63)66495	6373	C/s No 1. Damaged Nyagan' 25-6-03
RA-65930	Tu-134SKh	(63)66500	6374	Converted to passenger/cargo aircraft by 9-95, c/s No 1; sold to Kras Air by 2-00 and converted to Tu-134A-3M

There were subtle differences in the livery of individual aircraft. Most Tu-134s retain the blue Aeroflot cheatline, except that the pinstripe below it has a yellow background, and the titles are applied in ordinary block letters above the windows (c/s No 1). On two aircraft, however, the cheatline itself is blue/yellow and the titles are applied in italics below the windows.

On 30th November 2003 the airline's operating licence was withdrawn, probably as a result of the Nyagan' accident; the fate of the aircraft is not yet known.

In September 1999 Gromov Air Tu-134AK RA-65939 was leased to start-up Moscow carrier **VTS-TRANS**, a subsidiary of the Vneshtorgservis trading company (hence the VTS; Vneshtorgservis means 'foreign trade service'). The 72-seat aircraft received an all-new VIP interior with two five-seat de luxe cabins and 32 business class seats for the retinue; the interior was designed by ANTK Tupolev and installed at the company's flight test facility in Zhukovskiy. Interestingly, the aircraft was equipped with additional white navigation lights at the wingtips to meet ICAO norms.

VTS-Trans took delivery of the aircraft on 26th September 1999. In March 2001 RA-65939 was sold to Chernomor-Avia and reverted to 72-seat configuration.

Transaero Express Tu-134A-3 'Salon' RA-65088 on the GosNII GA ramp at Moscow/Sheremet'yevo-1. The basic colour scheme and tail logo are those of the Rosneft' oil company; note the additional Aeroleasing titles.
Dmitriy Petrochenko

Displaying all the tell-tale operational stains, Tu-134A RA-65960 in the smart livery of Tyumen' Airlines awaits its next flight in brilliant sunshine at Moscow-Domodedovo. The mobile gangway is a later-model SPT-154 identifiable by the angular 'bodywork'. Yuriy Kirsanov

Tyumen'AviaTrans leases Tu-134s as required; this is Tu-134A RA-65618 leased from Komiinteravia and seen at Moscow/Vnukovo-1 on 22nd March 2001 in basic Komiavia livery, including tail logo. The cheatline and the anti-glare panel originally extended onto the radome. Author

Seen on approach to Moscow-Domodedovo, Tu-134A-3 RA-65847 of Tyumen'AviaTrans has been leased from Orenburg Airlines, as revealed by the blue rudder. Note the angle of the main gear bogies in no-load condition. Yuriy Kirsanov

The **YERMOLINO FLIGHT TEST & RESEARCH ENTERPRISE** (YeLIIP – *Yermolinskoye lyotno-ispytahtel'noye issledovatel'skoye predproyatiye*) [–/EFE] based at Yermolino airfield near Moscow purchased two Tu-134AKs, RA-65099 and RA-65908, in 1998, leasing them to SBS-Bank and Aviazapchast' (later to Rusair) respectively. In 1999 YeLIIP was renamed **YERMOLINO AIRLINES**. By August 2000 RA-65099 had exchanged its red/blue/white SBS-Bank colour scheme for an all-white scheme with a thin emerald green cheatline and a registration reduced to almost illegible size.

In 2002 Yermolino Airlines ceased operations. RA-65099 was sold to Sirius Aero while RA-65908 was purchased by co-located Antex-Polus.

YUGANSKNEFTEGAZ, an oil and natural gas company from Nefteyugansk, briefly leased Tu-134B-3 YL-LBC (c/n (03)63221, f/n 5706) from Latavio Latvian Airlines in 1993.

YUKOSAVIA, the flying division of the Yukos Oil Co (likewise headquartered in Nefteyugansk), operated five Tu-134s on and off. Most of them were ordinary passenger aircraft used for carrying shifts of oil workers to airports located close to major oilfields. The airline suspended operations in 1998, intending to restart – which it never did.

Registration	Version	C/n	F/n	Notes
RA-65043	Tu-134A	(63)49400	3801	Leased from Nizhegorodskiye Avialinii ?-98; basic Nizhegorodskiye Avialinii c/s, Yukosavia titles
RA-65065	Tu-134AK*	(73)49890	4007	Lsf Nizhegorodskiye Avialinii ?-98
RA-65606	Tu-134AK/r.n.	(63)46300	3405	Lsf Komiavia ?-97, executive aircraft
RA-65610	Tu-134AK/r.n.*	(53)40150	3204	Lsf Komiavia ?-97
RA-65823	Tu-134A	(43)09073	2402	Lsf Nizhegorodskiye Avialinii 10-93

YAMAL AIRLINES [YL/LLM] based in Salekhard on the Yamal Peninsula in the Russian High North operated nine Tu-134s. The smart colour scheme varies from aircraft to aircraft; the cheatline may be broken by a white diamond with a blue 'shadow' on the nose (c/s No 1) or unbroken, tapering off at the front (c/s No 3) or widening to include the flightdeck glazing (c/s No 2). RA-65906, the latest addition to the fleet, introduced livery No 4 with a narrower cheatline going below the windows (instead of across them) and fanning out over the tail.

Registration	Version	C/n	F/n	Notes
RA-65132	Tu-134A-3	(83)60639	4804	Ex-Tu-134A-3 'Salon'. Bought from AVL Arkhangel'sk Airlines 9-99, c/s No 2
RA-65143	Tu-134A-3	(93)60967	4908	Bought from AVL Arkhangel'sk Airlines ?-98, c/s No 1, later No 3
RA-65552	Tu-134AK*	(43)66270	6358	D-30-III engines. Bought from GTK Rossiya by 3-00, c/s No 3
RA-65554	Tu-134AK*	(43)66320	6360	D-30-III engines. Bought from GTK Rossiya by 5-00; leased to Alliance Avia
RA-65613	Tu-134AK/r.n.*	3352106		Bought from Komiaviatrans 9-98, c/s No 1; sold to Karat 5-99
RA-65906	Tu-134AK*	(33)66175	6345	Bought from Tulpar 1-01, c/s No 4, named 'Salekhard'
RA-65914	Tu-134AK*	(33)66109	6337	D-30-III engines. Bought from GTK Rossiya 8-99, c/s No 3
RA-65915	Tu-134AK*	(33)66120	6338	D-30-III engines. Bought from GTK Rossiya ?-00
RA-65916	Tu-134AK*	(33)66152	6343	D-30-III engines. Bought from GTK Rossiya ?-00, c/s No 3. Leased to UTair by 8-03

Tu-134A-3M RA-65721 was purchased by an unknown private owner by February 2002. The aircraft wears a red/white corporate colour scheme vaguely reminiscent of the DHL International livery.

ARMENIA

By July 2001 **ARMAVIA** [U8/RNV] had bought Tu-134A-3 RA-65575 (c/n (93)62350, f/n 5209) from Chernomor-Avia. The aircraft was reregistered EK-65575, gaining new titles and logo but retaining the 'stormy sea' cheatline.

ARMENIAN AIRLINES [R3/RME] based at Yerevan-Zvartnots had nine Tu-134A-3s.

Registration	C/n	F/n	Notes
EK-65044	(63)49450	3802	C/s No 2
EK-65072	(73)49972	4107	C/s No 1, later No 2. To Government flight as
			Tu-134A-3 'Salon' by 1998
EK-65650	0351006		C/s No 1. SOC by 1998
EK-65731	1351401		SOC Gyumri by 6-97
EK-65822	(43)09071	2401	SOC by 2003
EK-65831	(43)17102	2502	C/s No 1
EK-65848	(43)23136	2702	C/s No 1
EK-65884	(53)36150	3101	SOC Yerevan-Zvartnots by 6-97
EK-65975	3352006		Ex-Government flight Tu-134A-3 'Salon'.
			Stored Yerevan-Zvartnots

Volga Airlines Tu-134A-3 RA-65903 during a quick turnaround at Moscow-Domodedovo on the afternoon of 25th November 1998. A technician checks the port engine's compressor blades for damage. The VAZ-21213 Niva jeep on the right is an East Line Airport Security car which carted this author about the place. Author

Voronezhavia Tu-134A-3 RA-65762 uses reverse thrust after landing on runway 06 at Moscow-Vnukovo. Like many former Aeroflot divisions, the airline made only minimum changes to the basic Aeroflot livery; even the 'chicken' (Aeroflot logo) is still there. Yuriy Kirsanov

RA-65929, the last remaining Tu-134SKh, seen visiting Novosibirsk-Tolmachovo; it retained the characteristic markings after Voronezhavia titles were applied. The SLAR pods have been removed. Dmitriy Petrochenko

Yamal Airlines Tu-134AK RA-65914 is just about to leave runway 25L at Moscow-Sheremet'yevo, turning right towards the domestic terminal after arriving from Salekhard on 26th February 2000. The airline bought a sizeable number of Tu-134AKs from Russia State Transport Co. Author

This page, top: **Private-owned Tu-134A-3M RA-65721 seen at Moscow/Vnukovo-1 on 18th June 2002 in a DHL-style colour scheme.** Author

Initially all aircraft retained Aeroflot colours without titles and with an Armenian flag on the tail in lieu of the Soviet flag. The first livery introduced in 1993 (c/s No 1) was predominantly white, with a grey belly, an *AAL* nose badge (the letters were orange, blue and red respectively), small titles (in English and Armenian script) and a round tail logo in the same national flag colours. Soon, however, this gave way to a striking new livery with a dark blue belly and rear fuselage/tail, a yellow cheatline and an 'AA' tail logo.

In October 1994 Tu-134A EK-65848 was briefly leased by now-defunct **GYUMRI AIRLINES** based at Gyumri (formerly Leninakan).

The **ARMENIAN GOVERNMENT FLIGHT** initially operated 36-seat Tu-134A-3 'Salon' EK-65975 as the presidential aircraft of Levon Ter-Petrosyan (and later of his successor Robert Kocharyan). At least until late March 1994 the aircraft retained basic Aeroflot colours with an Armenian flag on the tail, the state coat of arms ahead of the entry door and large blue titles in Armenian. Afterwards it gained a much more impressive colour scheme with a white top, a dark blue belly and 'Armenian Republic' titles. By 1998 EK-65975 was stripped of its plush interior and 'traded in' to Armenian Airlines for a newer Tu-134A-3 (EK-65072) which was according refitted as a Tu-134A-3 'Salon', receiving the same colour scheme as its forerunner.

AZERBAIJAN

AZAL AVIA [J2/AHY], alias **AZERBAIJAN AIRLINES** or **AHY – AZERBAIJAN HAVA YOLLARI**, operated 11 Tu-134B-3s from Baku-Bina airport.

Registration	C/n	F/n	Notes
4K-65702	(03)63375	5901	C/s No 1, named 'Trabzon'
4K-65703	(03)63383	5902	C/s No 1. Crashed Nakhichevan' 5-12-95
4K-65704	(03)63410	5904	Ex-Latavio YL-LBJ, D/D 5-97
4K-65705	(03)63415	5905	
4K-65708	(03)63447	5908	Ex-AL-65708. C/s No 1
4K-65709	(03)63484	6002	C/s No 1
4K-65710	(03)63490	6003	Ex-AL-65710. C/s No 1; stored Baku-Bina since 1996?
4K-65711	(03)63498	6004	Ex-AL-65711; ex-Government flight. C/s No 1, later No 2
4K-65712	(03)63515	6006	Ex-Latavio YL-LBL, D/D 1997; basic Latavio c/s, Azerbaijan
			Airlines – AHY titles/logo; later c/s No 2
4K-65713	(03)63520	6007	C/s No 1
4K-65714	(03)63527	6008	C/s No 1/AZƏRBAYCAN – AHY titles

Back in 1992, when the former Soviet Union was in turmoil, some of AZAL's aircraft wore the provisional AL- prefix (which was rejected by ICAO)[14] or no prefix at all. Normally the AZAL livery features a blue/green/orange tail (c/s No 1), but some Tu-134Bs gained a revised colour scheme with a brighter-coloured cheatline and a white tail (c/s No 2). 4K-65712 originally retained red/white Latavio colours; the AZAL flying crane logo placed into the existing white circle on the tail was red instead of blue and the registration was applied Latvian-style low on the rear fuselage instead of the engine nacelles.

Baku-based **IMAIR** [IK/ITX], a division of the Improtex trade corporation, operates passenger and cargo aircraft leased as required. These included Tu-134A EW-65049 (c/n (73)49755, f/n 3808) leased from Gomel'avia in 1998, returning it in mid-2002. The aircraft retained basic Belavia colours with Imair titles/logo and an Azeri flag aft of the flightdeck. Additionally, Tu-134B-3 YL-LBI (c/n (03)63365, f/n 5810) was leased from Baltic Express Line at an unknown date.

The **AZERBAIJAN GOVERNMENT FLIGHT** operated Tu-134B-3 AL-65711 in a non-standard colour scheme with AZARBAYCAN titles (later reregistered 4K-65711 and repainted in nearly-standard AZAL colours, except for AZƏRBAYCAN – AHY titles). This was a Tu-134B-3 'Salon' conversion with a VIP interior but with no rear entry door. In late 1997 it was substituted by Boeing 727-30 VP-CMM (registered in the Cayman Islands as a 'flag of convenience') and transferred to AZAL. (Interestingly, Tu-134B-3 4K-65714 also wore AZƏRBAYCAN titles in late 1998 but it was a regular 80-seater, not a VIP aircraft!)

The **AZERBAIJAN MINISTRY OF DEFENCE** operates a quasi-civil Tu-134 *Balkany* ABCP equipped to Tu-134A-3 standard. Originally registered 4K-65985 (c/n (03)63468, f/n 5910), it was reregistered 4K-65496 in 1997 – apparently to confuse would-be spies; this is the only known registration in the 65400 block. The aircraft had basic Aeroflot colours with an Azeri flag on the tail, AZERBAIJAN titles and the registration painted on the engine nacelles.

BELARUS' (BELORUSSIA)

In 1992 the charter carrier **BELAIR** (Belorussian Airlines) [–/BLI] based at Minsk-2 airport took delivery of Tu-134AK EW-65565 built to Tu-134A-1 standard (ex-CCCP-65565, ex-DDR-SDT, c/n (33)63998, f/n 6335) and radar-nosed Tu-134A EW-65605 (ex-CCCP-65605 No 2, ex-D-AOBI, c/n (43)09070, f/n 2310). The aircraft were leased from ARZ No 407 and painted in the 'CIS-style' Belorussian flag colours of red and white. Both were returned to the lessor in 1995, going to Chernomorskiye avialinii as RA-65565 and RA-65605.

The Belorussian flag carrier **BELAVIA** [B2/BRU] operated 19 Tu-134s from Minsk-2 and Gomel'.

Registration	Version	C/n	F/n	Notes
EW-65049	Tu-134A	(73)49755	3808	C/s No 1. To Gomelavia ?-96.
EW-65082	Tu-134A	(73)60081	4209	C/s No 2
EW-65085	Tu-134A	(73)60123	4303	C/s No 1. To Gomelavia ?-96; returned ?-98
EW-65106	Tu-134A	(83)60315	4503	
EW-65108	Tu-134A	(83)60332	4506	C/s No 1, later No 2
EW-65133	Tu-134A-3	(83)60645	4806	C/s No 1, later No 2
EW-65145	Tu-134A	(93)60985	4910	C/s No 1, later No 2
EW-65149	Tu-134A 'Salon'	(93)61033	5004	C/s No 2. Later reconverted to 76-seater
EW-65664	Tu-134A	1351210		Scrapped Minsk 5-96
EW-65676	Tu-134AK*	1351502		D-30-III engines, c/s No 2. To Gomelavia ?-96
EW-65754	Tu-134A	(93)62154	5102	C/s No 2
EW-65772	Tu-134A-3	(93)62472	5307	C/s No 2
EW-65803	Tu-134A	3352103		C/s No 2. WFU Minsk by 1997, SOC 1998
EW-65821	Tu-134AK*	(43)08060	2306	C/s No 2
EW-65832	Tu-134A	(43)17106	2504	C/s No 1. WFU Minsk by 1997, SOC 1998
EW-65861 #1†	Tu-134A-3	(53)28269	2806	Ex-CCCP-65861. SOC Minsk 9-94
EW-65892	Tu-134A	(53)38050	3110	SOC by 1997
EW-65957	Tu-134AK*	2351802		C/s No 1. To Gomelavia ?-96
EW-65974	Tu-134A	3352004		C/s No 1. To Gomelavia ?-96

† See Techaviaservice

Originally (in 1992) the airline was incorporated under the trading name **BELARUS'**. Tu-134As CCCP-65082, -65133, -65149, -65803 and -65832 were painted up accordingly to feature the red/white Belorussian flag superimposed on a dark blue band on the tail, red Cyrillic BELARUS' titles in plain script above the windows and small Aeroflot titles/logo beneath the windows. (This was because the airline was not yet an ICAO member and operated under Aeroflot's SU flight code for the time being.)

EW-65085 was one of the first to receive the new italic 'BELAVIA' titles but had an all-white tail for a while. In August 1993 EW-65106 also had a white tail with a red Belavia logo and a Belorussian flag on the rudder (outlined in red). Later Belavia standardised on a dark blue tail with the logo in a white ellipse and dark blue engine nacelles with a lighter stripe outlined in white; this livery was designed in-house. Yet, variations persisted; some aircraft retained an Aeroflot cheatline (c/s No 1), while others had a cheatline with pinstripes above and below (c/s No 2). The Tu-134 nose titles could be applied in Russian (EW-65149) or English (EW-65772). Finally, when the Russian Federation and the Republic of Belarus began preparing for integration into a new union in April 1997, the 'CIS-style' Belorussian flag on the rudder was replaced by a new red/green flag (strongly resembling the flag of the former Belorussian SSR) on the centre fuselage.

Belavia Tu-134s were sometimes used for government flights. For instance, on 6th February 1995 Tu-134A 'Salon' EW-65149 took President Aleksandr Lukashenko to Vilnius for a meeting with the then President Algirdas Brazauskas. The aircraft was 'demoted' to standard configuration after the delivery of Tu-154M 'Salon' EW-85815 in 1998.

In 1996 the Gomel' division of Belavia became a separate entity called **GOMELAVIA** [YD/GOM], taking over EW-65049, -65085, -65676, -65957 and -65974. The only changes of exterior were the application of 'GOMELAVIA' titles and a new logo (a red G in a white circle).

By 1998 EW-65957 and -65974 had been retired, while EW-65085 reverted to Belavia. By September 2002 EW-65049 was sold to Orenburg Airlines as RA-65049.

In March 1998 the airline **TECHAVIASERVICE** [–/BTS] based at Minsk-2 had acquired Czech Air Force Tu-134AK '1407 White' (c/n 1351407). For reasons unknown the aircraft was registered EW-65861, assuming the identity of a Belavia Tu-134A retired in 1997 (see above)! In early 1999 EW-65861 No 2 was sold to the Russian company LUKoil as RA-65861.

Tu-134A EK-65650 displays Armenian Airlines' old livery as it climbs away from runway 24 at Moscow-Domodedovo. Yuriy Kirsanov

Azerbaijan Airlines Tu-134B-3 4K-65708 caught by the camera seconds before touchdown on runway 14L at Moscow-Domodedovo. Dmitriy Petrochenko

Tu-134A EW-65049 leased by Imair from Gomel'avia seen at Moscow-Domodedovo shortly after arriving from Gyandzha on 18th November 1998. The basic livery is that of Belavia; note that the Imair logo is applied over a crudely overpainted Gomel'avia logo and the aircraft carries an Azeri flag in spite of the Belorussian registration. Author

Tu-134A CCCP-65082, a Belorussian CAD/2nd Minsk UAD/104th Flight aircraft, was one of several to gain the livery of Belarus' (the predecessor of Belavia Belorussian Airlines) in 1992. Note the additional Aeroflot titles/logo. Ghennadiy Petrov archive

The **BELORUSSIAN AIR FORCE** operated a single Tu-134 *Balkany* ABCP, EW-63955 (c/n (23)63955, f/n 6313), inherited from the Belorussian Defence District. The aircraft was operated by Squadron 1 of the 50th OSAP at Lipki AB near Minsk. In 1994 the unit moved to nearby Machoolischchi AB and was renamed 50th Aviation Base, changing its name again to 50th Transport Aviation Base on 26th March 1996.

The colour scheme was patterned on Belavia's livery but the aircraft had Cyrillic 'BELARUS' titles in plain script and a blue fin with a large Belorussian flag at the bottom and a white stripe on which the registration was applied. In 2002 EW-63955 was stripped of mission equipment and sold to Sibaviatrans, receiving the registration RA-65571 on 18th July.

GEORGIA

ADJARIAN AIRLINES (Adjal) [–/ADJ] of Batumi operated a pair of Tu-134AKs (UR 65073 and UR 65877) on lease from Air Ukraine in 1997. They wore basic 1993-standard Air Ukraine colours and Adjarian Airlines titles/logos. Both aircraft were returned in 1998, and Tu-134B-3 4L-AAD was leased from Sukhumi Airlines as a replacement; this wore basic Lat-Charter livery with Batumi Adjarian Airlines titles.

Tbilisi-based **ORBI** [NQ/DVU], which used to be Georgia's flag carrier, operated 15 Tu-134As. Fourteen of them were inherited from the Georgian CAD. Some of these aircraft wore an attractive blue/white livery with an eagle tail logo; at least until January 1993 they had no prefix and no flag to reveal their 'nationality'. However, by October 1997 all 14 of the original aircraft had been sold or retired.

Registration	Version	C/n	F/n	Notes
4L-65053?	Tu-134A-3	(73)49838	3904	SOC by 1996? 4L- prefix unconfirmed†
4L-65061	Tu-134A-3	(73)49874	4003	Sold to Taifun
4L-65750	Tu-134A-3	(93)61042	5005	Full c/s. Sold to Georgian Airlines
4L-65774	Tu-134A-3	(93)62519	5309	Full c/s. Sold to Georgian Airlines
4L-65798	Tu-134A-3	(03)63179	5701	Full c/s. Sold to Georgian Airlines
4L-65808?	Tu-134A	3352109		Sold to Taifun? 4L- prefix unconfirmed (SOC as CCCP-65808?)
4L-65809?	Tu-134A	3352110		SOC by 1995? 4L- prefix unconfirmed†
CCCP-65810	Tu-134A-3	3352201		Aeroflot c/s. DBR Khar'kov-Osnova 29-8-92
4L-65817?	Tu-134A	4352301		Sold to Taifun? 4L- prefix unconfirmed (SOC as CCCP-65817?)
4L-65857	Tu-134A-3	(53)23255	2802	Sold to Air Zena
4L-65865	Tu-134A-3	(53)28286	2810	Basic Aeroflot c/s. Sold to GACo-Kavkasia
4L-65879	Tu-134A-3	(53)31265	3005	Sold to Taifun
CCCP-65886	Tu-134A	(53)36165	3103	Aeroflot c/s. Sold to Taifun, stored Tbilisi-International
CCCP-65959	Tu-134A	3351805		Aeroflot c/s. Sold to Taifun, stored Tbilisi-International
4L-AAE	Tu-134A-1	8360282	4409	Ex-ČSA Czech Airlines OK-IFN, basic ČSA colour scheme.

† CCCP-65053 and 65809 (no prefix) were possibly destroyed at Sukhumi-Babushara on 23rd September 1993 during the Georgian/Abkhazian war.

In mid-1998 ORBI's fleet consisted of a single aircraft – Tu-134A-1 4L-AAE. This could not save the day and in 1999 the airline finally ceased operations. After sitting in storage at Kutaisi-Osnovnoy for a year the aircraft was sold to Roos' Air Transport Co on 6th December 2000.

GACO KAVKASIA [–/GAK], an airline based at Sukhumi (Abkhazia), leased Tu-134A-3 4L-65865 from ORBI in January 1995, eventually buying it. In 1997 the aircraft was withdrawn from use at Tbilisi-International; to replace it, Tu-134A-3 ER-65071 was leased from Air Moldova.

The three newest Tu-134A-3s in the original ORBI fleet (4L-65750, 4L-65774 and 4L-65798) passed to newly formed **GEORGIAN INTERNATIONAL**

AIR LINES [3P/GEG], later renamed **GEORGIAN AIR LINES** [6R/GEG].[15] The first aircraft was all-white with Georgian Air Lines titles/logo, while 4L-65798 retained basic ORBI colours.

TAIFUN [–/GIG] of Sukhumi started off by leasing Tu-134As from ORBI as required. For instance, 4L-65798 operated the Sukhumi – Moscow (Vnukovo) service in the summer of 1994 in Taifun colours with a white top, dark blue belly/wings/tail and red cheatline but no titles.

In 1994 the airline bought Tu-134As 4L 65061, 4L-65808, 4L-65817, 4L 65879, CCCP-65886 and CCCP-65959 from ORBI. Some of them wore the same colour scheme with tiny 'Taifun' titles, an equally small logo and Georgian flag. 4L-65808 and 4L-65817 were retired by 1997.

In April-May 1997 **SUKHUMI AIRLINES** [–/LOA] purchased three Tu-134B-3s from Lat-Charter. Originally they retained the varied colours of their ex-owner without titles; two out of three were later repainted in a livery patterned on that of Lat-Charter.

Registration	C/n	F/n	Notes
4L-AAB	(03)63340	5807	Ex-YL-LBH. Basic Lat-Charter 'yuck' green/dark blue c/s; to white/dark blue c/s ?-98. Sold to Aviaexpresscruise by 2-00 as RA-65569
4L-AAC	(13)63536	6009	Ex-YL-LBM; basic Latavio red/white c/s. Sold to Alrosa by 7-01 as RA-65715
4L-AAD	(03)63295	5802	Ex-YL-LBF. Basic Lat-Charter 'cool' white/light blue/light green c/s; to white/light blue c/s ?-98. Sold to Daghestan Airlines 9-01 as RA-65579

By 1999 Tu-134As 4L-65061 (now again painted normally with a dash!) and 4L 65879 were sold to **ABAVIA** (*Abkhazskiye avialinii* – Abkhazian Airlines) [–/BVZ], retaining basic Taifun colours without titles. Only the former aircraft remained active by 2001.

TRANSAIR GEORGIA was one of the first carriers to appear in post-Soviet Georgia. Among other things it operated Tu-134As CCCP-65001 (c/n (53)42235, f/n 3210) and 65893 (c/n 5340120, f/n 3201) in Aeroflot colours. Tragically, the latter aircraft was shot down at Sukhumi-Babushara on 21st September 1993 and CCCP-65001 was destroyed at the same location just two days later during the Georgian/Abkhazian war. Transair Georgia had no alternative but to lease Tu-154Ms from Russian carriers.

On 1st November 1999 **AIR ZENA** [A9/TGZ] of Tbilisi gobbled up Georgian Air Lines; consequently 4L-65750, 4L-65774 and 4L-65798 got a new livery. Judging by the bold 'GEORGIA' titles, the latter aircraft became a Tu-134A 'Salon' operated for the government. Additionally, Air Zena bought Tu-134A 4L-65857 from ORBI. In 2000 one of the airline's Tu-134As was reregistered 4L-AAI (its c/n remains unknown). In early 2001 4L-65798 was sold to East Line, becoming RA-65798. 4L-65750 was sold to Avial in 2003.

In July 1997 the **GEORGIAN AIR FORCE** purchased Tu-134 *Balkany* RA-65993 from the Russian Air Force. Reregistered 4L-65993, it retained basic Aeroflot colours without titles and with a Georgian flag on the tail.

By May 2003 4L-65993 was sold to the **TBILISI AIRCRAFT FACTORY** (Tbilaviamsheni) [L6/VNZ], stripped of its *Balkany* HF comms suite and reregistered 4L-AAJ. The aircraft now wears 'Georgia' titles in English and Georgian.

By September 2003 an **UNKNOWN GEORGIAN AIRLINE** had acquired Tu-134A-3 4L-65730 (ex-Tajikistan Airlines EY-65730, c/n 1351310). The aircraft was basically white without titles.

In 2003 the airline **AVIAL** (not to be confused with Avial' of Russia!) purchased Tu-134A-3 4L-65750 from Air Zena. A few months later, however, the aircraft was sold to Altyn Air as EX-020.

Top: **Belavia Tu-134A EW-65149, a former presidential VIP aircraft, sits under threatening skies at Moscow-Domodedovo on 3rd November 1998, making an unexpected visit due to Sheremet'yevo shutting down because of bad weather. Note the 'union-style' Belorussian flag introduced in 1997.** Author

Above: **Tu-134AK UR 65073 (*sic*) in the full colours of Adjarian Airlines rotates just as it passes the intersection with runway 20 at Moscow-Vnukovo, taking off from runway 24. The aircraft was initially operated in the basic livery of the lessor, Air Ukraine.** Yuriy Kirsanov

Below: **ORBI Georgian Airlines Tu-134A-3 4L-65750 landing at Moscow-Vnukovo.** Dmitriy Petrochenko

Top: **Abavia Tu-134A 4L 65061 (*sic* – no dash) in basic Taifun colours on approach to Moscow-Vnukovo.** Dmitriy Petrochenko

Above: **Tu-134AK UN 65900 in full Kazakstan Airlines colours taxying at Moscow-Sheremet'yevo, with the GosNII GA compound (left) and the Sheremet'yevo-1 maintenance base (right) in the background.** Yuriy Kirsanov

Below: **Air Kazakstan Tu-134A-3 UN 65130 at Moscow-Domodedovo on a bleak snowy day in late November 1998.** Author

KAZAKSTAN (KAZAKHSTAN)

By January 2003 **AQUALINE LEASING** had bought the last two remaining Tu-134B-3s from Lat-Charter. The aircraft were reregistered UN 65695 (ex-YL-LBE, c/n (03)63285, f/n 5801) and UN 65699 (ex-YL-LBG, c/n (03)63333, f/n 5806) and promptly leased to Air Libya Tibesti (see next chapter). Some sources, though, say UN 65699 belongs to a company with the weird-sounding name of Marsland!

ASIA SERVICE AIRLINES [–/ASQ] of Almaty leases Tu-134As from Tajikistan Airlines as required.

ATYRAU AIR WAYS/ATYRAU AUE ZHOLY [IP/JOL] based in Atyrau (formerly Goor'yev) operates four Tu-134s purchased form Komi(inter)avia. Contrary to normal Kazakh practice, they have the registrations applied with a dash.

Registration	Version	C/n	F/n	Notes
UN-65069	Tu-134A-3	(73)49908	4102	Ex-RA-65069, D/D ?-98, named 'Kashagan'
UN-65070	Tu-134A-3	(73)49912	4104	Ex-RA-65070, D/D ?-97, named 'Tungysh'
UN-65610	Tu-134AK/r.n.*	(53)40150	3204	Ex-RA-65610, D/D ?-00, named 'Bayterek'
UN-65619	Tu-134AK/r.n.	(53)31218	3001	Ex-RA-65619, D/D 1-02, named 'Venera'; VIP interior reinstated

KAZAKHSTAN AIRLINES/KAZAKHSTAN AUE ZHOLY or **KAZAIR** [K4/KZA] was this Central Asian republic's first flag carrier. Its large fleet included nine Tu-134As.

Registration	Version	C/n	F/n	Notes
UN 65115	Tu-134A-3	(83)60405	4603	C/s No 3. **Sold or retired by 2003**
UN 65121	Tu-134A-3	(83)60505	4701	**SOC by 1998**
UN 65130	Tu-134A-3	(83)60635	4802	C/s No 3. **Sold or retired by 2003**
UN 65138	Tu-134A	(83)60907	4902	C/s No 3. **Sold or retired by 2003**
UN 65147	Tu-134A-3	(93)61012	5002	C/s No 1. **WFU Almaty by 1-03**
UN 65767	Tu-134A-3	(93)62335	5208	C/s No 2. **WFU Almaty by 6-99**
UN 65776	Tu-134A-3	(83)62545	5401	**Sold to KazTransAir by 9-00**
UN 65787	Tu-134A	(03)62798	5506	
UN 65900	Tu-134AK*	(13)63684	6109	D-30-III engines, colour scheme No 3. **Sold to Kazair West ?-98**

Originally flown in basic Aeroflot colours with the Kazakh flag and without titles (c/s No 1), some aircraft later got a blue tail with the sun-and-eagle motif of the national flag and 'казакhstan airlines' titles, which required the registration to be relocated to the engine nacelles (c/s No 2). A stylish new livery (No 3) appeared in late 1994; incidentally, the titles now read 'казакstan airlines', without the 'h'.

On 20th August 1996 Kazakstan Airlines filed for bankruptcy, with debts of 19 billion tenge (more than US$ 180 million). Rather than attempt to rescue the ailing giant, the government chose to liquidate the airline and establish a new flag carrier, **AIR KAZAKSTAN** [9Y/KZK], which inherited most of Kazair's fleet, including all of the Tu-134s. The only changes to the livery were the 'Air Kazakstan' titles and the new logo – an arrow on a yellow circle. (Note: as there is no point in repeating the ex-Kazair fleet list, post-takeover changes of status for Air Kazakstan Tu-134s are marked in the above table in bold type.)

The **KAZAKSTAN GOVERNMENT FLIGHT** initially had a single Tu-134AK registered 65551 (later UN-65551, c/n (43)66212, f/n 6353) and equipped as a Tu-134A-3; the aircraft wore basic Aeroflot colours with Cyrillic 'KAZAKSTAN' (КАЗАКСТАН) titles and the Kazakhstan coat of arms. Later it was repainted in basic Kazair livery (again with КАЗАКСТАН titles) and the registration was applied with no dash. In

March 1999 the government flight took delivery of Tu-134B-3 'Salon' UN-65799 (ex-Latavio YL-LBN, c/n (93)63187, f/n 5702).

In 2000 the Tu-134AK was sold to KazTransAir, the other aircraft going to Kazair West by the end of 2002. However, both retain their VIP interiors and are apparently still used for government duties as required.

In 1998 **KAZAIR WEST** [–/KAW] based in Atyrau purchased Tu-134AK UN 65900 from Air Kazakstan. In late 2002 this was augmented by Tu-134B-3 'Salon' UN-65799 bought from the government flight.

In 2000 start-up carrier **KAZTRANSAIR** bought Tu-134AK UN 65551 from the government flight and Tu-134A-3 UN 65776 from Air Kazakstan. The latter aircraft retained ex-Kazakstan Airlines tail colours but the blue cheatline below the windows was deleted, leaving only the blue and yellow double pinstripe; the latter was broken on the nose and small 'Kaz-TransAir' titles applied in the gap. The registration was painted on the centre fuselage.

In late 2002 UN 65551 and UN 65776 were sold to **EURO-ASIA AIR/ YEVRO AZIYA AUE ZHOLY** [5B/EAK]; UN 65776 was converted to a Tu-134A-3 'Salon' in so doing. Both retain their ex-owner's markings.

SAN [S3/SND], a Kazakh-German joint venture based in Karaganda, leased Tu-134A-3s EY-65763 and EY-65788 from Tajikistan Airways in 1997; both were returned by the autumn of 1999.

From its early days the **KAZAKSTAN AIR FORCE** operated Tu-134 Balkany UN-65683 (c/n (93)62199, f/n 5106). In January 2000 it was announced that several more Tu-134 Balkany ABCPs were to be purchased from the Russian Air Force. As of August 2002, however, the only known acquisition was Tu-134A (apparently a 'Salon') registered 65025 (ex-Tyumen' Airlines RA-65025). It is in basic Aeroflot colours with the Kazakh flag on the tail.

KYRGHYZSTAN

KYRGHYZSTAN AIRLINES/KYRGHYZSTAN ABA ZHOLDORU [K2/KGA, later R8/KGA], the republic's flag carrier, operated six Tu-134A-3s from Bishkek-Manas airport.

Registration	Version	C/n	F/n	Notes
EX-65111	Tu-134A-3	(83)60346	4509	Sold or retired by 2003
EX-65119	Tu-134A-3 'Salon'	(83)60475	4608	Operated for Kyrgyz government; converted to 66-seater and leased to ITEK Air ?-00
EX-65125	Tu-134A-3	(83)60575	4706	Sold or retired by 2003
EX-65778	Tu-134A	(93)62590	5405	
EX-65779	Tu-134A-3	(93)62602	5406	
EX-65789	Tu-134A-3	(03)62850	5510	

In 2000 Tu-134A-3 EX-65119 was leased to **ITEK AIR** [–/IKA], operating in the airline's striking blue/white livery.

Around 1999 EX-65779 was leased to an unidentified company, gaining a rather strange colour scheme. The very weathered Kyrghyzstan Airlines cheatline with its green pinstripes above and below remained but the titles were removed; the vertical tail was painted bright red with a skewed five-pointed star in black and white. To top it all, the Kazakh flag was carried in an improbable (and most unbecoming) position – near the APU exhaust. The aircraft has since been returned.

In 2003 Bishkek-based **ALTYN AIR** [QH/LYN] purchased Tu-134A-3 4L-65750 from Georgian Airlines. The aircraft was reregistered EX-020 but the digits of the old registration still remained on the engine nacelles.

Top: **Kyrgyzstan Airlines Tu-134A EX-65779 taxies in at Moscow-Domodedovo after landing on runway 32R.** Yuriy Kirsanov

Above: **Itek Air Tu-134A-3 EX-65119 lines up for take-off from runway 14R at Moscow-Domodedovo; note the unusual placement of the 'Tupolev-134A-3' titles.** Yuriy Kirsanov

Below: **A fine shot of Tu-134A ER-65791 on short finals to Moscow-Vnukovo in the latest livery of Air Moldova.** Dmitriy Petrochenko

MOLDOVA (MOLDAVIA)

AIR MOLDOVA [9U/MLD], the national flag carrier, operated eleven Tu-134s from Kishinyov (Chișinău).

Registration	Version	C/n	F/n	Notes
ER-65036	Tu-134A-3	6348700	3703	C/s No 2
ER-65050	Tu-134A-3	(73)49756	3809	C/s No 2
ER-65051	Tu-134A-3	(73)49758	3810	C/s No 1, later No 2
ER-65071	Tu-134A-3	(73)49915	4106	C/s No 2. Leased to GACo-Kavkasia in 1997
ER-65094	Tu-134AK*	8360255	4403	D-30-III engines. Transferred from government flight ?-00, c/s No 3
ER-65140	Tu-134AK*	(83)60932	4905	D-30-III engines. C/s No 1, later No 2/No 3. Leased to unknown operator early 2000, returned by 25-5-00. Sold or retired by 2003
ER-65707	Tu-134AK*	(03)63435	5907	D-30-III engines. C/s No 1, later No 2
ER-65736	Tu-134A-3	1351501		SOC by 1999
ER-65741	Tu-134A-3	2351601		SOC by 1999
ER-65791	Tu-134A-3	(03)63110	5602	C/s No 2, later No 3
ER-65897	Tu-134A-3	(53)42210	3206	C/s No 1, later No 2

For many years the aircraft wore basic Aeroflot colours with an all-white tail, red 'AIR MOLDOVA' titles and the Moldovan flag on the centre fuselage (c/s No 1); the old CCCP- prefix was retained for a while. A new livery strongly reminiscent of the pre-1973 Aeroflot Tu-134A colour scheme was introduced in 1994 (c/s No 2).

The current livery with a white fuselage and a dark blue tail (No 3) was adopted in the spring of 2000, and the recently transferred Tu-134AK ER-65094 was the first to receive it ('last in, first out'?). Curiously, ER-65791 had the registration incorrectly applied to the underside of the wings as ER-65971 (see Russia/Komiavia) during repaint to livery No 2; this error was rectified during repaint to livery No 3.

In August 1996 Kishinyov-based **MOLDAVIAN AIRLINES** [2M/MDV] leased Tu-134A-3 ER-65036 from Air Moldova. After returning it the airline leased Tu-134AK ER-AAZ from Vichi (see below) in May 1997. Receiving a new interior layout with 12 business class seats and 56 tourist class seats, the aircraft was painted in an attractive three-tone green/white livery; soon afterwards it was purchased by Moldavian Airlines and reregistered ER-TCF. The fairing under the APU exhaust readily identifies it as a former Tu-134 *Balkany*. In 2003, however, ER-TCF was reportedly sold back to Vichi!

TIRAMAVIA [–/TVI], yet another Kishinyov-based airline, bought Tu-134A-3 OM-GAT (c/n 6348565, f/n 3701) from the Slovak carrier Air Transport Europe in November 2000. Reregistered ER-TCH, the aircraft retained the green/white livery of its previous owner, complete with titles! As early as June 2001, however, it was sold to the Ukrainian carrier South Airlines as UR-BZY.

The **MOLDOVAN GOVERNMENT FLIGHT** operated a 36-seat Tu-134AK, ER-65094, as the presidential aircraft of Mircea Snegur and later his successor Pyotr Luchinskiy (or, to use *their* spelling, Petru Lucinschi). The basic livery was again that of Aeroflot, but the aircraft had MOLDOVA titles, the national coat of arms aft of the flightdeck and the Moldovan flag was carried on the tail, not on the fuselage. In early 2000 the aircraft was sold to Air Moldova and converted again to passenger configuration – Moldova's third President Vladimir Voronin uses a Yak-42D 'Salon' (ER-YCA).

The **MOLDOVAN AIR FORCE** (FARM – *Forțele Aeriene de Republica Moldova*) operated a single Tu-134 *Balkany* (ER-65686, c/n (93)62390, f/n 5301) equipped to Tu-134A-3 standard. Since Moldova had no real use for an ABCP, the aircraft was promptly transferred to

VICHI AIRLINES [–/VIH], the commercial division of FARM, and stripped of the *Balkany* suite, receiving the new registration ER-AAZ (the last three letters caused this particular aircraft to be nicknamed 'Aziza' – possibly an association with a female singer who enjoyed notoriety in the CIS at the time). In 1997 Vichi leased and then sold the aircraft to Moldavian Airlines (see story above).

TAJIKISTAN

TAJIKISTAN AIRLINES [W5/TZK, later 7J/TZK], originally known as **TAJIK AIR**, operated 12 Tu-134A-3s based at Khujand.

Registration	C/n	F/n	Notes
EY-65003	(53)44040	3302	C/s No 1/no titles; later No 2? Was lst Stigl as 65003 before becoming EY-65003
EY-65022	(63)48395	3505	Ex-Estonian Air ES-AAE, D/D 1-97; c/s No 2
EY-65127	(83)60627	4709	Ex-Estonian Air ES-AAJ, bought 9-93; c/s No 1. Sold to Tyumen' Airlines 11-93 as RA-65127
EY-65730	1351310		C/s No 1. Sold to Georgia as 4L-65730
EY-65763	(93)62299	5204	C/s No 1, later No 2. Lst Shaheed Air ?-02
EY-65788	(03)62835	5509	C/s No 1, later No 2
EY-65814	4352208		C/s No 1/no titles. SOC by 2000
EY-65820	(43)08056	2305	C/s No 1. SOC by 2002
EY-65835	(43)17112	2507	C/s No 1/no titles; later No 2?
EY-65875	(53)29317	2910	SOC by 1997
EY-65876	(53)31220	3002	C/s No 1, later No 2
EY-65895	(53)40140	3203	C/s No 1. SOC by 1997

Again, at first they wore basic Aeroflot colours with a red/green/white 'bird in a circle' tail logo (c/s No 1) and TAJIK AIR titles. The latter were subject to variations – EY-65127 had Cyrillic 'TOCHIKISTON' (Tajikistan) titles, and several other aircraft were anonymous. The current blue/white livery with TAJIKISTAN titles appeared in 1994 (c/s No 2); EY-65763 has English titles to starboard and Tajik titles to port.

THE UKRAINE

AIR UKRAINE/AVIALINIĬ UKRAÏNY [6U/UKR], the Ukrainian flag carrier, had no fewer than 27 Tu-134s operated by the Borispol' (Kiev), Khar'kov and Chernovtsy divisions.

Registration	Version	C/n	F/n	Notes
UR-65037	Tu-134A-3	(63)48850	3704	Based Khar'kov, c/s No 1. To Air Kharkov
UR-65048	Tu-134A-3	(73)49750	3806	Based Kiev, c/s No 2. SOC by 2000
UR-65073†	Tu-134AK*	(73)49980	4108	Based Khar'kov. D-30-III engines, c/s No 5. To Air Kharkov
UR-65076†	Tu-134A-3	(73)60001	4202	Based Chernovtsy, c/s No 1, later No 5. To UM Air ?-98; bought back by 9-02
UR-65077†	Tu-134A-3 'Salon'	(73)60028	4203	Based Kiev, c/s No 2, later No 5
UR-65089	Tu-134A-3	(73)60180	4308	Based Chernovtsy. To Bukovyna Airlines
UR-65092	Tu-134A-3	(83)60206	4401	Based Khar'kov. Lst Imperial Air ?-93 as OB-1553; damaged Lima 15-4-93/stored
UR-65093	Tu-134AK*	(83)60215	4402	Based Khar'kov. D-30-III engines. Lst Imperial Air 1993-96 as OB-1552. Sold to Pulkovo ?-97 as RA-65093
UR-65107	Tu-134A	(83)60328	4505	Based Kiev
UR-65109	Tu-134AK*	(83)60339	4507	Based Khar'kov. C/n sometimes reported in error as (83)60342 or (83)60432. Sold to Pulkovo ?-98 as RA-65109
UR-65114	Tu-134A-3	(83)60395	4602	Based Khar'kov, c/s No 1. To Air Kharkov
UR-65123	Tu-134A-3	(83)60525	4703	Based Khar'kov. Lst Imperial Air 12-92 as OB-1490; stored Lima

UR-65134	Tu-134A-3	(83)60647	4807	Based Kiev, c/s No 4 (later No 5?); sold or retired by 2003
UR-65135	Tu-134A-3	(83)60648	4808	Based Kiev, c/s No 2, later No 5
UR-65718	Tu-134AK	(13)63668	6108	Based Kiev. D-30-III engines, c/s No 5. Sold to Ukraine Air Enterprise ?-97
UR-65746	Tu-134AK*	2351608		Based Khar'kov. D-30-III engines. To Air Kharkov
UR-65752	Tu-134A-3	(93)61079	5008	Based Khar'kov, c/s No 1. To Air Kharkov
UR-65757	Tu-134A-3	(93)62215	5108	Based Kiev, colour scheme No 1, later No 4, still later No 5
UR-65761	Tu-134AK*	(93)62244	5201	Based Khar'kov. D-30-III engines, c/s No 5. To Air Kharkov
UR-65764	Tu-134A-3	(93)62305	5205	Based Khar'kov. To Air Kharkov
UR-65765	Tu-134A	(93)62315	5206	Based Kiev, c/s No 3, later No 5
UR-65773	Tu-134AK*	(93)62495	5308	D-30-III engines. Based Khar'kov, c/s No 5. To Air Kharkov
UR-65782	Tu-134A-3	(93)62672	5410	Based Kiev, c/s No 5. Sold to Ukraine Air Enterprise ?-97
UR-65790	Tu-134A-3	(03)63100	5601	Based Chernovtsy, colour scheme No 5. To Bukovyna Airlines
UR-65826	Tu-134A-3	(43)12083	2405	SOC by 1997
UR-65841	Tu-134A	(43)18120	2603	SOC Yerevan ?-97
UR-65852	Tu-134A	(43)23244	2706	C/s No 1, later No 2. SOC by 1997
UR-65864	Tu-134A-3	(53)28284	2809	Based Kiev, c/s No 2. SOC by 1997
UR-65877†	Tu-134AK*	(53)31250	3003	Based Khar'kov. D-30-III engines, c/s No 5. To Air Kharkov
UR-65888	Tu-134AK*	(53)36175	3105	D-30-III engines. SOC by 1997

Until 1993 the airline had a truly baffling variety of colour schemes – the various divisions of the large Ukrainian CAD applied Air Ukraine titles and logos as they saw fit. Thus some Tu-134s retained basic Aeroflot colours with a Ukrainian flag and Air Ukraine titles above the windows, 'Авіалінії Украïни' titles below the windows and a tail logo consisting of a stylised yellow bird on a blue circle (c/s No 1). Others had a reversed logo – a blue bird on a yellow circle (c/s No 2). Still others featured white undersides and engine nacelles combined with a 'blue bird' tail logo (c/s No 3). 'Still still others' also had white undersides but 'Авіалінії Украïни' titles above the windows and a 'yellow bird' tail logo (c/s No 4).

Soon, however, the airline's management rightly decided that having such a motley fleet 'ain't no good nohow'.[16] Thus a fleetwide standard livery featuring the national flag colours of yellow and blue was introduced, starting in late 1993. After repaint in c/s No 5 some aircraft had the registration applied with no dash (such aircraft are marked with †).

It deserves mention here that two ex-Polish radar-nosed Tu-134AKs – CCCP-65559 and CCCP-65623 No 2 – briefly wore full Air Ukraine colours, albeit with the CCCP- prefix (!), an incorrectly painted 'bird' and additional Aeroflot titles/logo. In reality they were never operated by Air Ukraine and delivered straight to Aeroflot Russian International Airlines (which see). The reason is probably that, being ex-Polish Air Force aircraft, they were considered military equipment for legal purposes (airliners though they be!). Since Russian trade legislation prohibits purchase

Moldovan Government Tu-134AK ER-65094 moments after landing on runway 06 at Moscow-Vnukovo. Though operated by the Moldovan CAD/Kishinyov UAD/269th Flight as a 76-seater since at least 1987, the aircraft reverted to VIP configuration after the demise of the Soviet Union. Yuriy Kirsanov

Most Tajik Air Tu-134s, including Tu-134A-3 EY-65814 shown here on short finals to Moscow-Domodedovo, originally flew in basic Aeroflot colours with tail logo but no titles. The green-painted radome on this aircraft is most unusual. Yuriy Kirsanov

Tajikistan Airlines Tu-134A-3 EY-65763 at Ras al Khaimah on 4th March 2002. This aircraft is unusual in having Tajik titles to starboard; usually the titles are in English on both sides. Nikolay Ionkin

of military equipment by civilian organisations, the deal had to involve a third party to circumvent the inconvenient law.

In January 2001 at least one Air Ukraine Tu-134A-3 (UR-65135) wore a special colour scheme with pigeons carrying Ukrainian embroidered towels painted all over the aircraft.

Around 1998 the Khar'kov division of Air Ukraine became an independent airline called **AIR KHARKOV/AVIALINIÏ KHARKOVA** [–/KHV]. Its aircraft retained basic Air Ukraine colours with new titles and a stylised X (Cyrillic 'Kh') tail logo. (See Air Ukraine fleet list for details.)

By 2000 the Chernovtsy division also became a separate entity called **BUKOVYNA AIRLINES** [–/CHV] and operating two Tu-134A-3 – UR-65089 and UR-65790. Again it stuck to basic Air Ukraine colours with new titles and logo. Both aircraft were leased to UM Air in 2000, though UR-65790 has now been returned.

In March 2000 Donetsk-based **ISD-AVIA** [–/ISD] (ISD = Industrial Systems of Donbass, that is, 'Donetsk basin', a major coal mining region) purchased Tu-134B-1-3 RA-65720 from Tupolev-Aerotrans. Reregistered UR-BYY, the aircraft had the colour scheme amended to feature a white tail, blue engine nacelles and no titles. The aircraft was upgraded with new avionics, including TCAS; as of September 2001 it was a 70-seater, but a conversion to an executive layout was planned.

In 2000 Odessa-based **SOUTH AIRLINES/PIVDENNI AVIALINIÏ** [YG/OTL] leased Tu-134AK UR-65773 from Air Kharkov. The lessor's logo was retained, only the titles being replaced (in English to port and in Ukrainian to starboard). By July 2001 the airline doubled its fleet by purchasing Tu-134A-3 UR-BZY (ex-Tiramavia ER-TCH); this still wears Air Transport Europe colours and logo!

Khar'kov-based **SPAERO** [–/SPF] leased Tu-134s from other carriers as required.

Business charter operator **TRANSAGO** [–/AKO] based at Kiev-Borispol' operated three Tu-134A-3 'Salons'.

Registration	C/n	F/n	Notes
UR-65023	(63)48415	3508	Ex-Lithuanian Airlines LY-ABB, D/D 7-97; full c/s. Sold to Tatarstan Airlines as RA-65023
UR 65077	(73)60028	4203	Lsf Air Ukraine ?-95; full 1993-standard Air Ukraine c/s with additional AGO nose titles. Returned to lessor
UR-65081	(73)60076	4208	Ex-Lithuanian Airlines LY-ABE, D/D 3-97; full c/s, named 'Nina'. Opf UNEX Bank; fate unknown

During the spring of 1998 TransAGO was renamed **PRESTIGE-AVIA** [–/PGE]; the eye-catching blue/yellow livery remained the same, save for the titles and logo. In 2000, however, the airline ceased operations.

Founded in 1998 and based at Kiev-Borispol', **UM AIR** (Ukrainian-Mediterranean Airlines) [UF/UKM] operated three Tu-134A-3s.

Registration	C/n	F/n	Notes
UR 65076	(73)60001	4202	Leased from Air Ukraine; basic 1993-standard Air Ukraine c/s, UM Air titles/logo. Sub-leased to Sibaviatrans by 9-01; returned to lessor by 9-02
UR-65089	(73)60180	4308	Leased from Bukovyna Airlines, full c/s, named 'Yaroslav'
UR-65790	(03)63100	5601	Leased from Bukovyna Airlines, basic 1993-standard Air Ukraine c/s, titles unknown. Returned by 2003

Top: **Looking rather tatty, with Aeroflot titles showing through underneath the Air Ukraine titles, Tu-134A UR-65037 sits at Khar'kov-Osnova, its home base. This aircraft has the Air Ukraine logo in yellow on a blue background; in contrast, Kiev-based examples had the colours reversed.** Peter Davison

Below: **Spoilers deployed and engines roaring at reverse thrust, Tu-134A-3 'Salon' UR-65081 'Nina' completes its landing run at Moscow-Vnukovo. The stylish TransAGO livery is augmented by unobtrusive UNEX Bank titles.** Dmitriy Petrochenko

Above: **Tu-134A UR-65790 in 1993-standard Air Ukraine colours comes in to land at Moscow-Vnukovo.** Dmitriy Petrochenko

Opposite page: **Tu-134A-3 UR-65089 'Yaroslav' looks magnificent in the eye-catching livery of UM Air (Ukrainian Mediterranean Airlines). In passing, such artwork is commonly found on 'hot rods', and the analogy may be justified: the Tu-134 does behave rather like a fighter. (And sounds like one, too.)** Sergey and Dmitriy Komissarov archive

VETERAN AIRLINES [–/VPB], a commercial division of the Ukrainian Air Force based in Dzhankoy, leased Tu-134A OM-GAT (c/n 6348565, f/n 3701) from Air Transport Europe in 1999-2000.

The **UKRAINIAN GOVERNMENT FLIGHT** based at Kiev-Borispol' and known as the **UKRAINE AIR ENTERPRISE** [–/UKN] since 1996 has three Tu-134s.

Registration	Version	C/n	F/n	Notes
UR-65556	Tu-134AK	(43)66372	6364	Ex-65556; D-30-III engines, Tatra-M HF comms gear, basic Aeroflot c/s, Ukrainian flag on tail, UKRAÏNA titles; got Air Ukraine 'blue bird' logo as UR-65556; later full c/
UR-65718	Tu-134AK	(13)63668	6108	Ex-Air Ukraine, D/D ?-97; D-30-III engines. Basic 1993-standard Air Ukraine c/s, UKRAÏNA titles; later full c/s
UR-65782	Tu-134A-3 'Salon'	(93)62672	5410	Ex-Air Ukraine, D/D ?-97. Basic 1993-standard Air Ukraine c/s, UKRAÏNA titles; later full c/s

Tu-134AK 65556 was originally the presidential aircraft of Leonid Kravchuk and then of his successor Leonid Kuchma. In 1997 it became the unit's first aircraft to receive a white colour scheme with a thin yellow/blue cheatline and the Ukrainian coat of arms on the fuselage; the interior was refurbished by Diamonite. The other two examples were customised by Albatech. Since 1997 two IL-62M 'Salons' with intercontinental range are earmarked as the presidential jets and the Tu-134s take second place.

The **UKRAINIAN AIR FORCE** (UAF, or VPS – *Voyenno-povitryany seely*) had at least 16 Tu-134s on strength. First-line units included the 1st OSTAP (*otdel'nyy smeshannyy trahnsportnyy aviapolk* – independent composite airlift regiment, formerly 16th OSAP) at Kiev-Borispol', the 243rd OSAP at Sknilov AB near L'vov, and Squadron 3 of the 184th GvTBAP at Priluki AB. The Voroshilovgrad VVAUSh also found itself in the independent Ukraine after the break-up of the USSR (Voroshilovgrad has since been renamed back to Lugansk); however, the Ukraine had no need to train a lot of bomber crews and only a few Tu-134Sh-1s have been retained, the rest being transferred to Russia. The Tu-134UBLs are used for training Tu-22M crews, now that the Tu-160s at Priluki have been disposed of. Known aircraft are listed below.

Tactical code	Version	C/n	F/n	Notes
01 Yellow	Tu-134 *Balkany*	(23)63957	6314	1st OSTAP. Blue c/s with lightning bolt pinstripe. To UAF 63957† after 9-95, to 63957 after 1996
02 Yellow	Tu-134 *Balkany*	(23)63960	6315	[UR-63960] 243rd OSAP. Blue c/s with lightning bolt pinstripe;
03 Yellow	Tu-134 *Balkany*	(23)63982	6324	[UR-63982] Blue c/s with lightning bolt pinstripe; to 63982 and stripped of Balkany suite by 6-01
05 Blue	Tu-134Sh-1?	?	?	C/n reported as 36140 but cannot be correct
16 Blue	Tu-134Sh-1?	?	?	C/n reported as 37190 but cannot be correct
42 Red	Tu-134UBL	(23)64670	?	[UR-64670] 148th GvTBAP; Air Ukraine 'blue bird' logo!‡
43 Red	Tu-134UBL	(23)64678		[UR-64678] 148th GvTBAP
45 Red	Tu-134UBL	?	?	148th GvTBAP
71 Blue	Tu-134Sh-1?	?	?	C/n reported as 40105 but cannot be correct
72 Red	Tu-134UBK	(23)64728	?	[UR-64728] 33rd TsBP i PLS; recoded '83 Red'? WFU Nikolayev-Kul'bakino by 5-02, CCCP-64728 shows through!

† The unusual UAF prefix stood for Ukrainian Air Force.

‡ The Air Ukraine logo was applied because ARZ No 407 did not have stencils for UAF insignia.

The two quasi-civil Tu-134 *Balkany* ABCPs (63957 and 63982) nevertheless wear full UAF insignia (a blue shield with a trident on the tail and yellow/blue roundels on the wings), which is a fairly common occurrence for UAF transports. They also wear *Zbroyny Seely Ookraïny* (Ukrainian Armed Forces) titles.

UZBEKISTAN

The **UZBEKISTAN AIR FORCE** has at least one Tu-134 *Balkany*, UK 63979 (c/n (23)63979, f/n 6323). The aircraft makes a rather strange sight, as it wears the full livery of the national flag carrier **UZBEKISTAN AIRWAYS** (Uzbekiston Havo Yullari) [HY/UZB] and 'AIR FORCE' titles on the tail directly above the registration!

Above: **Ukrainian Air Force Tu-134 *Balkany* '03 Yellow' (c/n (23)63982) wears a colour scheme similar to that of Soviet/Russian Air Force red-painted examples. This aircraft was later stripped of the *Balkany* suite and became 63982, gaining *Zbroyny Seely Ookraïny* (Ukrainian Armed Forces) titles.** RART

Below: **Uzbekistan Air Force Tu-134 *Balkany* UK 63979 looks rather incongruous in Uzbekistan Airways livery.** Tupolev JSC

Chapter Seven

The Foreign Scene
Non-CIS Operators

The Tu-134 may be rightly called a bestseller among Soviet airliners. It was supplied to 13 nations, becoming the first jet aircraft for some of its operators; a total of 138 were exported. Additionally, the Tu-134 was leased by the airlines of seven more nations. Thus it has seen service almost all over the world!

Aircraft no longer operated by the respective carrier are shown in italics in the fleet lists (except when the airline itself no longer exists or *all* of its Tu-134s have been sold or retired). For aircraft leased to other carriers, only the last known lease is indicated for reasons of space. 'Tu-134AK*' (with an asterisk) means the aircraft is converted to passenger configuration. 'r.n.' denotes 'radar nose' (Groza-M134 radar).

ALBANIA

Deciding to finally come out of self-imposed political isolation, Albania launched economic reforms. Hence **ALBANIAN AIRLINES** [LV/LBC] were established in 1992 for furthering communication with the outside world. Since the impoverished country could not afford to buy aircraft, leasing them was the only option. In October 1996 Albanian Airlines leased radar-nosed Tu-134A-3 LZ-TUN from Hemus Air; a year later it was joined by Tu-134B-3 'Salon' LZ-TUT, followed by Tu-134A-1 LZ-TUH in March 1998. All have been returned now.

ANGOLA

The **ANGOLAN AIR FORCE** (FAA – *Força Aérea Angolana*) took delivery of radar-nosed Tu-134AK D2-ECC (c/n (73)49830, f/n 3903) in 1977. The aircraft was delivered with 'Força Aérea Angolana No 1' titles but these were changed to 'Republica Popular de Angola' by November 1981.

An FAA Tu-134AK serialled SG-104 was reportedly seen at Belgrade in June 1983; this was almost certainly the same aircraft which later again became D2-ECC.

BULGARIA

BALKAN BULGARIAN AIRLINES [LZ/LAZ], formerly TABSO – Bulgarian Air Transport, became the first foreign customer for the Tu-134 soon after being renamed on 1st April 1968, operating 13 of the type. The Tu-134s inherited the registrations of TABSO Li-2Ps; the choice of the TU… registration block was obviously intentional.

Registration	Version	C/n	F/n	Notes
LZ-TUA	Tu-134	8350405		D/D 22-9-68, SOC Sofia by 5-92; scrapped, tail to Bourgas museum
LZ-TUB	Tu-134	8350501		D/D 9-68. Crashed near Vratsa 16-3-78
LZ-TUC	Tu-134	9350807		D/D 6-69, SOC Sofia
LZ-TUD	Tu-134	9350808		D/D 6-69. Preserved Porein
LZ-TUE	Tu-134	9350914		D/D 12-69. Preserved on road 1km from Varna in amusement park
LZ-TUF	Tu-134	0350918		D/D 3-70. Preserved Sofia Golf Club, Ihtiman (previously reported as scrapped Sofia 29-5-87!)
LZ-TUK	Tu-134A	1351209		Ex-Bulgarian AF Tu-134A 'Salon', bought by 2-74. SOC Sofia by 4-95.
LZ-TUL	Tu-134A/r.n.	4352303		D/D 4-74. Sold to Hemus Air ?-94
LZ-TUM	Tu-134AK/r.n.*	3351906		D-30-III engines. Ex-Bulgarian AF, bought by 1986 (?). Sold to Tupolev-Aerotrans 7-95 as RA-65940
LZ-TUN	Tu-134A/r.n.	4352307		D/D 5-74. Sold to Hemus Air ?-94
LZ-TUO	Tu-134K*	0350922		Ex-Bulgarian AF '050 Red' No 1, D/D ?-78
LZ-TUR	Tu-134A/r.n.	4352308		D/D 5-74. Crashed Sofia 10-1-84
LZ-TUS	Tu-134A/r.n.	(83)60642	4805	D/D 9-78. Sold to 6-95 as RA-65941

The first revenue service from Sofia to Varna was performed in September 1968. Soon the Tu-134 *sans suffixe* had superseded the IL-18 on Balkan's international routes; the first foreign service was Sofia-London via Brussels. LZ-TUA and -TUB originally had a TABSO-style blue cheatline with 'feathers' at the front; it became red on subsequent aircraft. Tu-134A deliveries commenced in February 1974, making the first scheduled flight from Sofia to Prague on 4th April.

Along with the Tu-154, which was introduced in 1975, the Tupolev twinjets served 28 destinations abroad. Later the Tu-134s were repainted to match the fleetwide standard, with a heavier cheatline running across the windows instead of underneath. In the late 1980s Balkan introduced a new predominantly white livery matching the latest fashion, with curved stripes in the national flag colours of red, white and green; only one 'short' Tu-134, LZ-TUO, survived long enough to receive it.

Balkan's Tu-134 operations were quite intensive, with an average daily utilisation of 11-12 hours. For instance, on 22nd July 1986 LZ-TUL logged 11 hours 30 minutes in six flights, transporting a total of 530 passengers.

In the early 1990s, however, Balkan replaced the thirsty Tu-134As with three fuel-efficient Boeing 737-53As; the last remaining example was disposed of in 1995.

Sofia-based **HEMUS AIR** [DU/HMS] founded in 1986 operated eight Tu-134s. Most of the examples owned by the airline had a gaudy red/green/yellow/white livery, except for the ex-Czech machines which retain basic ČSA colours. The former VIP aircraft have been refitted as 76-seaters.

Registration	Version	C/n	F/n	Notes
LZ-TUH	Tu-134A-1	7360142	4305	Ex-ČSA OK-HFM, D/D 11-97
LZ-TUJ	Tu-134A/r.n.	7349913	4105	Ex-ČSA OK-HFL, D/D 12-97
LZ-TUL	Tu-134A-3/r.n.	4352303		Ex-Balkan, D/D ?-94
LZ-TUN	Tu-134A-3/r.n.	4352307		Ex-Balkan, D/D ?-94; basic Albanian Airlines c/s after lease
LZ-TUP	Tu-134AK*	1351303		Ex-Bulgarian AF LZ D 050, D/D ?-97
LZ-TUT	Tu-134B-3* 'Salon'	(23)63987	6326	Has rear door (≅ Tu-134AK); ex-Bulgarian AF, D/D ?-96. C/n sometimes reported in error as (43)66240
CCCP-65730	Tu-134A	1351310		Briefly leased from Aeroflot/Tajik CAD 7-90
CCCP-65875	Tu-134A	(53)29317	2910	Briefly leased from Aeroflot/Tajik CAD 7-90

The 16th Airlift Regiment (16 *Transporten Aviopolk*) of the **BULGARIAN AIR FORCE** (BVVS – *Bolgarski Voyenno Vozdooshni Seeli*) based at Dobroslavtzi AB near Sofia included a government VIP flight (formerly Sqn 1) operating from Sofia-Vrazhdebna airport. Among other things it operated nine Tu-134s – mostly civil-registered and in full Balkan colours to facilitate flights abroad. Only two BVVS Tu-134s ever wore military markings. Since 1964 the government flight was nominally part of Bulgaria's Ministry of Transport, but its entire flight and ground personnel consisted of BVVS officers on temporary duty at the Ministry. In 1972 the unit was renamed **28th GOVERNMENT FLIGHT**.

Regn / Serial	Version	C/n	F/n	Notes
LZ-TUG	Tu-134A-3 'Salon'	7349858	3907	Ex-Czech MoI OK-BYT, D/D 26-9-83, 47-seater; SOC by 2003
LZ-TUK	Tu-134A 'Salon'	1351209		D/D 27-3-71. Sold to Balkan by 2-74
LZ-TUM	Tu-134AK/r.n.	3351906		D/D 6-73, D-30-III engines. Sold to Balkan by 6-86 (?)
LZ-TUP	Tu-134AK	1351303		D/D 7-71. To '050 Red' No 2 ?-78; back to LZ-TUP 8-80. To LZ D 050† 7-95; sold to Hemus Air ?-97 as LZ-TUP
LZ-TUT	Tu-134B-3 'Salon'	(23)63987	6326	Has rear door (≅ Tu-134AK); c/n sometimes reported in error as (43)66240. Sold to Hemus Air ?-96
LZ-TUU	Tu-134AK	1351409		Ex-Czech MoI OK-BYQ, D/D 26-9-83, 47-seater, D-30-III engines. Sold to Tupolev-Aerotrans by 4-95 as RA-65939
LZ-TUV	Tu-134AK	1351408		Ex-Czech MoI OK-BYR, D/D 26-9-83, 47-seater, D-30-III engines
LZ-TUZ	Tu-134A-3	1351503		Ex-Czech MoI OK-BYS, D/D 26-9-83. WFU Sofia
050 Red No 1	Tu-134K	0350922		Ex-LZ-TUO? D/D ?-71. Sold to Balkan ?-78 as LZ-TUO

† The D was probably derived from Dobroslavtzi AB. The aircraft wore basic 1990s-standard Bakjan colours, BVVS roundels and 'Voyenno Vozdooshni Seeli' (port)/'Bulgarian Air Force' (starboard) titles.

LZ-TUG, -TUK and -TUU featured a non-standard L-shaped aerial above the flightdeck; on the latter two aircraft it was removed prior to sale.

Only Tu-134A 'Salon' LZ-TUG remained active by mid-1996; this aircraft was leased to Balkan from time to time. In late 1999 it gained 'РЕПУБЛИКА БЪЛГАРИЯ' (port)/'REPUBLIC OF BULGARIA' (starboard) titles.

In mid-2002 an airline called **TRANSAIR** operated a Tu-134 registered LZ-ACB (other reports say LZ-ACS). This was reportedly an ex-Latvian Tu-134B-3; this leaves YL-LBK, c/n (03)63425, f/n 5906) as the only possible previous identity, as all other Latvian Tu-134Bs were sold elsewhere.

All three Luftwaffe Tu-134AKs (11+10, 11+11 and 11+12 – see below) were ostensibly sold to Croatia in 1992 and registered 9A-ADP, 9A-ADL and 9A-ADR respectively on 16th December, with **RPL AIRPORTS RIJEKA** as the official owner. The aircraft retained basic Interflug or, in the case of 9A-ADL, East German Air Force colours. Actually, however, they were never delivered to Croatia; the real owner was a German financial group which wanted to sell them wholesale to the highest bidder. Thus in July 1993 the aircraft were sold to Aeroflot Russian International Airlines as RA-65567, RA-65566 and RA-65568 respectively.

In 1994 the **AEROMEDICAL SERVICES CYPRUS** non-profit organisation wet-leased radar-nosed Tu-134A-3 RA-65667 (c/n 1351207) from Tupolev-Aerotrans.

The nation's flag carrier **ČSA ČESKOSLOVENSKÉ AEROLINIE** (Czechoslovak Airlines) [OK/CSA] took delivery of 14 radar-nosed Tu-134As.

Registration	Version	C/n	F/n	Notes
OK-AFA†	Tu-134A	1351406		D/D 29-11-71, WFU 20-5-88, sold to the USSR 30-11-88
OK-AFB†	Tu-134A	1351410		D/D 9-1-72. DBR Prague 11-10-88, preserved Piešťany airport as bar
OK-CFC	Tu-134A	2351504		D/D 5-3-72, WFU 15-11-90, scrapped Prague; cockpit section preserved Au, Zürich Canton, Switzerland 1-98
OK-CFD	Tu-134A	2351505		D/D 10-3-72, DBR Prague 2-1-77, scrapped 30-8-77
OK-CFE	Tu-134A	2351602		D/D 12-5-72, WFU 9-11-90, flown to Ancona, Italy, 14-12-90 and preserved Aeropark Loreto (later to Porto Recanati)
OK-CFF	Tu-134A	2351603		D/D 19-5-72, WFU 4-7-89, scrapped Prague
OK-CFG	Tu-134A	2351710		D/D 15-1-73, WFU 14-12-90, scrapped Prague 1992. C/n often reported in error as 2351701 which is Tu-134AK CCCP-65749
OK-CFH	Tu-134A	2351801		D/D 22-1-73, WFU 4-7-91 (or 10-9-92?), preserved Brno-Tuřany as bar
OK-DFI	Tu-134A	3351908		D/D 4-7-73, WFU 20-1-92, scrapped Prague‡
OK-EFJ	Tu-134A	4323128	2607	D/D 20-11-74, WFU 23-1-95/scrapped; cockpit section preserved VM VHÚ, Prague-Kbely§
OK-EFK	Tu-134A	4323130	2608	D/D 22-11-74, WFU 29-1-95
OK-HFL	Tu-134A	7349913	4105	D/D 1-7-77; sold to Hemus Air 12-97 as LZ-TUJ
OK-HFM	Tu-134A-1	7360142	4305	D/D 22-12-77, 100th export aircraft. Sold to Hemus Air 11-97 as LZ-TUH
OK-IFN	Tu-134A-1	8360282	4409	D/D 10-3-78. Sold to ORBI 11-97 as 4L-AAE

† The registrations OK-AFA and OK-AFB were previously worn by Fokker F.VIIb-3m airliners.
‡ OK-DFI was to be preserved at Aéroklub Kolín, Prague, in February 1994 but was damaged beyond repair by a tornado!
§ VM VHÚ = *Vojenské muzeum Vojenského historického ústavu* – Military Museum of the Military Historical Society.

Incidentally, the Czechs and Slovaks have a unique civil aircraft registration system. The first letter following the nationality prefix denotes the year of registration, except B (see below) and Q (which is never placed first); for example, O = 1960, Z = 1970 and so on. The second letter denotes the type (for example, A = IL-18, later reused for Airbus A310-308) and the third letter is individual. In the case of OK-AFB, OK-CFG and OK-CFH the first letter did not match the year due to late delivery.

In April 1966 ČSA had ordered 12 Tu-134s *sans suffixe* scheduled for delivery in 1968-70 as a replacement for the airline's three Tu-124VEs.[1] When Tu-134A CCCP-65646 had been demonstrated to ČSA and Ministry of Transport executives at Prague-Ruzyne on 19th October 1970 the airline converted its order to radar-nosed Tu-134As. OK-AFA flew the inaugural service from Prague to Bratislava on 9th December 1971; the

Balkan Bulgarian Airlines LZ-TUA was the first Tu-134 to be exported. Seen here at the factory prior to delivery, it had a blue cheatline inherited from TABSO Bulgarian Air Transport. Tupolev JSC

Tu-134A-1 OK-IFN in the latest livery of ČSA Czech Airlines on approach to Moscow-Sheremet'yevo around 1996. The aircraft was sold to ORBI Georgian Airlines in December 1997 as 4L-AAE. Yuriy Kirsanov

second aircraft entered service on 21st January 1972, allowing the two surviving Tu-124VEs to be sold (the third aircraft had crashed).

The Tu-134A was the second aircraft (after the IL-62) to receive ČSA's 1969-standard livery with a red cheatline running across the windows and a red tail proudly bearing a large flag and the legend 'OK jet'. As you see, OK is both Czechoslovakia's country prefix and the airline's flight code, but the coincidence with the universally known slang word made a good selling point – 'that's an OK airline!' Later, however, someone objected to the 'jet' (which under the Czech language's phonetic rules is pronounced as 'yet'!) and in 1987 the legend was amended to 'OK čsa'. The natural metal undersurfaces were soon painted grey and the original white paint on the radomes gave way to a higher-quality black paint of Western provenance (although OK-CFD had a grey radome for a while); OK-CFF was the first 'black-nosed' example.

On 29th October 1973 Tu-134A OK-DFI carried various dignitaries on a special flight on occasion of the airline's golden jubilee. In 1975 for the first time in its history ČSA carried more than a million passengers, and OK-CFH had the honour of carrying the millionth passenger.

A new livery appeared in August 1990; the basically white aircraft featured a large red ČSA logo on the fuselage, a large red 'OK' tail logo, red/white/blue pinstripes and black 'Czechoslovak Airlines' (port)/ 'Československé Aérolinie' (starboard) titles. Until 1991 OK-EFJ and OK-EFK had a different colour scheme with a red/blue rear fuselage/tail and white 'OK' tail logo. Yet another standard introduced in 1992 featured triple red/blue 'pennants' on the tail instead of the 'OK' logo; the blue pinstripe became a cheatline carrying white 'Czechoslovak Airlines' titles. Finally, on 1st January 1993 the post-Communist Czech/Slovak Federal Republic divided into two independent states and the airline was renamed **ČSA CZECH AIRLINES** (České Aérolinie).

As a follow-on to the Tu-134A, ČSA originally viewed the Yak-42 (in 1983) and then the Tu-334 (1990). Eventually neither type was ordered; in 1992 the Tu-134As were supplemented by four Aérospatiale/Alenia ATR 72-202 turboprops and five Boeing 737-55S jets. The last five examples soldiered on a little longer and were even upgraded with a 'wide-body look' interior by Diamonite (the first aircraft thus modified, OK-HFL, re-entered service on 10th June 1994), but they could not compete with Western hardware. Hence in 1997 ČSA finally retired the type; the last revenue flight, a return service from Prague to Belgrade, was performed on 9th December, and the passengers included invited guests and journalists. During 26 years of sterling service ČSA Tu-134As had logged more than 175 million km (108,695,650 miles – that is, approximately 4,375 times around the globe!) and carried nearly 14,900,000 passengers. In these 26 years there had been only one material failure.

AIR MORAVIA CZECH CHARTER AIRLINE LTD [–/MAI] based at Prague-Ruzyne leased Tu-134As from ČSA in 1993, carrying tourists to Mediterranean holiday resorts.

ENSOR AIR [E9/ENR], likewise Prague-based, leased Tu-134B-3 CCCP-65704 (c/n (03)63410, f/n 5904) from the Latvian CAD/Riga UAD between 10th August and 12th September 1992.

On 16th December 1971 the **CZECHOSLOVAK AIR FORCE** (CzAF, or ČVL – *Československé Vojenské Létectvo*) took delivery of a 47-seat Tu-134AK serialled '1407 Black' (c/n 1351407). The aircraft was operated by the 61st Transport Air Regiment (61. *dopravní letecký pluk*) based at Prague-Kbely AB. As early as 9th May 1972 it was unveiled to the general public when it took part in the VE-Day parade in Prague, escorted by four Mikoyan/Gurevich MiG-21F *Fishbed-C* fighters.

On 15th February 1980 Czechoslovakia's Minister of Defence, Army General M Dzur, was due to visit Libya. The route took him across the territory of several countries that refused overflight rights to military aircraft belonging to Warsaw Pact nations. To circumvent this obstacle the aircraft was furnished with a civil registration, OK-AFD (although it should have been OK-KFD, judging by the year)[2] and the Czech flag; the crew was issued ČSA uniforms and civil papers, but the blue/white colour scheme having nothing in common with the red/white ČSA livery told too plain a tale. When the mission was over the aircraft reverted to military markings, but the fake registration was still assigned to it for similar occasions. Other non-standard missions included taking the Czechoslovak Olympic team to the 1992 Winter Olympics in Lillehammer, Norway, and carrying trade delegations to international airshows.

On 1st January 1993 the sole CzAF Tu-134 was taken over by the 'new' **CZECH AIR FORCE** (*České Vojenské Létectvo*). The aircraft now belonged to the 1.SDLP (*smišený dopravni letecký pluk* – Composite Transport Air Regiment) and wore a smart red/blue/white colour scheme, the serial changing to '1407 White'. In March 1998 was sold to the Belorussian airline Techaviaservice, becoming EW-65861 No 2. (The original EW-65861 No 1 was a Belavia Tu-134A (ex-CCCP-65861, c/n (53)28269, f/n 2806) retired in 1997.)

The **CZECH FEDERAL GOVERNMENT FLIGHT** (LOMV – *Letecký oddíl ministerstva vnitra*; also called LS FMV – *Letecká společnost federálního ministerstva vnitra*, Airline of the Federal Ministry of the Interior) operated four Tu-134s.

Registration	Version	C/n	F/n	Notes
OK-BYQ	Tu-134AK	1351409		D/D 17-1-72; 47-seater. Sold to Bulgarian AF as LZ-TUU
OK-BYR	Tu-134AK	1351408		D/D 19-1-72; 47-seater. Sold to Bulgarian AF as LZ-TUV
OK-BYS	Tu-134A	1351503		D/D 7-3-72. Sold to Bulgarian AF as LZ-TUZ
OK-BYT	Tu-134A 'Salon'	7349858	3907	D/D 5-4-77; 47-seater. Sold to Bulgarian Air Force as LZ-TUG

As already mentioned, the letter B was never used to denote the year of registration. All LOMV fixed-wing aircraft were registered in the BYx block; the B stood for [*Veřejná*] *bezpečnost* – 'public security' (that is, police). These registrations were reused time and time again; thus, OK-BYQ was previously a Li-2 while OK-BYT was an Avia-14 Salon (Czech-built IL-14S).[3]

The aircraft wore a red/white colour scheme and distinctive LOMV insignia resembling the CzAF roundels but having a quasi-triangular shape. Unlike ČSA's aircraft, they all had glazed noses.

On 26th September 1983 all four aircraft were sold to the Bulgarian Air Force's government flight, their role taken over by four Tu-154B-2 'Salons' delivered in 1980-85 (OK-BYA through OK-BYD). Interestingly, after this ČSA Tu-134As were occasionally used for government trans-

portation tasks; for instance, on 10th-14th December 1985 OK-CFG made the longest-ever Tu-134 flight in Czech service, taking a government delegation from Prague to Beijing and back.

EGYPT

In mid-1970 Aviaexport began negotiations with **UNITED ARAB AIRLINES** [MS/MSR], the Egyptian flag carrier, concerning the purchase of four Tu-134As and four Tu-154s *sans suffixe*. (The name was a leftover from the United Arab Republic, the union of Egypt and Syria which existed from February 1958 to September 1961; for some reason it persisted until 1972 when the airline was rebranded **EGYPTAIR**.) The aircraft were to replace UAA's IL-18Ds and Comet 4Cs on international services and An-24Vs on domestic services.

In January 1971 a Tu-134 *sans suffixe* captained by Distinguished Test Pilot Nikolay N Kharitonov made a promotional visit to Cairo where it was demonstrated to Minister of Civil Aviation Ahmed Nuh. On 5th April the Egyptian CAA formed a commission for preparing the service introduction of the Tu-134A. The Egyptians ordered two (some sources say four) radar-nosed 80-seat Tu-134As for delivery in 1972; a pair of Tu-134s *sans suffixe* was to be leased from Aeroflot pending the delivery of these aircraft, carrying tourists to Abu Simbel, one of Egypt's main tourist attractions. The British 'ran against the Soviets', offering UAA the BAC One-Eleven 475FU. Eventually the airline changed its mind, cancelling the Tu-134 order in January 1972 in favour of four more Tu-154s.

Much later the Tu-134 *did* see service in Egypt. On 11th May 1992 the carter carrier **PYRAMID AIRLINES** [–/PYR] leased Tu-134A CCCP-65106 (c/n (83)60315, f/n 4503) from the Belarus' airline (later Belavia). In November it was replaced by another Tu-134A, CCCP-65133 (c/n (83)60645, f/n 4806), leased from the same carrier.

EQUATORIAL GUINEA

Western sources reported that **EGA ECUATO GUINEANA DE AVIACION** [8Y/EGA] operated a single Tu-134A (identity unknown) – obviously leased in the CIS – in 1997.

In November 2003 **UTAGE** (Union de Transporte Aéreo de Guinea Ecuatorial) [–/UTG] based in Malabo leased Tu-134B-3 UN 65695 from Aqualine Leasing (see Kazakhstan).

ESTONIA

The national flag carrier **ESTONIAN AIR** [OV/ELL] had 12 Tu-134As based at Tallinn-Ylemiste. (Strictly speaking, Soviet-built aircraft operated by the Baltic States cannot be regarded as export aircraft – they are the legacy of the Soviet-era Aeroflot (in this case, the Estonian CAD/Tallinn UAD/141st Flight). Still, since Estonia, Latvia and Lithuania are *not* CIS republics, this author sees no option but to place the Tu-134s operated there in the export section.)

Estonian Air Tu-134A ES-AAL (ex-CCCP-65768) taxying at St Petersburg-Pulkovo past a Pulkovo Air Enterprise Tu-154B-2 (RA-85542). The aircraft was sold to Chernomorskie Airlines in 1996 as RA-65575. Pyotr Batuyev

ELK Airways' sole Tu-134A-3 ES-LTA taxies in at Moscow/Sheremet'yevo-1. Dmitriy Petrochenko

Pre-delivery shot of DM-SCB, the second Tu-134 *sans suffixe* received by Interflug. Delivered on 1st October 1968, this aircraft was retired on 13th November 1985 with 19,966 hours total time after carrying 612,755 passengers; three years later it became a café in Oschersleben near Magdeburg. Tupolev JSC

Registration	Version	C/n	F/n	Notes
ES-AAE	Tu-134A	(63)48395	3505	Ex-CCCP-65022. Sold to Tajikistan Airlines 1-97 as EY-65022
ES-AAF	Tu-134A-3	6348565	3701	Ex-CCCP-65034. Sold to Air Transport Europe 5-95 as OM-GAT
ES-AAG	Tu-134A	(73)49907	4101	Ex-CCCP-65068. Sold to Pulkovo AE 8-95 as RA-65068
ES-AAH	Tu-134A	(53)35270	3009	Ex-CCCP-65882, basic Aeroflot c/s, no titles. SOC Tallinn 1996 (late 1994 ?)
ES-AAI	Tu-134A	(83)60350	4510	Ex-CCCP-65112. Sold to Pulkovo AE 5-96 as RA-65112
ES-AAJ	Tu-134A-3	(83)60627	4709	Ex-CCCP-65127. Sold to Tajikistan Airlines 9-93 as EY-65127
ES-AAK	Tu-134A	(93)60977	4909	Ex-CCCP-65144. Sold to Orient Avia 7-96 as RA-65144
ES-AAL	Tu-134A	(93)62350	5209	Ex-CCCP-65768. Sold to Chernomorskie Airlines 1996 as RA-65575
ES-AAM	Tu-134A-3	(83)60380	4601	Ex-CCCP-65113. Sold to Pulkovo AE 8-95 as RA-65113
ES-AAN	Tu-134A	(83)60560	4705	Ex-CCCP-65124. Sold to Askhab Air ?-97 as RA-65124
ES-AAO	Tu-134A	(93)62239	5110	Ex-CCCP-65759. Sold to Pulkovo AE 8-95 as RA-65759
ES-AAP	Tu-134A-3	(53)38020	3107	Ex-CCCP-65890, basic Aeroflot c/s, no titles. WFU Tallinn as fire trainer

Initially they retained Aeroflot colours *with* titles but had all-white tails and wore Estonian registrations on the engine nacelles; the old Soviet registration was still carried on the wings. Later, Estonian Air titles were introduced. Finally, in 1994 all Tu-134s except the two oldest ones (ES-AAH and -AAP) received a white livery with a stylised swallow logo.

Estonian Air found it difficult to operate the Tu-134. According to Technical Director Aarne Tork, in less than four years (1992-95) the cost of maintenance at Minsk done every 6,000 hours rose from US$ 120,000 to US$ 350,000 and spares were hard to come by. Also, the Tu-134 was thirsty and had a crew of four. Hence in mid-1995 Estonian Air leased two Boeing 737-5Q8s designed for two-crew operations.

By July 1994 seven of the 12 Tu-134As had been grounded and were eventually auctioned off at a starting price of US$ 213,000. Two aircraft remained by 1997 and these, too, were sold by mid-year.

In mid-1998 Tallinn-based **ELK EESTI LENNUKOMPANII** (Estonian Airways), aka **ELK AIRWAYS** [S8/ELK], bought Tu-134A-3 RA-65091 (c/n 8360195, f/n 4310) from the defunct Orient-Avia. Reregistered ES-LTA, the aircraft received an attractive blue/white/black livery; unlike the airline's Tu-154Ms, it has 'ELK Airways' titles (instead of 'Estonian') and 'Flights to Moscow, Riga, St Petersburg, Turku' subtitles. On 31st December 2001 the airline suspended operations; the aircraft was presumably sold.

GERMANY (EAST GERMANY & POST-REUNIFICATION GERMANY)

The former East Germany (German Democratic Republic) was the largest foreign operator of the type, purchasing a total of 39 Tu-134s. All except one of them wore the livery of national flag carrier **INTERFLUG** [IF/IFL] at some time or other.[4] In fact, however, only 29 of them were actually operated by Interflug, for which the Tu-134 was the first jet type, and based at Berlin-Schönefeld.

Registration	Version	C/n	F/n	Notes
DM-SCA	Tu-134	8350502		D/D 18-9-68. DBR Dresden 17-10-72, sold to the USSR for spares
DM-SCB	Tu-134	8350503		D/D 1-10-68, to DDR-SCB 19-9-81; WFU Berlin 13-11-85, preserved as café Oschersleben 10-88
DM-SCD	Tu-134	9350702		D/D 2-69. Crashed Leipzig 1-9-75
DM-SCE	Tu-134K*	9350904		Transferred from EGAF 2-74. To DDR-SCE 13-4-81; WFU 5-85, scrapped Berlin 6-86
DM-SCF	Tu-134K*	9350905		Transf. from EGAF 6-74. To DDR-SCF 22-7-81; WFU 31-3-86, flown to Leipzig 12-5-86 and preserved Aeropark Leipzig
DM-SCG	Tu-134K*	9350912		Transferred from EGAF 2-74. To DDR-SCG 8-7-81; WFU 14-7-85, to Erfurt as fire trainer/burnt same day
DM-SCH	Tu-134	9350906		D/D 8-69, to DDR-SCH 16-4-81. WFU 3-12-83, instructional airframe at Berlin-Schönefeld; to Luftfahrthistorische Sammlung Finow
DM-SCI	Tu-134A/r.n.	3351903		D/D 10-1-73. To DDR-SCI 13-4-81, later D-AOBA. Sold as CCCP-65611 No 2
DM-SCK	Tu-134AK*	1351304		Ex-EGAF '183 Black', transferred 11-75. To DDR-SCK 1-7-81; D-AOBB allocated. WFU 9-9-90; flown to Augsburg 29-9-90 and preserved Das Fliegende Museum, later to Flugausstellung Leo & Peter Junior, Hermeskeil
DM-SCL	Tu-134AK*	1351305		Ex-EGAF '182 Black', transferred 12-5-77. To DDR-SCL 8-5-81; WFU 9-9-89, sold to Hydro-Gerätebau AG, flown to Lahr AB 29-1-90 and preserved Biberach (Baden-Württemberg)
DM-SCM	Tu-134A/r.n.	3351904		D/D 18-5-73. Crashed Berlin 22-11-77; nose section preserved Aeropark Diepensee near Berlin 5-94
DM-SCN	Tu-134AK/r.n.*	3352102		Transferred from EGAF 17-11-77. To DDR-SCN 2-4-81, later D-AOBC. Sold as CCCP-65612 No 2
DM-SCO	Tu-134AK/r.n.*	3352106		Transferred from EGAF 11-5-79. To DDR-SCO 19-5-81, later D-AOBD. Sold as CCCP-65613 No 2
DM-SCP	Tu-134AK/r.n.*	4352205		Transferred from EGAF 13-10-78. To DDR-SCP 15-7-81, later D-AOBE. Sold as CCCP-65615 No 2
DM-SCR	Tu-134AK/r.n.*	4352206		Ex-EGAF '176 Black', transferred 4-6-80. To DDR-SCR 10-6-81, later D-AOBF. Sold as CCCP-65616 No 2, D/D 15-10-91
DM-SCS	Tu-134AK/r.n.*	4352207		Transferred from EGAF 22-5-79. To DDR-SCS 13-4-81, later D-AOBG. Sold as CCCP-65614 No 2
DM-SCT	Tu-134A/r.n.	4308068	2309	D/D 10-5-74. To DDR-SCT 8-5-81, later D-AOBH. Sold as CCCP-65617 No 2 27-8-91
DM-SCU	Tu-134A/r.n.	(43)09070	2310	D/D 10-5-74. To DDR-SCU 22-7-81, later D-AOBI. Sold as CCCP-65605 No 2, D/D 6-12-90
DM-SCV	Tu-134A/r.n.	4312095	2410	D/D 18-7-74. To DDR-SCV 9-4-81, later D-AOBJ. Sold as CCCP-65618 No 2
DDR-SCW	Tu-134AK/r.n.*	(53)31218	3001	Trf. from EGAF 5-82. To D-AOBK. Sold as CCCP-65619 No 2
DM-SCX	Tu-134A/r.n.	6348320	3406	D/D 2-4-76. To DDR-SCX 19-5-81, later D-AOBL. Sold as CCCP-65621 No 2
DM-SCY	Tu-134A/r.n.	(83)60495	4610	D/D 23-6-78. To DDR-SCY 16-4-81, later D-AOBM. Sold as CCCP-65622 No 2
DM-SCZ	Tu-134K*	9350913		Ex-EGAF '177 Black', transferred 1-12-75. To DDR-SCZ 2-4-81, WFU 8-3-86; preserved Bernsdorf near Zwickau 4-86
DDR-SDC	Tu-134AK/r.n.*	(53)35180	3006	Ex-EGAF '181 Black', transferred 9-3-82. To D-AOBN. Sold as CCCP-65620 No 2
DDR-SDE	Tu-134AK/r.n.*	5338040	3109	Trf. from EGAF 3-85. To D-AOBO. Sold as CCCP-65608 No 2

Regn	Version	C/n	F/n	Notes
DDR-SDF	Tu-134AK/r.n.*	(53)40150	3204	Trf. from EGAF 3-83. To D-AOBP. Sold as CCCP-65610 No 2
DDR-SDG	Tu-134AK/r.n.*	(63)46155	3401	Ex-EGAF '186 Black', transferred 15-2-88. To D-AOBQ. Sold as CCCP-65609 No 2, D/D 21-8-91
DM-SDH	Tu-134AK/r.n.	(63)46300	3405	D/D 29-3-76, opb MfS. To DDR-SDH 4-6-81, later D-AOBR. Sold as CCCP-65606 No 2, D/D 21-12-90
DM-SDI	Tu-134AK/r.n.	(63)48560	3610	D/D 27-8-76, opb MfS. To DDR-SDI 13-4-81, later D-AOBS. Sold as CCCP-65607 No 2, D/D 30-12-90

In December 1967 Interflug General Director Karl Heiland announced the purchase of the first three Tu-134s. The first two Tu-134s *sans suffixe* delivered in September-October 1968 were initially used for flight and ground crew training. The first passenger flight was performed on 28th February 1969 by DM-SCD from Berlin to Leipzig on occasion of the Leipzig Spring Fair; hence the passengers were executives of Interflug, Aeroflot, ČSA, TAROM, SAS, KLM, SABENA, Swissair, TWA, Air France, British European Airways, JAL and Alitalia, as well as numerous journalists. Scheduled flights began soon afterwards; the first international service (to Beirut) was performed on 2nd April 1969.

In 1973 the airline began taking delivery of Tu-134As. Here it should be noted that the first two Tu-134AKs delivered to the East German Air Force (see below) back in 1971 – DM-SCK and DM-SCL – were standard 'glass-nosed' aircraft. All other East German Tu-134As and 'AKs had the Groza-M134 radar; this led some Western authors to claim they were delivered in 'glass-nosed' configuration and later converted to radar-nosed configuration, which of course is nonsense.

Interflug's first Tu-134A (DM-SCI) probably entered service in May 1973 on the Berlin-Moscow route. (The East German magazine *Flieger Revue* reported that the first Tu-134A service took place on 1st May 1973, but this is rubbish as well because DM-SCI was manufactured on 5th May 1973 and it seems improbable that an EGAF Tu-134AK would have been used!) The final Tu-134A (DM-SCY) delivered in 1978 as an attrition replacement was unusual in being custom-built with the old BSU-3P ALS (see Chapter 3).

The fleet included 14 Tu-134AKs, but most of them were ex-EGAF aircraft converted to 80-seaters. DM-SDH and DM-SDI were an exception, being operated by the Ministry of State Security (Ministerium für Staatssicherheit, or MfS) – the notorious StaSi – and retaining their VIP layout throughout. These aircraft were referred to off the record as *Fesselflieger* (translates loosely as 'flying con carrier'); this was because, apart from carrying StaSi chief Erich Mielke, they were occasionally used to bring East German citizens arrested abroad for attempting to 'go over the wall' home for trial.

On the Tu-134A/AK the registration was moved from the engine nacelles to the extreme rear fuselage (to make it less observable?); later, however, the last three letters were repeated on the nose gear doors. The undersides, which were originally natural metal, were later painted grey and the Interflug logo on the nose was deleted, remaining only on the fin.

In 1981 East Germany changed its nationality prefix from DM- to DDR-, resulting in a unique six-letter format, and the entire civil aircraft fleet was reregistered in the course of the year. Curiously, the DDR-prefix had already been in use in 1952-56. The reason why they reverted to the old prefix may be that someone in the government perceived the letters DM as a hint at the currency of the ideologically hostile West Germany (Deutschmark)! The first Tu-134 to have the new prefix from the start was EGAF Tu-134AK DDR-SDR.

The last of the Tu-134s *sans suffixe* was retired in March 1986. After German reunification on 3rd October 1990 the civil Tu-134s changed their identity again, receiving the West German registrations D-AOBA through D-AOBS.[5] However, when East and West Germany entered a financial and currency union on 1st July 1990 in preparation for reunification, Interflug began rapidly losing ground to Western air carriers. On 7th February 1991 the airline was declared bankrupt and the entire fleet

was sold off in due course. The last revenue service in Interflug's 32-year history, a round trip from Berlin to Vienna, was performed by Tu-134AK D-AOBC on 30th April 1991.

Starting in November 1969, the **EAST GERMAN AIR FORCE** (LSK/LV – *Luftstreitkräfte und Luftverteidigung der Deutschen Demokratischen Republik*, Air Force and Air Defence Force of the German Democratic Republic) took delivery of four Tu-134Ks which augmented and then supplanted the EGAF's three Tu-124K2-22s (the latter sold to the USSR in 1975). A total of 22 Tu-134AKs in 34-, 36- and 39-seat configurations followed in 1971-1983. Being constantly renewed, older aircraft were transferred to Interflug after the second overhaul.

The aircraft were operated by **STS-29** (*Selbständige Transportfliegerstaffel* – independent airlift squadron) at Marxwalde AB, Brandenburg District/Vorpommern.[6] The unit performed government VIP flights and hence was commonly known as *die Regierungsstaffel* (the government squadron). On 1st January 1973 STS-29 was reorganised, becoming **TFG-44 'Arthur Pieck'** (*Transportfliegergeschwader* – airlift wing) named after the first General Director of the East German Deutsche Lufthansa (and subsequently of Interflug).

The aircraft were mostly quasi-civil, wearing Interflug colours to facilitate flying abroad (although they did have EGAF serials assigned which were not worn visibly). Overt military insignia were only carried by the examples which were the current official transports of the East German Minister of Defence. Such aircraft wore a distinctive colour scheme with a lightning bolt pinstripe. They also had phony registrations in the DM-VBx block (V for *Nationale Volksarmee* – National People's Army) allocated as ATC callsigns.

Regn / Serial	Version	C/n	F/n	Notes
DM-SCE (175 #1)	Tu-134K	9350904		D/D 11-69. To Interflug 2-74
DM-SCF (178 #1)	Tu-134K	9350905		D/D 11-69. To Interflug 6-74
DM-SCG (179 #1)	Tu-134K	9350912		D/D 12-69. To Interflug 2-74
DM-SCK (183 #1)	Tu-134AK	1351304		D/D 2-8-71. To EGAF '183 Black' #1. To Interflug 11-75 as DM-SCK
DM-SCL (182)	Tu-134AK	1351305		D/D 2-8-71. To EGAF '182 Black' [DM-VBD] 1-76; to Interflug 12-5-77 as DM-SCL
DM-SCN (170)	Tu-134AK/r.n.	3352102		D/D 11-73. To Interflug 17-11-77
DM-SCO (171)	Tu-134AK/r.n.	3352106		D/D 27-12-73. To Interflug 11-5-79
DM-SCP (175 #2)	Tu-134AK/r.n.	4352205		D/D 7-3-74. To Interflug 13-10-78
DM-SCR (176 #1)	Tu-134AK/r.n.	4352206		D/D 15-3-74. To EGAF '176 Black' 27-5-77; to Interflug 4-6-80 as DM-SCR
DM-SCS (178 #2)	Tu-134AK/r.n.	4352207		D/D 20-3-74, to Interflug 22-5-79
DM-SCW (179 #2)	Tu-134AK/r.n.	(53)31218	3001	D/D 7-6-75. To DDR-SCW 23-10-81, to Interflug 5-82
DM-SDE (183 #2)	Tu-134AK/r.n.	5338040	3109	D/D 21-9-75. To DDR-SDE 7-7-81, to Interflug 3-85
DM-SDF (185)	Tu-134AK/r.n.	(53)40150	3204	D/D 24-10-75. To DDR-SDF 20-8-81, to Interflug 3-83
DM-SDG (186)	Tu-134AK/r.n.	(63)46155	3401	D/D 13-3-76. To EGAF '186 Black' 25-2-80; to Interflug 15-2-88 as DDR-SDG
DM-SDK (123)	Tu-134AK/r.n.	(73)49900	4009	D/D 27-5-77. To DDR-SDK 31-8-81. Sold to Vietnam Airlines 1-6-90 as VN-A122
DM-SDL (115)	Tu-134AK/r.n.	(73)60108	4301	D/D 22-11-77. To DDR-SDL 20-11-81. Sold to Vietnam Airlines 1-6-90 as VN-A124
DM-SDM (116)	Tu-134AK/r.n.	(83)60435	4605	Tu-134A-1 standard, D/D 7-6-78. To DDR-SDM 14-9-81. Sold to Vietnam Airlines 1-6-90 as VN-A126

DM-SDN (117)	Tu-134AK/r.n.	(83)60612	4708	Tu-134A-1 standard, D/D 25-8-78. To DDR-SDN 15-10-81. Sold to Vietnam Airlines 1-6-90 as VN-A128
DM-SDO (118)	Tu-134AK/r.n.	(93)62259	5202	Tu-134A-1 standard, D/D 31-5-79. To DDR-SDO 31-8-81. Sold to Vietnam Airlines 1-6-90 as VN-A130
DM-SDP (119)	Tu-134AK/r.n.	(03)63260	5710	Tu-134A-1 standard, D/D 6-6-80. To DDR-SDP 30-9-81. Sold to Vietnam Airlines 1-6-90 as VN-A132
DDR-SDR (176 #2)	Tu-134AK/r.n.	(23)63967	6318	Tu-134A-1 standard, D/D 27-5-82. To Luftwaffe 11+10
DDR-SDT (183 #3)	Tu-134AK/r.n.	(33)63998	6335	Tu-134A-1 standard, D/D 30-3-83. WFU Minsk 6-12-88; sold 23-4-90 as CCCP-65565†
DDR-SDU (193)	Tu-134AK/r.n.	(33)66135	6340	Tu-134A-1 standard, D/D 2-9-83. To Luftwaffe 11+12
177 Black	Tu-134K	9350913		[DM-VBB] D/D 12-69; to Interflug 1-12-75 as DM-SCZ
181 Black	Tu-134AK/r.n.	(53)35180	3006	[DM-VBC] D/D 1975; to Interflug 9-3-82 as DDR-SDC
184 Black	Tu-134AK/r.n.	(23)63952	6311	(DDR-SDS allocated). Tu-134A-1 standard, D/D 26-3-82. To Luftwaffe 11+11

† DDR-SDT was disposed of when structural damage caused by a hard landing was discovered during an overhaul at ARZ No 407. The aircraft was initially considered a write-off but eventually repaired and remains in service as of this writing.

As you see, some of the serials were reused – and not necessarily for other Tu-134s. For instance, later had Aero L-39V Albatros target tugs serialled '170 Black' and '171 Black', L-39ZO advanced trainers serialled '177 Black', '178 Black' and '182 Black'. The serials '179 Black', '181 Black' and '185 Black' passed to MiG-29UB combat trainers, while '119 Black' was later a Su-22UM-3K trainer.

After German reunification three Tu-134AKs built to Tu-134A-1 standard (DDR-SDR, DDR-SDU and '184 Black') were taken over by the unified **GERMAN AIR FORCE** (Luftwaffe) and reserialled 11+10, 11+12 and 11+11 respectively. Initially operated by the newly formed **65TH AIR TRANSPORT WING** (Lufttransportgeschwader 65) at Neuhardenberg (ex-Marxwalde), they later passed to the government flight of the **5TH AIR DIVISION** (LwDiv 5) known as **FBS** (Flugbereitschaftsstaffel, lit. 'duty squadron') and based at Köln-Wahn. The aircraft retained their basic Interflug (or EGAF) colours.

Soon, however, the Germans decided the Tu-134s were too noisy and thirsty; also, they were due for refurbishment and the costs proved prohibitive. Hence all three aircraft were sold via an agency called VEBEG which assessed and sold the assets of the former East Germany, including EGAF materiel. As already mentioned, the Tu-134AKs were bought by a German financial group but registered in Croatia; 11+10, 11+11 and 11+12 became 9A-ADP, 9A-ADL and 9A-ADR respectively on 16th December 1992.

Some Western publications say Tu-134 sans suffixe DDR-SCH (a ground instructional airframe) and Tu-134AKs DDR-SDH and DDR-SDI were allocated the Luftwaffe serials 11+13, 11+14 and 11+15.

Busy scene at Berlin-Schönefeld, with Interflug Tu-134AK DDR-SCR, Tu-134A DDR-SCY and Tu-134AK DDR-SCW heading a line-up of Interflug IL-62 sans suffixe DDR-SEC, Balkan Tu-154B-2 LZ-BTR, Aeroflot (Ukrainian CAD/Borispol' UAD/222nd Flight) Tu-154B-2 CCCP-85350, a Malév Tu-154 (version unknown) and another Interflug Tu-134AK. RART

East German Air Force Tu-134AK '181 Black' built to Tu-134A-1 standard (note large rear emergency exits) was the only German Tu-134 which never wore a civil registration. The livery makes an interesting comparison with that worn by Soviet/Russian Air Force Tu-134 Balkany ABCPs in overt military markings. RART

Conakry-based **AIR GUINÉE** [GI/GIB] leased Tu-134A-3 RA-65084 (c/n (73)60115, f/n 4302) from Polis Air between November 1993 and early 1995. The aircraft wore full beige/white Polis Air colours with additional Air Guinée titles and the Guinean flag aft of the flightdeck.

According to JP Airline-Fleets International, RA-65084 was leased by **GUINÉE AIRLINES** [G7/GIF] in November 1993.

HUNGARY

MALÉV HUNGARIAN AIRLINES [MA/MAH] (that is, Magyar Légiközlekedesi Vallalat – Hungarian Air Transport Co) had 13 Tu-134s. Again, the Tu-134 was the first jet operated by the Hungarian flag carrier.

Registration	Version	C/n	F/n	Notes
HA-LBA	Tu-134	8350604		D/D 22-12-68. DBR Istanbul 19-11-69
HA-LBC	Tu-134	8350605		D/D 17-1-69. Crashed near Bucharest 21-9-77
HA-LBD	Tu-134	9350801		D/D 31-12-68 as HA-LBB (reregistered 1-69)! Crashed near Kiev-Borispol' 16-9-71
HA-LBE	Tu-134	9350802		D/D 3-4-69. SOC 18-12-87, to Malév Training Centre at Budapest-Férihegy 8-88; Transport Museum, Budapest-Férihegy, 8-91
HA-LBF	Tu-134	0350923		D/D 6-5-70. To Magyar Repülöstörteneti Múzeum (Hungarian Air Force Museum), Szolnok, 19-5-88
HA-LBG	Tu-134K*	0350924		Ex-Government flight HA-924, D/D 10-74; red/white c/s, later full c/s. SOC 12-3-88, to Malév Training Centre at Budapest-Férihegy
HA-LBH	Tu-134K*	0350925		Ex-Government flight HA-925, D/D 10-74; red/white c/s, later full c/s. SOC 12-7-88; to Auto & Technik Museum, Sinsheim, Germany, 18-7-88
HA-LBI	Tu-134A-3	1351301		D/D 19-6-71, Selcal CS-KQ. Last flight 15-11-94; grounded Budapest 18-11-94, SOC 10-12-94/for spares; scrapped 6/14-2-97
HA-LBK	Tu-134A-3	1351302		D/D 29-6-71, Selcal CS-KR. Damaged Budapest 18-11-94, SOC 10-12-94/for spares; scrapped 24-2/4-3-97
HA-YSA	Tu-134AK/r.n.*	(43)12096	2501	Ex-Government flight, D/D 4-5-81. Departed for overhaul 13-10-81 and reregistered as, see next line
HA-LBN				Redelivered 17-12-81. D-30-III engines, Selcal CS-LM. Sold to ARZ No 407 23-6-98; to Lukoil 5-99 as RA-65944
HA-YSB	Tu-134AK/r.n.*	(43)17103	2503	Ex-Government flight, D/D 11-3-81. Departed for overhaul ?-8-81 and reregistered as, see next line
HA-LBO				Redelivered 15-10-81. D-30-III engines, Selcal CS-LP. Sold to ARZ No 407 1-7-98; to Lukoil 5-99 as RA-65942
HA-LBP	Tu-134A-3/r.n.	(13)63560	6101	Ex-Government flight, D/D 1-1-88, Selcal CS-LQ. Last flight 9-2-94; DBR Budapest 22-2-94, scrapped 10/24-1-97
HA-LBR	Tu-134A-3/r.n.	(13)63580	6102	Ex-Government flight, D/D 1-1-88, Selcal CS-LR. Sold to ARZ No 407 9-7-98; to Lukoil 4-99 as RA-65943
CCCP-65892	Tu-134A	(53)38050	3110	Leased from Aeroflot (Belorussian CAD/ 2nd Minsk UAD) 1-4-78 to 24-1-80; full Aeroflot c/s plus Malév titles and Hungarian flag on fuselage

Originally Malév had intended to buy the Tu-124VE as an IL-14P/IL-14M replacement due for delivery in 1966; however, the more modern Tu-134 was already undergoing trials at the time, and the airline opted for the latter type. An initial order for five 64-seat Tu-134s was placed in April 1965, and the first aircraft arrived at Budapest-Férihegy on 22nd December 1968. The inaugural service to Moscow was flown on 1st January 1969, and before the end of the year the IL-14 had been phased out.

Starting with HA-LBE, the Tu-134s *sans suffixe* were delivered with an updated communications suite featuring a Mikron HF radio and associated 'beak' at the top of the fin. Later Malév had Western radios (identifiable by the non-standard blade aerials on the forward fuselage) and a Sundstrand cockpit voice recorder fitted to its Tu-134s.

Deliveries of the Tu-134A began in 1971; the first two aircraft delivered were probably the last two Tu-134As to have 16 cabin windows to port. On 30th June 1971 HA-LBI performed the first service to Berlin. From 1st January 1983 Malév's Tu-134As and 'AKs had their interiors reconfigured to feature the so-called comfort (that is, business) class, thereby reducing seating capacity to 68.

The veteran Tu-134s *sans suffixe* remained on strength until December 1988, serving 22 foreign destinations. During that year the airline introduced its current livery with a basically white fuselage and a dark blue tail on which three stripes in the Hungarian flag colours of red, white and green form a stylised M (Later, when Malév signed a code-sharing agreement with Alitalia, the aircraft were adorned with 'Alitalia partner' titles.) In due course Malév's Tu-134As and 'AKs were equipped with the Selcal emergency HF communications system, receiving individual four-letter callsigns; also, their interiors were refurbished by Diamonite.

Still, back in 1988 Malév had begun re-equipping with Western hardware, supplementing the Tu-134s with leased Boeing 737-200s and -300s. In July 1997 the airline's General Director Sandor Száthmary was quoted as saying that Malév had decided to definitely shed the socialist touch and would not operate Russian-built aircraft any more as a matter of principle. The last four Tu-134s were replaced by Fokker 70 twinjets, starting in December 1995. On 31st December 1997 Tu-134A-3 HA-LBR flew the final service to Warsaw and back. On 8th January 1998 the same aircraft performed a farewell pleasure flight over Budapest, and that was it.

The **HUNGARIAN GOVERNMENT FLIGHT** operated a total of six Tu-134s. Some of them wore standard Malév colours, masquerading as ordinary airliners, while others sported a distinctive livery with a red cheatline, the Hungarian coat of arms on the tail and Magyar Népköztársaság (port)/Hungarian People's Republic (starboard) titles. Moreover, such aircraft wore (at least temporarily) non-standard alphanumeric registrations. All six were eventually transferred to Malév and stripped of VIP interiors.

The same aircraft in post-unification Luftwaffe markings as 11+11. The engines are covered by tarpaulins. RART

HA-LBF, Malév Hungarian Airlines' last Tu-134 *sans suffixe* (apart from the two Tu-134Ks transferred from the government flight, that is) taxies out at Berlin-Schönefeld; retirement to the Air Force Museum in Szolnok is only a few years away. Note the KLM City Hopper Fokker F.28 at the far end of the row. RART

Radar-nosed Tu-134A-3 HA-LBR taxies at Moscow/Sheremet'yevo-2, displaying the current Malév colours with additional 'Alitalia partner' titles. Note the non-standard blade aerial aft of the nose gear and the characteristic smutty stripes on the engine nacelles caused by oil leaking from the accessory gearbox – a persistent problem plaguing the D-30 engines. Yuriy Kirsanov

Registration	Version	C/n	F/n	Notes
HA-LBG	Tu-134K	0350924		D/D 20-7-70, Malév c/s. Reregistered 1-9-72 as, see next line
HA-924				Red/white c/s. Transferred to Malév as HA-LBG, rereg. 5-10-74
HA-LBH	Tu-134K	0350925		D/D 5-8-70, Malév c/s. Reregistered 1-9-72 as, see next line
HA-925				Red/white c/s. Transferred to Malév as HA-LBG, rereg. 5-10-74
HA-926	Tu-134AK/r.n.	(43)12096	2501	D/D 28-8-74, red/white c/s. Departed for overhaul 13-3-78 and reregistered as, see next line
HA-YSA				Redelivered 23-5-78, red/white c/s. Transferred to Malév 4-5-81
HA-927	Tu-134AK/r.n.	(43)17103	2503	D/D 29-8-74, red/white c/s. Departed for overhaul 5-1-78 and reregistered as, see next line
HA-YSB				Redelivered 7-3-78, red/white c/s. Transferred to Malév 11-3-81
HA-LBP	Tu-134A-3/r.n.	(13)63560	6101	Tu-134A 'Salon'? D/D 13-2-81 (4-2-81?), Malév c/s; occasionally opf Malév. Transferred to Malév 1-1-88
HA-LBR	Tu-134A-3/r.n.	(13)63580	6102	Tu-134A 'Salon'? D/D 14-2-81 (17-2-81?), Malév c/s; occasionally opf Malév. Transferred to Malév 1-1-88

In May 1993 **AIR SERVICE HUNGARY** (MÉM RSz – Repülögépes Szolgalat Allami Vallalat) [–/RSZ], an agency performing crop-spraying and other aerial work, leased Tu-134A RA-65824 (c/n (43)09074, f/n 2403) from Kaliningrad-Avia as an executive transport. The aircraft was reregistered HA-LBS and wore basic Aeroflot colours with Air Service Hungary titles/logo; in 1995 it was returned, regaining its former identity.

IRAN

In April 1992 the charter carrier **KISH AIR** [–/IRK], a subsidiary of the Kish Development Organisation (a free zone enterprise on Kish Island), leased radar-nosed Tu-134AK LZ-TUM (c/n 3351906) from Balkan. Later Kish Air considered buying or leasing more Tu-134s but leased Yak-42Ds and Tu-154Ms instead.

IRAQ

In 1970 a single Tu-134K registered YI-AED (c/n 9350916) was delivered to **IRAQI AIRWAYS** [IA/IAW]. The aircraft was used for government VIP duties and hence almost certainly operated by the **IRAQI AIR FORCE** (IrAF, or *al Quwwat al-Jawwiya al-Iraqiya*). Its career proved to be brief; after a minor accident at Jeddah in June 1971 the aircraft was returned to become CCCP-65669.

In January 1987 the *Interavia* magazine reported that the IrAF had two Tu-124s and two Tu-134s serialled 634 and 635. This must be an error; there is no other evidence of further Tu-134s being delivered to Iraq, but it has been reported that the IrAF had four Tu-124s, and 634 and 635 must be Tu-124Ks.

KAMPUCHEA (CAMBODIA)

KAMPUCHEA AIRLINES [KT/KMP] had two Tu-134AKs equipped to Tu-134A-3 standard. 'Glass-nosed' XU-101 was a former Aeroflot/235th United Air Detachment aircraft (ex-CCCP-65065, c/n (73)49890, f/n 4007), whereas radar-nosed XU-102 (c/n (63)66550, f/n 6375) – the last Tu-134 built as a passenger/VIP aircraft – was apparently delivered new.

The aircraft were operated for the Kampuchean government, carrying delegations to Hanoi and Bangkok where negotiations were held in order to end the civil war in Kampuchea. (In late 1988 the country reverted to its former name, Cambodia.)

Both aircraft originally wore basic Aeroflot colours with titles in the Khmer language. In October 1992 XU-102 was given a smart new livery with a white top, a grey belly, a triple green/blue cheatline and a tail logo showing a bird superimposed on the sun. In 1995 both were sold to Nizhegorodskiye Avialinii, becoming RA-65065 and RA-64451 respectively.[7]

LATVIA

The original national flag carrier, **LATAVIO LATVIAN AIRLINES** (Latvijas Aviolinijas) [PV/LTL], operated nine Tu-134B-3s inherited from the Latvian CAD/Riga UAD/280th Flight based at Riga-Skul'te.

Registration	Version	C/n	F/n Notes
YL-LBA	(93)61000	5001	Ex-CCCP-65146. WFU Moscow/Sheremet'yevo-1 ?-95; restored and sold to Alrosa by 6-99 as RA-65146
YL-LBC	(03)63221	5706	Ex-CCCP-65693. Sold to Aviaenergo ?-96 as RA-65693
YL-LBD	(03)63235	5707	Ex-CCCP-65694. WFU Riga 9-94; sold to Aeroflot-Plus by 1-01 as RA-65694
YL-LBE	(03)63285	5801	Ex-CCCP-65695. Sold to Lat-Charter ?-96
YL-LBG	(03)63333	5806	Ex-CCCP-65699. Sold to Lat-Charter ?-96
YL-LBH	(03)63340	5807	Ex-CCCP-65700. Sold to Lat-Charter ?-96
YL-LBI	(03)63365	5810	Ex-CCCP-65703. Sold to Baltic Express Line
YL-LBJ	(03)63410	5904	Ex-CCCP-65704. Sold to AZAL ?-97 as 4K-65704
YL-LBL	(03)63515	6006	Ex-CCCP-65712. Sold to AZAL ?-97 as 4K-65712
YL-LBN	(93)63187	5702	Ex-CCCP-65799. WFU Riga 7-94; restored and sold to Kazakstan government flight 3-99 as UN-65799

Initially Latavio's Tu-134Bs operated in basic Aeroflot colours with the titles, flag and Soviet registration crudely painted out; the Latvian registration was carried beneath the windows just aft of the wings. YL-LBH was an exception, wearing a large Latvian flag on the tail and *LATAVIO LATVIAN AIRLINES* titles. In due course part of the fleet was repainted at ARZ No 402 (Moscow-Bykovo), receiving a smart red/white livery with black-painted wings; curiously, the last three digits of the former Soviet registration were carried on the nose gear doors. The tips of the main gear fairings were Dayglo orange to minimise the risk of damage by airport vehicles.

Since the relations between Russia and the Baltic States were rather strained in the early 1990s, Latavio soon ran into maintenance problems with the Tu-134s. As a way out, YL-LBD and YL-LBN were cannibalised for spares to keep the others flyable. Fortunately, both were restored to airworthy condition and sold.

YL-LBA has a different case history. In 1995 it was impounded at Moscow-Sheremet'yevo due to persistent non-payment of airport handling fees. While the aircraft sat at the Sheremet'yevo-1 maintenance base, waiting to be bailed out, Latavio ceased operations in 1996. After that, the unwanted airliner was gradually stripped of usable parts and was in very poor condition by August 1998; luckily it found a new owner in 1999.

BALTIC INTERNATIONAL AIRLINES [TI/BIA], a Latvian-US joint venture, operated Tu-134B-3s YL-LBK (ex-CCCP-65706, c/n (03)63425, f/n 5906) and YL-LBM (ex-CCCP-65715, c/n (13)63536, f/n 6009). They wore the same basic Latavio livery with different titles; YL-LBK had a black radome.

In 1996 the airline underwent a major reorganisation, changing its name to **AIRBALTIC** [BT/BTI] and becoming Latvia's flag carrier. The Tu-134s had to make way for three Avro RJ70s and two SAAB SF340As. YL-LBM was sold to Lat-Charter, while YL-LBK was presumably bought by Transair as LZ-ACB or LZ-ACS.

BALTIC EXPRESS LINE [S8/LTB] purchased Tu-134B-3 YL-LBI from the defunct Latavio in 1996. The basic livery of the ex-owner was suitably amended to feature a new 'EL' tail logo and *'BALTIC express line'* titles. In 2001 the aircraft was sold to the Russian airline Avcom and reregistered RA-65701 on 16th November.

Riga-based **LAT CHARTER LTD** [–/LTC] had six Tu-134B-3s.

Registration	C/n	F/n	Notes
YL-LBB	(03)63215	5705	Ex-CCCP-65692. Sold to SkyField 11-96 as RA-65692
YL-LBE	(03)63285	5801	Bought from Latavio ?-96. Sold to Aqualine Leasing by 1-03 as UN 65695
YL-LBF	(03)63295	5802	Ex-CCCP-65696. Sold to Sukhumi Airlines ?-96 as 4L-AAD
YL-LBG	(03)63333	5806	Bought from Latavio ?-96. Sold to Aqualine Leasing by 1-03 as UN 65699
YL-LBH	(03)63340	5807	Bought from Latavio. Sold to Sukhumi Airlines ?-96 as 4L-AAB
YL-LBM	(13)63536	6009	Bought from Baltic International. Sold to Sukhumi Airlines ?-96 as 4L-AAC

Almost all aircraft wore different colour schemes (that is, following the same general pattern but using different colours). YL-LBB was a 'study in scarlet': the fuselage from the lower edge of the windows up and from just aft of the flightdeck, the bottom one-third of the tail and the upper three quarters of the engine nacelles were bright red, everything else was white. On YL-LBH the red colour was substituted by a swampy green and the white colour by dark blue, and the result was... well... yuck! YL-LBE and YL-LBF were identical and had a really attractive version with sapphire blue upper fuselage, lower fin and engine nacelles, curved bright green stripes just aft of the flightdeck and on the fin (these stripes were red on YL-LBB and swampy green on YL-LBH), a white belly/nose and upper fin. YL-LBG was the reverse, featuring a white fuselage top, lower fin and engine nacelles, a navy blue belly/nose and upper fin, and the same green stripes. YL-LBM was the 'odd man out' – it never received full colours, retaining the basic Latavio red/white livery.

YL-LBB was initially operated for Riga-based Baltija Bank and accordingly converted to a 16-seat Tu-134B-3 'Salon' (with no rear door); the navigation suite was upgraded with a GPS receiver. The outfitting and painting job was done by Diamonite Aircraft Furnishings at Bristol-Filton and the aircraft was delivered on 27th October 1993. When the bank went bust in 1995, the aircraft was reconverted to passenger configuration and the Baltija titles on the nose were removed.

Some Lat Charter aircraft, including YL-LBF, had improved (but not VIP) interiors fitted by Bedek, a division of Israel Aircraft Industries (IAI). Curiously, *Jane's Aircraft Upgrades* calls these aircraft Tu-134M for some reason!

Smartly painted Tu-134AK HA-927 at Khar'kov-Sokol'nikovo shortly before delivery to the Hungarian government flight; the titles on the port side read 'Magyar Népköztársaság' (Hungarian People's Republic). Tupolev JSC

Kampuchea Airlines Tu-134AK XU-102 in post-1992 colours; the rear entry door is not outlined. This was the last Tu-134AK built and the last example at large completed as a passenger aircraft. Sergey and Dmitriy Komissarov archive

Latavio Latvian Airlines Tu-134B-3 YL-LBA takes off from runway 07R at Moscow-Sheremet'yevo. The last three digits of the former Soviet registration, CCCP-65146, are painted on the nose gear doors. Yuriy Kirsanov

By January 2003 **AQUALINE LEASING** had bought the last two remaining Tu-134B-3s from Lat-Charter. The aircraft were reregistered UN 65695 (ex-YL-LBE, c/n (03)63285, f/n 5801) and UN 65699 (ex-YL-LBG, c/n (03)63333, f/n 5806) and promptly leased to **AIR LIBYA TIBESTI** (see next chapter).

LITHUANIA

The nation's flag carrier **LITHUANIAN AIRLINES** (Lietuvos Avialinijos) [TE/LIL] operated nine Tu-134As inherited from the Lithuanian CAD/Vilnius UAD/277th Flight.

Registration	Version	C/n	F/n	Notes
LY-ABA	Tu-134A-3	3352003		Ex-CCCP-65973. Transferred to Lietuva
LY-ABB	Tu-134A	(63)48415	3508	Ex-CCCP-65023. Sold to TransAGO 7-97 as UR-65023
LY-ABC	Tu-134A	6349100	3708	Ex-CCCP-65040. Sold to Bashkirian Airlines ?-94 as RA-65040
LY-ABD	Tu-134A	(73)60054	4206	Ex-CCCP-65079. Sold to Aurela Inc. ?-96 as LY-ASK
LY-ABE	Tu-134A-3	(73)60076	4208	Ex-CCCP-65081. Sold to TransAGO 6-96 as UR-65081
LY-ABF	Tu-134A-3	(73)60172	4307	Ex-CCCP-65088. Sold to Avialeasing Co ?-96 as RA-65088
LY-ABG	Tu-134A-3	8360195	4310	Ex-CCCP-65091. Sold to Orient-Avia 12-96 as RA-65091
LY-ABH	Tu-134A-3	(83)60308	4502	Ex-CCCP-65105. Sold to Samara Airlines ?-95 as RA-65105
LY-ABI	Tu-134A	(83)60628	4710	Ex-CCCP-65128. Sold to Pulkovo AE 3-97 as RA-65128

Originally the aircraft wore basic Aeroflot colours without titles, their ownership indicated only by the Lithuanian flag and registration on the tail. In 1993 the airline adopted a white livery featuring a salad green cheatline with a black pinstripe across the windows, 'Lithuanian Airlines' titles and a $L\Delta L$ tail logo. Hardly had the entire fleet been resprayed in this fashion, however, when a new and much more inspiring colour scheme appeared in January 1994, with bright orange lower/rear fuselage and tail and a grey cheatline below the windows curving upwards ahead of the fin. The logo was now an '*L*' with its 'mirror image' underneath (together they formed a sort of stylised bird) in a circle; the logo was worn both on the tail and on the belly. At least two Tu-134As (LY-ABF and LY-ABH) received the new livery.

From 1995 onwards the Tu-134As were mostly used for charter flights, giving up scheduled services to the quieter Boeing 737-200s and Yak-42s. All of the airline's Tu-134As had been sold off by mid-1997.

Kaunas-based **LIETUVA** [TT/KLA] (pronounced *Letoova* – the native name of Lithuania; also known as Air Lithuania) took delivery of a single Tu-134A-3 (CCCP-65973) which was surplus to Lithuanian Airlines' requirements. After sitting in storage at Vilnius until April 1994 it was refurbished, receiving at last its allocated registration LY-ABA and a red/white livery with *Lietuva* titles. The aircraft superseded the Yak-40 (Lietuva's principal type) on high-density routes. By October 1999, however, it was sold to Tatarstan Airlines as RA-65973.

The Vilnius-based enterprise **AURELA INC** [–/LSK] purchased Tu-134A LY-ABD from Lithuanian Airlines in 1996. Reregistered LY-ASK, the aircraft was refitted as a Tu-134A 'Salon' with 11 seats for the VIPs and 32 for the retinue, gaining a pleasing red/grey/white colour scheme. In December 2000 the aircraft was sold to Kazan'-based Tulpar as RA-65079.

In 1969 a single Aeroflot Tu-134 *sans suffixe* (identity unknown) was leased to **MIAT** (originally Mongolyn Irgeniy Agaaryn Te'ever – Mongolian Air Transport Directorate; now **MONGOLIAN INTERNATIONAL AIR TRANSPORT** [OM/MGL]) for evaluation purposes. During the five-month lease the aircraft was used mainly for government VIP flights. As one might imagine, the Mongolian comrades were very pleased with the Tu-134, but no orders followed (although some aviation magazines did announce a purchase!).

MOZAMBIQUE

On 30th September 1980 the **MOZAMBIQUE GOVERNMENT FLIGHT** (some sources say the **MOZAMBIQUE PEOPLE'S AIR FORCE** (FPA – *Força Popular Aérea de Moçambique*) took delivery of a radar-nosed Tu-134AK (c/n (03)63457, f/n 5909). Originally it was serialled 63457, sporting a blue cheatline below the windows and a blue/white tail adorned by an obscure emblem resembling the famous Sputnik-1 satellite on a blue/red/black/yellow rectangle. By 1981 the aircraft had been reregistered C9-CAA and the tail now sported the elaborate coat of arms of the Mozambique People's Republic. On 1st August 1986 the aircraft was upgraded to Tu-134A-3 standard.

The aircraft was operated by a Soviet flight crew on secondment from the Leningrad CAD/1st Leningrad UAD/344th Flight. Unfortunately on 19th October 1986 C9-CAA crashed fatally near Nelspruit, South Africa, as a result of unlawful interference with the purpose of eliminating President Samora Machel.

NIGERIA

In 1992-94 **HARCO AIR SERVICES** [–/HCO] operated eleven Tu-134s leased in Russia and Latvia. The name was derived from the airline's home base, Port Harcourt.

Registration	Version	C/n	F/n	Notes
CCCP-65608 #2	Tu-134AK/r.n.*	5338040	3109	Leased from Komiavia 8-92 to ?-94, basic Interflug c/s
RA 65609	Tu-134AK/r.n.*	(63)46155	3401	Leased from Komiavia 8-92 to ?-94, basic Interflug c/s
CCCP-65610 #2	Tu-134AK/r.n.*	(53)40150	3204	Leased from Komiavia 8-92 to ?-94, basic Interflug c/s
RA 65612	Tu-134AK/r.n.*	3352102		Leased from Komiavia 8-92 to ?-94, basic Interflug c/s
RA-65614	Tu-134AK/r.n.*	4352207		Leased from Komiavia 8-92 to ?-94, basic Interflug c/s
RA 65616	Tu-134AK/r.n.*	4352206		Leased from Komiavia 8-92 to ?-94, basic Interflug c/s
RA 65617	Tu-134A/r.n.	4308068	2309	Leased from Komiavia 8-92 to ?-94, basic Interflug c/s
RA-65618	Tu-134A-3/r.n.	4312095	2410	Leased from Komiavia 8-92 to ?-94, basic Interflug c/s
CCCP-65621 #2	Tu-134A-3/r.n.	6348320	3406	Leased from Komiavia 8-92 to ?-94, basic Interflug c/s; reregistered RA-65621 during lease
YL-LBC	Tu-134B-3	(03)63221	5706	Lsf Latavio 9-94 to 10-94; basic Aeroflot c/s, Harco Air titles/logo
YL-LBG	Tu-134B-3	(03)63333	5806	Lsf Latavio 9-94 to 10-94; basic Aeroflot c/s, Harco Air titles/logo

In mid-1994 the abovementioned RA-65608 through RA-65610, RA 65612 and RA 65616 through RA-65618, plus Tu-134AK RA-65611 (c/n 3351903), were leased by another airline with a very similar name, **HARKA AIR**.

Top: **Lat-Charter Tu-134B-3 YL-LBG shows just one of the many colour schemes worn by the airline's aircraft. Note the quasi-oval windows.**
Sergey and Dmitriy Komissarov archive

Above: **Tu-134A LY-ABF in 1994-standard Lithuanian Airlines colours a few seconds before touchdown at Moscow-Sheremet'yevo.**
Yuriy Kirsanov

Below: **Tu-134A LY-ABG in Lithuanian Airlines' 1993-standard livery seconds after landing on runway 25L at Moscow-Sheremet'yevo.**
Yuriy Kirsanov

They were still in basic ex-Interflug colours, to which were added red Harka Air titles and a blue swallow logo on the nearly all-white tail.

The airline was popular with its passengers, with consistently high load factors; even the presidential family used Harka Air aircraft occasionally. However, the lessee proved reluctant to pay, running up big debts; Komiavia had to do some arm-twisting, suspending flights periodically to make the Nigerians cough up the money. The fatal crash of Tu-134A RA 65617 at Lagos-Mohammed Murtala International on 24th June 1995 came at a most inopportune time when the financial conflict was at its peak. Eventually the Russians virtually fled from Nigeria on 3rd October 1995 in the last Tu-134 remaining there (RA-65609), abandoning some of the support equipment – and then it took a lot of time and effort to get the money payable to Komiavia.

Some sources say Harka Air also leased Tu-134A-3 RA-65805 (c/n 3352105) from Komiavia.

KOLKOL AIRLINES [–/KKL] intended to lease three Tu-134As – ER-65051 (c/n (73)49758, f/n 3810), ER-65736 (c/n 1351501) and ER-65741 (c/n 2351601) – from Air Moldova in 1994. However, when Kolkol Airlines had been applied to the aircraft (which retained basic 1994-standard Air Moldova colours), the lease fell through because the lessee was insolvent.

Western sources reported in 1996 that **MAINA AIR** operated five Tu-134As. However, no proof has been found, and the *JP Airline-Fleets* yearbook does not mention this airline at all!

NORTH KOREA

In 1984 North Korea's sole airline, **CHOSONMINHANG** (that is, Civil Aviation Administration of Korea – CAAK), took delivery of two two Tu-134B-3s registered P-813 (c/n (43)66215, f/n 6354) and P-814 (c/n (43)66368, f/n 6363). The c/n of the latter aircraft has also been stated as (43)66362. By 1994 the airline had been renamed **AIR KORYO** [JS/KOR] – and it's just as well, because the old name was a real tongue-twister. ('Koryo' is apparently how 'Korea' is pronounced in the native language.)

A third example, P-812, was also reported but no proof of its existence has been found. This is either a mis-sighting or the registration was temporarily altered to confuse spies. The North Koreans have done this; for instance, IL-62M P-881 was at one time disguised as 'P-884'.

PERU

In December 1992/May 1993 **AERO TUMI**, an airline based at Lima-Jorge Chavéz International, operated Tu-134A-1 OB-1489 and Tu-134A-3 OB-1490 (the latter was leased from Air Ukraine). The first service from Lima to Tarapoto via Trujillo was performed on 24th February 1993. Both aircraft later passed to Imperial Air (see below).

IMPERIAL AIR [7I/IMP] based at the same location operated four Tu-134s.

Registration	Version	C/n	F/n	Notes
OB-1489	Tu-134A-1	1351203		Ex-CCCP-93930, named 'Inca Roca'. WFU Lima 5-94
OB-1490	Tu-134A-3	(83)60525	4703	Ex-UR-65123, named 'Atahualpa'; lsf Air Ukraine. WFU/stored Lima
OB-1552	Tu-134AK*	(83)60215	4402	Ex-UR-65093, named 'Sinchi Roca'; leased from Air Ukraine. D-30-III engines. Returned ?-96 (27-4-94?) as UR-65093
OB-1553	Tu-134A-3	(83)60206	4401	Ex-UR-65092, named 'Yawar Huaca'; leased from Air Ukraine. Damaged Lima 15-4-93, WFU/stored

The three 'glass-nosed' aircraft were leased from Air Ukraine's Khar'kov division via the Ukrainian company Katran Leasing.[8] UR-65092 and UR-65093 were briefly operated by Imperial Air with their original registrations before being reregistered. (Imperial Air reportedly operated a fifth Tu-134A, OB-1492, but this is unconfirmed.)

The first service from Lima to Arequipa was performed on 23rd July 1993. However, on 6th January 1997 the airline suspended operations; three of the four aircraft have been in storage since.

POLAND

LOT POLISH AIRLINES [LO/LOT] (Polskie Linie Lotnicze LOT; 'lot' is the Polish word for 'flight') operated 12 Tu-134s.

Registration	Version	C/n	F/n	Notes
SP-LGA	Tu-134	8350602		D/D 6-11-68, named 'Ignacy Paderewski'. Sold as CCCP-65933
SP-LGB	Tu-134	8350603		D/D 23-11-68, named 'Władysław Reymont'. Crashed Warsaw-Okęcie 23-1-80
SP-LGC	Tu-134	9350804		D/D 29-4-69, named 'Marie Skłodowska-Curie'. Sold as CCCP-65923
SP-LGD	Tu-134	9350805		D/D 26-5-69, named 'Ludwik Zamenhoff'. Sold as CCCP-65922
SP-LGE	Tu-134	9350806		D/D 30-5-69, named 'Ignacy Domejko'. Sold as CCCP-65924 by 1-87
SP-LHA†	Tu-134A	2351808		D/D 29-3-73, named 'Paweł Strzelecki'. WFU Warsaw 10-90; sold to Polish Mol 18-9-97 for anti-terrorist training
SP-LHB†	Tu-134A	2351809		D/D 6-4-73, named 'Józef Bem'. WFU Warsaw 18-6-92; to *Muzeum Lotnictwa i Astronautyki* (Aerospace Museum), Kraków, 25-10-99
SP-LHC†	Tu-134A	2351810		D/D 10-4-73, named 'Janusz Kusociński'. WFU Warsaw 19-3-93; preserved Warsaw 10-9-97 in Szczesliwici housing estate; sold and installed as café in Chlapów late 1999?
SP-LHD†	Tu-134A	(63)48400	3506	D/D 10-6-76. WFU Warsaw 31-7-94; to *Lotnicze Zakłady Naukowe* (aviation tech school), Psie Pole near Wrocław 13-12-97 as ground instructional airframe; scrapped August/September 2002
SP-LHE†	Tu-134A	(63)48405	3507	D/D 3-6-76; c/n also reported as (63)48401. WFU Warsaw 5-11-93; to *Wystawa Sprzętu Lotniczego i Wojskowego* (Aviation & Military Equipment Expo), Łódz-Lublinek, 15-3-98
SP-LHF†	Tu-134AK/r.n.*	3352005		Ex-Polish Air Force '101 Red' No 1, D/D 2-8-77. WFU Warsaw 29-6-94; preserved as a restaurant Szymaki, 6km N of Płońsk/80km N of Warsaw
SP-LHG	Tu-134AK/r.n.*	3352008		Ex-Polish Air Force '102 Red' No 1, D/D 27-9-78‡. WFU Warsaw 29-6-94; preserved as a restaurant Władysławowo near Gdańsk (Restoracja Odlotowa – 'Departure Restaurant'), no reg on; opened 27-4-02

† The registrations SP-LHA through SP-LHF were used in 1949-59 for LOT's IL-12Bs (c/ns 93013501, 93013502, 93013506, 93013504, 93013505 and 93013515).

‡ The delivery date was also stated as 27th August 1978. The aircraft was reportedly returned to the Polish Air Force as '102 White' by September 1994 and finally retired by 1995, but this is unconfirmed.

The order for the five Tu-134s *sans suffixe* was placed in December 1967. The first of these was due for delivery in late November or early December 1968 but the Khar'kov aircraft factory and Aviaexport took great pains

Top: **Still wearing Kolkol Airlines titles from the lease that never was, Tu-134A ER-65051 taxies in at Moscow/Vnukovo-1 after arriving on the daily Air Moldova service from Kishinyov.**
Sergey and Dmitriy Komissarov archive

Above: **A fine study of Air Koryo Tu-134B-3 P-814.**
Sergey and Dmitriy Komissarov archive

Below: **Tu-134A SP-LHB in the stylish 1977-standard livery of LOT Polish Airlines.**
Sergey and Dmitriy Komissarov archive

Polish Air Force Tu-134AK '101 Red' No 1 (c/n 3352005). Yefim Gordon archive

On 4th May 1984 Tu-134AK '101 Red' No 2 (c/n 7349909) brought Polish leader Wójciech Jaruzelski (third from left) **to Moscow/Vnukovo-2. The welcoming committee included Defence Minister Marshal Dmitriy F Ustinov** (second from left) **and Minister of Foreign Affairs Andrey A Gromyko** (fourth from left). **Note that, unlike '101 Red' No 1, all doors and exits are outlined on this aircraft.** ITAR-TASS

to deliver the aircraft ahead of schedule, timing it to the 51st anniversary of the October Revolution, as well as to LOT's 40th anniversary. Such 'gifts' were the order of the day in Soviet times. The Poles 'answered in kind', speeding up the acceptance procedure insofar as possible to be in time for the 5th Congress of the Polish United Workers Party (and, according to LOT Technical Director Włodzimierż Wiłanowski, they were very proud of it).

In the course of four months the first two aircraft were used for flight and ground crew conversion training. On 1st April 1969 SP-LGA finally performed the first service from Warsaw to Leningrad, opening the jet age for LOT; SP-LGB also entered service on the same day. Curiously, *Flight International* wrote on 23rd May 1968: '*A twice-weekly Tu-124 service was inaugurated by LOT, Polish Airlines, between Leningrad and Warsaw on May 12*', although there never were any Tu-124s in Poland! This was obviously a misunderstanding and Aeroflot was probably the operator in question.

Soon the Tu-134 had ousted the An-24B from LOT's international services and partially replaced the IL-18V/IL-18E on medium-haul routes; the IL-18s were 'demoted' to cargo aircraft. To ensure observance of flight schedules LOT established so-called general maintenance facilities (SWOT – Stacja Wspólnej Obsługi Technicznej) in the remotest cities served by its aircraft; these could rapidly fix a minor malfunction, such as replacing a blown tyre. Tu-134s were handled by SWOTs located in London, Paris, Rome, Madrid and Lyon.

Deliveries of the Tu-134A began in March 1973, the first service with the type (to Damascus) taking place on 4th April. Despite insistent demands to deliver the aircraft with a three-man flightdeck (with no navigator's station), all five Tu-134s *sans suffixe* and all five Tu-134As supplied directly to LOT were 'glass-nosed' aircraft with an ROZ-1 radar. Not until 1977, when two radar-nosed Tu-134AKs were transferred from the Polish Air Force, did the airline receive the coveted three-crew aircraft.

With the exception of SP-LHD and SP-LHE, the Tu-134s' colour scheme represented a departure from LOT's then-current livery in that the cheatline was twin. In 1977 the airline introduced its current livery which was then the height of fashion and still does not look dated today; the reader may be interested to learn that a contest was announced via the *Skrzydlata Polska* (Winged Poland) magazine and a winner was selected from half a dozen liveries suggested by the readers.

In 1989 LOT started re-equipping with Western hardware when two Boeing 767-25D(ER)s and a Boeing 767-35D(ER) were acquired to replace the IL-62M fleet. (Poland had never been on really good terms with the Soviet Union; the smouldering anti-Russian sentiment goes back for centuries, and the reasons are outside the scope of this book. However, operating economics were the decisive factor in the decision to re-equip.) In 1991 it was the Tu-134's turn. The four surviving Tu-134s *sans suffixe* had been returned to the USSR by 1989; now the Tu-134As and 'AKs were replaced by Boeing 737-45Ds and Boeing 737-55Ds. On 31st March 1994 the aircraft were grounded at Warsaw-Okęcie and put up for sale – never to fly again. Incidentally, the registrations SP-LGA through SP-LGE later passed to Embraer RJ-145EP and RJ-145MP twinjets delivered from July 1999 onwards.

A total of six Tu-134s saw service with the **POLISH AIR FORCE** (PWL – *Polskie Wojsko Lotnicze*), although no more than two were in service at any one time. They were operated by the 36. SPLT (*Specjalny Pułk Lotnictwa Transportowego* – special transport air regiment) at Warsaw-Okęcie tasked with government VIP transport duties. Unlike regular PWL aircraft which have serials based on the construction number,[9] the fixed-wing aircraft of the 36. SPLT had serials which had nothing to do with the c/ns and were reused again and again. The radar-nosed Tu-134AKs came in 36-, 41- and 47-seat configurations.

Serial	Version	C/n	F/n	Notes
101 Red No 1	Tu-134AK/r.n.	3352005		D/D 1973. Transferred to LOT 2-8-77 as SP-LHF
101 Red No 2	Tu-134AK/r.n.	7349909	4103	D/D 26-6-77. Sold to Aeroflot Russian International Airlines ?-93 as CCCP-65559
102 Red No 1	Tu-134AK/r.n.	3352008		D/D 1973. Transferred to LOT 27-9-78 (27-8-78?) as SP-LHG; see comment to LOT fleet list!
102 Red No 2	Tu-134AK/r.n.	7349985	4109	D/D 28-7-77? To SP-LHI/LOT c/s 9-88, then to PWL '102 White' 6-91. Sold to Aeroflot Russian International Airlines ?-92 as CCCP-65623 No 2
103 White	Tu-134A	3351809		Ex/to SP-LHB, leased from LOT approx. 8-87 to 1-88; basic LOT c/s
104 White (No 1?)†	Tu-134A	3351808?		Ex/to SP-LHA? Leased from LOT in the spring of 1986 and approx. 4-90 to 10-90; basic LOT c/s

† *Euromil – Military Air Arms in Europe* lists Tu-134A '104' as c/n 4323526. However, firstly, c/n 23526 (f/n 2803) was Tu-134A-3 CCCP-65858 which was manufactured on 10th February 1975, which means the full c/n is (53)23256. Secondly, this aircraft belonged to the Chechen airline Stigl and was almost certainly destroyed at Groznyy-Severnyy on 11th December 1994.

On several occasions 'glass-nosed' Tu-134As were leased from LOT to 'bridge the gap' while the Air Force's own aircraft were undergoing refurbishment. Later, Tu-134AK '102 Red' No 2 became quasi-civil for several years to facilitate flying abroad.

Previously the serial '101 Red' had been worn by IL-18V 'Salon' c/n 180002504 (to LOT as SP-LSE in 1965), IL-18V 'Salon' c/n 185008305 (to CCCP-75593 in 1965) and IL-18E 'Salon' c/n 185008503 (to SP-LSK in 1988!); the serial '102 Red' had been worn by IL-18V 'Salon' c/n 185002701 (to SP-LSH in 1966) and IL-18E 'Salon' c/n 186008905 (to SP-LSI in 1975). After the Tu-134AKs had been phased out, the serials '101 Red' and '102 Red' were reused in 1996 for Tu-154M 'Salons' – formerly '837 Black' (c/n 90A837) and '862 Black' (c/n 90A862).

ROMANIA

As already mentioned, Romania never bought the Tu-134. However, the airline **MIRAVIA** [N3/MRV] based in Bucharest leases Tu-134As from Air Moldova as required.

SYRIA

SYRIANAIR (Syrian Arab Airlines) [RB/SYR], the sole national airline, operated six Tu-134B-3s. Three of them were built as Tu-134B-3 'Salon' VIP jets featuring a rear entry door/airstairs and were operated by the airline's government flight; these aircraft are often listed for the **SYRIAN AIR FORCE** (*al Quwwat al-Jawwiya al Arabiya as-Suriya*).

Registration	Version	C/n	F/n	Notes
YK-AYA	Tu-134B-3 'Salon'	(23)63992	6330	D/D 1982; WFU/stored Damascus by 3-01
YK-AYB	Tu-134B-3 'Salon'	(23)63994	6331	D/D 1982; WFU/stored Damascus by 3-01
YK-AYC	Tu-134B-3	(23)63989	6327	D/D 1982; WFU/stored Damascus by 3-01
YK-AYD	Tu-134B-3 'Salon'	(23)63990	6328	D/D 1982; WFU/stored Damascus by 3-01
YK-AYE	Tu-134B-3	(33)66187	6348	D/D 1983.
YK-AYF	Tu-134B-3	(33)66190	6349	D/D 10-10-84; WFU/stored Damascus by 3-01

In 1998 Syrianair began a large-scale fleet renewal programme. The Tu-134B-3s and the airline's three Tu-154Ms were replaced by six Airbus Industrie A320-232s; thus by March 2001 YK-AYE was Syrianair's last operational Tupolev aircraft.

SLOVAKIA

In 1994 the Moscow charter carrier ALAK [J4/LSV] (*aktsionernaya lizingovaya aviakompahniya* – joint-stock leasing airline) formed a joint venture with Bratislava-based **AIR SARAVI LTD** [–/SRV]. In October 1994 the venture operated Tu-134A-3 RA-65756 (c/n (93)62179, f/n 5106) leased from the Ivanovo Air Enterprise; the aircraft was in basic Aeroflot colours with ALAK AIR SARAVI titles. In 1998 ALAK suspended operations and the joint venture died with it.

AIR TRANSPORT EUROPE [–/EAT], originally a rotary-wing operator based in Poprad, owned a single Tu-134A registered OM-GAT and named 'Dávid'; the aircraft was purchased from Estonian Air in May 1995 (ex-ES-AAF, c/n 6348565, f/n 3701). Initially it flew in full Estonian Air colours with a Slovak registration; later Air Transport Europe titles and logo were applied. In 1999 the aircraft received a more attractive green/white livery. In November 2000 it was sold to Moldovan carrier Tiramavia as ER-TCH.

According to the Western press, **SLOVENSKÉ AEROLINIE BRATISLAVA** [6Q/SLL] operated a single Tu-134A. However, this is probably misinformation – they are known to operate three Tu-154-100s but no Tu-134s!

SUDAN

SASCO AIRLINES (Sudanese Air Services Co) [–/SAC] based in Khartoum leased Tu-134A-3 EY-65876 (c/n (53)31220, f/n 3002) from Tajikistan Airlines in late 1995, returning it by mid-1998. The aircraft was in basic Aeroflot colours without titles and with a yellow SASCO Air Lines tail logo.

Curiously, several Western publications reported Tu-134A RA-65868 (c/n (53)28305, f/n 2903) as operated by Khartoum-based **AZZA TRANSPORT COMPANY LTD** [–/AZZ]. Yet this is unconfirmed as, CCCP-65868 was most probably destroyed at Groznyy-Severnyy on 11th December 1994.

An airline with the strange name of **MARSLAND** (also reported as Marshland!) operated Tu-134B-3 ST-MRS (probably ex-UN 65699, c/n (03)63333, f/n 5806) in December 2003.

In September 2003 a Tu-134 registered ST-MGC (version and c/n unknown) was reported at Sharjah.

TURKEY

In March 1965 Aviaexport offered the Tu-134 *sans suffixe* to the nation's flag carrier **THY TURKISH AIRLINES** (Türk Hava Yollari) [TK/THY]. The aircraft were offered on *extremely* favourable terms – favourable to the point of disbelief; quite apart from the fact that they cost half as much as comparable Western jets, the Soviet Union offered a 20-year installment plan and offered to buy some of THY's existing aircraft. Still, the airline preferred the Boeing 727-2F2 Advanced. Apparently Aviaexport overdid it, making the whole affair look like an attempt to sell some total junk!

In 1988 **NESU AIR** wet-leased Tu-134A-1s YU-AHY (c/n 1351204) and YU-AJA (c/n 1351206) from Aviogenex. The aircraft were reregistered TC-ALV and TC-ALU respectively for the duration, retaining basic Aviogenex colours with new titles/logo.

In 1990 Istanbul-based charter carrier **GREENAIR** [–/GRN] wet-leased Tu-134AKs CCCP-65914 (c/n (33)66109, f/n 6337) and CCCP-65915 (c/n (33)66120, f/n 6338) equipped to Tu-134A-3 standard from the 235th Independent Air Detachment. Reregistered TC-GRD and TC-GRE respectively and repainted in the airline's inevitably green/white livery, the aircraft were delivered on 12th and 11th October respectively, receiving the names 'Başiktaş' and 'Galatasarayon'. They were returned to the lessor in 1993, regaining their original registrations – albeit with the RA- prefix.

TOP AIR [–/TOP] briefly wet-leased Tu-134A RA-65057 (c/n (73)49865, f/n 3909) from Voronezhavia in 1997.

UNITED KINGDOM

In 1998 a plan emerged to restore Latavio's Tu-134B-3 YL-LBD (which had been used for spares at Riga) to active status. The aircraft was allocated the Kazakh registration UN 65694; after outfitting as a Tu-134B-3 'Salon' it was to be operated by **BRISTOW HELICOPTERS** [–/BHL]. However, the plan never materialised and the 'undead' aircraft was eventually sold to Russia as RA-65694.

Soviet cosmonaut Col Aleksandr Viktorenko (left) and Syrian astronaut Muhammed Faris stand beside a Syrianair Tu-134B-3 'Salon' at Aleppo, displaying newly-awarded Soviet and Syrian orders, 1987. ITAR-TASS

Clintondale Aviation Tu-134A-3 'Salon' RA-65132 at its home base (Moscow/Sheremet'yevo-1). Dmitriy Petrochenko

Vietnam Airlines Tu-134AK VN-A126 completed to Tu-134A-1 standard (note the large rear emergency exits) was one of five such aircraft bought by what was then Háng Không Viêt Nam from the East German Air Force. It was damaged beyond repair in a landing accident at Ho Chi Minh City on 12th January 1991. RART

USA

In February 1994 the charter airline **CLINTONDALE AVIATION, INC** headquartered in Clintondale, New York, leased Tu-134A-3 'Salon' RA-65132 (c/n (83)60639, f/n 4804) from AVL Arkhangel'sk Airlines. Receiving full Clintondale colours, the aircraft was delivered on 4th March 1994, operating from Moscow/Sheremet'yevo-1 – mostly to Western Europe. Apart from carrying businesspeople, it delivered personnel shifts to and from the Baikonur Space Centre and even performed ambulance flights. Clintondale Aviation President Colin J Hamilton told this author 'the aircraft has left a very positive impression – there have never been any problems with it'.

Clintondale Aviation's clients included nearly all major Western oil companies represented on the CIS market (Chevron, Elf-Aquitaine, Exxon, Mobil Oil, Royal Dutch Shell, Statoil, Texaco), as well as General Motors Corporation, Motorola, Pratt & Whitney, Chase Manhattan Bank and the World Bank, the Price Waterhouse auditing company and foreign embassies.

In the summer of 1998 Clintondale Aviation leased Tu-134A-3 'Salon' RA-65088 (c/n (73)60172, f/n 4307) from Avialeasing. Unlike RA-65132, which was basically white with a white/blue/red band around the forward fuselage, red Clintondale titles and a large 'CG' (that is, Clintondale Group) tail logo, this aircraft still wore the gold/black cheatline and Rosneft' tail logo. The dark blue titles of previous lessee Transaero Express were replaced by red Clintondale titles and a small 'CG' logo aft of the flightdeck.

By March 1999 RA-65088 had been returned to the lessor, later going to the Pulkovo Air Enterprise as a 60-seater; RA-65132 was also returned by mid-year.

VIETNAM

HÁNG KHÔNG VIÊT NAM [VN/HVN] operated a total of 16 Tu-134s. Fourteen of them remained in service long enough to see the carrier renamed **VIETNAM AIRLINES** in 1990.

Registration	Version	C/n	F/n	Notes
VN-A102	Tu-134A/r.n.	(83)60925	4904	Crashed Bangkok 9-9-88
VN-A104	Tu-134A/r.n.	(93)61055	5006	D/D 2-79. WFU Hanoi late 1996
VN-A106	Tu-134AK*	(73)49752	3807	D/D 11-77. WFU Hanoi late 1996
VN-A108	Tu-134AK	6348430	3510	DBR Hanoi 17-2-88
VN-A110	Tu-134A/r.n.	(93)62144	5101	D/D 3-79. WFU Hanoi late 1996
VN-A112	Tu-134AK/r.n.*	(93)62458	5306	D/D 9-79. WFU Hanoi
VN-A114	Tu-134B-3 'Salon'*	(43)66220	6355	Has rear door (≅ Tu-134AK). D/D 4-84. Derelict Da Nang by 5-98; preserved 11-98
VN-A116	Tu-134B-3 'Salon'	(43)66230	6356	Has rear door (≅ Tu-134AK). D/D 4-84. WFU Hanoi by 3-99
VN-A118	Tu-134B-3 'Salon'*	(43)66250	6357	Has rear door (≅ Tu-134AK). D/D 5-84. WFU Hanoi by 3-99
VN-A120	Tu-134B-3	(43)66360	6362	D/D 7-84. Crashed Phnom Penh 3-9-97
VN-A122	Tu-134AK/r.n.*	(73)49900	4009	Ex-East German AF DDR-SDK, bought 1-6-90; D/D 17-6-90? WFU Hanoi late 1996
VN-A124	Tu-134AK/r.n.*	(73)60108	4301	Ex-East German AF DDR-SDL, bought 1-6-90; D/D 17-6-90? WFU Ho Chi Minh City by 3-96
VN-A126	Tu-134AK/r.n.*	(83)60435	4605	Tu-134A-1 standard. Ex-East German AF DDR-SDM, bought 1-6-90; D/D 2-7-90? DBR Ho Chi Minh City 12-1-91
VN-A128	Tu-134AK/r.n.*	(83)60612	4708	Tu-134A-1 standard. Ex-East German AF DDR-SDN, bought 1-6-90; D/D 17-6-90? WFU Ho Chi Minh City ?-96
VN-A130	Tu-134AK/r.n.*	(93)62259	5202	Tu-134A-1 standard. Ex-East German AF DDR-SDO, bought 1-6-90; D/D 2-7-90? WFU Hanoi late 1996
VN-A132	Tu-134AK/r.n.*	(03)63260	5710	Tu-134A-1 standard. Ex-East German AF DDR-SDP, bought 1-6-90; D/D 2-7-90? WFU Ho Chi Minh City by 3-96

One more Tu-134A or 'AK (identity unknown) was damaged at Phnom Penh on 25th November 1994. All Tu-134AKs and Tu-134B 'Salons' (except VN-A116) were converted to 72-seaters.

The first Tu-134A service was performed on 1st February 1977 on the Hanoi – Ho Chi Minh City route. At first the Vietnamese pilots took their training at the COMECON Civil Aviation Centre in Ul'yanovsk, but from April 1979 onwards conversion training took place at Hanoi under the supervision of Vietnamese instructors.

In July 1990 the fleet was expanded by the acquisition of six Tu-134AKs which were surplus to the East German Air Force. The renaming to Vietnam Airlines brought about a change in livery, which until then had been 'Aeroflotesque'; Tu-134AK VN-A112 was used for experiments with various colour schemes until the definitive one was chosen. (Incidentally, until then Háng Không Viêt Nam had no set standard – individual aircraft differed in the location of the titles, registration and flag. Tu-134AK VN-A108 initially had the 'Tu-134A' nose titles applied below the cheatline in the distinctive angular 'Tupolev typeface' of the 1950s/1960s.)

By 1993 only six Tu-134s remained flyable, the others being grounded by spares shortages. Besides, Vietnam Airlines had decided to raise passenger comfort and flight safety to world standards. In July 1996 – January 1997 the airline leased ten brand-new Airbus Industrie A320-214, while government VIP transportation was taken over by two Fokker 70s in executive configuration.

Delivered to Aviogenex in March 1978, YU-AJW was the last-but-one Tu-134A-1 built in airline configuration. Peter Davison

YUGOSLAVIA

The charter carrier **AVIOGENEX** [–/AGX] founded in 1969 as a subsidiary of the General Export trading company and a partner of the Jugotours travel agency operated 12 Tu-134s, most of which were named after Yugoslav cities.

Registration	Version	C/n	F/n	Notes
YU-AHH	Tu-134	8350701		D/D 1-69, named 'Beograd'; sold 11-5-71 as CCCP-65672
YU-AHI	Tu-134	9350705		D/D 27-3-69, named 'Zagreb'; sold 20-3-71 as CCCP-65673
YU-AHS	Tu-134/r.n.	0350921		D/D 30-4-70, named 'Skopje'; sold 26-7-71 as CCCP-65963
YU-AHX	Tu-134A/r.n.	1351203		D/D 24-3-71, named 'Beograd'; converted to Tu-134A-1 ?-75. Sold 24-12-90 as CCCP-93930
YU-AHY	Tu-134A/r.n.	1351204		D/D 15-4-71, named 'Zagreb'; converted to Tu-134A-1 1975/6. Lst Nesu Air 8-88 to 11-89 as TC-ALV. Sold 28-12-90 as CCCP-93926
YU-AHZ	Tu-134A/r.n.	1351205		D/D 22-4-71, named 'Skopje'. Crashed Rijeka 23-5-71
YU-AJA	Tu-134A/r.n.	1351206		D/D 29-4-71, named 'Titograd'; converted to Tu-134A-1 1975/6. Lst Nesu Air 8-88 to 7-89 as TC-ALU. Sold 28-12-90 as CCCP-93929
YU-AJD	Tu-134A/r.n.	2351508		D/D 4-72, named 'Skopje'; converted to Tu-134A-1 1975/6. Sold 24-12-90 as CCCP-93927
YU-AJS	Tu-134A-1	6348370	3501	D/D ?-76. Crashed Libreville 2-4-77
YU-AJV	Tu-134A-1	(73)60035	4204	D/D 8-77; sold 1985 as CCCP-65563
YU-AJW	Tu-134A-1	(83)60321	4504	D/D 24-3-78, named 'Priština'; sold 1985 as CCCP-65560
YU-ANE	Tu-134A-1	(93)63165	5609	D/D 3-80; sold 1985 as CCCP-65564

At the customer's request the aircraft were completed with improved cabin trim and a redesigned galley. The third and final Tu-134 *sans suffixe* (YU-AHS) was unique in featuring a radar nose and a three-man flightdeck.

By the end of 1969 the first two aircraft delivered that year had carried 50,000 passengers. However, the Tu-134 *sans suffixe* could not cope with the passenger loads at the peak of the season; therefore they were soon traded in for more capacious Tu-134As. The first five were delivered as 80-seaters, but soon the airline purchased lightweight seats of Western manufacture, which allowed the seating capacity to be increased to 84 and then to 86 by reducing the seat pitch to 70cm. Then the passenger evacuation problem arose, leading to the development of the Tu-134A-1. Four of the original five 'As were upgraded during the low season of 1975/1976; subsequent aircraft were custom-built as Tu-134A-1s. Another upgrade performed at the airline's request was the installation of a rain repellent spraying system for the windscreens. The system was manufactured by Boeing but installed in Khar'kov according to Soviet drawings.

The delivery of the Tu-134As increased the airline's passenger traffic to 250,000 passengers per year. Aviogenex Tu-134As linked Belgrade, Ljubljana and Rijeka with 150 destinations in 52 countries. During the winter season the aircraft were converted for cargo carriage.

Aviogenex really squeezed its aircraft to the last drop: at the height of the tourist season the Tu-134s achieved an average daily utilisation of 15 hours (Yugoslavia ranked first among Tu-134 operators in this respect). Moreover, having no maintenance hangar of its own, the airline had to service its aircraft in the open. The Tu-134s stood up to the challenge, demonstrating high reliability.

Aviogenex General Director Miroslav Spasić described the Tu-134A as 'an excellent aircraft', saying it was well liked by the passengers for its speed and comfort and by the pilots for its reliability and easy handling. Nevertheless, by 1989 the Tu-134As had been returned, giving way to Boeing 737-200s – whether it was because they, too, could no longer cope or because finicky Western travellers demanded greater comfort.

OPERATORS FROM UNKNOWN NATIONS

By August 2003 Tu-134A-3 4L-65061 (c/n (73)49874, f/n 4003) had been leased by an airline called **AIR BISEC**. The name does have an ex-Yugoslavian air but it's hard to tell...

In March 2002 Tajikistan Airlines Tu-134A-3 EY-65763 (c/n (93)62299, f/n 5204) was briefly wet-leased by an airline called **SHAHEED AIR**, operating from Ras al Khaimah in full Tajikistan Airlines colours with tine 'Shaheed Air' stickers.

Chapter Eight

Beneath the Skin

Type

Twin-engined short/medium-haul airliner. The airframe is of riveted all-metal construction and is largely made of D16T, D16AT, D16ATN, D16ATV, D16ATNV, D16AM and D16AMO duralumin. Some structural elements are made of V95T, V95T-1SV, V95AT, V95AT-1SV, AK-6 and AK-8 aluminium alloys, ML5-T4, MA1, MA2, MA5 and MA8 magnesium alloys, OT4-0 titanium alloy and 30KhGSA, 30KhGSNA, 30KhNMA and EI-643 steel. Large-scale use is made of chemical milling. To ensure corrosion protection the skin panels and internal structural members are electrochemically coated; additionally, the insides of the fuselage are given a coat of FL-086 primer.

Fuselage

Semi-monocoque stressed-skin structure of beam-and-stringer construction with 64 stringers and 65 (on the Tu-134 *sans suffixe*) or 70 (on subsequent versions) frames which are mostly set at 0.5m (1ft 7⅝in) intervals. Frames 2, 4, 6, 8, 15, 28, 34, 47, 48, 51, 55, 55a, 60, 63 and 64 are mainframes; frames 5 and 9 are reinforced and the others are ordinary extruded frames. Flush riveting in most areas, except the rear fuselage where rivets with lentil-shaped heads are used. The cross-section is circular, with a maximum diameter of 3.5m (11ft 5¾in).

Structurally the fuselage is divided into three sections: the forward fuselage (*Section F2*), the centre fuselage (*Section F3*) and the rear fuselage (*Section F4*). *Section F1* is the navigator's station glazing frame (a one-piece ML5-T4 casting) on 'glass-nosed' versions or a glassfibre radome of honeycomb construction on radar-nosed versions. On the Tu-134UBL Section F1 is a large structure with a metal upper half comprising 12 frames (2A, 1A, 0 and 1S-9S) and a dielectric radome forming the lower half; it is attached to Section F2 (which is identical to that of the Tu-134B-1) via an annular adapter with an aperture for the forward pressure bulkhead.

Sections F2/F3 (and, on 'glass-nosed' versions, F1) form a single pressure cabin. To ensure adequate pressurisation the structure is sealed by placing U-20A elastic tape between the skin, frames and stringers before they are riveted together. Additionally, in some places U-30MES-10 and UT-32 sealants are brushed on over the joint.

The *forward fuselage* (frames 2-15) includes the crew section; the flightdeck is located between frames 4-9. 'Glass-nosed' versions have a navigator's station between frames 2-4 and an unpressurised ventral bay for the radar antenna between frames 4-7 enclosed by a detachable teardrop-shaped glassfibre radome. On radar-nosed versions frame 2 is the forward pressure bulkhead mounting the radar dish covered by an upward-hinged radome, and the space between frames 2-4 is an avionics bay with a forward-hinged rectangular ventral access door.

The flightdeck glazing frame welded from V-section steel profiles is located between frames 5-8, resting on lateral beams. There are four optically-flat birdproof panes at the front made of PO-24 boron-silicate triplex glass, with four triangular side windows and eyebrow windows (four on the Tu-134 *sans suffixe* and two on later versions); the side and upper panes are made of SO-120 Plexiglas, with double or single glazing 4-22mm (0.157-0.86in) thick. The foremost side windows are sliding direct vision windows which can be used as emergency exits on the ground. The navigator's station features curved Plexiglas panels 16mm (0.62in) thick and an optically flat triplex elliptical lower panel.

The nosewheel well is located between frames 8-13. A 1.25 x 0.75m (49¼ x 29½ in; ICAO Type II) rectangular service door incorporating a window of 30cm (11¾in) diameter is located on the starboard side between frames 11-13; it is opened by pushing inwards and sliding forwards. The forward baggage compartment with an expandable-mesh door is located opposite. The Tu-134UBL, Tu-134B-1, Tu-134BV and Tu-134SKh feature a window of 40cm (15¾in) diameter to port between frames 12-13.

The *centre fuselage* (frames 15-55) is cylindrical up to frame 38, tapering gradually aft of it; the aft portion carries the fin fillet and the engine pylons. All frames except Nos 15, 28, 34 and 55 feature transverse beams at one third of the height to which the cabin floor and the seat tracks are attached. The seat tracks can withstand a longitudinal load of 9G in a crash landing. The floor is made of PVC foam plastic reinforced with two layers of plywood.

The front portion (frames 15-15D)[1] accommodates the galley/entry vestibule and, on the Tu-134A, part of the forward baggage compartment. A plug-type entry door measuring 1.61 x 0.7m (63⅜ x 27½in; ICAO Type I) is located on the port side between frames 15V-15D. It has a quasi-oval shape (the aperture is 'flattened' at the bottom to provide an even threshold), incorporating a window of 40cm diameter, and opens inward and forward. On the Tu-134A *et seq.* a 30-cm window is often located on the starboard side between frames 15-15A, and a 40-cm window is always located between frames 15V-15G to starboard. On the Tu-134AK and new-build Tu-134B 'Salon' part of the galley is moved from starboard to port at the expense of the forward baggage compartment, and a toilet is located between frames 15B-15G to starboard.

The passenger cabin(s) occupies (occupy) the space between frames 15D-45 on the Tu-134A/B or 15D-41 on the Tu-134AK/new-build Tu-134B 'Salon'. The latter two versions feature a rear galley/entry vestibule between frames 41-45, with a 1.42 x 0.87m (56 x 34¼in) rectangular entry door of similar design to the forward one on the port side between frames 42-44. Three-section airstairs are mounted on frame 45, turning manually through 90° into the doorway and deploying electrically within 60 seconds by means of linkages and cables. All doors are provided with rain gutters.

The centre fuselage features numerous windows of 40cm diameter. Each window has double glazing, with a 16-mm outer pane absorbing the pressure differential at high altitude, a 5-mm (0.19-in) inner pane and a 30mm (1.18in) wide spacer in between; both panes are made of SO-120 Plexiglas.

Most versions have two 0.586 x 0.6m (23 x 23⅝in; ICAO Type IV) rectangular overwing emergency exits on each side between frames 29-31 and 34-36. The Tu-134A-1 and Tu-134B feature ICAO Type III rear emergency exits measuring 0.916 x 0.6m (36 x 23⅝in). Some special mission versions have an incomplete set of windows and/or emergency exits (see Chapter 3).

Two toilets are installed between frames 45-48 on passenger versions, with 30-cm windows in the roof between frames 46-47; a toilet service panel is located ventrally between frames 41-42 and a water filling panel between frames 46-47. VIP aircraft featuring a forward toilet have a second toilet service panel between frames 15B-15V offset to starboard, and the starboard rear toilet is replaced by a coat closet.

Further aft is the rear baggage compartment (frames 48-55) terminating in the rear pressure dome. Loading/unloading takes place via a rectangular door measuring 0.905 x 1.22m (35⅝ x 48in) on the starboard side between frames 48-51 (under the starboard engine pylon). It slides inwards/upwards and is balanced by

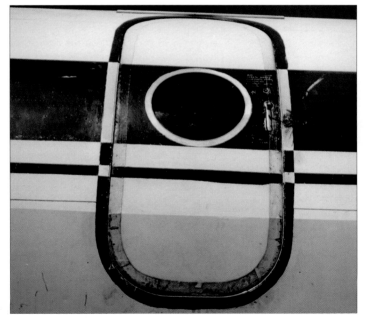

Top left: **The forward fuselage of most Tu-134s featured a glazed navigator's station and an ROZ-1 radar in a chin radome (illustrated here by Tu-134AK RA-65939). The upper aerials of the SRO-2M IFF transponder are just visible.** Author

Top right: **The export version of the Tu-134A/AK, as well as the Tu-134B, featured a Groza M-134 radar in a nose radome (illustrated by Tu-134A-3 RA-65667).** Author

Centre left: **The radome of the Groza M-134 is not blended completely into the nose contour, creating a 'dog nose' effect, and has four external stiffening ribs. Note the RIO-3 icing detector just aft of the radome on the starboard side and the avionics bay access hatch ahead of the nose gear.** Author

Centre right: **The starboard side service door with a window of 30cm diameter slides inwards and forwards.** Author

Bottom left: **The port side entry door with a full-size window swings inwards and forwards, measuring 1.61 x 0.7m from Batch 3 onwards (illustrated by Tu-134A-3 RA-65667). The handle pops out at the push of a button and is here sealed against unauthorised entry by a seal made of modelling clay!** Author

a pneumatic damper with cables and pulleys; when the door is open the starboard engine cannot be started. The compartment is also accessible via a door in the forward bulkhead. A 30-cm window in the roof offset to starboard provides natural lighting and allows inspection of the tail unit from within. On military trainer versions the baggage door is hinged at the top and opened inwards by a pneumatic ram for bailing out in an emergency.

The Nos 1 and 2 avionics/equipment bays are located between frames 15-28 and 34-45; they are accessible via inward/starboard-opening hatches located between frames 20-22 and 39-41 respectively, as well as via numerous removable panels in the cabin floor. The No 3 electrics bay is located under the rear baggage compartment floor.

The inside of Sections F2/F3 is covered with AZT heat- and soundproofing mats, except for the rear baggage compartment where ATM-3 heat insulation is used.

The unpressurised *rear fuselage* (frames 55-64) incorporates attachment points for the fin spars (at mainframes 55 and 60) and engine pylons. It accommodates the No 4 equipment bay (frames 55-60) housing air conditioning system equipment, with an outward-opening access door on the starboard side between frames 56-58. The Tu-134 *sans suffixe* had a brake parachute housing with an aft-hinged cover between frames 62-64; later versions have an APU bay with clamshell cowling doors (frames 62-65) and frame 62 is a titanium firewall. A tailcone is attached to frame 65, featuring an orifice for the APU jetpipe on the Tu-134A *et seq.*

The Tu-134AK and new-build Tu-134B 'Salon' feature a rear entry door to port which encroaches on the wing/fuselage fairing. Author

This sequence shows how the Tu-134AK's powered airstairs unfold after being manually rotated into position. The handrails are erected manually. Author

Top left: **The overwing emergency exits are identical (Type IV) on the Tu-134 *sans suffixe* and Tu-134A/AK. The Tu-134A-1 and Tu-134B (illustrated by RA-65720) have exits of unequal size, the rear pair being Type III and being surrounded by external reinforcing plates.** Author

Centre left: **The rear baggage door is located under the starboard engine nacelle, sliding inwards/upwards on passenger versions (illustrated by Tu-134AK RA-65680); on military trainers it serves as an escape hatch.** Author

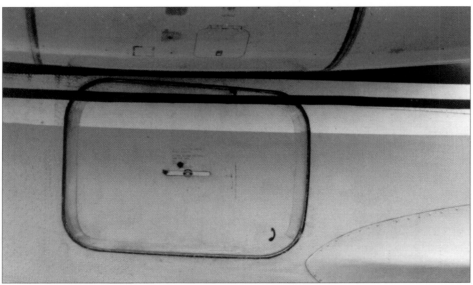

Bottom left: **The rear fuselage of a Tu-134 *sans suffixe* featuring a brake parachute bay with ventral door. This view also illustrates the shape of the rear ends of the initial version's engine pylons and nacelles. Note how the rudder trim tab terminates short of the fuselage and the tail navigation light is positioned on the tailcone.** Pyotr Batuyev

Bottom right: **The rear fuselage of a Tu-134Sh makes an interesting comparison. Note the reshaped engine nacelles with thrust reverser cascades; the APU bay (replacing the brake parachute bay) extended all the way aft, with cowling doors outlined in yellow and black; the strike camera fairing immediately ahead of these, flanked by auxiliary APU intake grilles (the port one is visible); the air conditioning system heat exchanger outlet just aft of the port engine pylon; the triangular IFF blade aerial and the ground power receptacle with a power cable connected.** Sergey Panov

Wings

Cantilever low-wing monoplane of modified trapezoidal planform, with small leading edge root extensions (leading-edge sweep 40°47' from root to rib 9 and 37°38' outboard); trailing edge broken by main landing gear fairings, with zero sweepback inboard of these. Sweepback at quarter-chord 35°, anhedral 1°30' from root to rib 15 and 0°33' outboard, incidence +1° at root and −1°55' at tip, camber −2°55', aspect ratio 6.5, taper 3.14.

The wings utilise TsAGI high-speed airfoils, including P35-13M. Thickness/chord ratio 9.75% at root, 13% at mid-span and 11% at tip; the lowest ratio at the roots is due to the top of the airfoil being cut away for better integration between wings and cabin floor.

The wings are a two-spar, stressed-skin structure with 57 ribs. Structurally they are built in five pieces: the centre section, inner wings and outer wings. The manufacturing joints are at ribs 0/1 and 15/15A; the sections are joined by flanges. Ribs 1, 9, 15 and 25 on each side are sealed; ribs 7-9, 10, 12, 14, 16, 18, 20, 22 and 24 are reinforced, serving as attachment points for the flaps, ailerons, spoilers and main gear fairings. The ribs are at right angles to the rear spar, except for the centre section ribs and ribs 1 and 25 which are parallel to the fuselage axis.

The *centre section* is integral with the fuselage, the spars being attached to mainframes 28 and 34 by fittings. It has five ribs forming four bays, the outer two accommodating control runs, hydraulic and fuel lines and electric cables; the inner two bays may house fuel tanks. The flat three-piece upper skin forms the pressure floor; the three-piece lower skin is attached by screws. The wing/fuselage joint is covered by a fairing located between frames 19-47.

The *inner wings* each have 15 ribs (1-15), six upper and two lower skin panels. Large pointed main landing gear fairings are attached to ribs 7-9 and inclined 3° up. The fairings have a basically rectangular cross-section changing to circular at the tips. They are of beam-and-stringer construction with 17 frames; each fairing has a manufacturing break at frame 8 and the front ends are split to fit around the wing torsion box. The wheel wells are located between frames 2-14.

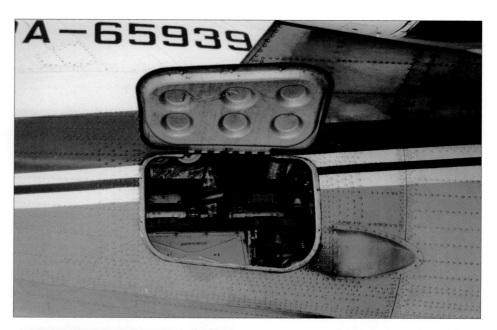

The open access door of the No 4 equipment bay housing air conditioning system equipment and the two DC batteries (in the grey box, marked 'No 1' and 'No 2'). Author

The port wing, showing the boundary layer fences and the detachable leading edge fairing/de-icer. Author

A view of the starboard wing, showing the spoiler outboard of the main gear fairing and the large aileron outboard of the outer fence. Sergey Panov

The *outer wings* each have 11 ribs (15A-25), three upper skin panels and one lower panel, plus tip fairings. All inner/outer wing skins have separate stringers and are attached by sealed flush rivets; some have variable thickness. The inner/outer wing torsion box incorporates integral fuel tanks with removable access panels for inspection (two on each inner wing and one on each outer wing).

The three-section leading edge is detachable, doubling as a de-icer. Each inner wing has two prominent boundary layer fences 16cm (6¼in) tall at ribs 9-11 and 13-15, designed to delay tip stall; they are built in several portions to avoid deformation as the wings flex.

The wings are equipped with two-section double-slotted flaps (inner sections, ribs 1-7; outer sections, ribs 10-15), two-section ailerons (see Control system) and one-piece spoilers on the outer wings. There are no leading-edge devices. The flaps are actuated by an MPZ-18A5 drive (*mekhanizm privoda zakrylkov*) with twin D-600-5 electric motors via drive shafts and angle drives/screw jacks (two for each inboard flap and three for each outboard flap. They move on curved tracks housed entirely inside the wings (two for each inboard flap and three for each outboard flap). The inboard and outboard flaps have two and three cove lip doors respectively; all were movable on early aircraft but the outboard flap cove lip doors were fixed from Tu-134AK c/n 3352005 (Polish AF '101 Red') onwards. The Tu-134A *et seq.* have an SEUZ-1 electronic flap synchroniser (*sistema elektronnovo oopravleniya zakrylkami*) preventing asymmetric deployment.

Flap settings were originally 9°/10° or 18°/20° (outboard/inboard) for takeoff and 35°/38° for landing; the maximum setting was later reduced to 30°. The difference in settings delays tip stall, improving roll stability, and reduces the pitch-down force when the flaps are deployed.

On most versions the spoilers are ground spoilers (lift dumpers) only, being armed before landing to deploy automatically 52° on

This view of Tu-134A CCCP-65747 at Minsk-2 shows the double-slotted flaps at full 35°/38° deflection (outboard/inboard) and the deployed ventral speedbrake. Note also the cabin pressurisation system outlet beneath the starboard rear emergency exit.
Ghennadiy Petrov archive

The tail unit of Tu-134 *Balkany* '05 Red' (c/n (23)63976), showing the detachable leading edge fairing/de-icer and the flush antennas; the lower two serve the RSBN-2S SHORAN, while the uppermost antenna is for the SOD-67M DME.
Author

The horizontal tail of Tu-134AK RA-65939, showing the elevator trim tabs and the tail navigation light on the fin top fairing flanked by static discharge wicks. Author

touchdown. Export Tu-134Bs and the Tu-134B-1 feature flight spoilers (airbrakes) deflected up to 40° in flight. Each spoiler is hinged on three brackets.

Aircraft up to and including Tu-134A CCCP-65111 (c/n (83)60346, f/n 4509) had a ventral speedbrake between fuselage frames 34-39. It was hinged to the wing centre section rear spar and actuated by a separate MPZ-18A5 electric drive with two screw jacks, deflecting 40°. The speedbrake was deleted from Tu-134A CCCP-65112 (c/n (83)60350, f/n 4510) onwards and permanently locked in the up position on earlier aircraft.

Tail Unit

Cantilever swept T-tail featuring symmetrical airfoils. The *vertical tail* consists of a large root fillet mounted on the centre fuselage between frames 47-55, a detachable fin and a one-piece rudder (see Control system). Sweepback at quarter-chord 40°, leading-edge sweep 44°36', aspect ratio 0.88 with root fillet or 0.933 less fillet, taper 1.75, thickness/chord ratio 10%.

The fin is bolted to fuselage mainframes 55 and 60. It is a two-spar stressed-skin structure with 18 ribs; all but the top and bottom ribs are at right angles to the rear spar. The three-piece leading edge is detachable, doubling as a de-icer, and incorporates an air conditioning system air intake. A cigar-shaped fairing at the top encloses the fin/stabiliser joint. There are three rudder mounting brackets and a lower rudder mounting post.

The variable-incidence *horizontal tail* is hinged to the fin rear spar, comprising two stabilisers and one-piece elevators (see Control system). Sweepback at quarter-chord 38°, thickness/chord ratio 11% at root and 10% at tip, aspect ratio 4.54, taper 2.46. Each stabiliser is of similar two-spar construction with 24 ribs, a tip fairing and five elevator mounting brackets at ribs 6, 10, 14, 18 and 22. The stabilisers are bolted together at the spars.

Landing Gear

Electrohydraulically retractable tricycle type; all three units retract aft. Maximum landing gear transition speed is 400km/h (248mph). Normal gear transition takes place within 7-10 seconds; emergency extension is accomplished within 20 seconds, using the brake hydraulic system, or 15-20 minutes, using the hand-driven pump as a last resort.

The nose unit attached to fuselage frame 8 has jury struts and an aft-mounted breaker strut. It is fitted with twin 660 x 200mm (26.0 x 7.87in) K-288B or K-288D non-braking wheels[2]

The nose landing gear unit of Tu-134 *Balkany* '05 Red' (c/n (23)63976); the torque link has been disconnected for towing. Note the mud/snow/slush guard and the earth connection wire running into the wheel well. Author

The port main gear unit, showing forward-mounted telescopic retraction strut. Author

and equipped with a mud/snow/slush guard. The nose unit features a steering mechanism/shimmy damper and is controlled by the rudder pedals. Steering angles for taxying are ±35° (Tu-134 *sans suffixe*) or ±55° (subsequent versions); when the flaps are deployed the nose gear steering angle is limited to ±5°30' or ±8°30' respectively, allowing evasive action during the take-off/landing run. For towing, the nose gear scissor link can be disengaged, allowing the wheels to turn through ±75°.

The semi-levered-suspension main units are attached to inner wing ribs 7-9; each unit has a forward-mounted telescopic retraction strut

and a four-wheel bogie. The bogies initially had 930 x 305mm (36.61 x 12.0in) KT-81/3 wheels equipped with four-disc brakes (KT = *koleso tormoznoye* – brake wheel); later aircraft have KT-153 wheels of identical size. An anti-skid unit is provided.

When extended, the main gear struts are inclined 12° aft. In no-load condition the bogies assume a slightly nose-down attitude. During retraction they are rotated aft through 180° by separate hydraulic rams/rocking dampers to lie inverted in the abovesaid fairings.

All three units have oleo-pneumatic shock absorbers and scissor links. Maximum oleo compression is 390mm (15⅜in) for the nose gear and 275mm (10⅞in) for the main gear; the bogies move aft by virtue of oleo compression in the event of hard braking or jolts. Tyre pressure is 9 bars (128.5psi).[3]

The nosewheel well is closed by two pairs of doors; the small forward doors are mechanically linked to the nose gear strut. Each main unit has two large main doors, two small clamshell doors in line with the gear fulcrum (mechanically linked to the strut) and a narrow curved strip attached to the retraction strut. The main doors are hydraulically actuated, opening only when the gear is in transit.

All three units have uplocks, downlocks (built into the retraction struts for the main units) and door locks. Landing gear position is indicated by pilot lights on the captain's instrument panel. A warning horn sounds if the throttles are retarded to flight idle when the gear is up; it is silenced automatically by gear extension.

For emergencies or wet/icy runway operations the Tu-134 *sans suffixe* was equipped with a PT-7546-61 brake parachute (*parashoot tormoznoy*) housed in the rear fuselage. The parachute had a 42-m² (451.6-ft²) main canopy and a 2-m² (21.5-ft²) auxiliary canopy, reducing the landing roll by 13-15%; its life expectancy was 30 landings over a ten-year period.

A D-30-III engine on a transportation dolly. It has just been removed from Tu-134A-3 RA-65667 on 23rd September 1999 and is ready for installation into the port engine nacelle of Tu-134B-1-3 RA-65720 as the latter is made airworthy again at Zhukovskiy; note the orange-coloured frame at the top used for hoisting the engine into the nacelle. Note also that the nacelle's tail fairing is attached directly to the engine. Author

Powerplant

The Tu-134 *sans suffixe* is powered by two Solov'yov D-30 (D-30 Srs I) turbofans rated at 6,800kgp (14,990 lbst) at ISA for take-off, with a cruise rating of 1,600kgp (3,530 lbst) at 11,000m (36,090ft) and 800km/h (500mph). The Tu-134A/AK, Tu-134B, Tu-134Sh and Tu-134UBL have identically rated D-30-II (D-30 Srs II) engines.

The D-30-II is a two-spool turbofan with a fixed-area subsonic air intake, a four-stage axial low-pressure (LP) compressor, a 10-stage axial high-pressure (HP) compressor, a can-annular combustion chamber, two-stage axial HP and LP turbines, a fixed-area subsonic jet-pipe featuring a 12-chute core/bypass flow mixer, and a cascade-type thrust reverser (no reverser on the D-30 Srs I).

Construction is mostly of titanium. The LP spool rotates in three bearings (in the air intake assembly, in the centre casing and in the rear support frame); the HP spool also has three bearings (in the centre casing, at the rear of the compressor and ahead of the turbine). The air intake assembly has a fixed spinner and 26 radial struts. Two-position variable inlet guide vanes are used on the HP compressor to min-imise blade vibration; the fourth and fifth HP compressor stages feature bleed valves. The centre casing carries two accessory gear-boxes; the upper one drives the generators while the lower one is for the fuel, oil and hydraulic pumps. The combustion chamber has 12 flame tubes, two of which feature ignit-ers. The first HP turbine stage has cooled blades in both rotor and stator; all turbine disks are air-cooled. The engine mounting lugs are located on the centre and turbine casings.

The thrust reverser grids are inclined 54° for-ward and 15° outward to direct the jet blast away from the main gear wheels. Maximum reverse thrust 2,500kgp (5,510 lbst). Reverse thrust is normally cancelled when the aircraft decelerates to 100-110km/h (62-68mph) to avoid exhaust gas ingestion and engine surge but may be used right down to zero speed if necessary.

The Tu-134A-3, Tu-134B-3 and Tu-134SKh are powered by D-30-III (D-30 Srs III) engines derived from the D-30-II by installing a five-stage LP compressor. The D-30-III has a 6,930-kgp (15,280-lbst) take-off rating at ISA, delivering 6,800kgp up to +25°C.

The D-30 Srs I is started by twin STG-12TMO-1000 starter-generators, using DC power from on-board batteries or ground power. The D-30-II/D-30-III is started by an STV-10 air turbine starter (*startyor vozdooshnyy*) using compressed air from the APU, ground supply or cross-feed from the other engine.

Bypass ratio 1.0. Maximum turbine speed 7,700rpm (LP)/11,600rpm (HP); overall engine pressure ratio at sea level 18.65 (LP compres-sor, 2.65/HP compressor, 7.1). Mass flow at take-off: Srs I, 126kg/sec (277 lb/sec); Srs II, 127kg/sec (280 lb/sec); Srs III, 128kg/sec (282 lb/sec). Turbine temperature: Srs I, 1,347°K; Srs II, 1,357°K; Srs III, 1,330°K. Specific fuel consumption (SFC) at take-off power: Srs I, 0.62kg/kgp·hr (1.36 lb/lbst·hr); Srs II, 0.605kg/kgp·hr (1.33 lb/lbst·hr); Srs III, 0.61kg/kgp·hr (1.34 lb/lbst·hr). Cruise SFC: Srs I/Srs II, 0.786kg/kgp·hr (1.73 lb/lbst·hr); Srs III, 0.793kg/kgp·hr (1.75 lb/lbst·hr).

Length overall: Srs I, 3.983m (13ft ¾in); Srs II/Srs III, 4.733m (15ft 6⅜in). Inlet diameter 0.963m (3ft 2in). Dry weight: Srs I, 1,550kg (3,420 lb); Srs II, 1,765kg (3,890 lb); Srs III, 1,809kg (3,990 lb). Design life was initially 7,500 hours for the D-30 Srs I, with a 2,500-hour time between overhauls. By 2000 this had been increased to 19,000 and 3,000 hours respectively.

The engines are mounted in individual cigar-shaped nacelles on large horizontal pylons (frames 46-58); the pylons are two-spar struc-tures with internal strut bracing whose spars are attached to fuselage mainframes 47/48 and 51. For aerodynamic reasons the nacelles are installed at 4° toe-out. On the Tu-134A *et seq.* the nacelles are 5.47m (17ft 11⅜in) long, with a maximum diameter of 1.36m (4ft 5½in).

Each nacelle is built in three pieces. The annular forward fairing with seven frames incor-porates the inlet duct, air intake de-icer and pylon leading edge; the inlets are angled 2° towards the fuselage. The centre portion is attached to the pylon by four bolts and features 17 frames and formers, five beams and six engine mounting struts; the inboard portion serves as a firewall. The large ventral cutout for engine installation/removal is closed by four outward-hinged cowling panels and a multi-segment rear strip; the centre portion features dorsal access hatches and a dorsal generator cooling air intake. The annular rear fairing fitting around the jetpipe is attached directly to the engine casing, featuring five frames; its trailing edge is made of heat-resistant steel.

The engines are controlled by a system of cables. On all versions except the Tu-134B and Tu-134UBL, which have a central control pedestal, each pilot has his own set of throttles and (except on the Tu-134 *sans suffixe*) only the captain has reverse thrust control levers. Air-craft built from 1979 onwards have an AT-5 autothrottle (*avtomaht tyaghi*) with a go-around function maintaining constant speed during landing approach.

The Tu-134A *et seq.* have a Stoopino Machinery Design Bureau TA-8 auxiliary power unit installed in the rear fuselage (frames 62-64) for self-contained engine starting, AC ground power supply and air conditioning. In 1984 it was superseded by the TA-8A (TA-8 Srs II) fea-turing drop-forged turbine disks instead of cast ones for greater reliability. Dimensions, 1.368 x 0.713 x 0.705m (4ft 5⅞in x 2ft 4 in x 2ft 3¾in), dry weight with GS-12TO generator 196kg (432 lb). Bleed air pressure 3.3 bars (47psi), delivery rate 0.75kg/sec (1.65 lb/sec), equivalent power 107kW. The APU can be started at altitudes up to 3,000m (9,840ft).

The APU has clamshell cowling doors and an upward-angled exhaust. On the ground it draws air via two upward-opening intakes at the base of the rudder which close automati-cally during rotation on take-off; in flight it breathes via a ventral intake grille between frames 60-62 (the Tu-134Sh and Tu-134UBK have two smaller grilles flanking the strike cam-era fairing).

Control System

Conventional mechanical dual control system with push-pull rods made of duralumin pipes, control cranks and levers (everywhere except for certain locations where KSAN ultra-pliant steel cables and rollers are used to transmit control inputs). Manual controls throughout, except for the rudder control circuit. The control rods and cables are provided with bronze/rubber pressure seals where they exit the pressure cabin. Gust locks are provided to prevent damage to the system by high winds while the aircraft is parked.

Directional control is provided by a one-piece rudder of single-spar construction. The rudder has aerodynamic and mass balancing. It features a trim tab hinged on four brackets; this has aerodynamic and mass balancing and is powered by an MP-100M-38 electric drive.

The rudder control circuit features a GU-108D irreversible hydraulic actuator (*ghidrousilitel'*), two artificial-feel units (one for take-off/landing and one for cruise flight) with MP-100M-36 and MP-100M-16 electric trim mechanisms respectively, and a DR-134M yaw damper (*dempfer ryskan'ya*). The actuator is powered by the main hydraulic system, switching to a backup system if hydraulic pressure falls; if this, too, fails, there is a manual emergency mode. The speed limit with the actuator or yaw damper inoperative is 550km/h (340mph). Maximum deflection is ±25° for the rudder with the flaps deployed (±5° in cruise mode) and ±17°30' for the servo tab.

Pitch control is provided by one-piece elevators with aerodynamic and mass balancing which are connected by a shaft with a universal joint. These are single-spar structures with a rear false spar; maximum deflection is +22°/–16°. Each elevator incorporates a trim tab controlled electrically (by a UT-15 drive) or manually by means of cables and handwheels; maximum deflection is ±4° in powered mode or ±8° in manual mode.

Top left: **The port engine nacelle of Tu-134AK RA-65939 with two of the four cowling panels open for inspection. Note the open tension locks at the top of the nacelle securing the generator access panel.** Author

Top right: **Upper view of the starboard nacelle and engine pylon of Tu-134Sh-1 '84 Red' (c/n 63550720), showing the generator cooling air intake. The engine air intake cover does not carry the c/n but is marked 'pravaya (starboard) – 84'. Note the windows for the starboard toilet and the rear baggage compartment.** Sergey Panov

Left: **The inside of the empty port engine nacelle of Tu-134A-3 RA-65667, with most of the cowling panels detached. The yellow and red pipes visible inside the nacelle are part of the fuel system and fire suppression system respectively.** Author

Above right: **The TA-8 APU with the cowling doors open for inspection; the port door is bulged to accommodate the air bleed duct. A GS-12TO generator is mounted on the front casing. Note the large ventral auxiliary intake grille ahead of the APU bay firewall, used by the APU in flight. The stainless steel tailcone carries static discharge wicks.** Author

To enhance pitch control at low speed and provide longitudinal trim the Tu-134 features variable-incidence stabilisers adjusted by an MUS-7A electric drive (*mekhanizm oopravleniya stabilizahtorom*) with twin D-600TV motors located on the fin front spar. Stabiliser settings are –1°30' in cruise mode, –3° for take-off and –4° for landing. Stabiliser trim change is possible up to 400km/h (248mph), taking 5.5 seconds or 11 seconds with one motor inoperative.

Roll control is provided by two-section ailerons on the outer wings (inner sections, ribs 15-19; outer sections, ribs 19-25); the inner and outer sections are suspended on two or three brackets respectively. The ailerons have both aerodynamic and mass balancing. The inner sections incorporate trim tabs with MP-100MT-20 electric drives and the outer sections have servo tabs; both are mass-balanced and suspended on three brackets each. The rudder control circuit features an artificial-feel unit. Maximum deflection is ±20° for the ailerons, ±6° for the trim tabs and ±3° for the servo tabs.

The Tu-134 *sans suffixe*, Tu-134Sh and early-production Tu-134As/AKs equipped with a BSU-3P ALS have an AP-6EM-3P autopilot; late Tu-134As/AKs and the Tu-134B featuring the ABSU-134 ALS are equipped with an AP-134 autopilot. The autopilot servos are connected to the control runs in parallel by means of cables and may be disengaged pyrotechnically at the push of a button if they jam. The servos feature overriding clutches, allowing the pilots to take corrective action when the autopilot is engaged.

Fuel System

The wing torsion box houses six integral fuel tanks (Nos 1, ribs 1-9; Nos 2, ribs 9-15 and Nos 3, ribs 15-25). They are sealed during manufacture by applying U-30MES-10 and UT-32 compounds over the joints.

Total capacity/fuel load is 16,300 litres/13.0 tons (3,586 Imp gals/28,660 lb) for the Tu-134 *sans suffixe* and 16 500 litres/13.2 tons (3,630 Imp gals/29,100 lb) for the Tu-134A/B. On the latter this is distributed as follows: No 1 tanks hold 4,910 litres (1,080.2 Imp gals) each; No 2 tanks, 2,190 litres (481.8 Imp gals) each and No 3 tanks, 1,150 litres (253 Imp gals) each.

The No 1 tanks are service tanks featuring two ETsN-45B delivery pumps (*elektricheskiy tsentrobezhnyy nasos* – electric centrifugal pump) each. The other tanks feature two DTsN-43P3T (on the Tu-134 *sans suffixe*) or ETsN-91 transfer pumps each. The fuel is heated in heat exchangers and fed to the engines by NR-30AR regulator pumps. The fuel filters are housed in the engine pylons.

Separate vent systems are provided for the port and starboard tanks, with ram air intakes in the wing/fuselage fairing.

On VIP and special mission aircraft the wing centre section houses two 750-litre (165-Imp gal) bag-type tanks made of kerosene-proof rubber; this brings the total to 17,800 litres/14.2 tons (3,916 Imp gals/31,305 lb) for the Tu-134K and 18,000 litres/14.4 tons (3,960 Imp gals/ 31,750 lb) for the Tu-134AK, Tu-134A/B 'Salon', Tu-134UBL and Tu-134SKh.

Normally the port and starboard halves of the system are isolated, but a cross-feed valve enables each engine to draw fuel from any group of tanks. The No 3 tanks are used up first, followed by the No 1/1A tanks until 2.24 tons (4,940 lb) of fuel remains, then the No 2 tanks and the remainder in Nos 1/1A. A warning light illuminates when the fuel is down to 2.4 tons (5,290 lb).

The Tu-134 has single-point pressure refuelling; a standard refuelling connector is located under the starboard wing leading edge. Refuelling at 4.5kg/cm² (64psi) takes no more than 23 minutes. Refuelling by gravity is also possible via three filler caps on each wing. Defuelling is done via two valves under the wing centre section; there is no provision for fuel jettisoning in flight. Fuel grades used are Russian T-1, TS-1 or RT, Western JP-1, Jet A-1, Avtur; grade 'I' special fluid is added in winter to prevent ice formation.

Oil System

Each engine has an open-type lubrication system using MK-8P mineral oil, VNII NP-50-1-4F synthetic oil[4] or equivalent. It features a 23-litre (5.06-Imp gal) oil tank installed in the front portion of the nacelle, a fuel/oil heat exchanger in the engine pylon, an OMN-30 delivery pump and an MNO-30 scavenging pump.

Hydraulics

Three separate hydraulic systems (main, brake and autonomous), each with its own reservoir, hydraulic accumulator and controls; common pressurisation system for the three.

The *main system* has two NP-43M/1 engine-driven pumps with a 70 litres/min (15.4 gals/min) total delivery rate. It operates the landing gear, nosewheel steering mechanism, spoilers, rudder actuator and windscreen wipers. A heat exchanger is provided.

The *brake system* has a Model 465D electric pump and an NR-01 hand-driven emergency pump. It operates the wheel brakes in normal and emergency mode, and is used for emergency landing gear extension.

The *autonomous system* has an NS-45 electric pump. It operates the rudder actuator if the main system fails and is activated automatically or manually.

All systems use AMG-10 oil-type hydraulic fluid (*aviatsionnoye mahslo ghidravlicheskoye*); total capacity is 48, 30 and 6 litres (10.56, 6.6 and 1.32 Imp gals) respectively. Nominal pressure 210kg/cm² (3,000psi) for the main and brake systems and 75-100kg/cm² (1,070-1,428psi) for the autonomous system.

Electrics

The electric system uses a single-wire layout with BPVLA (aluminium) and BPVLT (copper) wires having heat-resistant insulation to improve fire safety. Main 27V DC power supplied by four 12-kilowatt engine-driven STG-12TMO-1000 starter-generators on the Tu-134 *sans suffixe* or four 18kW/600 A GS-18TO generators on later versions. The APU features a GS-12TO generator supplying 12kW (10kW during engine starting). Backup 24V DC power provided by two 12SAM-55 lead-acid batteries (55 A·h) or, on the Tu-134UBL, 20NKNB-25 nickel-cadmium batteries (25 A·h) housed in the No 4 equipment bay.

115V/400Hz single-phase AC for the stabiliser and windscreen de-icers etc supplied by two (main and back-up) 4.5-kVA PO-4500 Srs VII AC converters (*preobrazovahtel' odnofahznyy*). 36V/400Hz three-phase AC for the radar, compass system, autopilot, navigation systems and flight instruments supplied by two (main and backup) 1-kVA PT-1000TsS or, on the Tu-134UBL, 1.5-kVA PT-1500TsB AC converters (*preobrazovahtel' tryokhfahznyy*).

DC power is distributed via seven distribution panels and circuit breaker panels in the flightdeck and galley. The central distribution panel is located in the rear baggage compartment on the port side of frame 48; the fuse box is located at frame 15 in the No 1 equipment bay. Two ground power receptacles (ShRAP-500 for DC power and ShRAP-200 for AC power) are provided on the fuselage underside between frames 48-49.

De-icing System

The wing and fin leading edges, engine air intake leading edges and spinners are de-iced by hot air bled from the 5th or 10th HP compressor stage (depending on rpm); the air exits through louvres at the wingtips and in the fin top fairing. Electric de-icing on the stabiliser leading edges, pitot heads, static ports (27V DC) and flightdeck/navigator's station glazing (115V AC); the heated panes are provided with an AOS-81 temperature regulator to prevent cracking. Engine inlet guide vanes are de-iced by hot oil circulating in the lubrication system.

An RIO-3 radioactive isotope icing detector (*rahdioizotopnyy indikahtor obledeneniya*) is installed on the starboard side of the nose at frame 3; on the ground it is closed by a lead cover to protect ground personnel against radiation. Early aircraft had DO-202M icing detectors in the engines but these were unreliable and were deleted.

Fire Suppression System

Six 8-litre (1.76-Imp gal) OS-8MF fire extinguisher bottles (*ognetooshitel' statsionarnyy* – stationary fire extinguisher) charged with 114V₂ grade chlorofluorocarbon in the No 1 equipment bay for fighting fires in the engine nacelles and in the APU bay. The system has a three-stage operating algorithm; the first shot is triggered automatically by flame sensors, the second and third shots are fired manually at the discretion of the crew. Impact sensors are installed under the wingtips, on the main gear retraction struts and immediately ahead of the nosewheel well to trigger all fire extinguishers automatically in a wheels-up landing.

A separate system featuring four 1-litre (0.22-Imp gal) OS-2IL or UBSh-2-1 bottles was originally installed in the No 2 equipment bay for fighting fires inside the engines proper (two shots per engine); however, it proved inefficient and was deleted. Additionally, portable fire extinguishers are provided in the cabin and flightdeck.

An SSP-2A fire warning system (*sistema signalizahtsii pozhahra*) with 27 DPS-1AG flame sensors provides audio and visual warnings; the engines feature a separate 2S7K fire warning system. Two DS-3M2 smoke sensors are installed in the rear baggage compartment.

Air Conditioning & Pressurisation System

The entire fuselage between frames 2-55 is pressurised by air bled from the 5th HP compressor stage. At 120-300°C (250-570°F) the air is fed first into a heat exchanger (its intake is located in the fin leading edge and the outlet just aft of the port engine pylon) and then into a cooling turbine. It is then and humidified before being fed into the pressure cabin.

Heating and ventilation air is processed separately. Ventilation air having a temperature of 10-40°C (50-104°F) is distributed by ducts running along the ceiling; additionally, there are individual ventilation nozzles for every seat. The cabin air is completely exchanged 24 to 32 times per hour. For heating, air with a temperature of 70°C (158°F) is distributed near the floor, passing between the cabin wall lining and the fuselage structure so that the walls act as 'radiators'. In the flightdeck, air is directed at the glazing to stop it from misting up.

On the ground, air for the ACS is supplied by the APU at 200°C (390°F) and 3.6 bars (51psi). Alternatively, a mobile air conditioner can be hooked up to a ventral connector located between frames 56-57. The ACS is adjusted by the flight engineer to automatically keep the cabin temperature anywhere between 16° and 25°C (60-77°F).

The Tu-134 has a duplex pressurisation system; the main and back-up systems maintain a pressure differential of 0.57 and 0.58kg/cm² (8.14 and 8.28psi) respectively. Sea level pressure is automatically maintained up to 6,300m (20,670ft); at 12,000m (39,370ft) the cabin pressure equals 2,400m (7,870ft) above sea level. Excess air is spilled to the atmosphere by a solenoid valve on the starboard side of the centre fuselage when the pressure differential reaches 0.63kg/cm² (9.0psi). A horn sounds and a warning light illuminates to alert the crew in the event of decompression.

Oxygen System

A 92-litre (20.24-Imp gal) oxygen bottle with five KP-24 masks (*kislorodnyy pribor*) is installed in the flightdeck, serving the flight crew to fight fatigue or in the event of decompression. One KP-19M portable breathing apparatus with a 7.8-litre (1.7-Imp gal) oxygen bottle is provided for the cabin crew, along with four KP-21 breathing apparatus with 1.7-litre (0.37-Imp gal) bottles in the event any of the passengers should feel unwell.

The Tu-134K, Tu-134AK and Tu-134B 'Salon' were completed with an automatic oxygen system having pop-out oxygen masks. Starting in 1993, many Tu-134A/Bs have been upgraded with automatic oxygen systems featuring chemical oxygen generators.

Avionics and Equipment

The Tu-134 is fully equipped for poor-weather day/night operation, including automatic flight assisted by an autopilot.

a) Navigation and piloting equipment: The Tu-134 *sans suffixe*, Tu-134Sh and early Tu-134As/AKs have a BSU-3P automatic flight control/landing system comprising an AP-6EM-3P autopilot, a Put'-4MPA-1K (Way) navigation system and an AT-2 automatic control trimming system (*avtomaht trimmeerovaniya*). The ALS automatically stabilises the aircraft around the CG at altitudes from 200m (650ft) up, maintains a preset heading in conjunction with the NAS-1A6K autonomous navigation system and permits automatic ICAO Cat I blind landing (decision altitude 60m/200ft, horizontal visibility 800m/2,600ft). The NAS-1A6K comprises a DISS-013 Trassa-A (Route-A) Doppler speed/drift sensor system (*doplerovskiy izmeritel' skorosti i snosa*) and an ANU-1 navigation computer.

Aircraft built from July 1977 onwards have the ABSU-134 ALS permitting Cat II landings (30-400m/100-1,300ft). It comprises an AP-134 autopilot, an STU-134 flight director system (*sistema trayektornovo oopravleniya*), an autothrottle, a VU-1 go-around system and built-in test equipment.

The Tu-134 *sans suffixe* has a Koors-MP1 (Heading) compass system (or Koors-MP2 on export aircraft) replaced by the Koors-MP2 or KS-8 on the Tu-134A *et seq*. It enables automatic route following, using VHF omnidirectional range (VOR) beacons, and automatic landing approach in conjunction with the ALS, using instrument landing system (ILS) beacons. The on-board part of the ILS includes a KRP-F localiser receiver, a GRP-2 glideslope beacon receiver, an MRP-56P marker beacon receiver and a module for working with Western ILS beacons.

The navigation/piloting equipment further includes main and backup ARK-11 automatic direction finders (ARK-15 on export aircraft), each with a buried loop aerial and a dorsal strake aerial; SD-67 distance measuring equipment (*samolyotnyy dahl'nomer*) and an RSBN-2S Svod short-range radio navigation system (or RSBN-PKV on the Tu-134UBL) with two flush antennas built into the fin on each side. An RV-4 (RV-UM) or, on export aircraft, RV-5 radio altimeter with dipole aerials under the fuselage is fitted, working in the 0-750m (0-2,460ft) altitude range together with the Vektor ground proximity warning system.

The Tu-134 *sans suffixe* (except c/n 0350921), Tu-134K, Tu-134UBL, Tu-134SKh and most Tu-134As/AKs are equipped with an ROZ-1 Lotsiya panoramic weather/navigation radar featuring an LTs-1 or LTs-2-12 revolving antenna in a chin radome. Tu-134 c/n 0350921, many export Tu-134As/AKs (including those built or modified to Tu-134A-1 standard) and the Tu-134B have a Groza-M134 weather radar in a forward-mounted radome. The Tu-134Sh-1 and Tu-134Sh-2 navigator trainers are fitted with an R-1 Rubin-1Sh or Initsiativa-1Sh panoramic navigation/bomb-aiming radar respectively in a deeper chin radome. The radar set is located under the navigator's station floor or in the avionics bay between frames 2-4.

The flight instrumentation includes AGD-1S artificial horizons, an AUASP-15KR AOA/speed/G load limiter, KUS-730/1100K or KUS-1200 combined airspeed indicators, a VD-20 barometric altimeter, a VM-15 mechanical altimeter indicator, EUP-53K turn and bank indicators, an AChS clock, a UVID-3015VK-2 cabin altitude and pressure indicator, VAR-30M and VAR-75M vertical speed indicators (the latter is used during emergency descent only) and an MS-1 Mach meter. The pitots are located under the extreme nose on 'glass-nosed' aircraft or aft of the flightdeck on radar-nosed versions.

b) Communications equipment: For long-range air/ground communications (up to 3,000km/1,860 miles), early Tu-134s *sans suffixe* had two 1-RSB-70 or R-807 HF communications/command link radios with a wire aerial running from the forward fuselage to the fin top. Later aircraft have a Mikron HF radio with a forward-pointing probe aerial on the fin top fairing. Short-range air/air and air/ground communications are catered for by two Landysh (or, on export aircraft, Lotos) UHF radios with AShS aerials above and below the forward fuselage. The Tu-134Sh has an R-802 HF radio with a wire aerial and an R-836 radio with an AShS-UD blade aerial, while the Tu-134UBL has an R-832M Evkalipt radio.

Communications equipment further includes an SPU-7 intercom (*samolyotnoye peregovornoye oostroystvo*) and, on passenger aircraft, an SGU-15 or SGS-25 public address system (*samolyotnaya gromkogovoryashchaya sistema*) with an Arfa-MB tape recorder for playing back music. The Tu-134AK may be equipped with secure HF communications suites (Tatra, Karpaty, Surgut, Balkany and so on).

c) IFF system: SRO-2M Khrom IFF transponder on civil aircraft, with characteristic triple rod aerials ahead of the flightdeck glazing and under the rear fuselage. Most military examples have the SRO-1P Parol'-2D transponder with equally characteristic triangular aerials; four other IFF antennas looking like penny-sized white buttons are located on the sides of the nose (just aft of the navigator's station glazing) and the wingtips.

The aircraft also features SOM-64 (*samolyotnyy otvetchik mezhdunarodnyy* – lit. aircraft-mounted international responder), SO-70 and SO-72M ATC transponders. These transmit the aircraft's registration, speed and altitude for presentation on ATC radar displays and may operate in 'Mayday' mode.

d) Data recording equipment: MSRP-12-96 primary flight data recorder in the No 4 equipment bay (frame 60), K-3-63 backup FDR in the No 2 equipment bay (frame 38) and MS-61B cockpit voice recorder on a rack in the forward baggage compartment (frame 9). The primary FDR captures 12 parameters, including barometric altitude, indicated airspeed, roll rates, vertical and lateral G forces, control surface deflection and throttle settings, as well as gear/flap transition and so on. The backup FDR records only altitude, IAS and vertical G forces. Aircraft built from late 1978 onwards have an MSRP-64-2 or MSRP-64M-2 primary FDR and a Mars-BM CVR. All recorders have armoured shells to ensure survival in a crash.

e) Lighting equipment: Port (red) and starboard (green) BANO-57 navigation lights at the wingtips, KhS-57 white tail navigation light at the aft end of the fin top fairing. Retractable PRF-4M landing/taxi lights on the sides of the nose (frames 5-6) and the inboard faces of the main gear fairings (frames 5-6). Red SPM-1 rotating anti-collision beacons (*samolyotnyy probleskovyy mayak* – 'aircraft-mounted flashing beacon') in teardrop-shaped Perspex fairings on the centre fuselage (lower, frame 19; upper, frame 20) on early Tu-134s *sans suffixe*, replaced from c/n 7350205 onwards by red SMI-2KM strobe lights (*samolyotnyy mayak impool'snyy*, same meaning) flashing sequentially at one-second intervals.

The flightdeck and baggage compartments feature PS-45 overhead lights. The cabin has SV overhead luminescent lights over the aisle, SBK auxiliary lights and individual reading lights over the seats, plus illuminated 'No smoking/Fasten seat belts' signs and, on late-production aircraft, exit signs.

Accommodation

The flightdeck is configured for a crew of four, with the navigator in the extreme nose, facing left, and the flight engineer on a fold-down chair behind the pilots. The Tu-134 *sans suffixe*/Tu-134K, Tu-134AK and Tu-134B 'Salon' have a crew of five with a radio operator sitting on a jump seat further aft. The cabin crew comprises two or three flight attendants.

The Tu-134 can be configured with first class (F), business class (C), tourist class (CY) and economy class (Y) seating. Possible layouts for Tu-134 the *sans suffixe* are:

- a 64-seat layout (F16+Y20+Y28) featuring 93cm (36⅝in) pitch in the forward cabin and 75cm (29½in) pitch in other two;
- a 68-seat tourist-class layout with 78cm (30¾in) seat pitch;
- a 72-seat all-economy layout with 44+28 seats at 75cm pitch.

The Tu-134K has two options:
- 29 seats (F5+F4+CY20) with 90cm (35½in) pitch in the rear cabin;
- 37 seats (F7+F6+CY24).

The Tu-134A has the following options:
- a 60-seater (F8+Y32+Y20) for the 235th IAD with 90cm and 75cm pitch respectively;
- a 60-seater (F4+ Y56);
- a 68-seater (F8+Y32+Y28) for TsUMVS with 90cm and 75cm pitch respectively;
- a 68-seater (F12+Y28+Y28) for TsUMVS with 93cm and 75cm pitch respectively;
- a 68-seater (C12+ Y56);
- a 68-seater (C16+ Y52) with 78cm and 75cm pitch respectively;
- a 72-seat tourist-class layout (44+28) for the 235th IAD;
- a 76-seat tourist-class layout (48+28);
- an 80-seat tourist-class layout;
- an 86-seat tourist-class layout (Tu-134A-1);
- a 96-seat all-economy layout (4+80+12 – see Chapter 3).

The Tu-134AK came in 11 standard layouts for 26, 27, 29, 34, 36, 37, 39, 41, 44, 45 or 47 passengers (see Chapter 3). The Tu-134B is usually an 80-seat 'tram'.

As standard the galley features a water boiler, an electric food heater, a sink with hot and cold water and storage lockers for tableware, food and drinks; aircraft with high-density seating lack the boiler and heater.

The lightweight seats have folding backs and armrests to facilitate getting in/out; the seat backs recline at the push of a button and incorporate meal trays. The seats feature seat belts and are stressed for longitudinal loads of 9G. A peculiarity of the Tu-134 is that the first row of seats usually faced aft, with tables between it and the second row.

As standard the cabin walls are upholstered in easily washable vinyl and the floor is covered with a carpet having a foam rubber base. The overhead luggage racks incorporate passenger service units.

Each toilet features a metal toilet bowl, a water heater tank and a wash basin with a pedal-driven pump and mixing tap. On passenger versions the two toilets located between frames 45-48 have a common 150-litre (33-Imp gal) septic tank in the No 3 equipment bay; VIP aircraft with a forward toilet have a second septic tank in the No 1 equipment bay. There is a circulation-type flushing system with electric pumps and filters which is charged with deodorant fluid. Water for the wash basins is stored in a 55-litre (12.1-Imp gal) tank.

Passenger evacuation in an emergency takes place via the overwing emergency exits (which are provided with escape ropes) and the entry and service doors. On the Tu-134A the entry door features a TN-3 inflatable slide (*trahp nadoovnoy*), whereas the service door has a canvas slide which must be stretched taut by assistants on the ground; on the Tu-134B this is replaced by a second inflatable slide. The flightdeck also features escape ropes. Additionally, a piece of fuselage skin between frames 17-20 on each side can be chopped out in an emergency if the regular exits are unusable and is clearly marked in colour. For overwater flights the aircraft is equipped with 12-man SP-12 inflatable rafts or 26-man rafts manufactured by the German company RFD, as well as life vests for all occupants.

The rear HF probe aerial associated with the HF communications suite of Tu-134 *Balkany* '05 Red' (c/n (23)63976). Note the open APU air intake (a second intake is located symmetrically to starboard). Author

Tu-134 Family Specifications

	Tu-134	Tu-134A	Tu-134A-3	Tu-134B-3	Tu-134Sh	Tu-134UBL
Powerplant	2 x D-30	2 x D-30-II	2 x D-30-III	2 x D-30-III	2 x D-30-II	2 x D-30-II
Take-off rating, kgp (lbst)	2 x 6,800 (2 x 14,990)	2 x 6,800 (2 x 14,990)	2 x 6,930 (2 x 15,280)	2 x 6,930 (2 x 15,280)	2 x 6,800 (2 x 14,990)	2 x 6,800 (2 x 14,990)
Length overall	34.95m (114' 8") *	37.1m (121' 8⅝") *	37.1m (121' 8⅝") *	37.322m (122' 5⅜")	37.1m (121' 8⅝")	41.918m (137' 6¼")
Wing span	29.01m (95' 2⅛")	29.01m (95' 2⅛")	29.01m (95' 2⅛")	29.01m (95' 2⅛")	29.01m (95' 2⅛")	29.01m (95' 2⅛")
Stabiliser span	11.8m (38' 8½") †	11.8m (38' 8½") †	11.8m (38' 8½") †	11.8m (38' 8½") †	11.8m (38' 8½") †	11.8m (38' 8½") †
Height on ground	9.02m (29' 7⅛")	9.02m (29' 7⅛")	9.02m (29' 7⅛")	9.02m (29' 7⅛")	9.02m (29' 7⅛")	9.144m (30' 0")
Landing gear wheelbase (static)	13.93m (45' 8⅝")	16.03m (52' 7⅛")	16.03m (52' 7⅛")	16.03m (52' 7⅛")	16.03m (52' 7⅛")	16.03m (52' 7⅛")
Landing gear track	9.45m (31' 0")	9.45m (31' 0")	9.45m (31' 0")	9.45m (31' 0")	9.45m (31' 0")	9.45m (31' 0")
Turning radius (measured by wingtip)	35.0m (114' 10")	26.3m (86' 3⅜")	26.3m (86' 3⅜")	26.3m (86' 3⅜")	26.3m (86' 3⅜")	26.3m (86' 3⅜")
Wing area, m² (ft²)	127.3 (1,168.81)	127.3 (1,168.81)	127.3 (1,168.81)	127.3 (1,168.81)	127.3 (1,168.81)	127.3 (1,168.81)
Flap area, m² (ft²): inboard	10.34 (111.18)	10.34 (111.18)	10.34 (111.18)	10.34 (111.18)	10.34 (111.18)	10.34 (111.18)
outboard	12.16 (130.75)	12.16 (130.75)	12.16 (130.75)	12.16 (130.75)	12.16 (130.75)	12.16 (130.75)
Speedbrake area, m² (ft²)	5.32 (57.2)	5.32 (57.2) §	none	none	5.32 (57.2) §	none
Spoiler area, m² (ft²)	4.48 (48.17)	4.48 (48.17)	4.48 (48.17)	4.48 (48.17)	4.48 (48.17)	4.48 (48.17)
Aileron area, m² (ft²)	9.68 (104.08)	9.68 (104.08)	9.68 (104.08)	9.68 (104.08)	9.68 (104.08)	9.68 (104.08)
Vertical tail area, incl fin fillet, m² (ft²)	21.25 (228.49)	21.25 (228.49)	21.25 (228.49)	21.25 (228.49)	21.25 (228.49)	21.25 (228.49)
Rudder area, m² (ft²)	5.76 (61.93)	5.76 (61.93)	5.76 (61.93)	5.76 (61.93)	5.76 (61.93)	5.76 (61.93)
Horizontal tail area, m² (ft²)	30.68 (329.89) †	30.68 (329.89) †	30.68 (329.89) †	30.68 (329.89) †	30.68 (329.89) †	30.68 (329.89) †
Elevator area, m² (ft²)	6.417 (69.0) †	6.417 (69.0) †	6.417 (69.0) †	6.417 (69.0) †	6.417 (69.0) †	6.417 (69.0) †
Baggage space, m³ (ft³): forward	4.5 (158.9)	6.0 (211.8) ‡	6.0 (211.8) ‡	2.6 (91.8)		none
aft	8.5 (300.1)	8.5 (300.1)	8.5 (300.1)	8.5 (300.1)	8.5 (300.1)	8.5 (300.1)
Operating empty weight, kg (lb)	27,500 (60,630)	29,000 (63,930)	29,500 (65,035)	29,600 (65,255)	n/a	28,840 (63,580)
MTOW, kg (lb)	44,000 (97,000)	47,600 (104,940)	49,000 (108,020)	49,000 (108,020)	46,500 (102,510)	44,250 (97,550)
Max landing weight, kg (lb): normal	37,000 (81,570)	43,000 (94,800)	43,000 (94,800)	n/a	n/a	43,000 (94,800)
emergency	44,000 (97,000)	47,000 (103,615)	n/a			n/a
Max payload, kg (lb)	7,700 (16,975)	8,200 (18,080)	9,000 (19,840)	9,000 (19,840)	3,100 (6,830)	8,200 (18,080)
Cruising speed, km/h (mph):						
at 8,600m (28,215ft)	820-850 (510-528)	885 (550)	882 (547)	895 (556)	800/860 (500/534) ¶	884 (549)
at 10,000m (32,810ft)	900 (560)	900 (560)	907 (563)	915 (568)	n/a	904 (561)
Unstick speed, km/h (mph)	248 (154)	290/275 (180/170.8) ‖	n/a	n/a	n/a	274 (170.1)
Landing speed, km/h (mph)	220 (136)	235-250 (146-155)	235-250 (146-155)	235-250 (146-155)	235-250 (146-155)	248 (154)
Stalling speed, km/h (kts) with 0° flaps	n/a	250 (155)	250 (155)	250 (155)	250 (155)	n/a
with 10° flaps	n/a	236 (146)	236 (146)	236 (146)	236 (146)	n/a
with 20° flaps	n/a	223 (138)	223 (138)	223 (138)	223 (138)	n/a
with 38° flaps	n/a	203 (126)	203 (126)	203 (126)	203 (126)	n/a
Take-off run, m (ft) at max take-off wt	1,000 (3,280)	1,400 (4,590)	n/a	n/a	1,380 4,530)	1,200 (3,940)
Take-off distance to 10.7m (35ft), m (ft)	1,880 (6,170)	2,300/2,150 (7,545/7,050) ‖	n/a	n/a	n/a	2,150 (7,050)
Landing run, m (ft) at max landing wt	865 (2,840)	800 (2,620)	n/a	n/a	760 (2,490)	1,100 (3,610)
Landing distance from 15m (50ft), m (ft)	1,200 (3,940)	1,200-1,350 (3,940-4,430)	n/a	n/a	n/a	1,980 (6,500)
Range, km (miles) with maximum fuel	3,500 (2,170)	3,000 (1,860)	3,200 (1,990)	3,200 (1,990)	3,900 (2,420)	3,400 (2,110)
with maximum payload	2,000 (1,240)	1,740 (1,080)	2,000 (1,240)	2,000 (1,240)	3,400 2,110)	n/a
Service ceiling, m (ft)	12,000 (39,370)	11,900 (39,040)	11,900 (39,040)	11,900 (39,040)	11,000 (36,090)	11,800 (38,710)

* 35.172m (115ft 4¾in) or 37.322m (122ft 5⅜in) respectively with Groza-M134 radar; † 9.2m (30ft 2¼in), 22.2m² (238.7ft²) and 4.492m² (48.3ft²) on first four aircraft; ‡ 2.6m³ (91.8ft³) on the Tu-134AK; § Aircraft built up to and including March 1978 only; ¶ With/without practice bombs; ‖ 10° and 20° flaps respectively

The flightdeck of Tu-134AK RA-65939 (c/n 1351409) manufactured on 28th December 1971. The turquoise colour of the instrument panels is typical of Soviet aircraft and is intended to reduce pilot fatigue. Note the blind flying training curtains (a standard fit on Soviet airliners) and the equally typical rubber-bladed cooling fans. Author

The captain's instrument panel of Tu-134AK RA-65939. The instruments are strictly electro-mechanical but the layout is quite rational, with the primary flight instruments in T fashion. Note the aircraft type marked on the hub of the control wheel which features a red autopilot override button and a guarded elevator trim switch; the blue insulating tape is a 'local modification', of course. The two red handles are for emergency engine shutdown; the aircraft was originally delivered to Czechoslovakia as OK-BYQ, and the 'Pull' inscription on the said handles is in Czech (Zatahnout k sobe). Author

The first officer's instrument panel of Tu-134AK RA-65939. Author

The instrument panels of the Tu-134 changed considerably over the years. Here, for comparison, is the flightdeck of Tu-134AK RA-65680 (c/n (63)49020, f/n 3706) manufactured on 2nd December 1976, and the difference in instrumentation is pretty obvious. The dark green colour of the instrument panels is decidedly non-standard. Interestingly, the registration plates still read '680' instead of '65680', dating back to the time when the aircraft was in full military markings and coded '680 Black'. Note the curtain covering the entrance to the navigator's station – a feature which once proved vital in foiling a hijack attempt. Author

The central instrument panel of Tu-134AK RA-65939 featuring engine instruments and navigation system controls. The autopilot is mounted above it. Author

The captain's side console of Tu-134AK RA-65939 featuring throttles, thrust reverse levers (captain's side only on the Tu-134A/AK!) and elevator trim wheel. The lever just aft of the throttles is the gust lock control lever; the red cock is for the windscreen wiper. Author

The first officer's side console. Note the totally different throttles. Author

The overhead circuit breaker panel of Tu-134AK RA-65939 featuring controls for the fuel system, de-icing system, fire suppression system, lighting etc. The flap selector handle is in the centre of the forward section, right above the autopilot; the landing gear selector handle is to the right of it, above the first officer's head. Author

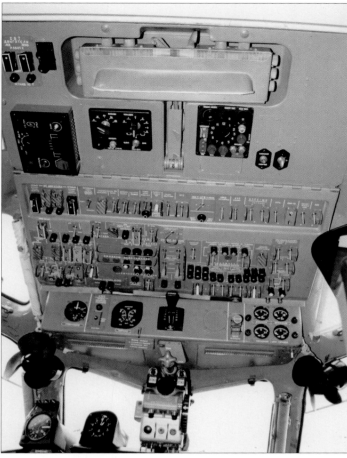

The navigator's station of Tu-134AK RA-65939. The navigator faces left, with navigation instruments and a map table in front of him; a circuit breaker/fuse panel occupies the other wall. Note the radar display with rubber sunblind on the starboard side of the glazing frame; the placard suspended above it advises maintenance personnel that the batteries have been removed. Author

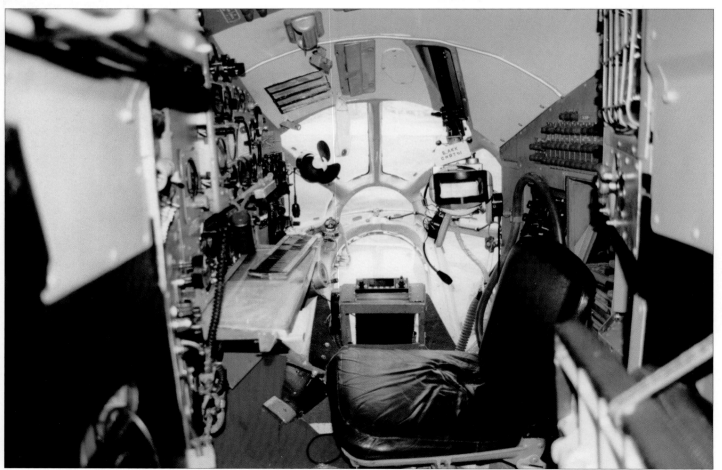

Far left: The flight engineer's station of Tu-134AK RA-65939. The right half of the main instrument panel is for the engines while the left half is for the APU. Author

Left: On some aircraft, such as Tu-134AK RA-65939, the flight engineer sits on a full-size tip-up seat with a back. The flightdeck door opens outwards and incorporates a peephole. Note the jump seat for the flight attendant beside the service door. Author

Below left: Here, for comparison, is part of the flight engineer's station of radar-nosed Tu-134A RA-65667 (c/n 1351207) manufactured on 14th May 1971; the flight engineer has to make do with a jump seat. Author

Below right: The flight engineer's station of Tu-134B-3 'Salon' RA-65694. Author

Opposite, top left: The flightdeck of radar-nosed export Tu-134As/AKs (illustrated by Tu-134A-3 RA-65667) lacks the passage to the navigator's station; instead, it features an instrument panel incorporating the radar display. On this aircraft the registration plate is located on top of the central instrument panel to the left of the autopilot and almost invisible in this view. Author

Opposite, top right: The Tu-134B (illustrated by Tu-134B-3 'Salon' RA-65694) features a central control pedestal mounting the throttles, elevator trim wheels, navigation system controls and flight spoiler controls (if any). Author

Opposite, centre left and right: The Tu-134B's two radar displays are mounted symmetrically on the side consoles. Author

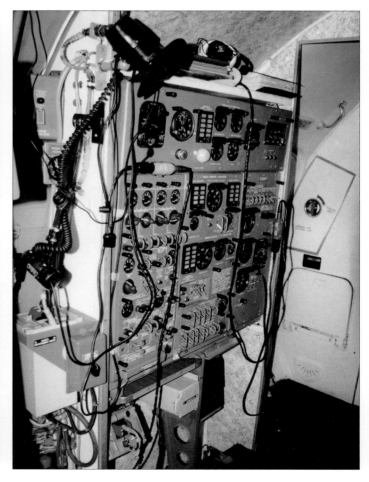

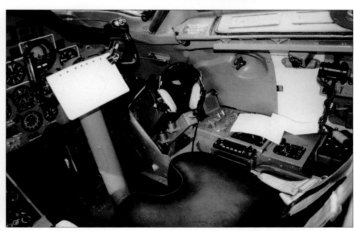

The galley of a Batch 1 Tu-134 *sans suffixe* featuring a square-shaped forward baggage door (note hinges); part of the 'kitchen table' tips up together with this door. There is ample storage space, together with electric food and water heaters on the rear wall; the control panel for these is located on the side wall above the window. Tupolev JSC

On the Tu-134AK (illustrated by RA-65680) the galley is configured differently from the Tu-134A because the forward toilet eats up part of the space in the forward vestibule. This is the food heater on the starboard side, with the cabin ventilation and temperature controls above it. Author

The water heaters on the other side, just ahead of the forward entry door, with the stewardess call/cabin lighting/galley equipment control panel above them. Author

Top left: **The cabin of a very early-production Tu-134 *sans suffixe* (note the folding overhead baggage racks).** Tupolev JSC

Top right: **A later example featuring seats with built-in meal tables; the seat cushions are tipped up in this view. The cabin partition is installed at fuselage frame 34.** Tupolev JSC

Left: **The forward cabin of an early-production Tu-134 *sans suffixe*, with decorative patterns on the wall trim and curtains. This view illustrates the design of the seat modules; the first two rows of seats face each other, with tables in between.** Tupolev JSC

Bottom left: **On later aircraft the patterned wall trim gave way to a simple, sterile-looking white finish. This is Moldavian Airlines Tu-134AK ER-TCF, a former Tu-134 *Balkany* refitted as a 68-seater, with minimum lighting on. The forward cabin has business class seating for 12 and the seats are upholstered in real leather!** Author

Bottom right: **This is how the non-functional rear entry door looks from inside on a Tu-134AK converted to airline configuration (again ER-TCF); the window curtain rails pass right across the door! The hinges are just visible in this view.** Author

The No 1 VIP cabin of 44-seat Tu-134AK RA-65680, looking aft, with the No 2 VIP cabin visible beyond. There are two comfortable armchairs with a table in between to port and a sofa for three to starboard; in the No 2 VIP cabin, it is vice versa. The bulkhead with a sold door at the far end separates the VIP cabins from the two tourist-class rear cabins to keep the retinue from eavesdropping on the bosses. The horrid green cloth in the aisle is meant to protect the carpet from the hordes of trampling visitors (the picture was taken during the 1999 open doors day at Chkalovskaya AB). Author

The rearmost cabin of Tu-134AK RA-65680. The bulge on the port side of the rear bulkhead is a recess for the jump seat in the rear entry vestibule. Author

The cabin of Azerbaijan Airlines Tu-134B-3 4K-65714 (note airline logo on the seat backs) in 80-seat configuration with no partition at frame 34. Author

Production list

Tu-134 production is presented in construction number/fuselage number order, with all identities worn consecutively by each aircraft. 'Deceased' (that is, crashed or destroyed) examples are marked with † (RIP crosses) followed by the date of the accident. Registrations followed by * indicate this is a quasi-civil aircraft, while § indicates the aircraft was military at first but was subsequently sold to a civil operator. Registrations given in square brackets were allocated but not taken up; while those given in parentheses are ATC callsigns (not worn visibly) of aircraft in overt military markings – for example, East German AF '181 Black' (DM-VBC).

Passenger and Special Versions (except trainers) – System 1

Construction number	Version	Registration/ tactical code/serial	Manufacture date'
00-00	Tu-134	CCCP-45075	
4350001	Tu-134	CCCP-45076 † *14-1-1966*	
no c/n	Tu-134	static test airframe	
no c/n	Tu-134	fatigue test airframe	
5350002	Tu-134	CCCP-65600	
6350003	Tu-134	CCCP-65601	
6350004	Tu-134	CCCP-65602	
6350005	Tu-134	CCCP-65603	
6350101	Tu-134	CCCP-65604 No 1	
6350102	Tu-134	CCCP-65605 No 1	
6350103	Tu-134	CCCP-65606 No 1	
6350104	Tu-134	CCCP-65607 No 1 † *17-7-1972*	
6350105	Tu-134	CCCP-65608 No 1	
6350201	Tu-134	CCCP-65609 No 1	30-11-1967
6350202	Tu-134	CCCP-65610 No 1	
6350203	Tu-134TS?	Soviet AF '01 Red'?	
7350204	Tu-134	CCCP-65611 No 1	
7350205	Tu-134	CCCP-65612 No 1	
7350301	Tu-134K	CCCP-65618 No 1	?-12-1967
7350302	Tu-134K	CCCP-65614 No 1; EW-65614?	?-12-1967
7350303	Tu-134K	CCCP-65615 No 1	?-12-1967
7350304	Tu-134K	CCCP-65616 No 1, Soviet AF '77 Blue', CCCP-65616 No 1	?-12-1967
7350305	Tu-134	CCCP-65617 No 1	
8350401	Tu-134	CCCP-65619 No 1	
8350402	Tu-134	CCCP-65620 No 1	
8350403	Tu-134	CCCP-65613 No 1	
8350404	Tu-134	CCCP-65621 No 1	
8350405	Tu-134	LZ-TUA	
8350501	Tu-134	LZ-TUB † *16-3-1978*	
8350502	Tu-134	DM-SCA † *17-10-1972*	
8350503	Tu-134	DM-SCB	
8350504	Tu-134	CCCP-65622 No 1	
8350505	Tu-134	CCCP-65623 No 1	
8350601	Tu-134A	CCCP-65624, 65624	?-4-1969
8350602	Tu-134	SP-LGA, CCCP-65933	
8350603	Tu-134	SP-LGB † *23-1-1980*	
8350604	Tu-134	HA-LBA † *19-11-1969*	
8350605	Tu-134	HA-LBB, HA-LBC † *21-9-1977*	
8350701	Tu-134	YU-AHH, CCCP-65672	6-1-1969
9350702	Tu-134	DM-SCD † *1-9-1975*	
9350703	Tu-134	CCCP-65625	
9350704	Tu-134A	CCCP-65626, RA-65626	
9350705	Tu-134	YU-AHI, CCCP-65673	26-3-1969
9350801	Tu-134	HA-LBD † *16-9-1971*	
9350802	Tu-134	HA-LBE	21-3-1969?
9350803	Tu-134	CCCP-65627	
9350804	Tu-134	SP-LGC, CCCP-65923	
9350805	Tu-134	SP-LGD, CCCP-65922	
9350806	Tu-134	SP-LGE, CCCP-65924	27-5-1969
9350807	Tu-134	LZ-TUC	
9350808	Tu-134	LZ-TUD	
9350809	Tu-134	CCCP-65628	
9350810	Tu-134	CCCP-65629	
9350901	Tu-134	CCCP-65630	
9350902	Tu-134	CCCP-65631	
9350903	Tu-134	CCCP-65632	
9350904	Tu-134K	DM-SCE§, DDR-SCE	
9350905	Tu-134K	DM-SCF§, DDR-SCF	

Construction number	Version	Registration/ tactical code/serial	Manufacture date'
9350906	Tu-134	DM-SCH, DDR-SCH, [Luftwaffe 11+13]	
9350907	Tu-134	CCCP-65633	
9350908	Tu-134	CCCP-65634	
9350909	Tu-134	CCCP-65635	
9350910	Tu-134	CCCP-65636	
9350911	Tu-134	CCCP-65637	
9350912	Tu-134K	DM-SCG§, DDR-SCG	
9350913	Tu-134K	East German AF '177 Black' (DM-VBB), DM-SCZ, DDR-SCZ	
9350914	Tu-134	LZ-TUE	
9350915	Tu-134	CCCP-65638	
9350916	Tu-134K	YI-AED*, CCCP-65669§, RA-65669	
9350917	Tu-134	CCCP-65639	
9350918	Tu-134	LZ-TUF	
0350919	Tu-134	CCCP-65640	6-4-1970
0350920	Tu-134	CCCP-65641	
0350921	Tu-134/r.n.	YU-AHS, CCCP-65963	24-4-1970
0350922	Tu-134K	LZ-TUO*?, Bulgarian AF '050 Red' No 1, LZ-TUO	
0350923	Tu-134	HA-LBF	30-4-1970?
0350924	Tu-134K	HA-LBG, HA-924, HA-LBG	19-5-1970?
0350925	Tu-134K	HA-LBH, HA-925, HA-LBH	27-5-1970?
0350926	Tu-134	CCCP-65642	
0350927	Tu-134	CCCP-65643	
0350928	Tu-134	CCCP-65644	
0351001	Tu-134A	CCCP-65646	?-6-1970
0351002	Tu-134A	CCCP-65647, RA-65647	
0351003	Tu-134A	CCCP-65648	
0351004	Tu-134A	CCCP-65649 † *31-5-1979*	18-8-1970
0351005	Tu-134A	CCCP-65645	
0351006	Tu-134A	CCCP-65650, EK-65650	31-10-1970
0351007	Tu-134A	CCCP-65651, RA-65651	31-10-1970
0351008	Tu-134A	CCCP-65652	
0351009	Tu-134A	CCCP-65653, RA-65653	31-10-1970
0351010	Tu-134A	CCCP-65654	
0351101	Tu-134A	CCCP-65655	
0351102	Tu-134A	CCCP-65656	
0351103	Tu-134A	CCCP-65657 † *17-6-1983*	22-10-1970
0351104	Tu-134A	CCCP-65658	
0351105	Tu-134A	CCCP-65659	
0351106	Tu-134A	CCCP-65660	
0351107	Tu-134A	CCCP-65661, RA-65661	28-10-1970
0351108	Tu-134A	CCCP-65662	5-2-1971
0351109	Tu-134A	CCCP-65663	
0351110	Tu-134AK	CCCP-65670* † *28-7-1989*	31-3-1971
1351201	Tu-134AK	CCCP-65665	
1351202	Tu-134AK	CCCP-65666, RA-65666	*11-6-1971*
1351203	Tu-134A/r.n., Tu-134A-1	YU-AHX, CCCP-93930, OB-1489	
1351204	Tu-134A/r.n., Tu-134A-1	YU-AHY, TC-ALV, YU-AHY, CCCP-93926, 93926, RA-93926	
1351205	Tu-134A/r.n.	YU-AHZ † *23-5-1971*	
1351206	Tu-134A/r.n., Tu-134A-1	YU-AJA, TC-ALU, YU-AJA, CCCP-93929, RA-93929	17-4-1971
1351207	Tu-134A/r.n.	CCCP-65667, RA-65667	14-5-1971
1351208	Tu-134AK?	CCCP-65671, RA-65671	13-5-1971
1351209	Tu-134A 'Salon'	LZ-TUK§	
1351210	Tu-134A	CCCP-65664, EW-65664	
1351301	Tu-134A	HA-LBI	8-6-1971?
1351302	Tu-134A	HA-LBK	17-6-1971?
1351303	Tu-134AK	LZ-TUP*, Bulgarian AF '050 Red' No 2, LZ-TUP*, LZ D 050*, LZ-TUP	
1351304	Tu-134AK	DM-SCK*, East German AF '183 Black'?, DM-SCK§, DDR-SCK, [D-AOBB]	22-6-1971?
1351305	Tu-134AK	DM-SCL*, East German AF '182 Black' (DM-VBD), DM-SCL§, DDR-SCL	
1351306	Tu-134AK?	CCCP-65668? † *30-6-1973*	
1351307	Tu-134A	CCCP-65727	31-7-1971

Construction number	Version	Registration/ tactical code/serial	Manufacture date
1351308	Tu-134A	CCCP-65728	
1351309	Tu-134A	CCCP-65729	23-8-1971
1351310	Tu-134A	CCCP-65730, EY-65730, 4L-65730	**31-8-1971**
1351401	Tu-134A	CCCP-65731, EK-65731	14-9-1971
1351402	Tu-134A	CCCP-65732	
1351403	Tu-134AK	CCCP-65733	
1351404	Tu-134AK?	CCCP-65734	
1351405	Tu-134AK	CCCP-65735 † *11-8-1979*	5-11-1971
1351406	Tu-134A/r.n.	OK-AFA	
1351407	Tu-134AK	Czechoslovak AF '1407 Black', OK-AFD*, Czechoslovak AF '1407 Black', Czechoslovak/ Czech AF '1407 White', EW-65861 No 2, RA-65861	?-12-1971
1351408	Tu-134AK	OK-BYR, LZ-TUV*	
1351409	Tu-134AK	OK-BYQ, LZ-TUU*, RA-65939	28-12-1971
1351410	Tu-134A/r.n.	OK-AFB † *11-10-1988*	
1351501	Tu-134A	CCCP-65736, ER-65736	12-2-1972
1351502	Tu-134AK	CCCP-65676§, EW-65676	25-4-1972
1351503	Tu-134A	OK-BYS, LZ-TUZ*	
2351504	Tu-134A/r.n.	OK-CFC	
2351505	Tu-134A/r.n.	OK-CFD † *2-1-1977*	
2351506	Tu-134A	CCCP-65737	
2351507	Tu-134A	CCCP-65738, RA-65738	
2351508	Tu-134A/r.n., Tu-134A-1	YU-AJD, CCCP-93927, RA-93927	?-3-1972
2351509	Tu-134A	CCCP-65739, RA-65739	
2351510	Tu-134A, Tu-134A-1510	CCCP-65…*, CCCP-65740§, RA-65740	
2351601	Tu-134A	CCCP-65741, ER-65741	28-4-1972
2351602	Tu-134A/r.n.	OK-CFE	
2351603	Tu-134A/r.n.	OK-CFF	
2351604	Tu-134A	CCCP-65742	
2351605	Tu-134A	CCCP-65743	
2351606	Tu-134A	CCCP-65744?	
2351607	Tu-134A	CCCP-65745	
2351608	Tu-134AK	CCCP-65746, UR-65746	31-7-1972
2351609	Tu-134A	CCCP-65747	
2351610	Tu-134AK	CCCP-65748	
2351701	Tu-134AK	CCCP-65749	
2351702	Tu-134AK	CCCP-65950, RA-65950	21-11-1972
2351703	Tu-134A	CCCP-65951 † *13-1-1990*	29-9-1972
2351704	Tu-134AK?	CCCP-65952*?, Soviet AF '10 Blue'?, CCCP-65952§?	
2351705	Tu-134AK	CCCP-65675§ † *27-2-1988*	**28-12-1972**
2351706	Tu-134A	CCCP-65953	
2351707	Tu-134AK	CCCP-65954, RA-65954	*1-12-1972*
2351708	Tu-134A	CCCP-65955, RA-65955	*29-12-1972*
2351709	Tu-134AK	CCCP-65956, RA-65956	17-1-1973
2351710	Tu-134A/r.n.	OK-CFG	
2351801	Tu-134A/r.n.	OK-CFH	
2351802	Tu-134AK	CCCP-65957, EW-65957	6-4-1973
2351803	Tu-134AK	CCCP-65965*, RA-65965*	
3351804	Tu-134A	CCCP-65958, RA-65958	22-2-1973
3351805	Tu-134A	CCCP-65959, [4L-65959]	*2-3-1973*
3351806	Tu-134A	CCCP-65960, RA-65960	26-3-1973
3351807	Tu-134AK	CCCP-65961, RA-65961	15-5-1973
3351808	Tu-134A	SP-LHA, Polish AF '104 White'?, SP-LHA, Polish AF '104 White'?, SP-LHA	
3351809	Tu-134A	SP-LHB, Polish AF '103 White', SP-LHB	
3351810	Tu-134A	SP-LHC	
3351901	Tu-134AK	CCCP-65962*, Soviet AF '16 Blue'?, RA-65962§	
3351902	Tu-134A	CCCP-65966, RA-65966	*18-8-1973*
3351903	Tu-134A/r.n.	DM-SCI, DDR-SCI, D-AOBA, CCCP-65611 No 2, RA-65611	7-5-1973
3351904	Tu-134A/r.n.	DM-SCM † *22-11-1977*	
3351905	Tu-134A	CCCP-65967, RA-65967	31-5-1973
3351906	Tu-134AK/r.n.	LZ-TUM§, RA-65940	
3351907	Tu-134A	CCCP-65968	
3351908	Tu-134A/r.n.	OK-DFI	
3351909	Tu-134A	CCCP-65969, RA-65969	13-7-1973
3351910	Tu-134AK	CCCP-65970, RA-65970	*6-10-1973*
3352001	Tu-134A	CCCP-65971, RA-65971, ER-65971	31-7-1973
3352002	Tu-134A	CCCP-65972, RA-65972	17-8-1973
3352003	Tu-134A	CCCP-65973, LY-ABA, RA-65973	30-8-1973
3352004	Tu-134A	CCCP-65974, EW-65974	*30-8-1973*
3352005	Tu-134AK/r.n.	Polish AF '101 Red' No 1, SP-LHF	
3352006	Tu-134A	CCCP-65975, EK-65975	27-9-1973
3352007	Tu-134A	CCCP-65976, RA-65976	29-9-1973
3352008	Tu-134AK/r.n.	Polish AF '102 Red' No 1, SP-LHG	
3352009	Tu-134A	CCCP-65800, RA-65800	*22-2-1974*
3352010	Tu-134AK	CCCP-65801, RA-65801	*20-11-1973*
3352101	Tu-134AK	CCCP-65802, RA-65802	16-11-1973
3352102	Tu-134AK/r.n.	DM-SCN§, DDR-SCN, D-AOBC, CCCP-65612 No 2, RA 65612	20-11-1973
3352103	Tu-134A	CCCP-65803, EW-65803	12-11-1973
3352104	Tu-134A	CCCP-65804	
3352105	Tu-134A	CCCP-65805, RA-65805	20-12-1973
3352106	Tu-134AK/r.n.	DM-SCO§, DDR-SCO, D-AOBD, CCCP-65613 No 2, 65613, RA 65613, RA-65613	*18-12-1973*
3352107	Tu-134A	CCCP-65806	

Construction number	Version	Registration/ tactical code/serial	Manufacture date
3352108	Tu-134A	CCCP-65807 † *18-11-1983*	17-12-1973
3352109	Tu-134A	CCCP-65808, 4L-65808	*23-12-1973*
3352110	Tu-134A	CCCP-65809, 65809, 4L-65809 † *23-9-1993?*	21-1-1974
3352201	Tu-134A	CCCP-65810 † *29-8-1992*	*10-1-1974*
3352202	Tu-134A	CCCP-65811, RA-65811	6-3-1974
3352203	Tu-134A	CCCP-65812	
3352204	Tu-134A	CCCP-65813, RA-65813	26-3-1974
4352205	Tu-134AK/r.n.	DM-SCP§, DDR-SCP, D-AOBE, CCCP-65615 No 2, RA-65615	*28-2-1974*
4352206	Tu-134AK/r.n.	DM-SCR*, East German AF '176 Black', DM-SCR, DDR-SCR, D-AOBF, CCCP-65616 No 2, RA 65616, RA-65616	*11-3-1974*
4352207	Tu-134AK/r.n.	DM-SCS§, DDR-SCS, D-AOBG, CCCP-65614 No 2, RA-65614	*11-3-1974*
4352208	Tu-134A	CCCP-65814, EY-65814	15-3-1974
4352209	Tu-134A	CCCP-65815, RA-65815	23-3-1974
4352210	Tu-134A	CCCP-65816 † *11-8-1979*	24-3-1974
4352301	Tu-134A	CCCP-65817, 4L-65817	
4352302	Tu-134A	CCCP-65818 (c/n also reported as (43)05043)	
4352303	Tu-134A/r.n.	LZ-TUL	
4352304	Tu-134A	CCCP-65819, RA-65819	23-4-1974
4352305	not used, see c/n (43)08056		
4352306	not used, see c/n (43)08060		
4352307	Tu-134A/r.n.	LZ-TUN	
4352308	Tu-134A/r.n.	LZ-TUR † *10-1-1984*	
4352309	not used, see c/n 4308068		
4352310	not used, see c/n (43)09070		

System 2

Construction number	Fuselage number	Version	Registration / tactical code/serial	Manufacture date
(43)08056	2305	Tu-134A	CCCP-65820, EY-65820	26-4-1974
08060	2306	Tu-134AK	CCCP-65821*, Soviet AF '02 Blue'?, CCCP-65821§, EW-65821	14-6-1974
4308068	2309	Tu-134A/r.n.	DM-SCT, DDR-SCT, D-AOBH, CCCP-65617 No 2, RA 65617 † *24-6-1995*	*17-5-1974*
09070	2310	Tu-134A/r.n.	DM-SCU, DDR-SCU, D-AOBI, CCCP-65605 No 2, EW-65605, RA-65605	*11-5-1974*
09071	2401	Tu-134A	CCCP-65822, EK-65822	31-5-1974
09073	2402	Tu-134A	CCCP-65823, RA-65823	*21-6-1974*
09074	2403	Tu-134A	CCCP-65824, RA-65824, HA-LBS, RA-65824	7-6-1974
09078	2404	Tu-134A	CCCP-65825, RA-65825	12-6-1974
12083	2405	Tu-134A	CCCP-65826, UR-65826	17-6-1974
12084	2406	Tu-134A	CCCP-65827, RA-65827	25-6-1974
12086	2407	Tu-134A	CCCP-65828, RA-65828	*29-6-1974*
12087	2408	Tu-134A	CCCP-65829, RA-65829	30-6-1974
12093	2409	Tu-134AK	CCCP-65830§, RA-65830	28-11-1974
4312095	2410	Tu-134A/r.n.	DM-SCV, DDR-SCV, D-AOBJ, CCCP-65618 No 2, RA-65618	*12-7-1974*
12096	2501	Tu-134AK/r.n.	HA-926, HA-YSA, [HA-LBM], HA-LBN, [EW-65944], RA-65944	22-7-1974
17102	2502	Tu-134A	CCCP-65831, EK-65831	31-7-1974
17103	2503	Tu-134AK/r.n.	HA-927, HA-YSB, HA-LBO, [EW-65942], RA-65942	25-7-1974?
17106	2504	Tu-134A	CCCP-65832, EW-65832	16-8-1974
17107	2505	Tu-134A	CCCP-65833	
17109	2506	Tu-134A	CCCP-65834, RA-65834	27-8-1974
17112	2507	Tu-134A	CCCP-65835, EY-65835	30-8-1974
17113	2508	Tu-134A	CCCP-65836 † *14-8-1982*	23-8-1974
17114	2509	Tu-134A	CCCP-65837, RA-65837	18-9-1974
18116	2510	Tu-134A	CCCP-65838, RA-65838	23-9-1974
18117	2601	Tu-134A	CCCP-65839 † *19-5-1979*	29-9-1974
18118	2602	Tu-134A	CCCP-65840, RA-65840	30-9-1974
18120	2603	Tu-134AK?	CCCP-65841, UR-65841	22-10-1974
18121	2604	Tu-134A	CCCP-65842, RA-65842	22-10-1974
18123	2605	Tu-134A	CCCP-65843, RA-65843	26-10-1974
18125	2606	Tu-134A	CCCP-65844, RA-65844	31-10-1974
4323128	2607	Tu-134A/r.n.	OK-EFJ	
4323130	2608	Tu-134A/r.n.	OK-EFK	
23131	2609	Tu-134A	CCCP-65845, RA-65845	23-11-1974
23132	2610	Tu-134A	CCCP-65846, RA-65846	28-11-1974
23135	2701	Tu-134A	CCCP-65847, RA-65847	*4-12-1974*
23136	2702	Tu-134A	CCCP-65848, EK-65848	11-12-1974
23138	2703	Tu-134A	CCCP-65849	19-12-1974
23240	2704	Tu-134A	CCCP-65850	18-12-1974
23241	2705	Tu-134A	CCCP-65851, RA-65851	23-12-1974
23244	2706	Tu-134A	CCCP-65852, UR-65852	13-12-1974
(53)23245	2707	Tu-134A	CCCP-65853, RA-65853	14-1-1975
23248	2708	Tu-134A	CCCP-65854, RA-65854	10-1-1975
23249	2709	Tu-134AK	CCCP-65679*, RA-65679*	22-2-1975
23252	2710	Tu-134A	CCCP-65855, RA-65855	10-1-1975
23253	2801	Tu-134A	CCCP-65856 † *3-5-1985*	20-2-1975
23255	2802	Tu-134A	CCCP-65857, 4L-65857	20-2-1975

Construction number	Fuselage number	Version	Registration / tactical code/serial	Manufacture date
23256	2803	Tu-134A	CCCP-65858 † 11-12-1994?	10-2-1975
23264	2804	Tu-134A	CCCP-65859, RA-65859	13-2-1975
28265	2805	Tu-134A	CCCP-65860, RA-65860	28-2-1975
28269	2806	Tu-134A	CCCP-65861, EW-65861 No 1	28-2-1975
28270	2807	Tu-134A	CCCP-65862, RA-65862	28-2-1975
28283	2808	Tu-134A	CCCP-65863, RA-65863	18-3-1975
28284	2809	Tu-134A	CCCP-65864, UR-65864	15-3-1975
28286	2810	Tu-134A	CCCP-65865, 4L-65865	27-3-1975
28292	2901	Tu-134A	CCCP-65866, RA-65866	4-4-1975
28296	2902	Tu-134A	CCCP-65867, RA-65867	17-4-1975
28305	2903	Tu-134A	CCCP-65868; 65868? † 11-12-1994	15-4-1975
28306	2904	Tu-134A	CCCP-65869, RA-65869	17-4-1975
28310	2905	Tu-134A	CCCP-65870, RA-65870	16-4-1975
28311	2906	Tu-134A	CCCP-65871 † 28-6-1981	25-6-1975
29312	2907	Tu-134A	CCCP-65872, RA-65872	29-4-1975
29314	2908	Tu-134A	CCCP-65873	
29315	2909	Tu-134A	CCCP-65874	
29317	2910	Tu-134A	CCCP-65875, EY-65875	21-5-1975
31218	3001	Tu-134AK/r.n.	DM-SCW*, DDR-SCW§, D-AOBK, CCCP-65619 No 2, RA-65619, UN-65619	22-5-1975
31220	3002	Tu-134A	CCCP-65876, EY-65876	29-5-1975
31250	3003	Tu-134AK	CCCP-65877, UR-65877	30-6-1975
31260	3004	Tu-134A	CCCP-65878	17-6-1975
31265	3005	Tu-134A	CCCP-65879, 4L 65879	7-6-1975
35180	3006	Tu-134AK/r.n.	East German AF '181 Black' (DM-VBC), DDR-SDC, D-AOBN, CCCP-65620 No 2, RA-65620	30-6-1975
35200	3007	Tu-134AK	CCCP-65880, RA-65880	20-8-1975
35220	3008	Tu-134AK	CCCP-65881, RA-65881	3-6-1975
35270	3009	Tu-134A	CCCP-65882, ES-AAH	
35300	3010	Tu-134A	CCCP-65883	
36150	3101	Tu-134A	CCCP-65884, EK-65884	30-7-1975
36160	3102	Tu-134A	CCCP-65885, RA-65885	
36165	3103	Tu-134A	CCCP-65886, [4L-65886]	27-7-1975
36170	3104	Tu-134A	CCCP-65887, RA-65887	13-8-1975
36175	3105	Tu-134AK	CCCP-65888§, UR-65888	19-8-1975
38010	3106	Tu-134A	CCCP-65889, RA-65889	18-8-1975
38020	3107	Tu-134A	CCCP-65890, ES-AAP	
38030	3108	Tu-134A	CCCP-65891, RA-65891	30-8-1975
5338040	3109	Tu-134AK/r.n.	DM-SDE*, DDR-SDE§, D-AOBQ, CCCP-65608 No 2, RA-65608	18-9-1975
38050	3110	Tu-134A	CCCP-65892, EW-65892	15-9-1975
5340120	3201	Tu-134A	CCCP-65893, 65893 † 21-9-1993	25-9-1975?
40130	3202	Tu-134A	CCCP-65894, RA-65894	30-9-1975
40140	3203	Tu-134A	CCCP-65895, EY-65895	29-10-1975
40150	3204	Tu-134AK/r.n.	DM-SDF*, DDR-SDF§, D-AOBP, CCCP-65610 No 2, RA-65610, UN-65610	20-10-1975
42200	3205	Tu-134A	CCCP-65896, 65896 † 11-12-1994	31-10-1975
42210	3206	Tu-134A	CCCP-65897, ER-65897	14-11-1975
42220	3207	Tu-134A	CCCP-65898, RA-65898	25-11-1975
42225	3208	Tu-134A	CCCP-65899, RA-65899	29-11-1975
42230	3209	Tu-134A	CCCP-65000, RA-65000	12-12-1975
42235	3210	Tu-134A	CCCP-65001 † 23-9-1993	8-12-1975
44020	3301	Tu-134A	CCCP-65002, RA-65002	26-12-1975
44040	3302	Tu-134A	CCCP-65003, 65003, EY-65003	23-12-1975
(63)44060	3303	Tu-134A	CCCP-65004, RA-65004	25-2-1976
44065	3304	Tu-134AK	CCCP-65005, RA-65005	20-4-1976
44080	3305	Tu-134A	CCCP-65006, RA-65006	31-1-1976
46100	3306	Tu-134A	CCCP-65007, RA-65007	31-1-1976
46105	3307	Tu-134A	CCCP-65008, RA-65008	13-2-1976
46120	3308	Tu-134A	CCCP-65009, RA-65009	19-2-1976
46130	3309	Tu-134A	CCCP-65010, RA-65010	30-6-1976
46140	3310	Tu-134A	CCCP-65011, RA-65011	19-3-1976
46155	3401	Tu-134AK/r.n.	DM-SDG*, East German AF '186 Black', DDR-SDG, D-AOBQ, CCCP-65609 No 2, RA 65609, RA-65609	22-2-1976
46175	3402	Tu-134A	CCCP-65012, RA-65012	3-3-1976
46180	3403	Tu-134A	CCCP-65013	4-3-1976
46200	3404	Tu-134A	CCCP-65014, 65014 † 11-12-1994	1-3-1976
46300	3405	Tu-134AK/r.n.	DM-SDH, DDR-SDH, [D-AOBR], [Luftwaffe 11+14], CCCP-65606 No 2, RA-65606	29-3-1976
6348320	3406	Tu-134A/r.n.	DM-SCX, DDR-SCX, D-AOBL, CCCP-65621 No 2, RA-65621	31-3-1976
48325	3407	Tu-134A	CCCP-65015, RA-65015	30-5-1976
48340	3408	Tu-134A	CCCP-65016, RA-65016	31-3-1976
48360	3409	Tu-134AK	CCCP-65017, RA-65017	31-5-1976
48365	3410	Tu-134A	CCCP-65018, RA-65018	17-4-1976
6348370	3501	Tu-134A-1	YU-AJS † 2-4-1977	
48375	3502	Tu-134A	CCCP-65019, RA-65019	27-4-1976
48380	3503	Tu-134A	CCCP-65020, RA-65020	28-4-1976
48390	3504	Tu-134AK	CCCP-65021, RA-65021	4-5-1976
48395	3505	Tu-134A	CCCP-65022, ES-AAE, EY-65022	19-5-1976
48400	3506	Tu-134A	SP-LHD	
48405	3507	Tu-134A	SP-LHE	
48415	3508	Tu-134A	CCCP-65023, LY-ABB, UR-65023, RA-65023	31-5-1976
48420	3509	Tu-134A	CCCP-65024, RA-65024	16-6-1976
6348430	3510	Tu-134AK	VN-A108 † 17-2-1988	
48450	3601	Tu-134A	CCCP-65025, RA-65025, 65025* (Kazakstan AF)	22-6-1976
48470	3602	Tu-134A	CCCP-65026, RA-65026	24-6-1976
48485	3603	Tu-134A	CCCP-65027, RA-65027	30-6-1976
48490	3604	Tu-134AK	CCCP-65028, RA-65028	14-7-1976
48500	3605	Tu-134A	CCCP-65029, RA-65029	15-7-1976
48520	3606	Tu-134A	CCCP-65030, 65030 † 11-12-1994	15-7-1976
48530	3607	Tu-134A	CCCP-65031 † 22-3-1979	27-7-1976
48535	3608	Tu-134A	CCCP-65032	27-7-1976
48540	3609	Tu-134A	CCCP-65033, RA-65033	20-7-1976
48560	3610	Tu-134AK/r.n.	DM-SDI, DDR-SDI, [D-AOBS], [Luftwaffe 11+15], CCCP-65607 No 2, RA-65607	12-8-1976
6348565	3701	Tu-134A	CCCP-65034, ES-AAF, OM-GAT, ER-TCH, UR-BZY	2-8-1976
48590	3702	Tu-134A	CCCP-65035, RA-65035	30-8-1976
6348700	3703	Tu-134A	CCCP-65036, ER-65036	27-8-1976
48850	3704	Tu-134A	CCCP-65037, UR-65037	17-9-1976
48950	3705	Tu-134A	CCCP-65038, RA-65038	30-9-1976
49020	3706	Tu-134AK	CCCP-65680*, Soviet/Russian AF '680 Black', RA-65680*	2-12-1976
49080	3707	Tu-134A	CCCP-65039, RA-65039?	18-10-1976
6349100	3708	Tu-134A	CCCP-65040, LY-ABC, RA-65040	25-11-1976
49200	3709	Tu-134AK?	CCCP-65041 (*?)	
49350	3710	Tu-134AK	CCCP-65042, RA-65042	26-11-1976
49400	3801	Tu-134A	CCCP-65043, RA-65043	14-12-1976
49450	3802	Tu-134A	CCCP-65044, 65044, EK-65044	20-12-1976
49500	3803	Tu-134AK	CCCP-65045, RA-65045	24-1-1977
49550	3804	Tu-134A	CCCP-65046, RA-65046	28-12-1976
(73)49600	3805	Tu-134A	CCCP-65047, RA-65047	26-8-1977
49750	3806	Tu-134A	CCCP-65048, UR-65048	7-9-1977
49752	3807	Tu-134AK	VN-A106	
49755	3808	Tu-134A	CCCP-65049, EW-65049, RA-65049	12-1-1977
49756	3809	Tu-134A	CCCP-65050, ER-65050	23-3-1977
49758	3810	Tu-134A	CCCP-65051, ER-65051	23-3-1977
49760	3901	Tu-134AK	CCCP-65681*, Soviet/Russian AF '681 Black', RA-65681*	27-12-1977
49825	3902	Tu-134A	CCCP-65052, RA-65052	24-2-1977
49830	3903	Tu-134AK/r.n.	D2-ECC*, Angolan AF 'SG-104'?, D2-ECC*	
49838	3904	Tu-134A	CCCP-65053, 4L-65053 † 23-9-1993?	20-2-1977
49840	3905	Tu-134A	CCCP-65054, RA-65054	28-2-1977
49856	3906	Tu-134A	CCCP-65055, RA-65055	15-4-1977
7349858	3907	Tu-134A 'Salon'¤	OK-BYT, LZ-TUG*	
49860	3908	Tu-134A	CCCP-65056, RA-65056	26-3-1977
49865	3909	Tu-134A	CCCP-65057, RA-65057	21-3-1977
49868	3910	Tu-134A	CCCP-65058 † 27-8-1992	30-3-1977
49870	4001	Tu-134A	CCCP-65059, RA-65059	31-3-1977
49872	4002	Tu-134A	CCCP-65060, RA-65060	4-5-1977
49874	4003	Tu-134A	CCCP-65061, 4L 65061, 4L-65061	8-4-1977
49875	4004	Tu-134A	CCCP-65062, RA-65062	19-4-1977
49880	4005	Tu-134A	CCCP-65063, RA-65063	24-4-1977
49886	4006	Tu-134A	CCCP-65064, RA-65064	3-5-1977
49890	4007	Tu-134AK	CCCP-65065, XU-101, RA-65065	24-5-1977
49898	4008	Tu-134A	CCCP-65066, RA-65066	4-7-1977
49900	4009	Tu-134AK/r.n.	DM-SDK*, DDR-SDK*, VN-A122	
49905	4010	Tu-134A	CCCP-65067, RA-65067	7-7-1977
49907	4101	Tu-134A	CCCP-65068, ES-AAG, RA-65068	15-7-1977
49908	4102	Tu-134A	CCCP-65069, RA-65069, UN-65069	15-7-1977
7349909	4103	Tu-134AK/r.n.	Polish AF '101 Red' No 2, CCCP-65559, RA-65559	
49912	4104	Tu-134A	CCCP-65070, RA-65070, UN-65070	28-7-1977
7349913	4105	Tu-134A/r.n.	OK-HFL, LZ-TUJ	
49915	4106	Tu-134A	CCCP-65071, ER-65071	20-7-1977
49972	4107	Tu-134A	CCCP-65072, EK-65072	30-7-1977
49980	4108	Tu-134AK	CCCP-65073, UR-65073	19-12-1977
7349985	4109	Tu-134AK/r.n.	Polish AF '102 Red' No 2, SP-LHI, Polish AF '102 White', CCCP-65623 No 2, RA-65623	23-7-1977
49987	4110	Tu-134A	CCCP-65074, RA-65074	7-9-1977
49998	4201	Tu-134A	CCCP-65075, 65075 † 11-12-1994	19-9-1977
60001	4202	Tu-134A	CCCP-65076, UR-65076	23-9-1977
60028	4203	Tu-134A	CCCP-65077, UR-65077	29-8-1977
60035	4204	Tu-134A-1	YU-AJV, CCCP-65563, RA-65563	26-8-1977
60043	4205	Tu-134A	CCCP-65078, RA-65078	26-9-1977
60054	4206	Tu-134A	CCCP-65079, LY-ABD, LY-ASK, RA-65079	26-9-1977
60065	4207	Tu-134A	CCCP-65080, RA-65080	19-7-1977
60076	4208	Tu-134A	CCCP-65081, LY-ABE, UR-65081	19-10-1977
60081	4209	Tu-134A	CCCP-65082, EW-65082	29-9-1977
60090	4210	Tu-134A	CCCP-65083, RA-65083	15-10-1977
60108	4301	Tu-134AK/r.n.	DM-SDL*, DDR-SDL*, VN-A124	
60115	4302	Tu-134A	CCCP-65084, RA-65084	30-10-1977
60123	4303	Tu-134A	CCCP-65085, EW-65085	30-11-1977
60130	4304	Tu-134A	CCCP-65086, RA-65086	12-12-1977
7360142	4305	Tu-134A-1	OK-HFM, LZ-TUH	
60155	4306	Tu-134A	CCCP-65087, RA-65087	23-12-1977
60172	4307	Tu-134A	CCCP-65088, LY-ABF, RA-65088	9-1-1978
60180	4308	Tu-134A	CCCP-65089, UR-65089	26-12-1977
60185	4309	Tu-134A	CCCP-65090, RA-65090	30-12-1977
8360195	4310	Tu-134A	CCCP-65091, LY-ABG, RA-65091, ES-LTA	6-1-1978
60206	4401	Tu-134AK?	CCCP-65092, UR-65092, OB-1553	9-2-1978
60215	4402	Tu-134AK	CCCP-65093, UR-65093, OB-1552, UR-65093, RA-65093	18-2-1978

Construction number	Fuselage number	Version	Registration / tactical code/serial	Manufacture date
8360255	4403	Tu-134AK	CCCP-65094, ER-65094	13-3-1978
60256	4404	Tu-134A	CCCP-65095	31-1-1978
60257	4405	Tu-134A	CCCP-65096, RA-65096	22-2-1978
60258	4406	Tu-134A	CCCP-65100, RA-65100	22-2-1978
60260	4407	Tu-134A	CCCP-65101, RA-65101	22-2-1978
60267	4408	Tu-134A	CCCP-65102, RA-65102	28-2-1978
8360282	4409	Tu-134A-1	OK-IFN, 4L-AAE, no registration [RA-65...]	28-2-1978
60297	4410	Tu-134A	CCCP-65103, RA-65103	28-2-1978
60301	4501	Tu-134A	CCCP-65104, RA-65104	20-3-1978
60308	4502	Tu-134A	CCCP-65105, LY-ABH, RA-65105	20-3-1978
60315	4503	Tu-134A	CCCP-65106, EW-65106	23-3-1978
60321	4504	Tu-134A-1	YU-AJW, CCCP-65560, RA-65560	22-3-1978
60328	4505	Tu-134A	CCCP-65107, UR-65107	25-3-1978
60332	4506	Tu-134A	CCCP-65108, EW-65108	30-3-1978
60339	4507	Tu-134AK	CCCP-65109, RA-65109?, UR-65109, RA-65109	27-9-1978
60343	4508	Tu-134A	CCCP-65110, RA-65110	31-3-1978
60346	4509	Tu-134A	CCCP-65111, EX-65111	24-3-1978
60350	4510	Tu-134A	CCCP-65112, ES-AAI, RA-65112	25-4-1978
60380	4601	Tu-134A	CCCP-65113, ES-AAM, RA-65113	27-4-1978
60395	4602	Tu-134A	CCCP-65114, UR-65114	12-5-1978
60405	4603	Tu-134A	CCCP-65115, UN-65115	25-4-1978
60420	4604	Tu-134A	CCCP-65116, RA-65116	24-5-1978
60435	4605	Tu-134AK/A-1	DM-SDM*, DDR-SDM*, VN-A126 † 12-1-1991	
60450	4606	Tu-134A	CCCP-65117, RA-65117	24-5-1978
60462	4607	Tu-134A	CCCP-65118, RA-65118	12-6-1978
60475	4608	Tu-134A	CCCP-65119, EX-65119	14-6-1978
60482	4609	Tu-134AK	CCCP-65120 † 2-7-1986	24-6-1978
60495	4610	Tu-134A/r.n.	DM-SCY, DDR-SCY, D-AOBM, CCCP-65622 No 2, RA-65622	16-6-1978
60505	4701	Tu-134A	CCCP-65121, UN-65121	24-6-1978
60519	4702	Tu-134A	CCCP-65122, RA-65122	30-6-1978
60525	4703	Tu-134A	CCCP-65123, UR-65123, OB-1490 † 27-9-1994?	
60540	4704	Tu-134AK	CCCP-65097, RA-65097	29-7-1978
60560	4705	Tu-134A	CCCP-65124, ES-AAN, RA-65124	13-7-1978
60575	4706	Tu-134A	CCCP-65125, EX-65125	29-7-1978
60588	4707	Tu-134A	CCCP-65126, RA-65126	8-8-1978
60612	4708	Tu-134AK/A-1	DM-SDN*, DDR-SDN*, VN-A128	
60627	4709	Tu-134A	CCCP-65127, ES-AAJ, EY-65127, RA-65127	27-8-1978
60628	4710	Tu-134A	CCCP-65128, LY-ABI, RA-65128	30-8-1978
60630	4801	Tu-134A	CCCP-65129 † 30-8-1983	31-8-1978
60635	4802	Tu-134A	CCCP-65130, UN 65130	31-8-1978
60637	4803	Tu-134A	CCCP-65131, RA-65131	22-9-1978
60639	4804	Tu-134A	CCCP-65132, RA-65132	25-9-1978
60642	4805	Tu-134A/r.n.	LZ-TUS, RA-65941	?-9-1978
60645	4806	Tu-134A	CCCP-65133, EW-65133	30-9-1978
60647	4807	Tu-134A	CCCP-65134, 65134, UR-65134	30-9-1978
60648	4808	Tu-134A	CCCP-65135, UR-65135	24-10-1978
60650	4809	Tu-134AK	Soviet/Russian AF '01 Red', Russian AF '01 Blue'	
60885	4810	Tu-134A	CCCP-65136, RA-65136	4-10-1978
60890	4901	Tu-134A	CCCP-65137, RA-65137	21-11-1978
60907	4902	Tu-134A	CCCP-65138, UN-65138	21-11-1978
60915	4903	Tu-134A	CCCP-65139, RA-65139	17-11-1978
60925	4904	Tu-134A/r.n.	VN-A102 † 9-9-1988	27-12-1978
60932	4905	Tu-134AK	CCCP-65140, ER-65140	29-12-1978
60945	4906	Tu-134A	CCCP-65141, RA-65141	25-12-1978
(93)60955	4907	Tu-134A	CCCP-65142 † 22-6-1986	10-1-1979
60967	4908	Tu-134A	CCCP-65143, RA-65143	18-1-1979
60977	4909	Tu-134A	CCCP-65144, ES-AAK, RA-65144	12-1-1979
60985	4910	Tu-134A	CCCP-65145, 65145, EW-65145	18-1-1979
61000	5001	Tu-134B	CCCP-65146, YL-LBA, RA-65146	31-3-1980
61012	5002	Tu-134A	CCCP-65147, UN-65147, UN 65147	6-2-1979
61025	5003	Tu-134A	CCCP-65148, RA-65148	6-2-1979
61033	5004	Tu-134A	CCCP-65149, EW-65149	22-1-1979
61042	5005	Tu-134A	CCCP-65750, 65750, 4L-65750, EX-020	26-1-1979
61055	5006	Tu-134A/r.n.	VN-A104	
61066	5007	Tu-134A	CCCP-65751, RA-65751	16-2-1979
61079	5008	Tu-134A	CCCP-65752, RA-65752	28-2-1979
61099	5009	Tu-134A	CCCP-65753, RA-65753	2-3-1979
62120	5010	Tu-134AK, Tu-134 Balkany	CCCP-65682*, RA-65682§ ['Balkany' HF comms suite removed]	
62144	5101	Tu-134A/r.n.	VN-A110	
62154	5102	Tu-134A	CCCP-65754, EW-65754	27-3-1979
62165	5103	Tu-134A	CCCP-65755, RA-65755	31-3-1979
62179	5104	Tu-134A	CCCP-65756, RA-65756	20-3-1979
62187	5105	Tu-134AK	CCCP-65760, RA-65760 † 9-9-1994	
62199	5106	Tu-134AK, Tu-134 Balkany	CCCP-65683*, UN-65683*	
62205	5107	Tu-134AK, Tu-134 Balkany	CCCP-65684*, RA-65684*	
62215	5108	Tu-134A	CCCP-65757, UR-65757	28-4-1979
62230	5109	Tu-134A	CCCP-65758, RA-65758	29-4-1979
62239	5110	Tu-134A	CCCP-65759, ES-AAO, RA-65759	30-4-1979
62244	5201	Tu-134AK	CCCP-65761, UR-65761	11-5-1979
62259	5202	Tu-134AK/A-1	DM-SDO*, DDR-SDO*, VN-A130	
62279	5203	Tu-134A	CCCP-65762, RA-65762	23-5-1979
62299	5204	Tu-134A	CCCP-65763, EY-65763	31-5-1979
62305	5205	Tu-134AK?	CCCP-65764, UR-65764, EW-65764	22-6-1979
62315	5206	Tu-134A	CCCP-65765, UR-65765	18-6-1979
62327	5207	Tu-134A	CCCP-65766 † 20-10-1986	28-6-1979
62335	5208	Tu-134A	CCCP-65767, UN-65767	28-6-1979
62350	5209	Tu-134A	CCCP-65768, ES-AAL, RA-65575, EK-65575	?-6-1979
62375	5210	Tu-134AK	CCCP-65685*, Soviet/Russian AF '685 Black', RA-65685*	
62390	5301	Tu-134AK, Tu-134 Balkany	CCCP-65686*, ER-65686*, ER-AAZ§ ['Balkany' suite removed], ER-TCF	
62400	5302	Tu-134AK	CCCP-65687§ † 17-6-1982	
62415	5303	Tu-134A	CCCP-65769, RA-65769	8-8-1979
62430	5304	Tu-134A	CCCP-65770, RA-65770	29-8-1979
62445	5305	Tu-134AK	CCCP-65771, RA-65771	31-8-1979
62458	5306	Tu-134AK/r.n.	VN-A112	
62472	5307	Tu-134A	CCCP-65772, EW-65772	19-9-1979
62495	5308	Tu-134AK	CCCP-65773, UR-65773	5-11-1979
62519	5309	Tu-134A	CCCP-65774, 65774, 4L-65774	24-9-1979
62530	5310	Tu-134A	CCCP-65775, RA-65775	23-9-1979
62545	5401	Tu-134A	CCCP-65776, UN 65776	29-9-1979
62552	5402	Tu-134A	CCCP-65777, RA-65777	17-10-1979
62561	5403	Tu-134AK	XU-122?, CCCP-65604 No 2, RA-65604	2-11-1979
62575	5404	Tu-134AK, Tu-134 Balkany	CCCP-65688*, RA-65688*	
62590	5405	Tu-134A	CCCP-65778, EX-65778	26-10-1979
62602	5406	Tu-134A	CCCP-65779, EX-65779	11-11-1979
62622	5407	Tu-134A	CCCP-65780, RA-65780	13-11-1979
62645	5408	Tu-134A	CCCP-65781, RA-65781	16-11-1979
62655	5409	Tu-134AK, Tu-134 Balkany	CCCP-65689*, RA-65689*	18-12-1979
62672	5410	Tu-134A	CCCP-65782, UR-65782	8-12-1979
62708	5501	Tu-134A	CCCP-65783, RA-65783	9-12-1979
62715	5502	Tu-134A	CCCP-65784, RA-65784	15-1-1980
62732	5503	Tu-134LK	Soviet/Russian AF '02 Red', Russian AF '02 Blue'/RA	8-5-1980
62750	5504	Tu-134A	CCCP-65785§, RA-65785	
62775	5505	Tu-134A	CCCP-65786, RA-65786	29-12-1979
(03)62798	5506	Tu-134A	CCCP-65787, UN-65787	25-1-1980
62805	5507	Tu-134AK, Tu-134 Balkany	CCCP-65690*, RA-65690*	6-2-1980
62820	5508	Tu-134B-1	CCCP-65720, RA-65720, UR-BYY	19-2-1981
62835	5509	Tu-134A	CCCP-65788, EY-65788	22-2-1980
62850	5510	Tu-134A	CCCP-65789, EX-65789	1-2-1980
63100	5601	Tu-134A	CCCP-65790, UR-65790	22-2-1980
63110	5602	Tu-134A	CCCP-65791, ER-65791	26-2-1980
63121	5603	Tu-134A	CCCP-65792, RA-65792	27-2-1980
63128	5604	Tu-134A	CCCP-65793, RA-65793	18-2-1980
63135	5605	Tu-134A	CCCP-65794, RA-65794	28-2-1980
63145	5606	Tu-134A	CCCP-65795 † 12-12-1986	18-3-1980
63150	5607	Tu-134A	CCCP-65796, RA-65796	17-3-1980
63158	5608	Tu-134AK, Tu-134 Balkany	CCCP-65979§ ['Balkany' suite removed]	
63165	5609	Tu-134A-1	YU-ANE, CCCP-65564, RA-65564	13-3-1980
63173	5610	Tu-134A	CCCP-65797, RA-65797	19-3-1980
63179	5701	Tu-134A	CCCP-65798, 65798, 4L-65798	31-3-1980
63187	5702	Tu-134B	CCCP-65799, YL-LBN, UN-65799	30-4-1980
63195	5703	Tu-134A	CCCP-65691, RA-65691	29-4-1980
63207	5704	Tu-134AK, Tu-134 Balkany	CCCP-65980*, Soviet AF '980 Black'?, RA-65980*	24-4-1980
63215	5705	Tu-134B	CCCP-65692, YL-LBB, RA-65692	26-5-1980
63221	5706	Tu-134B	CCCP-65693, YL-LBC, RA-65693	27-5-1980
63235	5707	Tu-134B	CCCP-65694, YL-LBD, [UN-65694], RA-65694	16-6-1980
63245	5708	Tu-134A	CCCP-65977, RA-65977	28-5-1980
63250	5709	Tu-134AK, Tu-134 Balkany	CCCP-65981*, RA-65981*	
63260	5710	Tu-134AK/A-1	DM-SDP*, DDR-SDP*, VN-A132	
63285	5801	Tu-134B	CCCP-65695, YL-LBE, UN 65695	16-6-1980
63295	5802	Tu-134B	CCCP-65696, YL-LBF, 4L-AAD, RA-65579	19-6-1980
63307	5803	Tu-134A	CCCP-65697, RA-65697	10-6-1980
63315	5804	Tu-134AK, Tu-134 Balkany	CCCP-65982*, RA-65982*	20-6-1980
63325	5805	Tu-134B	CCCP-65698 † 6-1-1981	28-6-1980
63333	5806	Tu-134B	CCCP-65699, YL-LBG, UN 65699	30-6-1980
63340	5807	Tu-134B	CCCP-65700, YL-LBH, 4L-AAB, RA-65569, ST-MRS	30-6-1980
63350	5808	Tu-134AK, Tu-134 Balkany	CCCP-65983*, RA-65983§ ['Balkany' suite removed]	25-7-1980
63357	5809	Tu-134AK	CCCP-65978, RA-65978	
63365	5810	Tu-134B	CCCP-65701, YL-LBI, RA-65701	31-7-1980
63375	5901	Tu-134B	CCCP-65702, 65702, 4K-65702	14-8-1980
63383	5902	Tu-134B	CCCP-65703, 4K-65703 † 5-12-1995	28-8-1980
63400	5903	Tu-134AK, Tu-134 Balkany	CCCP-65984*, RA-65984*	30-8-1980
63410	5904	Tu-134B	CCCP-65704, YL-LBJ, 4K-65704	
63415	5905	Tu-134B	CCCP-65705 No 2 (No 1 was a Lisunov Li-2), 65705, 4K-65705	23-9-1980
63425	5906	Tu-134B	CCCP-65706, YL-LBK; LZ-ACB?	25-9-1980
63435	5907	Tu-134AK	CCCP-65707, ER-65707	?-10-1980
63447	5908	Tu-134B	CCCP-65708, AL-65708, 65708, 4K-65708	14-10-1980

Construction number	Fuselage number	Version	Registration / tactical code/serial	Manufacture date
63457	5909	Tu-134AK/r.n.	Mozambique AF '63457', C9-CAA † *19-10-1986*	18-10-1980
63468	5910	Tu-134AK, Tu-134 *Balkany*	CCCP-65985*; 65985*, 4K-65985*, 4K-65496*	
63475	6001	Tu-134AK, Tu-134 *Balkany*	CCCP-65986*, RA-65986*	14-11-1980
63484	6002	Tu-134B	CCCP-65709, 65709, 4K-65709	23-12-1980
63490	6003	Tu-134B	CCCP-65710, AL-65710, 4K-65710	29-11-1980
63498	6004	Tu-134B	CCCP-65711, AL-65711, 65711, AL-65711, 4K-65711	30-11-1980
63505	6005	Tu-134AK, Tu-134 *Balkany*	CCCP-65987*, RA-65987*	16-12-1980
63515	6006	Tu-134B	CCCP-65712, YL-LBL, 4K-65712	30-12-1980
63520	6007	Tu-134B	CCCP-65713, 65713, 4K-65713	9-12-1980
63527	6008	Tu-134B	CCCP-65714, 65714, 4K-65714	30-12-1980
(13)63536	6009	Tu-134B	CCCP-65715, YL-LBM, 4L-AAC, RA-65715	*6-2-1981*
63550	6010	Tu-134AK, Tu-134 *Balkany*	CCCP-65988*, RA-65988*	4-1-1981
63560	6101	Tu-134A/r.n.	HA-LBP † *22-2-1994*	4-1-1981?
63580	6102	Tu-134A/r.n.	HA-LBR, *EW-65943*, RA-65943	*30-1-1981*
63595	6103	Tu-134B	CCCP-65716, RA-65716	*2-2-1981*
63605	6104	Tu-134AK, Tu-134 *Balkany*	CCCP-65989*, RA-65989*	12-2-1981
63620	6105	Tu-134LK-2	Soviet/Russian AF '03 Red', Russian AF '03 Blue'/RA-	
63637	6106	Tu-134AK	CCCP-65719, RA-65719	25-2-1981
63657	6107	Tu-134A	CCCP-65717, RA-65717	*6-3-1981*
63668	6108	Tu-134AK	CCCP-65718, UR-65718	31-3-1981
63684	6109	Tu-134AK	CCCP-65900, UN-65900	16-4-1981
63690	6110	Tu-134AK, Tu-134 *Balkany*	CCCP-65990*, RA-65990* ['Balkany' suite removed]	
63700	6201	Tu-134AK	CCCP-65099, RA-65099	3-4-1981
63720	6202	Tu-134AK	CCCP-65726, RA-65726	31-3-1981
63731	6203	Tu-134A	CCCP-65901, RA-65901	8-4-1981
63742	6204	Tu-134A	CCCP-65902, RA-65902	*24-4-1981*
63750	6205	Tu-134A	CCCP-65903, RA-65903	29-4-1981
63757	6206	Tu-134AK, Tu-134 *Balkany*	CCCP-63757*, Soviet/Russian Navy (tactical code unknown), RA 63757*	
1363761	6207	Tu-134AK, Tu-134 *Balkany*	CCCP-63761*?, Soviet/Russian AF '25 Red' (RA-63761?)	
63769	6208	Tu-134AK?		
63775	6209	Tu-134AK; Tu-134 *Balkany*?	CCCP-63775*, Soviet/Russian AF '35 Red'?, RA-63775	
63780	6210	Tu-134AK?		
63820	6301	Tu-134AK?		
63825	6302	Tu-134AK, Tu-134 *Balkany*	CCCP-65996*?, Soviet AF '50 Black'?, CCCP-65996*?, RA-65996*?	20-11-1981
63832	6303	Tu-134AK?		
63845	6304	Tu-134AK, Tu-134 *Balkany*	CCCP-65991*, RA-65991*	
63850	6305	Tu-134AK, Tu-134 *Balkany*	CCCP-65992*, RA-65992*	26-11-1981
63860	6306	Tu-134AK, Tu-134 *Balkany*	CCCP-65993*, Soviet AF '993 Black', CCCP-65993*, RA-65993*, 4L-65993*, 4L-AAJ ['Balkany' suite removed]	
(23)63870	6307	Tu-134AK	CCCP-65908, RA-65908	22-1-1982
63880?	6308	Tu-134AK?		
63900	6309	Tu-134AK?		
63950	6310	Tu-134AK?		
63952	6311	Tu-134AK/A-1	East German AF '184 Black' (DDR-SDS), Luftwaffe 11+11, 9A-ADL, RA-65566	18-3-1982
63953	6312	Tu-134AK	CCCP-65904, RA-65904	
63955	6313	Tu-134AK, Tu-134 *Balkany*	CCCP-63955*, EW-63955*, RA-65571 ['Balkany' suite removed]	
63957	6314	Tu-134AK, Tu-134 *Balkany*	CCCP-63957*, Ukraine AF '01 Yellow', UAF 63957*, 63957*	
63960	6315	Tu-134AK, Tu-134 *Balkany*	CCCP-63960*, Ukraine AF '02 Yellow' (UR-63960)	
63961	6316	Tu-134AK, Tu-134 *Balkany*	CCCP-63961*?, Soviet/Russian AF '10 Black' (RA-63961?)	29-4-1982
63965	6317	Tu-134AK	CCCP-65905, RA-65905	
63967	6318	Tu-134AK/A-1	DDR-SDR*, Luftwaffe 11+10, 9A-ADP, RA-65567	*4-5-1982*
63969	6319	Tu-134AK	CCCP-65910 † *1-2-1985*	11-5-1982
63972	6320	Tu-134AK	CCCP-65911, 65911, RA-65911	
63975	6321	Tu-134AK, Tu-134 *Balkany*	CCCP-63975*, Soviet/Russian AF '01' (Black?), RA-63975*/'01 Blue'	
63976	6322	Tu-134AK, Tu-134 *Balkany*	CCCP-63976*, Soviet/Russian AF '05 Red' (RA-63976)	
63979	6323	Tu-134AK, Tu-134 *Balkany*	CCCP-63979*, UK 63979*	
63982	6324	Tu-134AK, Tu-134 *Balkany*	CCCP-63982*, Ukraine AF '03 Yellow' (UR-63982), 63982* ['Balkany' suite removed]	
63985	6325	Tu-134AK	CCCP-65912, RA-65912	30-9-1982
63987	6326	Tu-134B 'Salon'	LZ-TUT§	
63989	6327	Tu-134B	YK-AYC	
63990	6328	Tu-134B 'Salon'	YK-AYD*	
(33)63991	6329	Tu-134SKh	CCCP-65917, RA-65917, UR-65917 [converted to Tu-134A-3M]	
63992	6330	Tu-134B 'Salon'	YK-AYA*	
63994	6331	Tu-134B 'Salon'	YK-AYB*	
63995	6332	Tu-134SKh	CCCP-65918, RA-65918	*28-4-1984*
63996	6333	Tu-134AK	CCCP-65907, RA-65907	
63997	6334	Tu-134AK	CCCP-65921, RA-65921	5-3-1983
63998	6335	Tu-134AK/A-1	DDR-SDT*, CCCP-65565, EW-65565, RA-65565	28-2-1983
66101	6336	Tu-134AK	CCCP-65926, RA-65926	30-5-1983
66109	6337	Tu-134AK	CCCP-65914, TC-GRD, RA-65914	*19-6-1983*
66120	6338	Tu-134AK	CCCP-65915, TC-GRE, RA-65915	31-7-1983
66130	6339	Tu-134SKh	CCCP-65721, RA-65721 [converted to Tu-134A-3M]	19-9-1984
66135	6340	Tu-134AK/A-1	DDR-SDU*, Luftwaffe 11+12, 9A-ADR, RA-65568	17-8-1983
66140	6341	Tu-134IK	CCCP-64454*, RA-64454*	
66143	6342	Tu-134AK	CCCP-65934, RA-65934	17-8-1983
66152	6343	Tu-134AK	CCCP-65916, RA-65916	
66168	6344	Tu-134AK	CCCP-65919, RA-65919	26-10-1983
66175	6345	Tu-134AK	CCCP-65906, RA-65906 [IMARK; reconverted]	31-10-1983
66180	6346	Tu-134AK	CCCP-65935, RA-65935	28-11-1983

Construction number	Fuselage number	Version	Registration / tactical code/serial	Manufacture date
66185	6347	Tu-134BV	CCCP-65931, RA-65931	2-12-1983
66187	6348	Tu-134B	YK-AYE	
66190	6349	Tu-134B	YK-AYF	
(43)66198	6350	Tu-134AK	CCCP-65927, RA-65927	17-2-1984
66200	6351	Tu-134AK	CCCP-65550, RA-65550	23-2-1984
66207	6352	Tu-134AK	CCCP-65994, RA-65994	
66212	6353	Tu-134AK	CCCP-65551, 65551, UN-65551, UN 65551	31-3-1984
66215	6354	Tu-134B	P-813	
66220	6355	Tu-134B 'Salon'	VN-A114	
66230	6356	Tu-134B 'Salon'	VN-A116	
66250	6357	Tu-134B 'Salon'	VN-A118	
66270	6358	Tu-134AK	CCCP-65552, RA-65552	31-5-1984
66300	6359	Tu-134AK	CCCP-65553, RA-65553	
66320	6360	Tu-134AK	CCCP-65554, RA-65554	26-7-1984
66350	6361	Tu-134AK	CCCP-65555, RA-65555	16-8-1984
66360	6362	Tu-134B	VN-A120 † *3-9-1997*	27-7-1984
66368	6363	Tu-134B	P-814	
66372	6364	Tu-134AK	CCCP-65556, 65556, UR-65556	30-8-1984
66380	6365	Tu-134AK	CCCP-65557, 65557, RA-65557	6-11-1984
66400	6366	Tu-134AK	CCCP-65995, RA-65995	
66405	6367	Tu-134A 'Salon'	CCCP-65932, 65932, RA-65932	29-9-1984
66420	6368	Tu-134SKh	CCCP-65722, RA-65722 [converted to Tu-134A-3M]	
66440	6369	Tu-134SKh	CCCP-65723, RA-65723 [converted to Tu-134A-3M]	30-6-1989
66445	6370	Tu-134SKh	CCCP-65724, RA-65724 [converted to Tu-134A-3M]	
66472	6371	Tu-134SKh	CCCP-65725, RA-65725 [converted to Tu-134A-3M]	
66491	6372	Tu-134SKh	CCCP-65928, RA-65928 [converted to Tu-134A-3M]	
66495	6373	Tu-134AK	CCCP-65929, RA-65929	24-6-1987
66500	6374	Tu-134SKh	CCCP-65930, RA-65930 [converted to Tu-134A-3M]	
66550	6375	Tu-134AK/r.n.	XU-102, CCCP-64451, XU-102, RA-64451, RA-65570	15-12-1986

Tu-134Sh – System 1 (known c/ns only)

Construction number	Version	Registration/ tactical code/serial	Manufacture date
0350001	Tu-134Sh-1	Soviet/Russian AF '01 Red'	29-1-1971
0350002	Tu-134Sh-2?		17-3-1971
1350101			?-12-1971
1350102			?-12-1971
2350103			
2350104	Tu-134Sh-1?	Soviet/Russian AF '63 Blue'?	
2350105			
2350201	Tu-134Sh-1	?, CCCP-65562, RA-65562 [converted to Tu-134LL]	
2350202	Tu-134Sh-2	? † *25-5-1984*	30-8-1972
2350203	Tu-134Sh-1?	Soviet AF '92 Red'	
2350204			
2350205			
2350206			
2350207			
2350208		?, CCCP-65561	
3350301?			
3350302	Tu-134Sh-1	Soviet AF '76 Blue'	
3350303	Tu-134Sh-1	Soviet AF '10 Red' [converted to SL-134Sh]	
3350304		Soviet AF '77 Blue'?	
3350305		Soviet AF '51 Blue'	
3350401	Tu-134Sh-1	Soviet AF '78 Blue'	
3350402			
3350403		Soviet AF '87 Blue'	
4350404?			
4350405?			

System 3 (known c/ns only)

Construction number	Fuselage number	Version	Registration / tactical code	Manufacture date
53550550	0501?		Soviet/Russian AF '74 Blue'	
53550580	0503?		Soviet/Russian AF '86 Blue', Russian AF '78 Blue'	
53550650	0505?	Tu-134Sh-1	Soviet/Russian AF '82 Red'	
63550705		Tu-134Sh-1	Soviet AF '01 Red'	
63550720		Tu-134Sh-1	Soviet/Russian AF '84 Red'	17-9-1976
73550752		Tu-134Sh-1	Soviet/Russian AF '57 Red'	
73550795		Tu-134Sh-1?	?, Russian Navy '07 Blue'?	
73550815	0805?	Tu-134Sh-1	?, CCCP-65098, 65098 [converted to Tu-134SL (SL-134Sh)]	
83550920				
83550945		Tu-134Sh-1		
83550968		Tu-134Sh-2	Soviet/Russian AF '38 Blue'	15-5-1979
93550970		Tu-134Sh-2	Soviet/Russian AF '34 Blue'	19-4-1979
93550983		Tu-134Sh-2	Soviet/Russian AF '40 Blue'	
93550999		Tu-134Sh-1	Soviet/Russian AF '52 Red'	
93551050		Tu-134Sh-1	Soviet/Russian AF '31 Red'	
93551120	1201?	Tu-134Sh-2?	Soviet AF '40 Red'	
93553016		Tu-134Sh-2	Soviet/Russian AF '21 Blue'	10-12-1979

Tu-134UBL (known c/ns only)

Construction number	Fuselage number	Registration / tactical code	Manufacture date[i]
(13)64010	6401	CCCP-64010, Soviet/Russian AF '11 Red' (RA-64010) [converted to 'Tu-134B-3' RA-65945]	?-1-1981
64020	6402	CCCP-64020, Soviet AF '02 Red', ?	
64035	6403?	CCCP-64035, Soviet/Russian AF '21 Red' (RA-64035)	
64065		CCCP-64065, Soviet/Russian AF '12 Red' (RA-64065)	
64073		CCCP-64073; Soviet/Russian AF '16 Red' (RA-64073)?	
64083		CCCP-64083, ?	
64095		CCCP-64095, ?	
64105 [vi]		*CCCP-64105, Soviet/Russian AF '11 Red' (RA-64105)*	
64121		CCCP-64121, ?, 64121* (RA-64121)	
64140		CCCP-64140, Soviet AF '02 Red'	
64148		CCCP-64148, Soviet AF '11 Red'	
64175		CCCP-64175, ? (RA-64175)	
64182		CCCP-64182, Soviet/Russian AF '34 Red' (RA-64182)	
64188		CCCP-64188, ?	
64235		CCCP-64235, ?	
64245		CCCP-64245, Soviet/Russian AF '11 Red' (RA-64245)	
(23)64270		CCCP-64270, Soviet/Russian AF '15 Red' (RA-64270)	?-?-1982
64277		CCCP-64277, ?	
64310		*CCCP-64310, Soviet/Russian AF '14 Red' (RA-64310)*	
64315		CCCP-64315, ?	
64325		CCCP-64325, Soviet AF '21 Red'	
64350		CCCP-64350, Soviet AF '23 Red'	
64365?		CCCP-64365?, ?	
64375		CCCP-64375, ?	
64392		CCCP-64392, Soviet/Russian AF '26 Red' (RA-64392)	
64400		CCCP-64400, Soviet/Russian AF '27 Red' (RA-64400)	
64435		CCCP-64435, Soviet AF '30 Red'	
64505		*CCCP-64505, Soviet/Russian AF '18 Red' (RA-64505)*	
64585		CCCP-64585, ?	
64630		CCCP-64630, Soviet/Russian AF '25 Red' (RA-64630) [converted to Tu-134UBKM]	
64640		CCCP-64640, Soviet AF '40 Red', Soviet AF '22 Red'	
64650?		CCCP-64650?, ?	
64670		CCCP-64670, Soviet/Ukraine AF '42 Red' (UR-64670)	
64678		CCCP-64678, Soviet AF '43 Red'; to Ukraine AF (UR-64678)?	
64728		CCCP-64728, Soviet/Ukraine Navy '72 Red' (UR-64728) [converted to Tu-134UBK]	?-12-1982
(33)64740		CCCP-64740, Soviet AF '21 Red', no tactical code (RA-64740)	
64753		CCCP-64753, Soviet/Russian AF '17 Red' (RA-64753); Russian AF '17 Blue'?	
64775		CCCP-64775, ?	
64800		CCCP-64800, Soviet/Russian AF '18 Red' (RA-64800)	
64830		CCCP-64830, Soviet/Russian AF '48 Red' (RA-64830)	
64835		CCCP-64835, Soviet/Russian AF '30 Red' (RA-64835)	
64845		CCCP-64845, Soviet AF '42 Red'?, Soviet/Russian AF '30 Red' (RA-64845)	
64950		*CCCP-64950, Soviet/Russian AF '23 Red' (RA-64950)?*	

Footnotes

i Chronologically the manufacture dates do not always follow the c/n order; this is explained by the need to eliminate any defects discovered during the first flight and by the higher complexity of outfitting jobs on VIP and special mission aircraft as compared to Tu-134s in ordinary passenger configuration.

Manufacture dates followed by a question mark come from Western sources and are not yet confirmed by Russian ones. In some cases different documents give different manufacture dates for the same aircraft (such dates are given in bold italics in the table). For instance, the manufacture date of CCCP-65000 has also been stated as 1st November 1975. Other 'alternative' dates are 27th December 1975 for CCCP-65003, 13th February 1976 for CCCP-65005, 21st January 1976 for CCCP-65008, 9th February 1976 and 20th February 1976 for CCCP-65011, 21st March 1976 and 30th March 1976 for CCCP-65015, 6th April 1976 for CCCP-65018, 31st May 1976 for CCCP-65021, 18th June 1976 for CCCP-65024, 21st October 1976 for CCCP-65040, 21st November 1976 for CCCP-65043, 21st January 1977, 27th January 1977 and 16th June 1976 for CCCP-65045 (the latter date is impossible), 31st January 1977 for CCCP-65049, 8th April 1977 for CCCP-65060, 29th April 1977 and 8th September 1977 for CCCP-65061, 22nd April 1977 for CCCP-65062, 19th April 1977 and 29th April 1977 for CCCP-65063, 28th July 1977 for CCCP-65071, 20th October 1977 for CCCP-65082, 20th January 1978 for CCCP-65087, 31st January 1978 for CCCP-65089, 29th June 1978 for CCCP-65097, 26th April 1978 for CCCP-65113, 28th April 1978 for CCCP-65115, 5th December 1978 for CCCP-65136, 18th July 1979 for CCCP-65143, 25th December 1978 and 18th November 1979 for CCCP-65145 (the latter date is highly improbable), 12th May 1982 for RA-65567, 24th May 1974 for RA-65605 (ex-DM-SCU), 20th March 1976 for RA-65606 (ex-DM-SDH), 15th September 1975 for RA-65608 (ex-DM-SDE), 2nd April 1976 for RA-65621 (ex-DM-SCX), 15th June 1971 and 31st January 1972 for CCCP-65666, 17th November 1972 for CCCP-65675, 24th May 1980 for CCCP-65693, 16th May 1980 for CCCP-65694, 30th June 1980 for CCCP-65697, 26th February 1981 for CCCP-65715, 28th February 1981 for CCCP-65716, 18th February 1981 for CCCP-65717, 30th August 1971 for CCCP-65730, 22nd February 1979 for CCCP-65750, 26th February 1979 for CCCP-65751, 23rd March 1979 for CCCP-65753, 17th March 1979 for CCCP-65755, 31st May 1979 for CCCP-65762, 22nd June 1979 for CCCP-65767, 28th July 1979 for CCCP-65769, 3rd August 1979 and 28th August 1979 for CCCP-65770, 11th October 1979 for CCCP-65775, 24th July 1979 for CCCP-65776 (which is extremely doubtful), 29th October 1979 for CCCP-65777, 20th November 1979 for CCCP-65779, 30th November 1979 for CCCP-65780, 5th December 1979 for CCCP-65781, 20th December 1979 for CCCP-65783, 16th January 1980 for CCCP-65784, 25th December 1979 for CCCP-65786, 23rd January 1980 for CCCP-65787, 29th February 1980 for CCCP-65793, 18th March 1980 for CCCP-65796, 21st February 1974 for CCCP-65800, 23rd January 1974 for CCCP-65808, 7th January 1974 for CCCP-65810, 31st May 1974 for CCCP-65823, 19th June 1974 for CCCP-65828, 11th December 1974 for CCCP-65847, 7th April 1975 for CCCP-65866, 21st November 1975 for CCCP-65881, 28th July 1975 for CCCP-65886, 25th February 1973 for CCCP-65893 (which is impossible!), 25th November 1975 for CCCP-65899, 18th April 1981 for CCCP-65902, 19th April 1983 for CCCP-65914, 22nd September 1984 for CCCP-65918, 28th December 1972 for CCCP-65954, 29th February 1972 for CCCP-65955 (which again does not make sense), 14th March 1973 for CCCP-65959, 27th July 1973 for CCCP-65966, 16th October 1973 for CCCP-65970, 21st July 1973 for CCCP-65974 and 14th May 1980 for CCCP-65977.

Western sources state 22nd November 1973 as the manufacture date for CCCP-65801, 3rd December 1973 for DM-SCO, 6th February 1974 for DM-SCP, 16th February 1974 for DM-SCR, 20th February 1974 for DM-SCS, 5th May 1974 for DM-SCT, 6th July 1974 for DM-SCV, 14th May 1975 for DM-SCW, 19th March 1976 for DM-SCX, 8th June 1978 for DM-SCY, 16th June 1975 for DDR-SDC, 1st September 1975 for DM-SDE, 10th October 1975 for DM-SDF, 18th February 1976 for DM-SDG, 27th August 1976 for DM-SDI and 8th January 1981 for HA-LBR.

ii Radar nose (Groza-M134 radar); iii Only Tu-134A 'Salons' originally built and delivered as such are listed.
iv Tu-134AK manufactured to Tu-134A-1 standard; v The sole Tu-134B-1 was completed late.
vi Built as such (with a rear entry door and built-in airstairs à la Tu-134AK).
vii C/ns given in italics are unconfirmed. 64950 may be a misread for (23)64350!

Until recently Avcom had no standard livery of its own, and every aircraft in the fleet was painted differently. This is RA-65701, a refitted Tu-134B 'Salon' (ex-Baltic Express Line YL-LBI, c/n (03)63365, f/n 5710) placed on the Russian register on 16th November 2001; the aircraft has a curved red/blue cheatline.
Yuriy Kirsanov

Accident Attrition

The Tu-134's accident statistics as of 1st January 2003 are detailed below. Only fatal and non-fatal accidents of varying seriousness are listed here; flight incidents and cases of ground damage to parked aircraft are not dealt with because with most aircraft types the number of such incidents per year runs into the hundreds.[1] Full accounts cannot be given for reasons of space, so only the basic facts are described. (A list of aircraft accidents in chronological order admittedly makes pretty depressing reading. However, lest the reader should get the wrong idea that the type in question is 'inherently unsafe', remember that all these events occurred over a 35-year period. Also, fortunately most flights end in a safe landing, and this goes for the Tu-134 as well!)

1988 and 1989 were the worst years, with ten accidents each, not all of them resulting in total hull losses. The largest number of write-offs was in 1994 (eight, including five destroyed in a single day during the First Chechen War). Discounting wars, the worst attrition was in 1979 and 1986, five aircraft being lost in each case.

As already mentioned, the second prototype Tu-134 *sans suffixe* (CCCP-45076, c/n 4350001) was the first to be lost, crashing near Chkalovskaya AB on 14th January 1966 due to pilot error. All eight crewmembers were killed.

In July 1968 a Tu-134 *sans suffixe* belonging to Aeroflot's International Services Directorate/207th Flight was flying the Moscow-Bucharest service with 15 passengers and nine crew. 1 hour 8 minutes after departure from Moscow-Sheremet'yevo the starboard engine disintegrated at 11,000m (39,370ft); turbine fragments punctured the fuselage, decompressing it and igniting bales of cotton wool in the rear baggage compartment. After making an emergency descent to 5,000m (16,400ft) the aircraft landed safely at Kiev-Borispol'; the first officer managed to extinguish the fire. All members of the flight crew were subsequently decorated for their bravery and excellent airmanship.

On 7th October 1969 Malév Hungarian Airlines Tu-134 *sans suffixe* HA-LBC (c/n 8350605) had its starboard main landing gear unit collapse on landing at Amsterdam-Schiphol. The aircraft was repaired, remaining in service for another eight years.

Due to crew error another Malév Tu-134 *sans suffixe*, HA-LBA (c/n 8350604), overran at Istanbul-Atatürk International airport on 19th November 1969 when landing in heavy rain, suffering heavy damage to the wings and fuselage. Nobody was hurt but the aircraft was a write-off.

On 23rd May 1971 Aviogenex Tu-134A YU-AHZ (c/n 1351205) crashed in the Yugoslav resort city of Rijeka, inbound from Manchester with a load of British tourists. Rijeka airport is located on Krk Island and the runway thresholds are located right next to the shore. Landing in heavy rain and poor visibility, the captain got the illusion that the aircraft was too high and close to the runway. Fearing an overrun into the Mediterranean, he increased the sink rate to 10m/sec (1,968ft/min). The jet touched down hard with a vertical acceleration of 4G and broke up, rolling inverted and bursting into flames (the destructive G load for the Tu-134's wings is 3.75).

All four emergency exits jammed as the fuselage buckled; also, a stewardess unwittingly locked the entry door, complicating evacuation. As a result, 75 passengers and all three stewardesses died, mostly overcome by smoke; the four flight crew and the sole surviving passenger were injured.

On 22nd June 1971 the Iraqi Government Tu-134K YI-AED (c/n 9350916) was damaged at Jeddah airport but repaired and returned to the USSR.

On 16th September 1971 Malév Tu-134 *sans suffixe* HA-LBD (c/n 9350801) crashed at Kiev-Borispol', inbound from Budapest. The weather at the destination was poor, yet the Hungarian captain obstinately pressed on towards Kiev instead of diverting to one of the designated alternate airports where fine weather prevailed – a decision that would have been all the more logical because the main electric system had failed 31 minutes before the crash.

Landing in adverse weather (rain, fog, cloudbase 60m/200ft, horizontal visibility 700m/2,300ft) the crew messed up the final approach and initiated a go-around. In so doing the Tu-134 dived into clouds; losing sight of the ground, the captain unintentionally started a descent. At 09:44 GMT the aircraft hit the ground, disintegrating utterly and killing all 49 on board.

On 22nd December 1971 Tu-134 *sans suffixe* CCCP-65635 (c/n 9350909) operated by the Ukrainian CAD (possibly the Khar'kov UAD/87th Flight) suffered a port main gear collapse during a night landing at Tyumen'-Roschchino due to fatigue failure of the retraction strut.

On 4th April 1972 the nose and starboard landing gear units of Tu-134 *sans suffixe* CCCP-65672 (c/n 8350701) belonging to the Volga CAD/Gor'kiy UAD/220th Flight retracted spontaneously after touchdown at Gor'kiy-Strigino due to a short circuit. The aircraft suffered damage to the nose and the starboard wing but was repaired.

On 17th July 1972 both engines of GosNII GA's Tu-134 *sans suffixe* CCCP-65607 No 1 (c/n 6350104) failed at 400m (1,310ft) on approach to Moscow-Sheremet'yevo; the crew had no choice but to ditch in the Moscow Canal. The flameout was caused by a vapour lock in the fuel line because the flight engineer had not switched on the fuel transfer pumps in time. The aircraft stayed in one piece and was salvaged but then written off, becoming an evacuation trainer.

On 20th September 1972 a chip detector warning light illuminated as Tu-134 *sans suffixe* CCCP-65634 of the Leningrad CAD (c/n 9350908) was departing from Warsaw-Okęcie. Shutting down the affected engine, the crew made a circuit of the field and force-landed – too fast, touching down at 370km/h (230mph). The brake parachute was deployed but failed immediately; during the ensuing emergency braking the port main gear collapsed and the port wing scraped along the runway, catching fire. Luckily nobody was hurt; the aircraft was repaired.

On 17th October 1972[2] Interflug Tu-134 *sans suffixe* DM-SCA (c/n 8350502) was written off after a heavy landing at Dresden-Klotzsche. Subsequently it was ferried to Minsk and cannibalised for spares.

On 14th March 1973 Soviet Air Force Tu-134AK CCCP-65675 (c/n 2351705) operated by GK NII VVS made an off-field emergency landing. No details are known, but the aircraft was repaired to fly for another 15 years.

On 17th May 1973 Tu-134A CCCP-65647 (c/n 0351002) of the Moldavian CAD/Kishinyov UAD/269th Flight had the starboard main gear collapse when landing at Moscow-Vnukovo, the bogie and fairing catching fire. Again the cause was a short circuit in an electric connector.

On 30th June 1973, as Tu-134AK* (?) CCCP-65668 (c/n 1351306?)[3] of the Armenian CAD/Yerevan UAD/279th Flight was starting on a flight from Amman to Moscow, the captain erroneously believed that one of the engines had failed at rotation speed. He aborted the takeoff – a fatal error in the circumstances; being just 500-550m (1,640-1,800ft) from the

Tu-134 *sans suffixe* CCCP-65607 No 1 after ditching on the Moscow Canal. RART

runway's end, the aircraft overran at 13:39 Moscow time,[4] colliding with an apartment building. Two of the seven crew (the navigator and radio operator) and seven of the 78 passengers died.

On 11th July 1973 the starboard engine of Tu-134A CCCP-65742 (c/n 2351604) of the Azerbaijan CAD/Baku UAD/339th Flight exploded at 230km/h (142mph) during takeoff at Baku-Bina. The jet was stopped with no further consequences; the cause was traced to a defective turbine disc.

On 12th June 1974 an Aviogenex Tu-134A-1 damaged its landing gear in a hard landing at Brussels-Zaventem. The six crew and 80 passengers were unhurt.

On 11th August 1975 Tu-134A CCCP-65742 (by then transferred to the North Caucasian CAD) suffered another mishap. A defective retraction strut broke at 100km/h (62mph) during a night landing at Volgograd-Goomrak and the starboard main gear collapsed, resulting in damage to the outer wing and the ventral speedbrake. Yet again the aircraft was repaired.

On 1st September 1975 Interflug Tu-134 *sans suffixe* DM-SCD (c/n 9350702) undershot 300m (990ft) when landing at Leipzig-Schkeuditz and exploded, killing 26 of the 34 occupants.

On 22nd November 1975 Tu-134A CCCP-65658 of the Armenian CAD/Yerevan UAD/279th Flight (c/n 0351104) had its port main gear collapse as it began its takeoff run at Moscow-Domodedovo – again due to fatigue failure of the retraction strut.

On 24th December 1975 Tu-134A CCCP-65876 (c/n (53)31220, f/n 3002) of the Tajik CAD/Leninabad UAD/292nd Flight/1st Squadron was landing at an unknown location on a rainy and foggy night. At the point of flareout the captain briefly lost sight of the ground; taken aback, he misjudged the altitude and landed hard. Bouncing, the aircraft touched down on the runway's right shoulder, damaging the landing gear.

On 16th July 1976, Tu-134A CCCP-65743 of the Volga CAD (c/n 2351605) suffered a port

main gear collapse at 100km/h after touchdown in Ufa. Once again the accident was attributed to a defective retraction strut. Later the aircraft was presumably transferred to the Ukrainian CAD.

On 3rd November 1976 Tu-134 *sans suffixe* CCCP-65606 No 1 of the Moldavian CAD/Kishinyov UAD/269th Flight (c/n 6350103) ran onto the runway's left shoulder when landing at Kishinyov and struck several high-intensity lights (HILs), snapping off the nose gear and smashing the radar. Nobody was hurt and the damage was repairable.

In the late afternoon of 2nd January 1977 the crew of ČSA Czechoslovak Airlines Tu-134A OK-CFD (c/n 2351505) failed to maintain horizontal separation while landing at Prague-Ruzyne. Seconds after touchdown the jet's port wing struck the tail of another ČSA aircraft, IL-18B OK-NAA (c/n 189001604), just as the latter was vacating the runway. Losing control, the Tu-134A slewed off the runway and came to rest with the nose and port main gear units collapsed.

There were no fatalities but both aircraft were declared write-offs. After serving as a rescue trainer for eight months OK-CFD was finally scrapped on 30th August. The IL-18B had a happier fate – on 8th March 1979 it was donated to the Military Museum (VM VHÚ) at Prague-Kbely.

In the evening of 17th January 1977 Tu-134K* CCCP-65614 No 1 (c/n 7350302), by then transferred to the Leningrad CAD and converted to all-economy configuration, struck the ground with one of the wingtips during a messed-up landing at Murmansk-Murmashi during a blind landing training session.

On 2nd April 1977 Aviogenex Tu-134A-1 YU-AJS (c/n 6348370, f/n 3501)[5] was flying a cargo charter from Frankfurt/Main to Libreville, Gabon. When the aircraft was on short finals the crew suddenly saw a Boeing 707 taxiing out onto the runway tail-first, using reverse thrust to get out from a dead-end taxiway; the Tu-134's crew had not been warned of the situation in time. As the Aviogenex captain initiated a go-around, a downpour began, instantly reducing visibility to zero. The tired pilot involuntarily jerked the control wheel, causing the aircraft

to side-slip; seconds later it clipped a 60-m (196-ft) baobab standing in line with the runway (!) and crashed, killing all eight occupants.

On 1st August 1977 Tu-134K* CCCP-65616 No 1 (c/n 7350304) of the Ukrainian CAD landed hard in heavy rain at L'vov due to late flareout in poor visibility, collapsing the nose gear.

On 3rd September 1977 Interflug Tu-134A DM-SCI (c/n 3351903) was damaged in a heavy landing at Berlin-Schönefeld. The repairs dragged on until August 1978.

On the evening of 21st September 1977 Tu-134 *sans suffixe* HA-LBC crashed 32km (19.8 miles; other sources say 38.7km/24 miles) east of Bucharest-Otopeni, inbound from Istanbul. All eight crew and 21 of the 45 passengers lost their lives. The crew had repeatedly requested permission to land on runway 08, which was equipped with an ILS; the controller insisted that HA-LBC should land on runway 26, even though this involved a visual approach. Eventually the captain complied, but in order to land on a westerly heading the aircraft had to lose a lot of altitude. To speed up the descent the captain increased the sink rate to 8-10m/sec (1,570-1,990ft/min). At this point the crew lost track of the altitude – partly because of the dusk, partly because they were too busy discussing personal matters. When the captain saw trees ahead two seconds before the first impact, it was too late for corrective action. The only survivors were the 24 passengers who sat at the rear of the cabin when the fuselage broke up.

On 30th September 1977 Tu-134A CCCP-65829 (c/n (43)12087, f/n 2408) of the Volga CAD/Gor'kiy UAD/220th Flight had its port main gear collapse at the line-up point at Kuibyshev-Kurumoch; once again the retraction strut had failed.

On 22nd November 1977 Interflug Tu-134A DM-SCM (c/n 3351904) crashed at Berlin-Schönefeld while arriving on a scheduled flight from Moscow. The passengers included East German government officials and an Interflug instructor pilot; the latter decided to show off and talked the crew into making an automatic approach 'at the request of the passengers' (to whom he had 'sold' the idea earlier). However, when the aircraft reached decision altitude

(30m/100ft) the captain, who did not have an ALS rating, panicked; instead of disengaging the autopilot normally he hauled back on the control column, overriding the autopilot. The airliner pitched up; then the captain pushed the control column forward, causing the jet to descend sharply and land so hard that one wing broke off and the aircraft overturned. Fortuitously, there was no fire and no fatalities but the aircraft was totalled, of course.

On 20th December 1977 Tu-134A CCCP-65806 (c/n 3352107) of the Lithuanian CAD/Vilnius UAD/277th Flight missed the runway during a night landing at Vilnius in driving snow, landing on the right-hand shoulder and collapsing the nose gear. The landing lights had created a so-called reflection screen, causing the crew to become disoriented at 25-30m (82-100ft) above ground level.

On 16th March 1978 Balkan Bulgarian Airlines Tu-134 *sans suffixe* LZ-TUB (c/n 8350501) lost control at 4,900m (16,080ft; some sources say 6,000m/19,685ft) ten minutes after takeoff from Sofia-Vrazhdebna. Turning through 150°, the airliner dived into the ground near the town of Vratsa and exploded, killing all 73 occupants. The cause of the crash was never determined.

On 28th October 1978 Tu-134A CCCP-65800 (c/n 3352009) of the Volga CAD/1st Kuibyshev UAD/173rd Flight touched down on the right runway shoulder at Kuibyshev-Kurumoch on a foggy night and the starboard main gear bogie struck HILs, suffering minor damage. The captain was held responsible, since he had landed without having adequate ground visibility; yet the blame also rested with the air traffic controllers who did not divert the aircraft to an alternate airfield.

On 1st February 1979 Tu-134AK* CCCP-65954 (c/n 2351707) of the Moldavian CAD/Kishinyov UAD/269th Flight encountered a sudden blizzard during a late night approach to Kishinyov. Briefly losing sight of the surroundings because of the 'reflection screen', the captain made an error and the airliner ran off the side of the runway, collapsing the nose gear. The inefficient operation of the airport's weather service was a contributing factor. Following repairs the jet was transferred to the Komi CAD.

On 22nd March 1979 Tu-134A CCCP-65031 (c/n (63)48530, f/n 3607) of the Latvian CAD/Riga UAD/280th Flight crashed at Liepaja, Latvia, inbound from Omsk on a cargo flight. By midnight the weather in Liepaja had deteriorated below minima, with ground fog and wet snow. Nevertheless, the approach controller did not divert the jet to an alternate destination or even warn the crew.

Trying to establish visual contact with the ground on finals, the captain unintentionally increased the sink rate to 8m/sec (1,570ft/min) and the airliner dropped below the glideslope. The crew was unaware that the aircraft was overloaded by 752kg (1,658 lb), with the CG too far forward at 19.8% mean aerodynamic chord (the Tu-134's permissible CG range is 21-38% MAC); possibly this proved fatal, making it impossible to climb immediately. When the GPWS horn sounded at 60m (200ft) AGL the captain initiated a go-around. Still, the aircraft continued losing altitude; at 00:57 CCCP-65031 clipped trees, impacted the ground, cartwheeled and exploded. Of the five crew-members, only the flight engineer survived.

At 23:46 on 19th May 1979 Tu-134A CCCP-65839 (c/n (43)18117, f/n 2601) of the Moldavian CAD/Kishinyov UAD/269th Flight crash-landed at Ufa, inbound from Novosibirsk on flight 7732 with an ultimate destination of Kishinyov. The aircraft approached runway 14 too fast and above the glideslope. Realising he might land long, the captain applied reverse thrust and stood on the brakes two seconds before touchdown (which was against the flight manual), rendering the anti-skid system inoperative. The wheels locked and the tyres blew, whereupon the wheels of the port bogie caught fire.

The jet skidded out onto the right runway shoulder, the port wing striking the ground violently; the No 1 port fuel tank was ruptured and a massive fire ensued, destroying the airliner totally within minutes. There were no fatalities but two of the six crew and eight of the 83 passengers suffered injuries.

On 31st May 1979 Tu-134A CCCP-65649 (c/n 0351004) of the Tyumen' CAD/2nd Tyumen' UAD/259th Flight was making repeated circuits at Tyumen'-Roschchino as the crew practiced the approach/go-around procedure with single-engine failure simulation. At 18:06 a wheel on the port main gear bogie exploded due to overheating when the aircraft was making the fourth consecutive take-off. A tyre fragment ruptured a hydraulic line; as the gear retracted, hydraulic fluid leaked onto the hot wheels and ignited.

When the gear was extended the fire flared up due to the slipstream and the influx of hydraulic fluid, the flames engulfing the entire port wing. At 18:25 the aircraft made a flapless emergency landing (the flaps could not be deployed due to the danger of structural failure). The landing gear collapsed, the jet ground-looped to the right and came to rest across the runway. The wings and fuselage suffered massive fire and structural damage, and CCCP-65649 was declared a write-off; the four instructor crew and two trainee pilots were unhurt. The crash had been caused by non-observance of the flight manual which prescribes a pause of at least 15 minutes between consecutive landings in order to cool down the wheels.

On 16th July 1979 the port main gear of Tu-134A CCCP-65056 (c/n (73)49860, f/n 3908) operated by the Urals CAD/Izhevsk UAD collapsed on landing at Moscow-Domodedovo due to a defective downlock; the aircraft was repaired.

On 11th August 1979 ATC incompetence caused the worst air disaster in Soviet history, with a death toll of 178. On that day Tu-134AK* CCCP-65735 (c/n 1351405) of the Belorussian CAD/2nd Minsk UAD/104th Flight headed from Tashkent to Minsk on flight 7880 with a crew of seven and 77 passengers. Concurrently Tu-134A CCCP-65816 (c/n 4352210) of the Moldavian CAD/Kishinyov UAD/269th Flight was winging its way from Chelyabinsk to Kishinyov on flight 7628. There were six crewmembers and 88 passengers aboard, including six children.

A young and inexperienced air traffic controller of the Khar'kov Regional ATC Centre repeatedly denied CCCP-65816 permission to climb from 8,400m (27,560ft) to 9,600m (31,470ft) for no valid reason. Then, incorrectly estimating the airliners' overflight times, he instructed CCCP-65735, which was cruising along a crossing airway, to climb to 8,400m – without checking where CCCP-65816 was, as he was confident that the airliners would pass the intersection with a three-minute interval.

A senior ATC officer on the shift smelled a rat at the last moment and took over to provide vertical separation between the jets, ordering CCCP-65735 to climb to 9,000m (29,530ft). However, due to static on the line he mistook another aircraft's transmission for the Tu-134AK captain's reply and was satisfied that CCCP-65735 had complied – which it had not because the crew never received the instruction. At 13:35.38 the Tu-134s collided in thick overcast 8km (5 miles) north of Dneprodzerzhinsk; the wreckage was scattered over an area of more than 20km² (7.7 miles²).

On 23rd January 1980 LOT Polish Airlines Tu-134 *sans suffixe* SP-LGB (c/n 8350603) overran runway 11 at Warsaw-Okęcie; hitting an earthen dike, the aircraft broke up and burst into flames. There were no fatalities but the aircraft was a total loss.

On 15th August 1980 Tu-134A CCCP-65766 (c/n (93)62327, f/n 5207) of the North Caucasian CAD/Rostov UAD/336th Flight was performing flight 6275 from Krasnodar to Tashkent. During approach to Tashkent-Yoozhnyy the first officer was to act as pilot in command down to the holding pattern altitude, whereupon the captain would take over because the F/O was not qualified to execute the landing. However, the captain remained aloof and the F/O remained in control throughout.

On final approach the aircraft 'popped up' above the glideslope because of a strong tailwind. The pilot increased the sink rate to get the jet back on the glideslope but misjudged the flareout altitude in poor visibility due to lack of experience. At 18:03 CCCP-65766 touched down with a force of 2.22G and bounced, collapsing the nose gear; all six crew and 71 passengers escaped without injury.

On 17th December 1980 Tu-134A CCCP-65142 (c/n (93)60955, f/n 4907) of the Volga CAD/Orenburg UAD/195th Flight collided with a snow plough while landing at Cheboksary, inbound from Moscow on flight 401. The crew did not see the vehicle standing on the runway

Tu-134A CCCP-65031 at Leningrad-Pulkovo in 1978. This aircraft was lost in a fatal crash at Liepaya on 22nd March 1979. Sergey Komissarov

centreline with a stalled engine and no lights until the moment of touchdown. The captain took evasive action as best he could, but there was simply not enough room. The aircraft struck the vehicle with the starboard wing at 110km/h (68mph), damaging the wingtip and outer aileron section; none of the six crew and 38 passengers were injured. The accident was due to the lousy operation of the airport's snow control desk, which was late in alerting the tower, and the ATC which should have ordered the incoming aircraft to go around.

On 6th January 1981 Tu-134B CCCP-65698 (c/n (03)63325, f/n 5805) of the Latvian CAD/Riga UAD/280th Flight/4th Sqn was performing cargo flight 8189 from Sukhumi to Sochi/Adler; it had originated from Riga the day before but diverted to Sukhumi due to poor weather.

The cleared runway 02 was short (2,200m/ 7,220ft), with rough terrain beyond. Hence the crew was intent on some aggressive braking so as to avoid an overrun. Due to pilot error the jet bounced and touched down again with the wheel brakes locked, blowing the tyres and causing the aircraft to skid. Groundlooping to the right, it ripped away both main gear units and came to rest on the runway shoulder in a nose-up attitude.

Sadly, the brand-new airliner was damaged beyond repair; the runway was blocked for 48 hours. The crew of six was unhurt. The forward fuselage of CCCP-65698 later found use as a cabin trainer.

On 24th January 1981 the crew of Tu-134A CCCP-65114 (c/n (83)60395, f/n 4602) of the Ukrainian CAD/Khar'kov UAD/87th Flight lost sight of the ground on finals to L'vov, inbound from Khar'kov on flight 7449. The weathermen had neglected to warn the crew that the weather had deteriorated below minima, with thick fog. Touching down on the left runway shoulder, the airliner bounced and then struck a HIL with the nose gear, collapsing it as it ran onto the

runway. The six crew and 36 passengers suffered no injury and the aircraft was repaired.

At 23:09 on 28th June 1981 Tu-134A CCCP-65871 (c/n (53)28311, f/n 2906) of the Ukrainian CAD/Borispol' UAD/208th Flight landed at Simferopol', inbound from Kiev on flight SU2682. Seconds later the forward wheels of the starboard bogie exploded as a result of overheating during an aborted take-off at Kiev-Borispol'. A wheel fragment punctured a fuel tank; leaking fuel doused the wing and fuselage underside, igniting as it made contact with the hot wheels. As the aircraft came to a standstill the fire flared up, severing the aft fuselage from the rest of the airframe. Of the 59 passengers 29 were injured during evacuation; the six crew were unharmed.

On 17th June 1982 Tu-134AK CCCP-65687 (c/n (93)62400, f/n 5302), an avionics testbed with a unique submarine detection system, crashed near the North Fleet air arm airbase of Severomorsk-1 (Murmansk Region) during a positioning flight from Zhukovskiy to undergo tests. During final approach the aircraft dropped below glide path and drifted off course, the captain not reacting to the GPWS horn, the ATC officer's commands or the crew's calls. At a distance of 12km (7.5 miles) from the runway CCCP-65687 clipped a radio mast, hit a hillside and burst into flames. Of the five flight crew, four engineers and technicians, and seven passengers (mostly designers of the ASW equipment), only the captain survived. The 'tin kickers' came to the conclusion that the crew had been psychologically unprepared for the flight…

On 14th August 1982 Tu-134A CCCP-65836 (c/n (43)17113, f/n 2508) of the Georgian CAD/Sukhumi UAD/297th Flight/1st Sqn was departing Sukhumi-Babushara on flight 974 to Moscow with six crew and 76 passengers. A Let L-410MA Turbolet feederliner registered CCCP-67191 (c/n 781120) and operated by the 2nd Squadron of the same Flight was due to take off next on flight G-73 to Kutaïsi. Runway 30 was active on that day; however, the L-410 captain contacted the circuit controller, requesting permission to take off on a recipro-

cal heading to save time, and got the go-ahead; the ground controller took no measures to stop this grave breach of the rules.

At 17:08 the Tu-134A began its take-off run on runway 30. Meanwhile the L-410MA taxied out on runway 12 without stopping at the holding point, the crew requesting permission to line up after they had done it. Despite evasive action by both crews and emergency braking by the Tu-134A, 33.5 seconds after brake release the jet struck the diminutive turboprop with its port wing at 210km/h (130.5mph), destroying it utterly; the two pilots and nine passengers died instantly. There were no casualties on the Tu-134A but the aircraft suffered serious damage to the starboard wing and fuselage and was declared a write-off.

On the evening of 24th January 1983 Tu-134A CCCP-65864 (c/n (53)28284, f/n 2809) of the Ukrainian CAD/Borispol' UAD/208th Flight was damaged at Yerevan-Zvartnots while arriving on cargo flight 86111 from Kiev. Seconds before touchdown a sudden blizzard created a 'reflection screen', causing the pilots to lose sight of the ground; the airliner landed on the right runway shoulder and hit a HIL at 19:08.02, snapping off the nose gear. The five crew were uninjured and the aircraft was repaired.

On 24th March 1983 the port main gear unit of ČSA Tu-134A OK-AFA (c/n 1351406) failed to extend on flight OK981 from Warsaw to Prague. The captain managed a two-point landing at Prague-Ruzyne, the aircraft suffering only superficial damage.

On 17th June 1983 Tu-134A CCCP-65657 (c/n 0351103) of the Armenian CAD/Yerevan UAD/279th Flight encountered a major storm front off Gali, Abkhazia, while cruising at 10,200m (33,460ft) en route from L'vov to Yerevan on flight 7190. The Sukhumi Regional ATC Centre had neglected to inform the crew that a storm warning had been issued or specify the location of storm cells. Trying to circumnavigate the front, CCCP-65657 hit storm turbulence where the radar did not indicate any storm activity; between 15:43.34 and 15:45.00 the aircraft was subjected to G loads of

+3.05/–0.65 and was hurled down to 10,000m (32,810ft) by wind shear. It then landed safely at Yerevan-Zvartnots, with no injuries to any of the occupants, but was written off when structural damage caused by the G loads was discovered.

At 23:52 on 28th August 1983 Tu-134AK* CCCP-65881 (c/n (53)35220, f/n 3008) of the Central Regions CAD/Voronezh UAD/243rd Flight suffered a fire in the port engine on the runway at Mineral'nyye Vody just as it was about to depart on flight 2552 to Voronezh. It turned out that the air turbine starter had failed to disengage and disintegrated due to over-speeding as the engines were run up. The six crew and 81 passengers were unhurt and the aircraft was repaired.

Two days later Tu-134A CCCP-65129 (c/n (83)60630, f/n 4801) of the Volga CAD/1st Kazan' UAD/261st Flight was approaching Alma-Ata, inbound from Kazan' on flight 5463. Due to a succession of crew errors and criminal negligence on the part of the landing pattern controller the aircraft departed from the prescribed landing pattern in the darkness in the midst of a mountainous area. At 20:17.23 Moscow time (23:17.23 local time), while still 36km (22.3 miles) out, the jet slammed into the 1,403-m (4,603-ft) Mount Dolan at 1,365m (4,478ft) ASL and exploded, killing all six crew and 84 passengers.

On 18th November 1983 Tu-134A CCCP-65807 (c/n 3352108) of the Georgian CAD/Tbilisi UAD/347th Flight outbound from Tbilisi on flight 6833 to Leningrad with a crew of seven and 59 passengers was hijacked by nine armed criminals (including three women) demanding to be flown to Turkey. A shootout broke out in which an inspector pilot and the flight engineer were mortally wounded, while one of the hijackers was shot dead and another wounded. As the aircraft headed back to Tbilisi, the bandits killed two passengers, wounding ten more; a stewardess was also killed after the jet landed.

After lengthy negotiations KGB commandos stormed the airliner the following morning; the remaining hijackers (except one who committed suicide to avoid capture) were arrested and tried, the men receiving death sentences. The aircraft, too, was a write-off, having sustained structural damage when the first officer made violent manoeuvres, pulling +3.15/–0.6G to stop the hijackers from taking aim.

On 10th January 1984 Balkan Bulgarian Airlines Tu-134A LZ-TUR (c/n 4352308) executed a go-around after a missed approach to Sofia-Vrazhdebna. Due to grave pilot error in almost zero visibility (there was heavy snow at the time) the aircraft hit power lines and crashed into a cattle farm 4km (2.5 miles) beyond the runway. There were no survivors among the 50 occupants.

At 21:04.59 on 10th January 1984, while taking off on flight 6678 from Simferopol' to Baku, Tu-134B-3 CCCP-65708 (c/n (03)63447, f/n 5908) of the Azerbaijan CAD/Baku UAD/339th

Flight struck lumps of wet snow left on the runway by a snow plough. The nose gear collapsed but the airliner was brought to a halt without further damage; the six crew and 39 passengers suffered no injury and the aircraft was repaired.

At 18:34 on 25th May 1984 a Tu-134Sh-2 operated by the Voroshilovgrad VVAUSh (tactical code unknown, c/n 2350202) broke up in mid-air 12 minutes 38 seconds after departing from Zhdanov airport,[6] killing all on board. Initially the investigation focused on storm turbulence as a cause, since the aircraft had attempted to pass between two storm fronts. However, examination of the wreckage revealed that the yaw damper's backup power supply cables had been cross-wired to the wrong connectors during maintenance at the Air Force's ARZ No 712 in Chelyabinsk. When the main AC converter failed at 4,200m (13,780ft) and backup power kicked in, the damper began *inducing* oscillations instead of damping them; in the course of 38 seconds the aircraft was subjected to G loads of +3.6/–1.9 which finally overstressed the airframe when the trainer was down to 2,750m (9,020ft). After this tragedy the wiring was modified so as to preclude improper connection.

Four days later the port engine of Tu-134A CCCP-65792 (c/n (03)63121, f/n 5603) operated by the Volga CAD/1st Kuibyshev UAD/173rd Flight failed at 09:54 just as the airliner was taking off at Donetsk, on the second leg of flight 5433 from Kuibyshev to Kishinyov with eight crew and 82 passengers. The take-off was aborted but the aircraft overran, crashing through the perimeter fence and colliding with a parked tractor at 115km/h (71mph). Nobody was hurt; despite suffering serious damage to the fuselage, starboard wing and nose/starboard landing gear units, the aircraft was repaired and returned to service.

On 10th June 1984 Tu-134A CCCP-65758 operated by the same Flight had its port main gear collapse due to fatigue failure of the retraction strut after touching down at Donetsk at 03:13, inbound from Kishinyov on flight 5560 with six crew and 54 passengers. The aircraft slewed off the runway as the port wing caught fire; one of the passengers was injured. Fortunately the fire was quickly extinguished and the aircraft was repaired.

On the evening of 21st June 1984 Tu-134A CCCP-65874 (c/n (53)29315, f/n 2909) of the Ukrainian CAD/Borispol' UAD/208th Flight became airborne from the stopway at Ivano-Frankovsk due to overloading, brushing the crash barrier at the end. (The barrier was there because the airfield was not only a civil airport but also a Soviet Air Force fighter base.)

On 1st February 1985 the port engine of Tu-134AK* CCCP-65910 (c/n (23)63969, f/n 6319) belonging to the Belorussian CAD/2nd Minsk UAD/104th Flight flamed out at 07:59, six seconds after the aircraft became airborne at Minsk-2 airport, taking off on flight 7841 to Leningrad. The crew requested an emergency

landing, but one minute later the starboard engine also flamed out at 220m (720ft). At 08:01 the airliner crashed and burned in thick woods near Nezhivka village 10km (6.2 miles) from the airport; three of the six crewmembers (the navigator, the flight engineer and a stewardess) and 55 of the 74 passengers lost their lives, the remaining occupants suffering injuries.

Ice ingestion was cited as the most likely cause for the flameouts, as the fuel was found to be of high quality and the engines serviceable. During the six days before the accident (26th–30th January) the fully fuelled aircraft had sat in the open in beastly weather with rain, sleet and temperatures fluctuating sharply from zero to –20°C (32° to –20°F). A large amount of ice had built up on the airframe; the aircraft had been de-iced with hot water and glycol at 5 AM, but possibly some of the ice had been missed because the apron was poorly lit. Alternatively, clear ice could have formed on the inner wings *after* the aircraft had been de-iced because these were much colder than the ambient air (–2°C/28°F), subsequently separating and entering the engine air intakes. It was impossible to prove or disprove it because most of the airframe had been consumed by the post-crash fire.

At 15:34 on 10th February 1985 Tu-134AK* CCCP-65045 (c/n (63)49500, f/n 3803) of the Volga CAD/Gor'kiy UAD/220th Flight suffered a fire in the port engine 32 seconds after taking off from Gor'kiy-Strigino on flight 5685 to Simferopol'. Making a circuit of the field, the aircraft landed at 15:43 without injuries to the eight crew and 70 passengers. Consequently changes were made to the engine's design by reinforcing the HP turbine bearing support; the aircraft returned to service after the engine and the charred nacelle had been replaced.

On 3rd May 1985 Tu-134A CCCP-65856 (c/n (53)23253, f/n 2801) of the Estonian CAD/Tallinn UAD/141st Flight approached L'vov on flight 8381 from Tallinn with an ultimate destination of Kishinyov. Meanwhile a Soviet Air Force/243rd OSAP An-26 staff transport coded '101 Red' (c/n 9506) took off from Sknilov AB near L'vov, heading for Chkalovskaya AB and using the ATC callsign CCCP-26492. As the jet descended to 4,200m, the L'vov airport approach controller made two grave errors, incorrectly determining the distance to the An-26 (which was then cruising at 3,900m/12,795ft) and then mistaking it for An-24RV CCCP-47353 which had crossed the Tu-134A's track a few minutes earlier. Hence he instructed the airliner's crew to turn onto final approach and descend to 3,600m (11,810ft). At 12:13.26 the two aircraft collided in clouds at 3,930m (12,890ft) near Zolochev 64.3km (40 miles) from the airport; both crews took evasive action at the last moment but too late. All six crew and 73 passengers on the Tu-134A were killed, as were all five crew and ten passengers on the An-26, including Carpathian DD Air Force Commander Maj Gen Yevgeniy I Krapivin.

On 24th June 1985 Tu-134A CCCP-65061 (c/n (73)49874, f/n 4003) of the Georgian CAD/Sukhumi UAD/297th Flight/1st Sqn was damaged at Batumi airport when a defective concrete slab covering an underground chamber of the centralised refuelling system gave way under the weight of the aircraft!

Four days later Tu-134A CCCP-65085 (c/n (73)60123, f/n 4303) of the Belorussian CAD/2nd Minsk UAD/104th Flight suffered an uncontained failure of the starboard engine at 9:12, one second after taking off from Grodno-Obukhovo on flight 2014 to Moscow. Making a circuit of the field, the aircraft landed safely without injuries to the six crew and 76 passengers. The failure was traced to operation with an excessively high turbine temperature.

On 20th September 1985 Tu-134A CCCP-65032 (c/n (63)48535, f/n 3608) of the Volga CAD/Ufa UAD/282nd Flight suffered an identical failure of the starboard engine at 04:45 while taking off at Orenburg-Tsentral'nyy on flight 5923 to Kiev. The take-off was aborted but the aircraft overran, crashing through the barbed wire perimeter fence; the six crew and 75 passengers were unhurt. Despite being a high-time airframe, the aircraft was returned to service.

On 22nd June 1986 Tu-134A CCCP-65142 met its fate. As the jet was taking off from Penza on flight 5569 to Simferopol' with six crew and 59 passengers, a 'Dangerous vibration' annunciator light illuminated at 21:35. Though only 300-350m (990-1,150ft) of runway length remained, the speed was below V_1 and the captain aborted the take-off. Yet the aircraft could not stop in time and overran into a ravine, breaking its back at the emergency exits. There was no fire or injuries, but one of the passengers died of a heart attack. The investigation showed that the engines had been delivering less thrust than they should due to improperly adjusted fuel pumps. To top it all, the vibration warning had been false!

On 2nd July 1986 Tu-134AK* CCCP-65120 (83)60482, f/n 4609) of the Komi CAD/Syktyvkar UAD/75th Flight took off from Syktyvkar on the second leg of flight 2306 from Vorkuta to Moscow. Twelve minutes later (at 10:07) a fire broke out in the rear baggage compartment. Attempts to tackle the blaze with hand-held fire extinguishers failed, as the fire had spread to the No 3 equipment bay. Sending out a distress call, the crew executed an emergency descent to 1,000m (3,280ft) and headed back to Syktyvkar.

Meanwhile the passengers were being smothered by the smoke pouring into the cabin, and at 10:18 the crew decided to make an off-field emergency landing. Unfortunately no suitable spot could be found; at 10:27.10 the aircraft crashed into a forest near Kopsa settlement 90km (56 miles) from the airport and burned. Two of the six crewmembers (the navigator and the flight engineer) and 52 of the 86 passengers died, evacuation being hampered by the jammed entry door and unusable overwing exits; all survivors were injured. The cause of the fire could not be determined due to post-crash damage.

On 19th October 1986 Mozambique Government Tu-134AK C9-CAA (c/n (03)63457, f/n 5909) took President Samora Moises Machel on a brief visit to Zambia. Apart from the President, there were 35 other passengers, a five-man Soviet flight crew and a four-man Mozambican cabin crew. On the way back from M'bala to Maputo the aircraft strayed off course 96km (60 miles) from the airport and hit the Lebombo mountain ridge near Nelspruit (Transvaal, South African Republic) at 19:21:39 GMT (21:21.39 local time), killing 26 of the passengers, including Samora Machel, and eight of the nine crewmembers. Eight passengers and the flight engineer were seriously injured, two more passengers escaping with bruises.

The investigation was initially performed by a Soviet/South African/Mozambican panel. Analysis of the wreckage and the 'black boxes' showed that the aircraft had been fully serviceable. The flight crew consisted of skilled and experienced airmen who knew the route, including the night landing procedure at Maputo, and were fit and well. Communication with the Maputo tower had been maintained throughout and the weather had been good.

The question now was, why did the aircraft turn on a heading of 221° instead of the required 184° at 19:10.41 GMT and follow this course for nearly 11 minutes until it crashed? If the aircraft and the crew were OK, surely the cause of the crash must be *on the ground*? The South African party did not answer this question and refused to co-operate further on 16th January 1987 when the accident report was being signed. The final report was to be completed by a South African court, with the Soviet and Mozambican parties acting as witnesses, which was deemed unacceptable.

Soviet specialists undertook a separate investigation and concluded that an illegal (and more powerful) transmitter had been operating on the same frequency as the Maputo VOR (VHF Omnidirectional Range) beacon to throw the aircraft off course. Three facts support this theory. Firstly, the cockpit voice recorder transcript contains a key phrase; when the captain commented the change of course at 19:11.28 the navigator replied, 'The VOR points that way'. The crew did not sense anything amiss, expecting a turn onto heading 231° for the approach to runway 23. (Later, the South African party claimed the compass system had been tuned in error to the VOR at Matsapha airport (Mbabane, Swaziland) but analysis of the wreckage disproved this; besides, the Matsapha VOR was obscured by Mount Bombegazi and the aircraft could not have received the signal. Also, the aircraft's actual course at the moment of impact was not the one for Matsapha.

Five-and-a-half minutes after the change of course the GPWS horn sounded because the radio altimeter had caught the signal of a Mozambican air defence radar, something that had happened more than once. Hence the next GPWS warning 30 seconds before the impact was dismissed as a false alarm because the crew was sure they were flying over even terrain near Maputo. Failing to discover any lights on the ground or detect any signals from the ILS, the crew decided there was a blackout in Maputo – a fairly common occurrence in Africa. The marker beacons at Maputo were not powerful enough to use them for navigation purposes.

Secondly, LAM Mozambique Airlines Boeing 737-2B1 C9-BAA bound from Beira to Maputo on flight TM103 fifty minutes later also strayed off course and followed the same heading (221°) until Maputo closed and the aircraft returned to Beira. Finally, a military camp was discovered just 150m (500ft) from the crash site; it had been abandoned the day after the crash. The bottom line is that the crash of C9-CAA was a carefully planned and executed act of terrorism with the purpose of assassinating Samora Machel.

On 20th October 1986 Tu-134A CCCP-65766 – now operated by the North Caucasian CAD/Groznyy UAD/82nd Flight since March 1984 – approached Kuibyshev-Kurumoch on flight 6502 from Sverdlovsk with an ultimate destination of Groznyy, carrying a crew of seven and 87 passengers, including 14 children. The crew had agreed that the captain would make a blind landing 'for training purposes' (!). During final approach the captain involuntarily increased the sink rate to 6m/sec (1,180ft/min), which was much higher than normal. When the blind flying curtain was opened one second before touchdown, it was too late for corrective action. At 15:50 the Tu-134A landed hard and broke up, rolling inverted and bursting into flames. The crash rescue team acted inefficiently and the medical team on site did not feature intensive care specialists. As a result, 60 passengers and all three stewardesses died on the spot, another six passengers and the first officer dying in hospital; of the remaining 24 occupants, only two passengers escaped uninjured. The captain was later sentenced to 15 years – the maximum applicable prison term.

On 12th December 1986 Tu-134A CCCP-65795 (c/n (03)63145, f/n 5606) of the Belorussian CAD/2nd Minsk UAD/104th Flight approached Berlin-Schönefeld on flight SU892 from Prague (where it had diverted due to poor weather as flight SU891 originating from Minsk on the same day).

Berlin-Schönefeld has two runways – 07L/25R and 07R/25L (used chiefly for landing and for take-off respectively). They are spaced 460m (1,500ft) apart but the threshold of runway 25L is located 2,300m 1.4 miles) further forward; hence ordering a go-around is often easier than redirecting an aircraft to the other runway. Runway 25L was the only active runway on that day, and the crew tuned the ILS accordingly to 109.9MHz for an automatic approach. A Malév Tu-154 inbound on flight MA808 was next in line, and at 16:01.49 GMT, when CCCP-65795 was 10km (6.2 miles) out, the flight dispatcher suddenly announced, 'Aeroflot-892 and Malév-808, for your information, runway and approach lights 25 Right in use for test, for test'. Nonplussed by this untimely information, the Tu-134 captain acknowledged, 'Aeroflot-892, roger, thank you, 25 Right' – and heard an 'OK!'. This was part of the other aircraft's transmission ('OK, what about that 25 Right, would you say again please, Malév-808').

Deciding they had been rerouted to runway 25R, the crew retuned the ILS to 110.3MHz and initiated an S-turn to the right. When CCCP-65795 was 6km (3.72 miles) from runway 25L, the error was discovered by the tower which advised the crew. The captain ordered the ILS retuned again and initiated another S-turn without noticing that the aircraft was below glide path. At 16:04.31 GMT the Tu-134A crashed into woodland 3km (1.86 miles) from the runway and exploded, killing all nine crew and 63 of the 72 passengers – a group of East German schoolchildren.

On 24th December 1986 Tu-134A-3 CCCP-65779 (c/n (93)62602, f/n 5406) of the Kirghiz CAD/Frunze UAD/250th Flight entered unpredicted fog on final approach to Frunze-Manas, inbound from Kustanai on flight 4672. Suddenly losing sight of the ground, the crew allowed the aircraft to drift and at 19:08 it landed on the left runway shoulder, destroying two HILs whose fragments then damaged the port engine and flap. The seven crew and 76 passengers were unhurt.

On 15th July 1987 the aforementioned Tu-134A CCCP-65876 suffered an APU explosion on the ground at an unspecified location.

On 17th February 1988 Háng Không Viêt Nam Tu-134AK VN-A108 (c/n 6348430, f/n 3510) was damaged beyond repair in a hard landing at Hanoi-Gia Lam.

Ten days later Tu-134AK* CCCP-65675, by then transferred to the Belorussian CAD/2nd Minsk UAD/104th Flight, was approaching Surgut on flight 7867 from Minsk with six crew and 45 passengers. On finals to runway 07 the aircraft entered a layer of smog; the landing lights created a 'reflection screen' and were switched off. Having no visual contact with the ground, the captain continued the approach, unaware that the aircraft was drifting off course to the right. In turn, not seeing this because of the inactive landing lights, the tower could not order a go-around. At 04:08 the airliner landed on the right runway shoulder with a vertical acceleration of 4.6G and broke up, rolling inverted as burning fuel from the ruptured tanks entered the cabin via a breach in the fuselage.

Quickly though the crash team put out the blaze, the first officer, both stewardesses and 17 passengers died, mostly overcome by smoke. Poor crew resources management and adverse weather were cited as the causes of the accident.

At 09:12 on 18th March 1988 Tu-134A-3 CCCP-65951 (c/n 2351703) of the North Caucasian CAD/Volgograd UAD/231st Flight lost its nose gear unit at 150-170km/h (93-105mph) while departing from Groznyy-Severnyy on non-scheduled flight 30159 to Noyabr'skiy (an 'oil support mission'). The aircraft was stopped with no injury to the four crew and 66 passengers. The cause was fatigue failure due to repeated shock loads; the aircraft was repaired to fly for two more years. (The runway at Groznyy-Severnyy was notorious for its horrible condition (it deserves to be called 'ruinway'); pilots were literally shaken out of their seats and their headsets came off! Still, the management of the Groznyy UAD did nothing to improve the situation…)

Three days later Tu-134AK* CCCP-65771 (c/n (93)62445, f/n 5305) of the North Caucasian CAD/Rostov UAD/336th Flight suffered an uncontained failure of the starboard engine at 23:42 while taking off from Tyumen'-Roschchino on flight 6120 to Rostov-on-Don. Shutting down the engine, the crew made an emergency landing 6.5 minutes later. The fire was extinguished within three minutes; the seven crew and 66 passengers were unhurt. The cause was a fatigue failure of a compressor disc; the aircraft returning to service after the engine and nacelle had been replaced.

The scenario was repeated on 4th April 1988. The starboard engine of Tu-134A CCCP-65066 (c/n (73)49898, f/n 4008) operated by the Arkhangel'sk CAD/1st Arkhangel'sk UAD/312th Flight exploded at 12:51 as the aircraft began its take-off run at Gor'kiy-Strigino on the second leg of flight 8915 from Arkhangel'sk to Mineral'nyye Vody. The take-off was aborted immediately and the fire-fighters were on the scene within three minutes, putting out the fire at 12:56. The seven crew and 37 passengers suffered no harm but the badly burnt nacelle had to be replaced.

On 31st July 1988 Tu-134AK* CCCP-65900 (c/n (13)63684, f/n 6109) of the Kazakh CAD/Alma-Ata UAD/240th Flight suffered an APU explosion at Djamboul while getting ready for the second leg of flight 4197 from Alma-Ata to Mineral'nyye Vody via Djamboul and Goor'yev. Fatigue failure of the turbine was the cause.

On 9th September 1988 Háng Không Viêt Nam Tu-134A VN-A102 (c/n (83)60925, f/n 4904) was approaching Bangkok-Don Muang on flight HVN831 from Hanoi. On final approach to runway 21R the aircraft dropped below glide path; at 04:37.05 GMT it struck a palm tree and plunged to the ground, bursting into flames. Four of the six crew and 72 of the 75 passengers were killed, the five survivors sustaining injuries. Wind shear was the most likely cause, as there was considerable storm activity in the area, but it is possible that the Tu-134A had hit wake turbulence from a Philippine Airlines McDonnell Douglas DC-10-30 flying 11.1km (6.89 miles) ahead.

At 19:06 on 26th September 1988 Tu-134B-3 CCCP-65711 (c/n (03)63498, f/n 6004) of the Azerbaijan CAD/Baku UAD/339th Flight approached runway 08 at Donetsk on flight 6718 from Tallinn, with an ultimate destination of Baku. The captain was late on the flareout and the aircraft landed with a vertical acceleration of 3.1G. Fortunately it stayed in one piece, suffering structural damage to the fuselage but being repaired; no one was hurt.

On 11th October 1988 ČSA Tu-134A OK-AFB (c/n 1351410) suffered structural damage in a hard landing at Prague-Ruzyne on a flight from Budapest. Being a high-time airframe, the aircraft was written off to become a café at Piešťany airport.

At 17:05 on 6th December 1988 Tu-134AK CCCP-65097 (c/n (83)60540, f/n 4704) of MRP/NPO Vzlyot landed on runway 20 at Moscow-Vnukovo on a flight from Yoshkar-Ola. Contrary to the flight manual, the captain applied reverse thrust before the nose gear was on the runway; in a 5.7m/sec (11.4 kt) side wind the aircraft swung and veered off the runway, snapping off the nose gear as it struck the verge of a taxiway and damaging the starboard engine. The icy runway was a contributing factor. The five crew and nine passengers suffered no harm and the aircraft was repaired.

On 28th July 1989 Soviet Air Force Tu-134AK CCCP-65670 (c/n 0351110) made a positioning flight to Ulan-Ude's Mookhino airport from an airbase located 25km (15.5 miles) away to pick up a group of US military inspectors. The weather was misty, with limited visibility. During final approach the captain lost awareness of the altitude; belatedly he called a go-around, but at 02:23 the aircraft landed 300m (990ft) short of the runway with a vertical acceleration of 2.65G. Next, the port main gear bogie hit a hummock; banking sharply, the aircraft struck the ground with the starboard wingtip and rolled over, disintegrating and bursting into flames as it slid forward. Luckily the five crewmembers walked away.

At 21:50 on 19th August 1989 Tu-134B-3 CCCP-65704 (c/n (03)63410, f/n 5904) of the Latvian CAD/Riga UAD/280th Flight was performing flight 8149 from Riga to Novosibirsk via Naberezhnyye Chelny. However, the flight was cut short when an APA-4G ground power unit with a faulty gearbox backed straight into the aircraft at Naberezhnyye Chelny-Begishevo at 21:50 after starting up the jet's APU.

On 5th October 1989 Tu-134AK CCCP-65099 (c/n (13)63700, f/n 6201), another NPO Vzlyot aircraft, was due to depart Moscow-Vnukovo, using the ATC callsign CCCP-80590. As the aircraft accelerated along runway 24 at 11:05, the port engine surged at 240-250km/h (149-155mph) and the flight was aborted. It transpired that CCCP-65099 had narrowly escaped the fate of Tu-134AK CCCP-65910 – the fuelled aircraft had spent more than 24 hours in heavy snowfall and had been sloppily de-iced, the surge being caused by snow ingestion. The seriously damaged engine had to be replaced.

The starboard engine nacelle of Tu-134A CCCP-65136 was virtually cut into three pieces when the engine disintegrated at Moscow-Domodedovo on 30th October 1989. Note the LP compressor disc visible through the hole.
Courtesy CIS Interstate Aviation Committee

At 21:08.53 on 30th October 1989 Tu-134A-3 CCCP-65136 (c/n (83)60885, f/n 4810) of the Volga CAD/Orenburg UAD/195th Flight suffered an uncontained failure of the starboard engine on Moscow-Domodedovo's runway 14L as it was about to depart for Orenburg on flight 733. The seven crew and 80 passengers were uninjured and the aircraft was repaired. The explosion was caused by fatigue failure of the LP compressor's second stage; the LP turbine then overspeeded and disintegrated.

At 15:34 on 5th November 1989 Tu-134A-3 CCCP-65053[7] (c/n (73)49838, f/n 3904) of the Georgian CAD/Sukhumi UAD/297th Flight/1st Sqn suffered an uncontained failure of the port engine at 9,750m (31,990ft) en route from Moscow-Vnukovo to Batumi on flight 969 with six crew and 70 passengers. The cabin decompressed as compressor fragments punctured the fuselage, the crew and passengers feeling ill. Executing an emergency descent, the aircraft made a safe emergency landing at Voronezh-Chertovitskoye. Again, fatigue failure was the cause; the aircraft was repaired.

On 27th November 1989 Tu-134A CCCP-65972 (c/n 3352002) of the North Caucasian CAD/Groznyy UAD/82nd Flight was performing 'oil support' flight 30509 from Groznyy to Noyabr'skiy via Ufa. At 21:48, seconds after touchdown at Ufa, the nose gear broke in a shower of sparks, the axle and wheels hitting the fuselage twice as they departed. As in the case of CCCP-65951, fatigue failure was the cause – no doubt because of the horrible runway at Groznyy. The six crew and 80 passengers were unhurt; following repairs the aircraft went to the Rostov UAD.

On 25th December 1989 Tu-134A CCCP-65756 (c/n (93)62179, f/n 5104) of the Central Regions CAD/Voronezh UAD/243rd Flight came in too low while landing on runway 12 at Voronezh-Chertovitskoye, inbound from Leningrad on flight 2606. At 01:49 the jet collided with the localiser antenna, destroying it and suffering minor damage. The eight crew and 77 passengers were uninjured. Poor weather and pilot fatigue were the causes this time; in heavy rain and fog the captain got the false impression that the aircraft was too high and took measures to avoid overrunning the short (2,200m) and wet runway.

Four days later Tu-134A CCCP-65849 (c/n (43)23138, f/n 2703) of the Ukrainian CAD/Khar'kov UAD/87th Flight/2nd Squadron had its port main gear collapse at the line-up point at Novyy Urengoy-Yaghel'noye just as it was about to depart on non-scheduled flight 36142 to Khar'kov, carrying gas industry workers. The fate of the aircraft is unknown.

Another Tu-134Sh reportedly coded '03 Red' crashed in 1989. No details are known (the c/n was reported as 46210, which is obviously incorrect).

Tu-134A-3 CCCP-65951 was also jinxed. An uncanny repetition of the 1986 Syktyvkar tragedy came on 13th January 1990. On that day the aircraft took off from Tyumen'-Roschchino, bound for Volgograd on flight 6246 with six crew and 65 passengers. Twenty-two minutes later, at 12:46, a fire broke out in the No 3 equipment bay at 10,600m (34,780ft). Requesting an emergency landing at Sverdlovsk-Kol'tsovo some 20km (12.4 miles) away, the crew began an emergency descent at more than 30m/sec (5,900ft/min), subsequently reducing the sink rate to 23-24m/sec (4,520-4,720ft/min).

At 12:55.20 a power supply cable melted, putting the main electric system and hence nearly all flight instruments out of action. Having no radio communication and not knowing their position, the crew stood no chance of reaching Sverdlovsk and did the only right thing, going for an off-field landing. The only suitable spot was a field near Pervoural'sk 49km (30.4 miles) from Sverdlovsk. Coming in for a very fast, flapless landing (the flaps were inoperative due to the electrics failure), the airliner touched down at 12:56.40, bounced several times and broke up, colliding with a power line pylon, irrigation pipes and trees before coming to rest inverted. The captain, the navigator and 22 passengers were killed outright, one more passenger and a stewardess later dying in hospital; the 32 survivors were seriously injured. The cause of the fire was clearly a short circuit but the exact location was never found.

On 6th June 1990 Tu-134A CCCP-65056 suffered a failure of the starboard engine necessitating a forced landing at Naberezhnyye Chelny-Begishevo.

On 27th August 1990 Tu-134A CCCP-65033 (c/n (63)48540, f/n 3609) of the Volga CAD/Gor'kiy UAD/220th Flight suffered a fire in the port engine at an unknown location when the air turbine starter failed to disengage and disintegrated as the engines went to full power. There were no casualties and the aircraft was repaired.

In late 1990 Vietnam Airlines Tu-134AK* VN-A112 (c/n (93)62458, f/n 5306) collided with an airport vehicle at Ho Chi Minh City (Tan Son Nhut airport) but was repaired.

On 12th January 1991 another Vietnam Airlines Tu-134AK*, VN-A126 (c/n (83)60435, f/n 4605) built to Tu-134A-1 standard, was damaged beyond repair in a hard landing at Ho Chi Minh City.

On 23rd April 1991 Tu-134A-3 CCCP-65780 (c/n (93)62622, f/n 5407) of the Komi CAD/Syktyvkar UAD/75th Flight was making a night approach to Moscow-Sheremet'yevo's runway 07R, inbound from Syktyvkar on flight 2310. The weather was bad, with sleet and a 8.2m/sec (16.4 kt) crosswind from the left, and the runway was covered with slush; the tower did not give the crew timely warning of this. At 02:11 the aircraft touched down and was pushed towards the right edge of the runway by the wind, the nose turning to the left. Believing the jet was heading towards the left runway verge, the captain applied right rudder – which only made it worse. Running onto the right runway shoulder, CCCP-65780 struck the edge of an elevated taxiway and the nose gear collapsed. The seven crew and 89 passengers, including 16 children, were OK and the aircraft was repaired.

On 19th July 1991 Tu-134A-3 CCCP-65767 (c/n (93)62335, f/n 5209) of the Kazakh CAD/Alma-Ata UAD/240th Flight flew from Moscow to Alma-Ata via Kustanai and Taldy-Kurgan on flight 579-Kh-6. Taldy-Kurgan was an air force base as well as an airport, and various military ground support vehicles were lined up along the main taxiway because a large group of military aircraft was due shortly. Taxiing out for the final leg of the journey, at 08:02 (05:02 local time) CCCP-65767 collided with a UPG-300 ground power unit which was parked a bit too close. The force of the collision was so great that the starboard outer wing separated, fuel gushing out onto the tarmac; luckily there was no fire. The six crew and 48 passengers were uninjured; the aircraft was repaired. Poor interaction between military and civil authorities, as well as the irresponsible actions of the captain, were the causes of the accident.

On 24th November 1991 the starboard main gear of Tu-134A-3 CCCP-65899 (c/n

(53)42225, f/n 3208) operated by the Tyumen' CAD/2nd Tyumen' UAD/259th Flight failed to lock down at the end of flight T-62 from Nadym to Tyumen'-Roschchino. At 10:27 the airliner touched down; 1,300m (4,265ft) further on the starboard main gear collapsed. The starboard wing suffered minor damage but the crew and 71 passengers were unhurt.

On 24th January 1992 Tu-134A-3 CCCP-65053 was damaged again, collapsing the nose gear after overrunning at Batumi. It is not clear whether it was repaired this time.

Three days later Tu-134A-3 CCCP-65776 (c/n (93)62545, f/n 5401) of the Kazakh CAD/Alma-Ata UAD/240th Flight drifted off course due to side wind on short finals to Arkalyk on flight 527 from Moscow. Touching down on the right runway shoulder, the aircraft ploughed through deep snow (which had no business being there) and the nose gear collapsed. The crew of seven escaped unhurt but one of the 34 passengers was injured. The damage appeared quite serious but was eventually repaired.

On 25th May 1992 the captain of Tu-134A-3 CCCP-65003 (c/n (53)44040, f/n 3302) operated by the Tajik CAD/Leninabad UAD/292nd Flight/1st Squadron misjudged the distance while taxiing at Yekaterinburg-Kol'tsovo. At 12:05 the aircraft, which had just arrived from Vladikavkaz on flight 4855, struck an unserviceable bus standing on the taxiway. The crew and 25 passengers suffered no injury and the damage to the port wingtip was minor.

On 13th June 1992 Tu-134A-3 CCCP-65902 (c/n (13)63742, f/n 6204) of the Komi CAD/Syktyvkar UAD/75th Flight struck the tail of Tu-134A-3 CCCP-65793 operated by the same unit while being pushed back at Syktyvkar for flight 8714 to St Petersburg. Both aircraft suffered only superficial damage.

On 27th August 1992 Tu-134A CCCP-65058 (c/n (73)49868, f/n 3910) of the Central Regions CAD/Ivanovo UAD/176th Flight departed from the designated approach pattern at Ivanovo-Yoozhnyy while inbound from Mineral'nyye Vody on flight 2808. This was a wilful action of the captain who was notorious for his 'I know better' attitude. As a result, the crew was pressed for time to complete the pre-landing checklists; the captain ignored repeated suggestions by the first officer to go around.

Six kilometres (3.72 miles) out the stabilisers were set to maximum incidence in one move (rather than incrementally as the flight manual requires) and the aircraft started climbing of its own accord. To compensate, the captain initiated a descent at 10-14m/sec (1,970-2,755ft/min), causing the aircraft to drop below glide path. At 22:43.31 CCCP-65058 clipped trees 3km (1.86 miles) out and crashed inverted, killing the seven crew and 77 passengers. In so doing it destroyed a house in Lebyazhiy Loog settlement – luckily without causing casualties. The approach controller at Ivanovo did nothing to avert the tragedy.

Two days later Tu-134A-3 CCCP-65810 (c/n

3352201) of the Georgian CAD/Tbilisi UAD/347th Flight landed too fast at Khar'kov-Osnova while arriving from Tbilisi on flight 6879. Reverse thrust was not used because the control levers were poorly adjusted, requiring considerable force to move them. As a result, the jet overran runway 26, careering over rough ground at high speed. The seven crew and 51 passengers were uninjured but the aircraft was damaged beyond repair, with skin wrinkling on the fuselage and starboard wing.

On 15th April 1993, just as Imperial Air Tu-134A-3 OB-1553 (c/n (83)60206, f/n 4401) was taking off at Cuzco, a wheel on the port main gear bogie exploded, damaging hydraulic lines. As a result, the port main gear would not deploy on approach to Lima-Jorge Chávez and the aircraft was substantially damaged in the ensuing crash landing; none of the 68 occupants was injured.

Sadly, the demise of the USSR sparked civil wars and ethnic strife in the former Soviet republics, including the Georgian-Abkhazi war. On 21st September 1993 an atrocious act of war demonstrated that airliners are not armoured assault aircraft designed to withstand enemy fire. At 16:25 Transair Georgia Tu-134A 65893 (c/n 5340120, f/n 3201) inbound from Sochi was shot down on finals to Sukhumi-Babushara by a 9K32M Strela-2M surface-to-air missile (NATO codename SA-7 Grail) launched from an Abkhazi separatist gunboat. The aircraft plunged into the Black Sea 8km (5 miles) from the shore; six crew and 22 passengers lost their lives.

Two days later another Transair Georgia Tu-134A, CCCP-65001 (c/n (53)42235, f/n 3210), was destroyed on the ground by a direct hit when the separatists shelled Sukhumi-Babushara. Different sources state one or ten fatalities for this. (Some sources claim Tu-134As CCCP-65053 and 65809 (c/n 3352110) were also destroyed at Sukhumi on that day.)

On 21st December 1993 Kazair Tu-134A-3 UN 65787 (c/n (03)62798, f/n 5506) performed flight 4194 from Mineral'nyye Vody to Almaty via Atyrau and Shimkent. Even though the weather in Almaty was below minima and deteriorating, the crew irresponsibly departed from Shimkent, ignoring warnings en route. Landing without secure visual contact with the ground, at 15:37 the crew landed the aircraft on the right runway shoulder covered with deep snow and the nose gear collapsed. The seven crew and 77 passengers were unhurt and the aircraft was repaired.

On 8th February 1994 Estonian Air Tu-134A ES-AAL (c/n (93)62350, f/n 5209) suffered a fire in the port engine en route from Amsterdam to Tallinn with 19 passengers, making a safe emergency landing in Hamburg.

On 22nd February 1994 Malév Tu-134A-3 HA-LBP (c/n (13)63560, f/n 6101) was damaged beyond repair by a flightdeck/galley fire during maintenance at Budapest-Ferihegy; one person died and several more were injured.

On 7th May 1994, as AVL Arkhangel'sk Airlines Tu-134A RA-65976 (c/n 3352007) was taking off from runway 07R at Moscow-Sheremet'yevo on flight 2315 to Arkhangel'sk, a defective maintenance plate on the starboard main gear broke loose, damaging hydraulic lines. As the gear was extended on approach to Arkhangel'sk-Talagi, the starboard unit failed to lock down. At 10:42 RA-65976 landed on runway 26; seconds later the starboard main gear collapsed and the aircraft groundlooped, crashing through the perimeter fence and collapsing the nose gear. The seven crew and 56 passengers were uninjured, but the aircraft was damaged beyond economical repair.

On 9th September 1994 LII's Tu-134AK RA-65760 (c/n (93)62187, f/n 5105) flew as chase plane for the Tu-22M3-LL *Backfire-C* laminar-flow research aircraft ('32 Red', c/n 4830156, f/n 3005). At the time of the accident the airliner was controlled by the first officer, a young pilot unaccustomed to close-formation flying. As the Tu-134AK moved from line abreast formation (off the bomber's starboard wing) to echelon port formation, passing under the bomber, the jets collided at 10,000-11,000m (32,810-36,090ft). The tailless airliner dove into the ground 20km (12.4 miles) northeast of Yegor'yevsk (Moscow Region), killing all eight crewmembers; the bomber managed a safe landing at Zhukovskiy.

On 27th September 1994 Imperial Air Tu-134A-3 OB-1490 (c/n (83)60525, f/n 4703) was reportedly written off after hitting high ground near Cuzco; all 40 occupants survived.

On 25th November 1994 a Vietnam Airlines Tu-134A ran off the side of the runway at Phnom Penh-Pochentong while landing on a flight from Ho Chi Minh City and struck HILs, collapsing the nose and starboard gear and suffering damage to the fuselage and starboard wing. The 40 occupants were unhurt.

11th December 1994 saw the outbreak of the First Chechen War. On the first day of the hostilities Russian Air Force Sukhoi Su-25 *Frogfoot-A* attack aircraft raided all Chechen airfields, knocking out nearly 100% of the maverick republic's aviation. Among other things, Tu-134A-3s 65014 (c/n (63)46200, f/n 3404), 65030 (c/n (63)48520, f/n 3606), 65075 (c/n (73)49998, f/n 4201), plus apparently Tu-134A CCCP-65858 (c/n (53)23256, f/n 2803) and Tu-134A-3 65896 (c/n (53)42200, f/n 3205), all operated by the Chechen airline Stigl, were destroyed at Groznyy-Severnyy along with a retired Tu-134 *sans suffixe* (CCCP-65631, c/n 9350902).[8] 65030 was reportedly the presidential aircraft of Gen Djokhar Dudayev.

On 24th June 1995 Harka Air Tu-134A RA 65617 (c/n 4308068, f/n 2309) wet-leased from Komiavia approached runway 19L at Lagos-Mohammed Murtala International, inbound from Kaduna, Nigeria. When the aircraft was down to 2m (6ft 6¾in), a freak gust of wind caught it from behind, lifting it to 5m (16ft 4⅞in) and increasing the approach speed; as a result, the aircraft landed long. Until then it had

been drizzling, but as soon as RA 65617 touched down at 15:10 GMT an almighty downpour began, flooding the runway instantly. Aquaplaning, the airliner could not stop in time and overran at high speed, careering over a concrete storm culvert. The landing gear collapsed and the starboard wing tanks were ruptured; the leaking fuel was ignited by a spark and the fire quickly engulfed the aircraft. The airport's rescue team acted extremely inefficiently, the fire engines getting stuck in the mud and the firemen having no heat protection suits. As a result, 15 of the 74 passengers suffocated in the rear baggage compartment where they had sought shelter from the smoke; the six crewmembers escaped unhurt.

Runway 01R/19L at Lagos was generally prone to flooding and extremely slippery in rainy weather. Also, the taxiways on both sides (that is, no runway shoulders) and the storm culverts left no chances of staying in one piece if an aircraft ran off the runway. In short, dangers have to be designed out of airports as well as aircraft.

On 15th September 1995 Kaliningrad Avia Tu-134A RA-65027 (c/n (63)48485, f/n 3603) came in off centre and above glide path while landing at St Petersburg-Pulkovo on flight 7905 from Kaliningrad with an ultimate destination of Murmansk. Instead of initiating a go-around the captain made an S-turn with 20° bank at the last moment to get the aircraft back on track. At 07:28.58 the starboard wingtip struck the run-

way and broke away, the wing catching fire. The seven crew and 29 passengers suffered no harm and the aircraft returned to service after the starboard outer wing had been replaced.

On 24th October 1995 Tu-134A-3 RA-65855 (c/n (53)23252, f/n 2710) of the Air Transport School was hit by several stray bullets at Sleptsovsk, Ingushetia, when Russian Commandos raided the airport, expecting to find Chechen guerrillas. Actually they found only innocent civilians – the intelligence report turned out to be false.

On 5th December 1995 the port engine of Azerbaijan Airlines Tu-134B-3 4K-65703 (c/n (03)63383, f/n 5902) failed at 17:53, 1.5 minutes after the aircraft had taken off from Nakhichevan' on flight A-56 to Baku. However, the flight engineer shut down the starboard engine in error, and the damaged engine failed to provide the required thrust. The error was caused by high workload and imperfect workstation ergonomics. Having no time for restarting the starboard engine, the crew opted for an off-field landing. However, trying to avoid a collision with the houses of Hanaï settlement straight ahead, the captain made a tight turn and did not manage to level out the aircraft before it ran out of altitude, coming down on a field at 17:54.06. Seconds later it struck a power line pylon and disintegrated completely; two of the six crew (the first officer and a flight attendant) and 50 of the 76 passengers were killed, the survivors receiving serious injuries.

Flight hours and cycles of Tu-134s written off in accidents (where known)

Aircraft	Registration	(c/n) / [f/n]	Total time since new		Total cycles since new	Overhauls
Tu-134A	CCCP-65649	(0351004)	12,295 hours		7,789	3
Tu-134A	CCCP-65657	(0351103)	17,870 hours		11,029	4
Tu-134AK	CCCP-65735	(1351405)	10,753 hours	26 mins	7,075	2
Tu-134A	CCCP-65951	(2351703)	30,755 hours	30 mins	18,102	5
Tu-134AK	CCCP-65675	(2351705)	18,900 hours		12,656	3
Tu-134A	RA-65976	(3352007)	33,606 hours		21,071	6
Tu-134A	CCCP-65807	(3352108)	13,273 hours		10,506	3
Tu-134A	CCCP-65810	(3352201)	26,173 hours		18,701	5
Tu-134A	CCCP-65816	(4352210)	12,739 hours	16 mins	7,683	2
Tu-134A	RA 65617	[2310]	24,844 hours	25 mins	15,740	4
Tu-134A	CCCP-65836	[2508]	14,007 hours		10,406	3
Tu-134A	CCCP-65839	[2601]	9,994 hours	36 mins	6,113	2
Tu-134A	CCCP-65856	[2801]	18,548 hours	5 mins	12,306	3
Tu-134A	CCCP-65871	[2906]	11,492 hours	50 mins	8,206	2
Tu-134A	CCCP-65031	[3607]	5,838 hours	52 mins	3,894	0
Tu-134A	CCCP-65058	[3910]	26,307 hours		16,388	4
Tu-134AK	CCCP-65120	[4609]	13,988 hours		7,989	2
Tu-134A	CCCP-65129	[4801]	9,976 hours	37 mins	6,515	1
Tu-134A	VN-A102	[4904]	4,069 hours	56 mins	1,537	0
Tu-134A	CCCP-65142	[4907]	15,938 hours	50 mins	10,397	2
Tu-134A	CCCP-65766	[5207]	16,154 hours	20 mins	9,689	2
Tu-134A	CCCP-65795	[5606]	12,658 hours	48 mins	8,482	2
Tu-134B	CCCP-65698	[5805]	1,416 hours		901	0
Tu-134B	4K-65703	[5902]	27,500 hours	29 mins	17,893	4
Tu-134AK	C9-CAA	[5909]	1,040 hours		565	1
Tu-134AK	CCCP-65910	[6319]	685 hours	47 mins	448	0
Tu-134B-3	VN-A120	[6362]	11,723 hours		8,209	2?
Tu-134Sh-2		(2350202)	3,173 hours		2,370	1?

The following evening an Aeroflot Russian International Airlines Tu-134A-3 suffered an engine fire soon after taking off from Tromsø, Norway, bound for Arkhangel'sk. The fire was quickly extinguished, using the on-board system, and the aircraft made an emergency landing at Tromsø with no injuries to the nine crew and 37 passengers.

On 25th March 1996 Komiavia Tu-134AK* RA-65616 (c/n 4352206) flew from Ukhta to Prague on flight AFL2101 with nine crew and 44 passengers. Fourteen minutes after take-off from Ukhta a titanium fire occurred in the starboard engine at 7,800m (25,590ft). Shutting down the engine and putting out the fire, the crew diverted to Syktyvkar where the aircraft landed at 10:18.

Exactly one month later Komiavia Tu-134A-3 RA-65902 was heading from Vorkuta to Moscow-Sheremet'yevo on flight 2308 when a fire broke out in the port engine. Extinguishing the fire, the crew executed a safe emergency landing at Vorkuta. The aircraft returned to service after an engine change.

At 17:19 GMT on 2nd July 1997 Tu-134AK RA-65097, by then leased to Antares Air, landed with a vertical acceleration of 3.25G at Orenburg-Tsentral'nyy due to pilot error when arriving from Noyabr'skiy on flight AF2082. Bouncing, the aircraft touched down again with the nose gear first, demolishing it. The six crew and 44 passengers were unharmed and the aircraft was repaired.

On 3rd September 1997 Vietnam Airlines Tu-134B-3 VN-A120 (c/n (43)66360, f/n 6362) approached flight Phnom Penh-Pochentong on flight VN815 from Ho Chi Minh City. Ten kilometres (6.2 miles) out the aircraft entered a swath of heavy rain which reduced visibility dra-

matically. At 06:43.33 GMT (13:43.33 local time) the approach controller informed the crew that the wind had changed and runway 05 was now active; the crew did not understand the carelessly worded transmission and continued the approach to the originally cleared runway 23. The situation in Cambodia was far from peaceful at the time; a few days earlier the ILS and the airport radar at Pochentong had been damaged during fighting between government forces and insurgents, which is why the approach controller could not monitor the aircraft's position.

Despite the poor visibility, the captain pressed on towards the airport, ignoring insistent entreaties by the crew to turn back and not realising the aircraft was off centre and below glide path. At 06:44.27 GMT the Tu-134 struck a 14-m (46-ft) palm tree 112m (367ft) from the runway and the starboard engine was damaged by ingested debris. Rolling left and pitching up to a post-critical angle of attack (17°), the aircraft stalled after climbing to 117m (383ft) and crashed in a rice paddy near Thmor Kol village at 06:44.51, exploding on impact. Of the six crew and 60 passengers, only two small children survived. Despite the downpour, the local populace converged on the scene like vultures and started plundering the wreckage; the police had to fire shots to run the robbers off!

On 21st November 1997 Air Moldova Tu-134A-3 ER-65036 (c/n 6348700, f/n 3703) came in too low in poor weather and undershot 179m (587ft) at Kishinyov while arriving from Moscow on flight 1741, colliding with approach lights and the localiser antenna. The seven crew and 65 passengers were unhurt and the aircraft suffered only minor damage.

The charred remains of Harka Air Tu-134A RA 65617 beyond runway 19L at Lagos-Mohammed Murtala International. The aircraft overran while landing in torrential rain on 24th June 1995 and was destroyed, 15 of the 74 occupants losing their lives. Courtesy CIS Interstate Aviation Committee

On 23rd September 1999 Russian Air Force attack aircraft raided Sheikh Mansur airport (Groznyy-Severnyy) during the early stage of the Second Chechen War waged in response to a series of savage terrorist acts in Russia. The target of the day's attack was an An-2 Colt biplane serialled '099 Red' which was used for supplying the extremists with weapons. In so doing Vaynakhavia Tu-134A RA-65626 parked nearby was also damaged – and apparently not repaired due to its advanced age.

On 16th July 2002 Kras Air Tu-134A RA-65605 (c/n (43)09070, f/n 2310) was damaged in a hard landing at Irkutsk-1 airport while arriving from Krasnoyarsk on flight 7B587 with 73 passengers. The nose gear collapsed but the aircraft stopped without further complications; nobody was hurt.

On 25th June 2003 Voronezhavia Tu-134SKh RA-65929 (c/n (63)66495, f/n 6373) overran the runway at Nyagan', Tyumen' Region, by 570m (1,870ft) after aborting a take-off at 230km/h (143mph) and may be a write-off.

Aeroflot Russian International Airlines Tu-134A-3 RA-65785 (c/n (93)62750, f/n 5504) was damaged at Moscow/Sheremet'yevo-2 at an unknown date when a lorry driven by a drunk driver collided with it. The aircraft was ferried to Minsk and, after careful examination at ARZ No 407, declared a write-off.

End Notes

Chapter One

1 OKB = *opytno-konstrooktorskoye byuro* – experimental design bureau; the number is a code allocated for security reasons. In 1991 it became the Tupolev Aviation Scientific & Technical Complex (ANTK imeni Tupoleva – *aviatsionnyy naoochno-tekhnicheskiy kompleks*). Since 1991 the company is known as the Tupolev Joint-Stock Company (OAO Tupolev – *otkrytoye aktsionernoye obschchestvo*).

2 This rendering of the Soviet country prefix (as actually applied) is used throughout. The L is an operator designator denoting the Main Directorate of the Civil Air Fleet which operated scheduled passenger/cargo services. Cf. N (that is, CCCP-Hxxx) for Polar Aviation, S (CCCP-Cxxxx) for the Osoaviakhim sports organisation running Soviet air clubs, A for the agricultural division, K for ambulance aircraft etc.

3 D = *dvigatel'* – engine. The P stands for *passazheerskiy samolyot* (passenger aircraft), implying this is a non-afterburning commercial version. The original D-20 was an afterburning turbofan intended to power the '113' (Tu-113) unmanned aerial vehicle which was never built.

4 Later renamed KhAPO (*Khar'kovskoye aviatsionnoye proizvodstvennoye obyedineniye* – Khar'kov Aviation Production Association). Now called KhGAPP, *Khar'kovskoye gosoodarstvennoye aviatsionnoye proizvodstvennoye predpriyahtiye* – Khar'kov State Aviation Production Enterprise).

5 The official title of Soviet OKB heads.

6 ROZ = *rahdiolokahtor obzora zemlee* – ground mapping radar. The radar had been borrowed from the An-12 *Cub-A* transport, hence the primary mission and the designation.

Seen here taxying in at Kazan'-Osnovnoy airport in December 2000, Tu-134A 'Salon' RA-65079 (ex-LY-ASK, c/n (73)60054, f/n 4206) retained the basic white/grey/red colours of ex-owner Aurela Co with Tulpar titles. Note the blanked-off cabin windows where closets or some such are located (in spite of the 'plug' in the first full-size window, this is not a Tu-134AK!). In January 2001 the aircraft was sold to Avcom. *Il'dar Valeyev*

7 Some sources mistakenly state the redesignation date as 20th November 1963. This is because until the 1970s it was common to state the month in Roman numerals in Soviet documents; apparently someone later misinterpreted '20.II.1963' in a typewritten document as '20-11-1963'.

8 There are also 10 or 15 registration blocks reserved for Aeroflot's Polar division (04xxx), the Ministry of Aircraft Industry (29xxx, 48xxx, 69xxx, 93xxx, 98xxx etc), the Ministry of Defence and so on. They do not correspond to any specific type and are a mixed bag of assorted aircraft.

Chapter Two

1 Now part of the Moscow Aviation Production Association (MAPO – *Moskovskoye aviatseeonnoye proizvodstvennoye obyedineniye*) named after Pyotr V Demen'tyev, ex-Minister of Aircraft Industry.

2 An official grade reflecting pilot expertise and experience.

3 Some Western sources claim the Tu-134 prototypes were converted from Tu-124s with the c/ns 5351608 and 5351609 for which the registrations CCCP-45075 and -45076 had been reserved. However, the c/ns suggest the year of manufacture is 1965, whereas the Tu-134 prototypes were flown in 1963-64!

4 In some cases the first digit does not match the actual year of production because the aircraft was delivered late due to complex modification/outfitting jobs or the need to eliminate defects. For instance, Tu-134A CCCP-65800 (c/n 3352009) was not released by the factory until 22nd February 1974, even though the c/n suggests 1973.

5 *Izdeliye* (product) such-and-such is a term often used for coding Soviet military hardware items. The choice of the number 3 may be due to the fact that the Tu-134 was the third Tupolev aircraft built in Khar'kov (after the Tu-104 and the Tu-124).

6 Unlike Western military aircraft which have *serials* allowing positive identification, since 1955 Soviet/CIS military aircraft usually have two-digit *tactical codes* which, as a rule, are simply the aircraft's number in the unit operating it, making positive identification impossible. Three- or four-digit tactical codes are rare and are usually worn by development aircraft, in which case they still tie in with the c/n or f/n. On military *transport* aircraft, however, three-digit codes are usually the last three of the former civil registration; many Soviet/Russian Air Force transports were, and still are, quasi-civilian.

7 *Euromil – Military Air Arms in Europe* handbook quotes several dozen Tu-134s with c/ns under System 2 which do not fit into the civil sequence and thus must be Tu-134Sh trainers. However, these c/ns are unconfirmed; it is the author's opinion that some data therein is questionable.

8 On civil Tu-134s the intake covers etc carry the *registration*; on military examples, however, there is little point in writing the tactical code (or the registration), as the code will surely change if the aircraft is transferred to another unit and a quasi-civilian aircraft may receive overt military markings anytime. Thus the c/n or f/n is the only reliable identification.

9 Western sources erroneously quote 14th August 1965 as the first flight date.

10 The transport aircraft division of (ex-) GK NII VVS is still located at Chkalovskaya AB; combat aircraft are tested at the main facility at Vladimirovka AB in Akhtoobinsk near Saratov, southern Russia. *Krasnoznamyonnyy* means that the institute was awarded the Order of the Red Banner of Combat.

11 Later called the Perm' Engine Production Association (PPOM – *Permskoye proizvodstvennoye obyedineniye motorostroyeniya*); now called the **Perm**skiye **Moto**ry Joint-Stock Company.

12 The registrations of 16 early-production Tu-134s and four Tu-134Ks (CCCP-65604 through -65623) were later reused for re-export aircraft (six Tu-134As and 14 Tu-134AKs) because the purchase deal had to be closed urgently and there was no time to get new registrations issued by the Air Force General Headquarters.

13 Aka '1971-model MiG-23'; this 'limited edition' was an intermediate version between the original MiG-23S *Flogger-A* and the MiG-23M *Flogger-B*.

Chapter Three

1 Various versions of this radar are fitted to the An-24 (the Groza-24), An-26 *Curl* (the Groza-26), An-32 *Cline*, An-30A/B/D *Clank* (the Groza-30), some versions of the Il'yushin IL-14 *Crate*, Tu-154 *Careless* (the Groza-154) and Yakovlev Yak-40 *Codling* (the Groza-40).

2 Now NPP Aerosila (= Aeropower Scientific & Production Enterprise)

3 From 1982 onwards production was largely limited to Tu-134AKs, Tu-134Bs and various special mission versions.

4 When referring to such aircraft the VIPs are quaintly referred to as *glahvnyy passazheer* – main passenger!

5 Other companies refurbishing and customising Tu-134 interiors include Sand Capital, the Aircraft Maintenance & Support Department of ANTK Tupolev (both based in Zhukovskiy), Kvand Aircraft Interiors, Plast-Avia (both based in Minsk, Belorussia), Dublin-based GPA Expressair Aviation Group, the Israeli company Bedek (a division of Israel Aircraft Industries) and the Dutch company Albatech (jointly with Moscow-based Rosaero).
6 Some sources quote a rating of 7,060kgp (15,565 lbst).
7 This error derives from the Cyrillic rendering of the designation (Ty-134CX).
8 AFA = *aerofotoappa**raht*** – aerial camera; TAFA = *topogra**fich**eskiy aerofotoapparaht* – topographic aerial camera; AFUS = *aerofotoustanovka* – aerial camera mount.
9 In some sources the Rubin radar has been called RBP-4 (***rah**diolokatsi**onn**yy bombardi**rov**ochnyy pri**tsel*** – radar bomb sight); other sources, however, say the RBP-4 is a different radar called Rubidiy-MM-II.
10 SRO = *samo**lyot**nyy **rah**diolokatsee**onn**yy ot**vet**chik* – aircraft-mounted radar [IFF] responder.
11 MBD = *mnogozam**kov**yy **bah**lochnyy der**zhah**tel'* – multiple beam-type rack; U = *oonifit**seer**ovannyy* – standardised. Thus, MBD3-U6-68 means 'MER, Group 3 (ie, capable of carrying ordnance up to 500kg/1,102 lb calibre), standardised, six-bomb version, 1968 model'.
12 Some sources claim the first prototype had an identical installation at one time.
13 Some of these registrations, including RA-64010, RA-64020 and RA-64035, were later reused for Tu-204 medium-haul airliners.
14 Possibly '11 Red' (RA-64105, c/n (13)64105); the existence of this c/n is unconfirmed.
15 'Tu-135s' coded '08 Red' (ex-'28 Red'), '20 Red', '21 Red' and '42 Red' have been reported by *Luftfahrt-Journal* but these were almost certainly reported in error and were actually Tu-134UBLs based at Engels-2.
16 These aircraft obviously had overt military markings before. RA-63975 may be ex-'01 Black'.
17 An instructor pilot who was killed together with the world's first spaceman Yuriy A Gagarin in the crash of an Aero CS-102 (Czech-built Mikoyan/Gurevich UTI-MiG-15 *Midget*) trainer coded '18 Red' (c/n 612739) near Chkalovskaya AB on 27th March 1968.
18 VNIIRA = *Vseso**yooz**nyy na**ooch**no-is**sle**dovatel'skiy insti**toot rah**dioapparat**oo**ry* – All-Union Electronics Research Institute; LNPO = *Lenin**grahd**skoye na**ooch**no-proiz**vod**stvennoye obyedi**nen**iye* – Leningrad Scientific & Production Association. LNPO Leninets is now the Leninets Holding Co.
19 The non-standard registration is very probably explained as follows: the aircraft was built using components of an unbuilt Tu-134UBL which was to receive the c/n (23)64454. On the other hand, some MAP aircraft had registrations in the CCCP-644xx block; cf. Tu-124K-36 CCCP-64452 No 1, An-32 CCCP-64452 No 2, An-8 CCCP-64457 and the two An-22PZ *Cock* special transports, CCCP-64459 and CCCP-64460.
20 RP = ***rah**diopri**tsel*** – lit. 'radio sight', as airborne intercept radars were referred to in the Soviet Union at the time. The identical names of the R-1 ground mapping radar and the RP-29 are pure coincidence.
21 The reference to the Taïfoon radar sounds a bit improbable, as this name applies to a 1960s-vintage fire control radar developed for the Sukhoi Su-15T *Flagon-E*/Su-15TM *Flagon-F* interceptor.
22 This Russian term is used indiscriminately and can denote any kind of testbed (avionics, engine, equipment, weapons etc), an aerodynamics research aircraft or control configured vehicle (CCV), a weather research aircraft, a geophysical survey aircraft etc.
23 Incidentally, in the West there were similar testbeds based on aircraft sharing the Tu-134's general layout – such as the Defence Evaluation and Research Agency's BAC 111-479FU ZE433 (c/n 245) with the Ferranti Blue Fox radar for the British Aerospace Harrier FA.2.
24 The c/n was also reported in error as 3350705 and 6350705.
25 The c/n has also been quoted as 2350104 and 2350204.
26 There are reasons to believe that the aircraft had worn a different, out-of-sequence registration in its Air Force days before being transferred to LII and reregistered CCCP-65740 (which is in sequence!). A photo taken in 1991 shows the CCCP- prefix on the tail was painted normally while the digits 65740 were applied over a blotch of dirty white paint, suggesting that another registration was overpainted there! Possible former identities are CCCP-65677, -65678 and -65964.
27 'ChR' supposedly stands for *chrezvy**chai**nyy re**zhim***, but this Russian term means 'contingency rating' and refers to engines!

Chapter Four

1 The Tupolev OKB had wanted to use Boeing-type doors on the Tu-154. However, tests on Tu-154 *sans suffixe* CCCP-85032 showed the design was ill-suited for this type because the doors were placed too high above the fuselage waterline and the hinge line was not vertical, making it hard to open and close the heavy door. However, Boeing-type doors found use on the Il'yushin IL-86, IL-96 and IL-114, as well as the Tu-204/Tu-214, Tu-334 and Yakovlev Yak-42.
2 Not to be confused with the Russian company headed by Vyacheslav P Kondrat'yev which developed the SM-92 Finist light utility aircraft, the SP-55M Slava aerobatic aircraft and so on.

Chapter Five

1 The registrations CCCP-65558, -65571 through -65574, -65576 through -65578, -65936 through -65938 and -65946 through -65949 have not been used to date. RA-65566 through -65570, -65575, -65579 and -65939 through -65944 are re-export aircraft purchased after 1993, while RA-65571 and RA-65945 are ex-military aircraft sold to civil operators in 2002, ie, they never had the CCCP- prefix.
2 42 aircraft were struck off charge and scrapped; another 25 An-10As in reasonably good condition were transferred to the Air Force and MAP.
3 Now called Bykovo Air Services Company (BASCO).
4 Called Western Group of Forces (ZGV – ***Zah**padnaya **groop**pa voysk*) in 1989-94.
5 These aircraft were reportedly reregistered EW-65614 and EW-65663.
6 The original intention was to use Tu-134A CCCP-65142 which crashed at Penza in 1986, but its fuselage had broken in two and it would be difficult to set it horizontally, which was a requirement.

Chapter Six

1 Askhab was a brother-in-arms of the Prophet Muhammad.
2 The flight code E6 previously belonged to Elf Air.
3 The name has nothing to do with the French oil company Elf-Aquitaine.The E6 flight code was used only briefly; in 2000 it was passed to the Russian charter carrier Aviaexpresscruise [E6/BKS].
4 Not to be confused with Volare [F7/VRE], one of the Ukrainian Air Force's many commercial divisions, and the Italian Volare Airlines [8D/VLE].
5 The OP flight code was transferred to Chalk's International Airlines [OP/CHK] of Miami, Florida.
6 **AAPO** = *Ar**sen**'yevskoye aviatsi**onn**oye proiz**vod**stvennoye obyedi**nen**iye '**Prog**ress'* – 'Progress' Arsen'yev Aircraft Production Association named after N I Sazykin (factory No 116) which builds the Mi-34S *Hermit* light helicopter and the Kamov Ka-50 Black Shark (*Hokum-A*) attack helicopter.
IAPO = *Ir**koot**skoye aviatsi**onn**oye proiz**vod**stvennoye obyedi**nen**iye* – Irkutsk Aircraft Production Association (factory No 39) at Irkutsk-2 which builds the Su-30 multi-role combat aircraft and the Beriyev Be-200 multi-purpose amphibian. The Tu-134s were operated by the factory's airline IRKUT-AVIA [–/UTK]; RA-65934 had an eye-catching three-tone blue/white livery.
KNAAPO [–/KNM] = *Komso**mol**'skoye-na-A**moor**e aviatsi**onn**oye proiz**vod**stvennoye obyedi**nen**iye* – Komsomol'sk-on-Amur Aircraft Production Association named after Yuriy A Gagarin (factory No 126) at Komsomol'sk-on-Amur/Dzemgi which produces single-seat versions of the Su-27 *Flanker* tactical fighter, the Be-103 light amphibian and the Su-80 light transport.
NAPO = *Novosi**beer**skoye aviatsi**onn**oye proiz**vod**stvennoye obyedi**nen**iye* – Novosibisk Aircraft Production Association named after Valeriy P Chkalov (factory No 153) at Novosibisk-Yel'tsovka which builds the An-38 regional airliner, the Su-34 fighter-bomber and is set to build the Su-49 primary trainer. The Tu-134s are operated by the factory's airline NAPO-AVIATRANS [–/NPO].
OAPO = ***Om**skoye aviatsi**onn**oye proiz**vod**stvennoye obyedi**nen**iye 'Po**lyot**'* – 'Flight' Omsk Aircraft Production Association (factory No 166) at Omsk-Severnyy performs An-2 to An-3 upgrades and manufactures the An-74 *Coaler* STOL transport; plans are in hand to build the An-70 four-propfan transport.
U-UAPO = *Oo**lahn**-oo**den**skoye aviatsi**onn**oye proiz**vod**stvennoye obyedi**nen**iye* – Ulan-Ude Aircraft Production Association (factory No 99) which manufactures the Mi-8/Mi-17 *Hip* multi-role helicopter family. From late 1998 onwards Tu-134A-1 RA-65560 was operated by the factory's airline BARGUZIN [–/BAZ]. (*Bargu**zin*** is the name of a river flowing into Lake Baikal, on the shores of which Ulan-Ude is situated.)
7 The UP flight code was transferred to Bahamasair [UP/BHS] of Nassau.
8 This is an old poetic-style name of Russia.
9 The original name and the graphic rendering of CGI Aero's logo suggest the airline is a member of the Clintondale Group, USA.
10 Also rendered as SP Air and Spaero; not to be confused with the Ukrainian Spaero, which see!
11 Formerly the COMECON Civil Aviation Centre (*Tsentr grazh**dahn**skoy avi**aht**siï SEV*). COMECON (aka CMEA) = Council for Mutual Economic Assistance (***So**vet eko**nomi**cheskoy vzai**mopo**moschchi*), the Soviet Union and its satellites' equivalent of the European Economic Council.
12 '*Vay**nakh***' is how the Chechens and the Ingushes call themselves collectively.
13 Some sources suggest RA-65626 was operated by IRS Aero [LD/LDF, later 5R/LDF]. Despite the fact that the airline's registered office was in Moscow, persistent rumours circulated that IRS Aero was in fact owned by the Chechens (with obvious negative implications).
14 Curiously, Albania had tried securing the AL- prefix before but this was likewise rejected and replaced with ZA.
15 The 3P flight code was transferred to Inter Tropical Aviation [3P/TCU] of Surinam.
16 The above colour schemes are *not* all that were used; some re-export An-24Bs and IL-62Ms had basic LOT Polish Airlines colours with Air Ukraine titles and the 'blue bird' logo!

Chapter Seven

1 The Tu-124VE was the export version of the 56-seat Tu-124V (E = ***eks**portnyy*).
2 The last letter D became available when Tu-134A OK-CFD was written off in an accident.
3 Czech sources also mention Avia-14 Salon OK-BYQ whose c/n remains unknown.
4 Established on 18th September 1958, Interflug (a contraction of Internationale Fluggesellschaft) was originally a charter airline serving international routes which were off limits to Deutsche Lufthansa because of its name. (Between 1955 and 1963 there were *two Deutsche Lufthansas* – one in East Germany and the other (the one which still exists) in West Germany. As long as the East German DLH flew domestic flights, nobody seemed to mind, but any attempt to venture outside the country would immediately result in a legal spat with its Western namesake.)
5 The 'O' may have stood for Ostdeutschland, hinting at the East German origin of the aircraft.
6 Marxwalde reverted to its original name, Neuhardenberg, after German reunification.
7 Some sources mention a third Tu-134, XU-122. This was probably a mis-sighting for XU-102, but if it was not, this may be a 'glass-nosed' Tu-134AK (c/n (93)62561, f/n 5403) which was returned by 1992 and became CCCP-65604 No 2.
8 Katran is a kind of shark found in the Black Sea, similar to the dogfish.
9 For instance, a) Mil' Mi-2T '2617 White' is c/n 512617092, ie, transport version (product code '51'), Batch 26, 17th aircraft in the batch out of 50, manufactured in September (09) 1972 (2); b) Mikoyan MiG-29 '70 Red' is c/n 2960526370, ie, Moscow Aircraft Production Association (factory code 296 – cf. IL-22), *izdeliye* 5 (first production version known at the Mikoyan OKB as *izdeliye* 9.12 and in the West as *Fulcrum-A*), the rest is the 'famous last five'.

Chapter Eight

1 That is, in Russian alphabetic sequence (15-15A-15B-15V-15G-15D).
2 Sometimes rendered as K2-88B.
3 Some sources say 7 bars (100psi) for the nosewheels and 5.5-6 bars (78.5-85.7psi) for the mainwheels.
4 VNII NP = *Vseso**yooz**nyy na**ooch**no-is**sled**ovatel'skiy insti**toot neftepro**dook**tov* – All-Union Petroleum Products Research Institute.

Appendix Two

1 The author uses Russian terminology here; the word 'accident' refers to fatal and non-fatal accidents when the aircraft suffers more or less serious damage to the airframe and/or engines, applying both to total hull losses and cases where the aircraft is repaired. 'Incident' means cases not serious enough to be rated as a non-fatal accident, such as avionics or systems malfunctions not causing major damage; in-flight engine shutdowns; tyre explosions; birdstrikes; lightning strikes; near-misses; departures from predesignated air routes; landings in below-minima conditions; go-around because of obstacles on the runway etc.
2 Accident date as per East German Civil Aircraft Register. Some Western sources, however, quote the date as 30th October or as 17th November!
3 Hereinafter Tu-134Ks and Tu-134AKs refitted to tourist/economy/mixed-class configuration are marked with an asterisk.
4 The indicated time is Moscow time unless stated otherwise.
5 Some sources state the c/n as (63)48350, in which case the f/n would be 3409, and the date of the crash as 3rd April.
6 The city was renamed Mariupol' back in Soviet times.
7 Some sources erroneously state the aircraft has a rear entry door (ie, is a Tu-134AK), but it does not.
8 Some sources claim a single Tu-134A was destroyed on 24th November by a Mil' Mi-24 *Hind* assault helicopter operated by the anti-Dudayev opposition and the others on 29th or 30th November by Russian Air Force Su-25s. Also, the six Tu-134s reported destroyed on the first day of the war may include Tu-134A CCCP-65868 (c/n (53)28305, f/n 2903), in which case the dead Tu-134 *sans suffixe* CCCP-65631 should be discounted.

Tu-134 Family Drawings

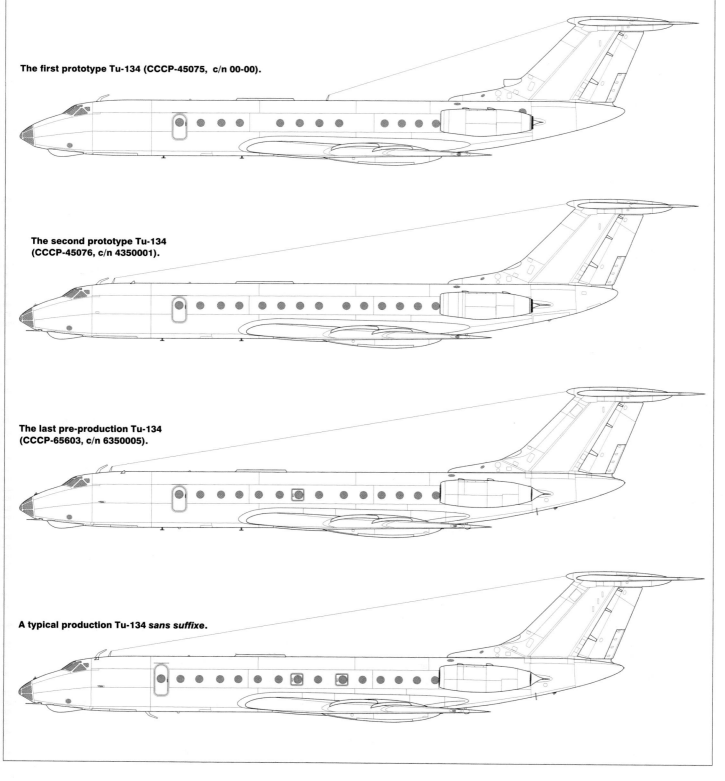

The first prototype Tu-134 (CCCP-45075, c/n 00-00).

The second prototype Tu-134
(CCCP-45076, c/n 4350001).

The last pre-production Tu-134
(CCCP-65603, c/n 6350005).

A typical production Tu-134 *sans suffixe*.

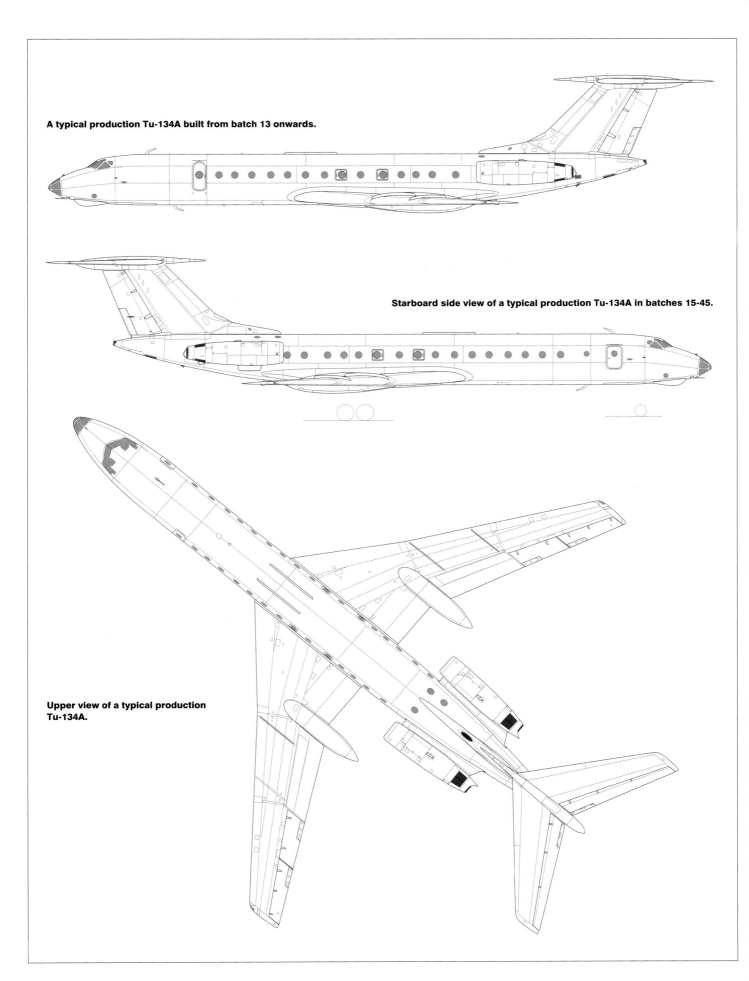

A typical production Tu-134A built from batch 13 onwards.

Starboard side view of a typical production Tu-134A in batches 15-45.

Upper view of a typical production
Tu-134A.

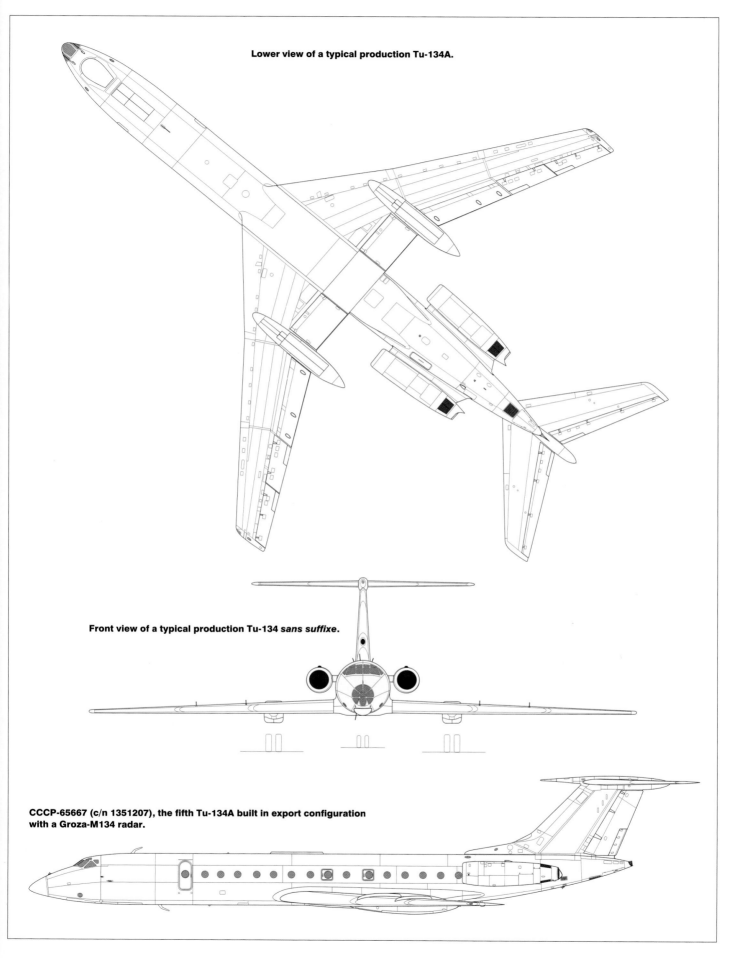

Lower view of a typical production Tu-134A.

Front view of a typical production Tu-134 *sans suffixe*.

CCCP-65667 (c/n 1351207), the fifth Tu-134A built in export configuration with a Groza-M134 radar.

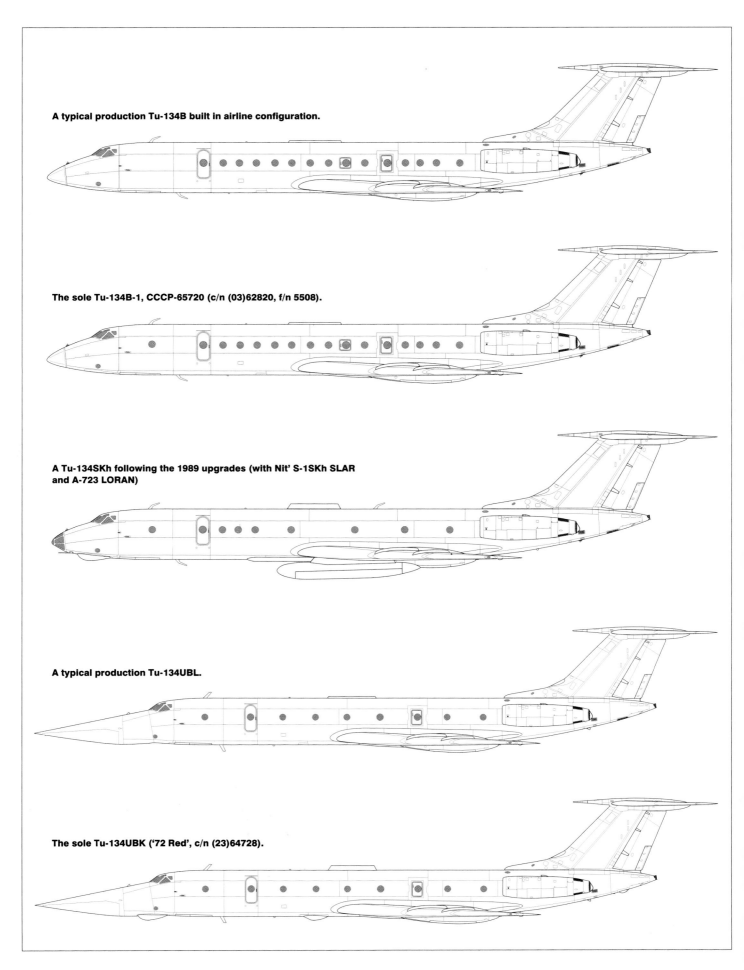

A typical production Tu-134B built in airline configuration.

The sole Tu-134B-1, CCCP-65720 (c/n (03)62820, f/n 5508).

A Tu-134SKh following the 1989 upgrades (with Nit' S-1SKh SLAR and A-723 LORAN)

A typical production Tu-134UBL.

The sole Tu-134UBK ('72 Red', c/n (23)64728).

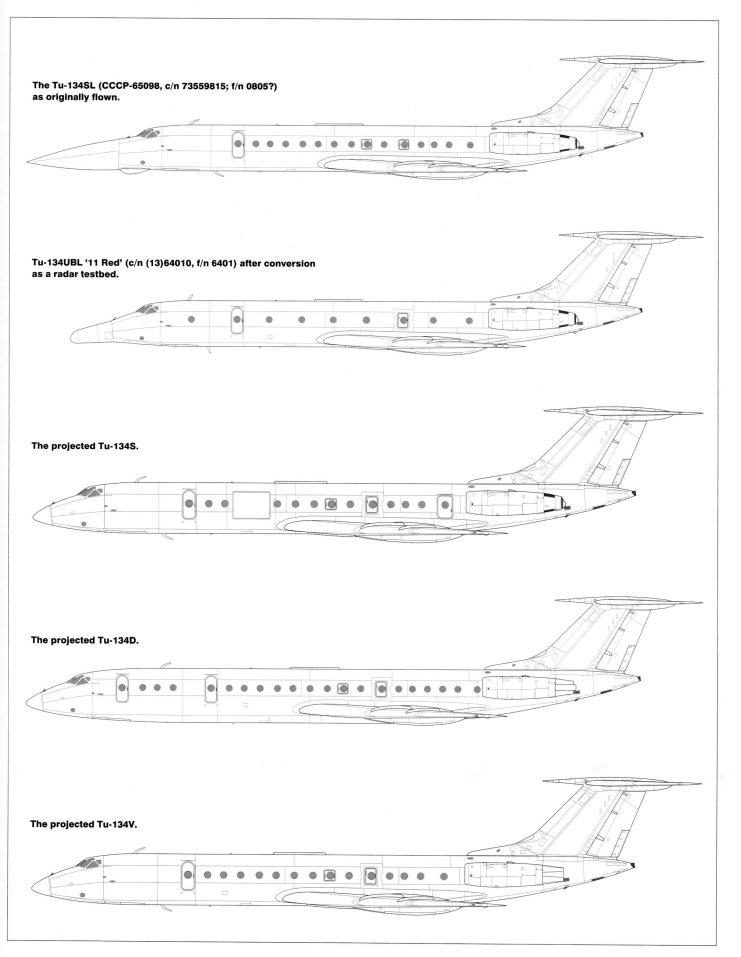

The Tu-134SL (CCCP-65098, c/n 73559815; f/n 0805?) as originally flown.

Tu-134UBL '11 Red' (c/n (13)64010, f/n 6401) after conversion as a radar testbed.

The projected Tu-134S.

The projected Tu-134D.

The projected Tu-134V.

Red Star Volume 12
ANTONOV'S TURBOPROP TWINS – An-24/26/30/32

Yefim Gordon

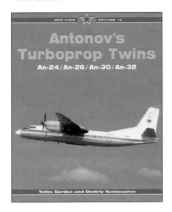

The twin-turboprop An-24 was designed in the late 1950s and was produced by three Soviet aircraft factories; many remain in operation.

The An-24 airliner evolved first into the 'quick fix' An-24T and then into the An-26. This paved the way for the 'hot and high' An-32 and the 'big head' An-30, the latter for aerial photography.

This book lists all known operators of Antonov's twin-turboprop family around the world.

Softback, 280 x 215 mm, 128 pages
175 b/w and 28 colour photographs, plus line drawings
1 85780 153 9 **£18.99**

Red Star Volume 14
MIL Mi-8/Mi-17
Rotary-Wing Workhorse and Warhorse

Yefim Gordon and Dmitriy Komissarov

Since 1961, when it first took to the air, the basic design of the Mi-8 has evolved. Every known version, both civil and military, is covered, including electronic warfare, minelaying and minesweeping and SAR. It also served as a basis for the Mi-14 amphibious ASW helicopter.

Over the years the Mi-8 family have become veritable aerial workhorses, participating in countless wars of varying scale. The type is probably best known for its service in the Afghan War.

Softback, 280 x 215 mm, 128 pages
179 b/w and 32 colour photographs, plus line drawings.
1 85780 161 X **£18.99**

Red Star Volume 15
ANTONOV AN-2
Annushka, Maid of All Work

Yefim Gordon and Dmitriy Komissarov

Initially derided as 'obsolete at the moment of birth' due to its biplane layout, this aircraft has put the sceptics to shame. It may lack the glamour of the fast jets, but it has proved itself time and time again as an indispensable and long-serving workhorse. The An-2, which first flew in 1947, has been operated by more than 40 nations.

The An-2 is the only biplane transport which remained in service long enough to pass into the 21st century!

Softback, 280 x 215 mm, 128 pages
c200 b/w and 28 colour photographs, plus line drawings.
1 85780 162 8 **£18.99**

Aerofax
BELL BOEING V-22 OSPREY
Multi-Service Tiltrotor

Bill Norton

This technologically challenging tiltrotor project established in 1982. A transport aircraft style fuselage, able to carry 24 troops, is topped by a wing with two swivelling pods housing Rolls-Royce engines, each driving three-bladed prop-rotors. The USAF should receive the CV-22B for special missions, the US Marines the MV-22B assault transports, and the Navy the HV-22B CSAR/fleet logistics version, but the program suffered setbacks, with initial operating capability now set for 2005.

Softback, 280 x 215 mm, 128 pages
186 colour, 54 b/w photos, dwgs
1 85780 165 2 April c**£16.99**

Aerofax
ILYUSHIN IL-18/20/22
A Versatile Turboprop Transport

Yefim Gordon and Dmitriy Komissarov

The IL-18 four-turboprop airliner first flew in 1957 and was supplied to many 'friendly nations' in Eastern Europe, Asia, Africa, Middle East and the Caribbean. Its uses included passenger and cargo, VIP transportation, support of Antarctic research stations, electronic espionage and various research programmes. All versions are described, as are many test and development aircraft, the IL-20M ELINT, IL-20RT space tracker, IL-22 airborne command post, IL-24N for ice reconnaissance and IL-38 ASW aircraft.

Softback, 280 x 215 mm, 160 pages
184 b/w, 67 colour photos, plus dwgs
1 85780 157 1 **£19.99**

Aerofax
ILYUSHIN IL-76
Russia's Versatile Jet Freighter

Yefim Gordon and Dmitriy Komissarov

The Soviet Union's answer to the Lockheed Starlifter first flew in 1971 and has become familiar both in its intended military guise and as a commercial freighter. It has also been developed as the IL-78 for aerial refuelling, and in AEW and other versions.

There is not only a full development history and technical description, but extensive tables detailing each aircraft built, with c/n, serial and so on, and detailed notes on every operator, both civil and military, and their fleets.

Softback, 280 x 215 mm, 160 pages
c250 b/w and colour photos, drawings
1 85780 106 7 **£19.95**

Aerofax
TUPOLEV Tu-95/Tu-142 'BEAR'

Yefim Gordon and Vladimir Rigmant

During the 'Cold War' Tupolev's Tu-95 'Bear' strategic bomber provided an awesome spectacle. It was the mainstay of the USSR's strike force, a reliable and adaptable weapons platform. Additional roles included electronic/photographic reconnaissance and maritime patrol, AEW and command and control.

The author has had unparalleled access to the Tupolev OKB archives, taking the lid off a story previously full of speculation to produce the most comprehensive study to date.

Softback, 280 x 216 mm, 128 pages
236 b/w, 24 col photos, 12 diagrams
1 85780 046 X **£14.95**